THE BRAZILIAN COMMUNIST PARTY

THE BRAZILIAN COMMUNIST PARTY

Conflict and Integration 1922-1972

RONALD H. CHILCOTE

New York ● Oxford University Press ● 1974

For all Brazilians committed and active in the
struggle against oppression and exploitation

Contents

Preface

The present study of the Communist party in Brazil has had to be exploratory and speculative, with tentative conclusions that await new data and documentation. Despite the fact that I have been observing Brazilian affairs since an initial visit in August of 1958, my investigation of the subject has necessarily been limited by current political conditions—at least after April of 1964, when the military seized power from the left-leaning administration of President João Goulart. The military regime, motivated by the alleged threat of Communism, arrested hundreds of party members and confiscated libraries of left-wing materials. (A similar crackdown had taken place after the aborted uprisings of 1935.)

Such conditions of course precluded any systematic survey of party attitudes and opinion, though it was possible for me to interview a number of present and former Communist party members, who will remain unnamed for reasons we hope are obvious to the reader. And it was possible to concentrate on party documents and statements by party leaders—though here again I was limited, since some of the material is held by the police and the military, having been confiscated from party files at one time or another. I have made use of such material as has become available in published form—including materials from the 1935 uprising, documents seized by Recife police in 1956, and documents published by a military police commission after 1964—but I made no attempt to obtain permission to consult unpublished material that might still be in police archives. Let me emphasize that I have been very careful with these materials, especially with police interpretations of archival documents. In the text I have made reference to PCB documents published by the police and military; in nearly every case the citation is to a document known to have been prepared by the party, not to an interpretation by the anti-Communist agency responsible for its release.

Considerable Communist documentation was accessible nonetheless— as is attested by the extent of the annotated bibliography at the end of this work—and more of it may be preserved also in some private collections that I was prevented from examining by the political situation. I had to content myself with whatever was available in the Biblioteca Nacional of Rio de Janeiro, with its broken runs of several Communist dailies and periodicals; in the Biblioteca Municipal of São Paulo; and in the Biblioteca Pública of Recife, which contains complete runs of three regional Communist dailies. In addition I was aided in my search by used-book dealers, and am grateful in particular to Roberto da Cunha of Rio, who uncovered certain items that would otherwise have been unavailable to me.

Inevitably my findings are based largely on documentary evidence, since considerable factual error and misinterpretation have invalidated much of the secondary writings. From the outset I have been aware that such limitations would affect this study, and yet I felt the need to fill the gap in analysis of Communist party politics, to the extent that such a study would contribute to the literature of Latin American party politics in general, for there are few scholarly studies in this area.

I am deeply indebted to many scholars for their advice and assistance, as for their interest and encouragement. I benefited first of all from the suggestion of Professor Jan Triska of Stanford University that my investigation be oriented to his theoretic framework for the comparative study of non-ruling Communist parties. This framework, developed by Triska and his colleagues at Stanford's Institute of Political Studies, focuses on the varieties of the non-ruling parties and their individual mutations from the prescriptive Bolshevik organizational model; the causes of these variations, and identification of those environments within which non-ruling parties operate and the consequences of these variations, in particular the conditions that make for similarities or differences among non-ruling parties. I was motivated by Professor Triska to undertake the present work, and in addition I have profited from his counsel and suggestions.

Then too, this study was to have been a collaboration with Amaury de Souza of the Instituto Universitário de Pesquisa in Rio de Janeiro; and although other commitments prevented him from making a contribution in words, many of his ideas and suggestions have been incorporated in the manuscript, and I am deeply grateful for his invaluable assistance. I should like to thank Maria Laura Menezes also, for her assistance in the Biblioteca Pública of Recife. A number of researchers in the Latin American Research Program of the University of California, Riverside, provided research assistance, and I wish to thank especially Paul Mason, who labored over portions of the bibliography and some of the statistical data in Chapter 3; Caesar Sereseres, who searched periodicals for documents and interpretive articles during an early phase of the investigation; Stuart Graham, who assisted with two of the charts; Marie Zentai, who painstakingly uncovered material in Brazilian periodicals; and Diane Radke, who typed the manuscript in its various drafts. I am deeply grateful also to my wife, Frances Bunker Chilcote, for her constructive suggestions, and to the publisher's staff, whose editing improved the manuscript considerably.

Professors Robert J. Alexander of Rutgers University, Rollie Poppino of the University of California, Davis, and Thomas E. Skidmore of the University of Wisconsin commented extensively on the manuscript and made a number of suggestions for revision, most of which are incorporated in the present version. Professor Timothy F. Harding of California State University, Los Angeles, offered invaluable advice as well as access to his collection of primary and secondary materials on the Brazilian labor movement. In addition, the work is the better for the criticisms of several other experts who reviewed the entire manuscript. I am in the special debt of Professors John W. F. Dulles of the University of Texas; Helio Jaguaribe and Wanderley Guilherme dos Santos, both of Rio de Janeiro; Robert Levine of the New York State University, Stony Brook; Teotônio dos Santos Barbosa, a Brazilian sociologist with the University of Chile; and my colleague, Howard Sherman, of the University of California, Riverside. I had also the benefit of assistance and advice from Professors Bradford Burns of the University of California, Los Angeles; Alberto Guerreiro Ramos of the University of Southern California; and John Martz of the University of North Carolina.

Ronald H. Chilcote

University of California, Riverside

Abbreviations in Text

ALN	Ação Libertadora Nacional
ANL	Aliança Nacional Libertadora
AP	Ação Popular
ARENA	Aliança Nacional Renovadora
BO	Bloco Operário
BOC	Bloco Operário e Camponês
BPR	Bloco Parlamentar Revolucionário
CA	Comitê de Ação
CCC	Comando da Caça aos Communistas
CEDPEN	Centro de Estudos e Defesa do Petróleo e da Economia
CGG	Comando Geral de Greve
CGT	Comando Geral dos Trabalhadores
CGTB	Confederação Geral dos Trabalhadores do Brasil
CNOP	Comissão Nacional de Organização Provisória
CNT	Confederação Nacional dos Trabalhadores
CNTC	Confederação Nacional dos Trabalhadores no Comércio
CNTI	Confederação Nacional dos Trabalhadores no Indústria
CONTEC	Confederação Nacional dos Trabalhadores em Emprêsas de Crédito
CNTTMFA	Confederação Nacional dos Trabalhadores em Transportes Marítimos, Fluvias e Aéreos

CNTTT Confederação Nacional dos Trabalhadores em Transportes Terrestres

COB Confederação Operária Brasileira

COLINA Comando de Libertação Nacional

CONTAG Confederação Nacional dos Trabalhadores na Agricultura

CPOS Comissão Permanente de Organizações Sindicais

CTB Confederação dos Trabalhadores do Brasil

FER Frente de Esquerda Revolucionária

FLN Frente de Libertação Nacional

FMB Federação de Mulheres do Brasil

FMP Frente de Mobilização Popular

FPN Frente Parlamentar Nacionalista

FSD Forum Sindical de Debates

FSRR Federação Sindical Regional do Rio de Janeiro

IBAD Instituto Brasileiro de Reforma Agrária

IMF International Monetary Fund

IPES Instituto de Pesquisas e Estudos Sociais

ISEB Instituto Superior de Estudos Brasileiros

LAR Liga de Ação Revolucionária

MAC Movimento Anti-Comunista

MDB Movimento Democrático Brasileiro

MR-8 Movimento Revolucionário 8 de Outubro

MR-26 Movimento Revolucionário 26 de Julho

MRT Movimento Revolucionário Tiradentes

MSD Movimento Sindical Democrático

MUT Movimento Unificador dos Trabalhadores

OCLAE Organización Continental Latinoamericana de Estudiantes

OLAS Organización Latino-Americana de Solidaridad (Organization of Latin American Solidarity)

ORIT Organización Regional Interamericana de Trabajadores

PCB Partido Comunista do Brasil 1922–61, Partido Comunista Brasileiro thereafter

PCBR Partido Comunista Brasileiro Revolucionário

PC do B	Partido Comunista do Brasil
PDC	Partido Democrata Cristão
PL	Partido Libertador
POC	Partido Operária Comunista
POLOP	Político Operária
PORT	Partido Operário Revolucionário Trotskista
PPS	Partido Popular Sindicalista
PR	Partido Republicano
PRI	Partido Revolutionario Institucional
PRT	Partido Republicano Trabalhista
PSB	Partido Socialista Brasileiro
PSB	Partido Socialista do Brasil
PSD	Partido Social Democrático
PSP	Partido Social Progressista
PSR	Partido Socialista Revolucionário
PST	Partido Social Trabalhista
PTB	Partido Trabalhista Brasileiro
PTN	Partido Trabalhista Nacional
PUA	Pacto de Unidade e Ação
PVR	Partido de Vanguarda Revolucionario
UDN	União Democrática Nacional
UFB	União Feminina do Brasil
UJC	União da Juventude Comunista
ULTAB	União dos Lavradores e Trabalhadores Agrícolas do Brasil
UNE	União Nacional dos Estudantes
UST	União Sindical dos Trabalhadores
VAR-Palmares	Vanguarda Armada Revolucionária Palmares
VPR	Vanguarda Popular Revolucionário
VR-1	Vanguarda Revolucionário-1

I • THE SETTING

1 • Introduction

Communism in Brazil, as elsewhere, has co-opted the political party as its principal organizational form. As such, the Partido Comunista do Brasil or Partido Comunista Brasileiro (PCB—the designation varies according to historical periods divided by the date 1961)—has conformed to a set of conditions now regarded as traditional requisites to the formation and maintenance of any political party. For one thing, the party in Brazil has existed for more than one-half century, and its continuity has not been totally dependent on the life span of its leadership. Then, too, insofar as possible—given an existence variously semi-legal and illegal—the party established itself as a permanent organization with regularized communications between national and local levels. Again, the leadership has managed to control party decision-making power at both national and local levels. Finally, throughout its existence, alone or in coalition, the party has sought followers and popular support.[1]

Comparative Party Theory

There are at least three theories to explain the origin and growth of political parties.[2] First are the institutional theories involving the relations between early parliaments and the formation of parties, common especially in nineteenth-century Europe. A second set focuses on parties emerging as the result of historical crisis, such as, for example, socialist parties of the late nineteenth century or Christian Democrat parties of the twentieth century, both of which types evolved with political demands in support of emerging working classes. Here Marxist-

Leninist theory is especially important, for the party as a vanguard force is rooted in the proletariat in opposition to traditional bourgeois parties. Third are the developmental theories relating party formation to the process of modernization, especially to socio-economic changes with which ruling groups may seek wider public support to maintain power. The second and third categories are especially pertinent to the PCB, since its emergence followed upon the failures of socialist and anarchist movements to unite, organize effectively, and formulate ideologies that satisfied workers' aspirations and demands; it was related, too, to the expansion of urban life and populations during a period of rapid industrialization, and to the impact of the Russian Revolution, which set the precedent for the implantation of Communism in Brazil.

There is an abundance of theoretical literature on political parties.[3] In particular, Roberto Michels and Maurice Duverger have provided us with a useful foundation and several generalizations for the comparative study of parties, and some of their ideas have been employed in the present volume. Both writers concentrate on European parties.[4] Duverger is less relevant to the study of a Communist party in a Third World country, however, principally because of his institutional focus. He postulates typical party development according to stages, beginning with the formation of parliamentary groups, proceeding to the organization of electoral committees, then achieving a formal linking of these elements.[5]

While the genesis and early evolution of the PCB seem related to these traditional considerations, and Brazilian efforts to bring about organized Communism were no doubt inspired by the European example, the further evolution and later development of the party were related to quite different circumstances. For one thing, the Brazilian party survived despite long periods of suppression and illegality (a fate suffered by rival parties as well). Parliamentary activity never achieved prominence and recognition by oligarchies, dictators, and military leaders in Brazil. Moreover, the temporary withdrawal from politics of Getúlio Vargas in 1945 allowed a return to civilian administration and the emergence of a multi-party system. The PCB's participation in that system depended directly upon the popularity of one personality, Luiz Carlos Prestes, a colorful military rebel in search of representative government. During the long march of his "column" through the backlands of Brazil (1924–27) Prestes had achieved hero status, and later became secretary general of the PCB. But the dominance of a

colorful figure was not an uncommon feature of the personalism
that characterized Brazilian party politics after 1945. For most parties
the result of this tendency was weak organization, loose ideology, lack
of discipline, and general ineffectiveness. Paradoxically, the PCB,
though dominated like other Brazilian parties by a major personality,
was not characteristically unorganized, undisciplined, or loosely ideological, even though it was undoubtedly somewhat ineffective throughout most of its existence. We shall have more to say about these concerns in Chapter 3.

Like so many writers investigating the political party, Michels focuses
on the two extremes—democracy and dictatorship—and the wide variations of party formulations. Like Neumann and many others, Michels
argues for parliamentary democracy but views the parties as essentially
"aristocratic in origin and in aim," since "they are forced to make use
of the masses." As he observes, "The *raison d'être* of the political
party is the push for power." [6] Although his example is Germany, and
his party type the social democrat, Michels still has applications for
the PCB. The PCB has pursued a policy of participation in the electoral
system, at least since Prestes came to exercise influence over its activities (perhaps as early as 1927, informally and certainly by 1931,
and officially in 1934). In times of legality the party won elections at
all levels; while banned, it sought participation through informal electoral alliances with other parties. Further, the PCB in general has been
distinctly conservative in its political maneuvering, as will become clear
in subsequent chapters. Michels, concerned with the conservative nature
of the political party, is helpful in his interpretation of that behavior.
Third, in its policy and actions the PCB has often assumed a typical
social-democrat posture, and Michels' attention to that party type provided insight for our understanding of a non-ruling Communist party
in Brazil.

If we were to follow Michels' reasoning, the styles of PCB politics
mentioned above might be explained as follows: Over the years, instead of becoming revolutionary and militant as its organization and
solidarity increased, the party grew increasingly prudent and timid, as
the direct result of the continuous threat posed by the state against its
very existence. Once the party achieved maturity and stature, it modified its original doctrines and frequently reacted against revolutionary
currents, those persisting within its own organization and sometimes
those from outside. In the struggle for power the PCB transformed it-

self from a workers' revolutionary party into a bourgeois party; became competitive rather than revolutionary, and harmonious rather than heterogeneous; and sought coalition and alliances in its determination to gain increased membership and a prominent role in the electoral system.[7]

The span of Communist history in Brazil reveals a degree of validity in this account of party behavior, although the threats of the state led to a revolutionary response on at least one occasion—that of the 1935 revolts. Further, as one of the few remaining alternative opposition forces, the PCB should continue to appeal to segments of the alienated masses, and there is little evidence against the possibility, given the appropriate circumstances, that the party could become a revitalized revolutionary force in the struggle to remold Brazilian society.[8]

Lenin departed from—while elaborating upon—the thought of Marx and Engels, and placed his emphasis upon the role of the political party. The proletarian party, he maintained, raises the consciousness, initiative, and energy of its members and becomes the vanguard force that publicly exposes the ruling class and government. Thus, he stated, "Only a party that will organize real, public exposures can become the vanguard of the revolutionary forces of our time." The party, he argued further, would engage in political agitation, preserving its political independence and taking advantage of spontaneous conflicts to unite "into one inseparable whole the pressure upon the government in the name of the whole people."[9] In its efforts to adapt to such a model, the PCB, as will unfold in succeeding chapters, has experienced both success and failure, and these outcomes have been conditioned largely by national developments in Brazil.

The comparative literature on non-ruling Communist parties is helpful if not too plentiful. We might cite the earlier studies of Gabriel A. Almond, Hadley Cantril, and Lucian W. Pye, all of which provide us with insights as to why individuals and groups become alienated from society. The object of Almond's investigation was to discover why people join a Communist party, how it affects their behavior, and why they eventually withdraw. In his study, based on extensive interviewing in depth with former party members in four advanced nations (the United States, England, France, and Italy), he has examined the processes of assimilation to and defection from a Communist party, and has described how such processes vary from one nation to another, one class to another, one generation to another, and one party level to another.[10]

While he may attribute the alienation to psychological maladjustment deriving from the problems encountered by the immigrant vis-à-vis the American or Anglo culture, he finds the responses of French and Italian Communists related to working-class frustrations and the feeling that the Communist party might fulfill many of their aspirations.[11]

Cantril interviewed the protest voter in two European nations (France and Italy)—that is, the person who votes for a Communist candidate or a Communist party but is not a member—by way of probing the nature of the psychological world such a voter builds for himself.[12] Cantril probes deeply, and constructs a model of beliefs to assist us in understanding the very important and complex phenomenon of commitment.[13] Why, we ask, have Brazilian Communists retained their party membership and militancy after years of suppression and (for some) imprisonment, and when the party itself has been weakened by schisms and a decline in prestige over the past several decades? In our present study we shall see that affiliation to a Communist party is generally a concomitant of a high level of politicization and social consciousness. In a society in which alternatives to existing conditions are rarely feasible, a conscious commitment to social change might well be retained only within the refuge of the party itself.

Pye's study—one of the few scholarly studies of a non-ruling Communist party in the Third World—is based on detailed interviews with Chinese who had once been members of the Malayan Communist party. His analysis and his findings on the personal psychological problems of people who had experienced social and political upheaval in contemporary Asia contain insights into relations between Communism and Chinese culture.[14] Thus, he hypothesizes—somewhat along traditional social-science lines—that identification with the party is related to an ongoing process in which large numbers of people in underdeveloped countries are losing their sense of identity with traditional ways of life and see in Communism a stable element in an otherwise unstable society. Often, too, they can expect reward in the form of recognition and prestige for effort in behalf of the party. For them Marxism provides a framework for explaining social, economic, and political reality, and the party represents the possibility of action to solve societal problems.[15]

In suggesting such comparisons, however, Pye emphasizes differences among parties of different cultures, pointing out that the historical experience of a specific party relates uniquely to a specific political and social setting: each party, that is, has been in varying degrees a "captive of its own particular history." [16] As we shall see, this proposition applies to our study of the Communist party of Brazil, for although there is indeed —as most scholars have observed—a congruence of Soviet and Brazilian party policy, many Brazilian party policies and actions have been determined largely by interaction with the national environment.

These investigators have relied heavily on depth interview and survey techniques that we have not been able to utilize—for reasons elaborated in our preface. Instead we have concentrated on documents by party leaders, the party itself, and splinter and rival Marxist groups, as well as on collateral interpretations, to the end of assessing the importance of party organization and doctrine, the impact of party policy upon Brazilian affairs, and the performance of party leaders and followers. When we turn from the theoretical and empirical literature to studies of non-ruling Communist parties in Latin America, we find little material, raw or published, based on survey technique or systematic interviewing. In fact, only a few scholarly monographs exist on individual parties in Latin America. [17]

In Latin America there are two dominant examples of ruling single-party systems, one non-Communist (the Mexican Partido Revolucionario Institucional) and the other Communist (the Partido Comunista de Cuba). [18] A non-ruling Communist party is found in all the other Latin American republics except Chile, and usually in a multi-party environment (in 1970 the Partido Comunista de Chile came to power in coalition with other parties). [19] With the exception of Robert Alexander's study of the Partido Comunista de Venezuela, we have no published investigation in English of a non-ruling Communist party in a country with a multi-party system. [20]

There are, however, several useful surveys of Communism in Latin America, [21] and they suggest that certain conditions unique to underdeveloped areas have both stimulated and retarded the growth of Communism in Latin America and, in particular, in Brazil. Gil, for example, notes that Communist influence may be attributed to two revolutions—industrial and social—which have confronted simultaneously the traditional order and archaic structures. The industrial revolution has given the repressed and exploited agricultural worker a hope for new social and economic freedom once he flees to the city. Frustration and unrest, however, are manifested by elements in the population, especially the middle class or national bourgeoisie but also the working class, and are related to Latin American aspirations for social revolution. That revolution is nationalist and anti-imperialist, with antagonism directed against U.S. intervention in the internal affairs of Latin American nations as well as U.S. domination and ownership of important segments of the economy. Communists in Latin America have associated themselves with the revolutionary cause, identifying with reform and change. Claiming to be authentic nationalists and anti-imperialists, they defend industrialization, change in the traditional social and political systems, and the principles of political democracy.[22]

These have been the appeals of Brazilian Communists, and they have been effectively manifested during times of crisis and instability. Yet those in power—the governing class of Brazil—have persistently maintained order throughout the evolving periods of industrial and social change. The Communists have occasionally contributed to that order, even though there has grown up the stereotype of a violent and revolutionary party. While Communists have influenced certain political and economic decisions in Brazil, they have generally been excluded from the formal decision-making process. This seems to be the result of pressures emanating from the close ties between Brazil and the Western world, especially the United States; the sharp divisions produced by the Cold War after the Second World War; and the dominance of powerful internal economic interests.

Characteristics of the Communist Party in Brazil

As our study suggests, the emergence, and evolution, of the PCB was not unlike Communist development elsewhere in Latin America. The Brazilian Communist movement passed through a series of distinct stages, each linked with policies of international Communism.[23] The beginnings of the party were influenced by the successes of the Russian Revolution and an interest in affiliation with the Communist International or Comintern. Divisions in the Soviet Union between Stalin and Trotsky engendered intra-party schisms in the late 1920's. Brazilian Communists adhered to the "third period" policy of extreme isolation from other political groups, and this resulted in ambivalent policy during the 1930 revolution. During the mid-thirties, however, the PCB became collaborationist, the result of popular-front policies of the Comintern. For the first time, the party began to appeal to a substantial following among workers and intellectuals.

With the end of the Second World War and the advent of the Cold

War, Communists advocated nationalism and hostility to the United States. Their subservience to the Soviet Union brought internal division after the death of Stalin in 1953 and his denunciation in 1956; thereafter, attempts to change the character of the party radically were thwarted by Prestes and his inner circle of supporters, although his hegemony was accompanied by a general decline in party prestige and membership, and an exodus of many elements in the intellectual membership. Subsequently the Cuban Revolution and the Sino-Soviet dispute exerted substantial impact on internal PCB developments.

While close ties between a national party and the Comintern were not uncommon to Communist parties in Latin America, the Latin American parties did differ from European working-class parties. In Europe the brunt of the organizational effort was carried out by the working-class elite: in Europe and Latin America intellectuals provided ideology for the movements. Although a working-class elite, characteristic of many movements outside Latin America, did emerge in the formative years of the many Latin American parties—the PCB, for example —the leadership base of these parties was not generally dominated by the working class. Halperin attributes this to education and to the inability of an illiterate working class to develop its own leadership elite —a generalization that probably has less validity in such nations as Argentina, Brazil, and Chile than in other Latin American nations. Another explanation was that populist politicians set up state-sponsored trade unions and extensive social legislation, thereby undermining working-class efforts to shape a counter-elite alienated from the existing order.[24] Then, too, there was the numerical weakness of the urban industrial working class, the result of the inability of most Latin American countries to establish a large-scale heavy industrial base.

In Brazil and in many other Latin American countries Communists obtained top leadership positions in the labor movement, and yet they were never numerous enough to establish an effective counter-elite. Indeed, Communist control and influence in the trade unions were considerably weakened by a dependence on government toleration. This in turn frequently led to compromises and diminishing party dynamism as well as to conservative voting patterns in unions dominated by Communists.

Another tendency, evident also outside Latin America, was the tension between intellectuals and working-class elements. In Brazil, the PCB—at least until the break with Stalinism but also thereafter—had considerable influence on the leftist intelligentsia. According to one writer, this was due to the Prestes prestige and the impact of his hero image and charisma upon the intellectuals.[25] Ironically, it may have been Prestes' own belief in a revolutionary proletariat that encouraged him to support anti-intellectual trends within his party.[26] No doubt over the years his decisions and actions antagonized many intellectuals, thereby undermining needed support for a party that could depend on only a very limited segment of the working-class vote.[27]

There are several characteristics distinguishing the Brazilian party from other Latin American Communist parties. For one thing, the PCB sprang from the anarchist movement, and was only slightly influenced by socialist developments of the late nineteenth and early twentieth century. Further, since the 1930's it has had connections with military men, a result of the popularity that Prestes maintained with his former comrades in the armed forces. Then too, Prestes' role made the party distinctly more personalist than other Communist units in Latin America.[28]

A number of hypotheses have been suggested by Jan Triska on the subject of non-ruling Communist parties in general. One is that although the immediate concern of the non-ruling party may be with other goals and objectives, its principal aspiration is to become a single ruling Communist party. Another, that the less the non-ruling Communist party is willing to support the interests of the ruling Communist party (the Soviet party, for example), the more the non-ruling party tends to deviate from its aspiration to become a ruling party. Again, that the non-ruling party tends to be progressively more nationally than cross-nationally oriented; this party is subject to growing interaction with its operational environment in direct proportion to growing differences in policy and action among the ruling parties. Finally, that the greater the coincidence of action and goals between the non-ruling party and the operational environment, the more influential will be the non-ruling party in that environment.

These hypotheses appear valid in the case of the PCB and especially so during its period of legality after 1945 and semi-legality after the Stalinist debates of 1956. Since the military intervention in 1964, however, there has been no way of assessing the validity of these hypotheses. Until the coup the party's aspiration to become the ruling party had become secondary to its involvement in the national environment. While its actions and goals tended to be those of mainstream Brazilian politics, deviating considerably from the demands of other Marxist and radical left groups, the PCB also remained more and more cautious in the face of conflicting policies in international Communism. Thus it discretely supported the Cuban Revolution, passively backed the Soviet Union, and tried to avoid breaking altogether with Communist China.

And now to summarize the content of the chapters to follow. At the start we look at Brazilian society in relation to the party. We are interested in how the PCB emerged: why it came into being; which were the precursor influences. In the third and fourth chapters we trace the evolution of the party, identifying the principal periods of activity and noting the impact upon the party of changes in the national environment and in the international Communist movement. Our focus in Chapter 5 involves party structure at the local, intermediary, and national levels, organizational principles, and leadership and membership. Party status (electoral and revolutionary) and influence are assessed, as well as degree of militancy and toleration within the national milieu. Membership is analyzed over periods of the party history, and leadership is distinguished from the rank and file membership as well as from active and other supporters. In Chapter 6 the party's ambivalence toward its national environment is assessed, with specific attention to relations with such organizations as trade unions, peasant associations, student groups, and special clubs and societies; electoral fronts; and ideological competitors. In Chapter 7 we examine the party at the local level. In Chapter 8 we look at party policy nationally and internationally, to determine the interaction with the cross-national environment, relations past and present with the ruling Communist parties in particular, but also with other non-ruling parties. In conclusion we describe the principal determinants of the Brazilian party's behavior, its actions and policies, and its successes and failures in contending with its national and cross-national environments.

II • THE HISTORICAL EXPERIENCE

2 • The Emergence of the Party

For the great part the conditions and aspirations that explain how and why the Communist party came into being in Brazil are similar to those prevailing in other countries during the period when Communist parties were formed: incipient industrialization, for example. Thus, the development of industry and of an industrial working class will be described, and precursor radical movements and ideologies are identified and analyzed in relation to major protest in the period 1848 to 1917. Then too, we must examine organizational activity by groups of radical militants, since this culminated in 1922 in the emergence of the Partido Comunista do Brasil (PCB).

Early Challenges to the National System

Historical cases of protest and challenge to the Brazilian system have long interested Marxist intellectuals, and the nineteenth- and twentieth-century demands for representative government and improvement of social conditions were emphasized in their literature well before the formation of the PCB. One can only hint at the causal relation between early challenges to the system and the formation of the party. That party theorists found these challenges relevant to a critical analysis of the structural weaknesses of the national society did not signify that the early challenges actually shaped the milieu in which the PCB emerged. Nevertheless, the patterns of conflict and the threads of resistance running throughout Brazilian history provided these theorists with a loose framework for analysis of contemporary conditions. Each event constituted a challenge to the Brazilian system in the form of demands for national independence, alleviation of miserable social conditions, and substitution of popular representation for hierarchical-paternal government. Furthermore, the challenge became not only a manifestation of protest but also a means of sensitizing broad segments of society to problems and possible solutions.

Marxist intellectuals and party theorists turned their attention to the Brazilian past, and uncovered three areas of conflict—racial, rural, and urban. Caio Prado Júnior, a distinguished Marxist historian, related such conflict to internal and external structural conditions.[1] Edison Carneiro found historical relevance in black slave rebellions.[2] Rural upheaval was a manifestation of fanatical movements in which millenarian ideology was paramount. The Marxist concerned himself with rural upheaval and social significance in an examination of past protest and conflict—circumstances ignored by most chroniclers of the events. The late PCB journalist, Rui Facó, gave his attention to the social implications of movements inspired by both messianism and "social banditry."[3] A conspicuous example was the war of Canudos fought by Antônio the Counsellor at the end of the nineteenth century.[4] The backlands revolt of Contestado caught the attention of Brasil Gerson and Maurício Vinhas de Queiroz.[5] In addition there were Catholic-inspired movements like those of Padre Cícero in Juàzeiro, in the northeastern state of Ceará, and his disciple Beato Lourenço.[6] Another index of rural unrest was the "social banditry" led by popular heroes like Antônio Silvino and Lampião.[7]

Considerable attention has been given to Luiz Carlos Prestes, who, as we related in the Introduction, became in 1935 honorary president of the popular front, Aliança Nacional Libertadora (ANL), and titular head of the PCB, which had prepared the broad plans for revolutionary insurrections occurring in November of that year.[8] Efforts to organize the peasantry have likewise received exposure. Thus we learn that Communists were the first to form peasant leagues in São Paulo and in Northeast Brazil.[9] Although the party was never very influential among peasants, it did set a precedent for Marxist lawyer-politician Francisco Julião,[10] as we shall see.

Urban discontent and popular rebellion have been represented in Brazilian Marxist literature. The social implications of the Inconfidência, a conspiracy organized in Minas Gerais in 1789 to overthrow the Portuguese regime,[11] have been examined by Brasil Gerson. Amaro

Quintas, a Pernambucan historian, published on the Inconfidência as well as the 1817 revolution in Pernambuco and the Praieira revolt in 1848 and 1849.[12] Manuel Correia de Andrade, a historian and geographer, explored the popular roots of the Cabanos war of the 1830's.[13] Paulo Cavalcanti, a respected journalist, analyzed nationalist agitation in Pernambuco during the late nineteenth century.[14]

Thus, early challenges to the Brazilian system are of relevance to the thought of Marxists and party intellectuals, although the causal link of the challenges to the emergence of the PCB is less clear in their writings. Certain conditions and forms of radical activity that contributed substantially to early party formation can be isolated, however. One was the existence of an incipient working class; another, the influence of precursor ideologies and organizations. And the Russian Revolution was a catalytic element. It is to these considerations that we now direct our attention.

Industrialization and the Working Class

Until World War I, industry played a very minor role in the Brazilian economy. Agriculture, divided between food production and export crops such as coffee, was the dominant economic activity. Cities were just beginning to expand beyond the status of large towns, and social and political life was still largely confined to the great landed estates. Such a social context was hardly conducive to early industrialization, and manufactured goods for the most part were imported from European markets. Existing industries were small—more in the manner of artisan shops—and industrial production occupied an insignificant proportion of the labor force.

But then two developments converged to bring about a period of rapid industrialization from 1914 onward. During the final two decades of the nineteenth century, a huge expansion of the coffee crop in southern Brazil took place as a result of growing demand from the international market, and in consequence, large amounts of capital became available for investment in other economic enterprises. In its turn, the expansion of the coffee economy demanded an increasingly large number of work hands. Slaves had provided most of the labor required by the coffee plantations until slavery was formally abolished, in May 1888. Immigration became particularly significant after the abolition of slavery, and more than one million one hundred thousand immigrants

—mostly Italian, Spaniards, and Germans—reached Brazil during the decade 1891–1900.[15] Therefore, when World War I prevented Europe from providing Brazilian consumers with manufactured goods, there were sufficient capital and work hands for new industries. From 1914 to 1919 the number of industrial enterprises almost doubled, and by 1920 reached a total of some fourteen thousand and employed about three hundred thousand workers.

Immigrant labor brought with it new ideas about social legislation and an experience of labor organization and agitation relatively unknown to Brazilian workers. From 1900 onward the labor movement was activated sporadically at the local level, especially in Rio and São Paulo. In the cities small unions sprang up to demand wage increases, an end to Sunday work, an eight-hour day, and like improvements. Thereafter, in the first significant development in labor organization, congresses were held in 1906, 1912, 1913, 1915, and 1920, and the Confederação Operária Brasileira (COB) was founded in 1908.[16]

The period of rapid industrialization thus coincided with—indeed, largely created—serious dislocations within Brazilian society. Industry attracted not only immigrants from Europe but also a large number of migrants from the countryside, especially the recently freed slaves. Cities began to grow at a rapid rate, and public and private bureaucracies expanded, thus stimulating the growth of the urban middle classes. One telling effect of these social dislocations was to produce a sizable class of residents in the large cities—chiefly workers and intellectuals—with very few ties to the established order. Those déclassé individuals, alienated from and hostile to the dominant oligarchic order, would in time provide the main impetus for radical movements.[17]

Precursor Radical Movements and Ideology: 1848-1917

In the period prior to the emergence of a Communist party in Brazil, two ideologies dominated radical thought and captured the imagination of progressive intellectuals and artisans: that of socialism, which provided the early roots of contemporary radicalism, especially in the intelligentsia; and that of anarchism and anarcho-syndicalism, which was significant particularly in the period from 1906 to about 1920. These ideologies were promoted by organizational activity and the aggregation of intellectuals and workers who favored alternatives to oligarchic rule.

In the case of socialism, several attempts to form a political party followed the establishment the Marx's anarcho-syndicalist International Workingmen's Association, headquartered in Berlin. These attempts also coincided with the early activities of the Social Democratic Second International and with Lenin's insistence on a centrally controlled party that would establish the "revolutionary democratic dictatorship of the proletariat and peasantry." [18] At the same time small socialist groups proliferated in the major Brazilian cities, Rio de Janeiro and São Paulo in particular, and in provincial urban centers such as Recife and Pôrto Alegre as well.

Like socialism, anarchism was influenced by European thought and international organization. Its appeal, however, was limited to the immigrant laborer and especially to the craft and industrial workers in the urban areas. It came to dominate the labor movement during the first important labor congress in Brazil, that initiated by the Federação Operária Regional of Rio de Janeiro in 1906; there, a minority faction of anarchists engineered the resultant theses and resolutions. [19] Despite such success, anarchism suffered from deep-rooted internal ideological differences that would result in proliferation and splintering into anarchist and anarcho-syndicalist organizations, and in a leadership that quickly became polarized by the Russian Revolution. Let us now take a closer view of the two ideologies.

Socialism

Less influential than anarchism, yet significant to early intellectual and radical thought in Brazil, socialism—and specifically the philosophy of Marx and Engels—constituted an ideology fundamental to the formation of the PCB. Although Brazilian socialists were overshadowed by anarchist influence, and their parties were undermined by ideological immaturity, there were several early attempts to establish or revive a socialist party. [20] The first attempt occurred on August 1, 1892, at the first Congresso Socialista Brasileiro in Rio de Janeiro, convened under the presidency of labor leader Luís da França e Silva. Although it failed to establish a party that united all workers politically, this first congress stimulated the formation of several socialist-oriented workers' groups, notably in Rio, São Paulo, and Rio Grande do Sul. [21] In São Paulo during the same year, however, another assemblage called the first Congresso Socialista do Brasil set up the Partido Socialista do Brasil (PSB). [22]

Three years later, four hundred workers and intellectuals founded the Partido Socialista Operário in Rio de Janeiro.[23] From May 28 to June 1, 1902, a second Congresso Socialista Brasileiro drew fifty delegates to São Paulo, and approved the statutes and program of the short-lived Partido Socialista Brasileiro.[24] Simultaneously, the Partido Socialista Colectivista was founded in Rio by Vicente de Sousa and Gustavo de Lacerda. A proliferation of small socialist movements followed, among them the Círculo Socialista França e Silva e Silva, founded by Inácio Ranzini in Jundiaí in September 1903; the Clube Internacional Filhos do Trabalho (a movement of socialist tendencies one of whose founders was Euclides da Cunha), in São José do Rio Pardo, also in September 1903; and the Círculo Socialista 14 de Julho in São Paulo founded two months later.[25] In July 1911 the socialist weekly, *A Vanguarda,* commenced publication in Rio de Janeiro.

Before the Russian Revolution, socialist activity seems not to have had a very substantial effect on radical thought. Thereafter, a variety of socialist organizations appeared. On May 1, 1917, the PSB was reactivated under the leadership of Nestor Peixoto de Oliveira and the influence of French theorist Jean Jaurès. Although the party disappeared a few years later, it published *Fôlha Nova,* first issued on January 4, 1919, and *Tempos Novos,* on June 30 of the same year. There were other attempts to organize socialist groups. In the city of Cruzeiro in São Paulo State, Hermogêneo Fernandes da Silva (later a founder of the PCB) founded the União Operário Primeiro de Maio, which functioned from 1917 to 1919. Cristiano Cordeiro and Rodolfo Coutinho organized the Círculo de Estudos Marxistas in Recife, active in 1919 and 1920. In Fortaleza a Partido Socialista Cearense was formed on July 14, 1919, and in Salvador the Partido Socialista Baiano was formed in August 1920.[26] A last attempt to organize a party in the early period prior to the formation of he PCB apparently had some connection with the activities in Rio de Janeiro of the Grupo da Clarté (which was influenced by the French Marxist writer Henri Barbusse), and similar groupings in Montevideo and Buenos Aires.[27] Its founding executive committee comprised Marxist activists Nicanor Nascimento, Evaristo de Moraes, Luiz Palmeira, Antônio Correia, and Everardo Dias. In the first issue (September 1921) of its publication entitled *Clarté,* the group advocated the formation of a socialist party which, while forgoing participation in Congress, would disseminate ideas and organize the working masses.[28]

That the early socialist movement never achieved any great influence may be attributed not only to the dominance of anarchism but also to the divisive tendencies of the socialist ideology; to its inability to build a broad national base of party organization; to a minimal following, both among workers and intellectuals, this owing perhaps to inaccessibility of publications through which ideas could be propagated in an effort to mobilize the masses; and, finally, to its failure to align with the workers' movement. It was the Russian Revolution that served as the catalyst for Brazilian socialist thought. In the few years between the Revolution and the founding of the PCB, socialists influenced by the Russian experience were able to disseminate their ideas and contribute to the formation of a Marxist-Leninist party in Brazil.

Anarchism and Anarcho-syndicalism
These ideologies influenced intellectual, labor, and immigrant thought and organization in Brazil during the first two decades of the twentieth century. Anarchism, defined by Woodcock as "a system of social thought, aiming at fundamental changes in the structure of society and . . . at the replacement of the authoritarian state by some form of non-governmental cooperation between free individuals," was inspired by the writings of Pierre-Joseph Proudhon and by later anarchists such as Michael Bakunin and Peter Kropotkin, as well as by earlier and later theoreticians such as William Godwin, Max Stirner, and Leo Tolstoy, who severally evolved anti-governmental systems without acceptance of anarchy.[29]

Traditional cultural and linguistic ties as well as similar social conditions favored the transmission of revolutionary (Bakuninist specifically) ideas from Spain and Portugal to Latin America in the nineteenth and early twentieth century. Spanish immigrants spread anarchist ideals in Mexico, Cuba, and Argentina, where nuclei were forming as early as 1870. These countries together with Uruguay were represented at the last Congress of the Saint-Imier International in 1877; a year later a Bakuninist league was founded in Mexico City. After that, anarchists quickly moved to organize craft and industrial workers until by 1920 most of the trade unions in Mexico, Peru, Chile, Argentina, and Brazil were anarcho-syndicalist-dominated.[30] In Brazil the anarchism of Bakunin in particular assumed a dominant role in the frequent and violent struggles to achieve social reforms and win economic benefits.[31] Anarchism dominated labor and intellectual circles during the period 1906–20, and constituted a strong preparation for the Communist tendencies that emerged later on.[32] Despite its substantial influence in Brazil, anarchism was beset by deep-rooted problems in its ideology, organization, and leadership.

Ideologically inflexible, anarchism and anarcho-syndicalism were unable to adapt to revolutionary alternatives that fit the Brazilian reality —a problem that continues to plague the left even today. This dilemma was reflected in the dispersion of ideas in a variety of sporadic, generally short-lived, journals and newspapers published in urban and industrial centers. Of thirty periodicals manifesting anarchist and anarcho-syndicalist views between 1894 and 1920, twenty were published in São Paulo, seven in Rio de Janeiro, two in Pôrto Alegre, and one in Curitiba; probably only five periodicals were issued consistently over a period of one year or more, and at least five ceased after their first issue.[33] The dissemination of anarchist views was largely the work of ex-European intellectuals and propagandists; and of course their periodicals projected the views of the many anarchists whose differences divided revolutionary movements in Europe. Still, although the diversity of views contributed also to divisions within Brazil, there is no doubt that anarchism aided the working-class struggle to achieve moderate reforms such as the eight-hour day and wage increases.

These ideological differences and leadership divisions mentioned above were evident among dispersed anarchist and anarcho-syndicalist organizations. Although anarchist activity centered in the COB, many intellectuals and workers supported organizations that sprang up around relevant issues of the times. In Rio the Nova Aurora group was founded in 1900 to propagate libertarian ideas. A year later the Centro Socialista Eurico Ferri in its May 1 manifesto issued a six-point program calling for modification of the penal and civil codes; recognition of free assembly and the right to strike; labor laws to protect women and children; and laws specifying maximum work hours, minimum salaries, and old-age pensions and disability benefits. The first Congresso Operário do Brasil, held in Rio April 5–20, 1906, resulted two years later in the formation of the COB not as a political party but as a workers' movement combining eight labor organizations of Rio de Janeiro, twenty-two organizations of São Paulo, and one of Pôrto Alegre. A proliferation of small anarchist groups accompanied the foundation of the COB.[34]

As noted earlier, the Russian Revolution was the catalyst coalescing the radical elements that would emerge five years later in the PCB.[35]

Yet it too generated dissension within the anarchists' ranks, polarizing them ideologically in two camps; and the anarchist press became a forum for pro- and anti-Bolshevik opinion.[36] Octávio Brandão and Astrojildo Pereira, founders of the PCB later on, called for intense propagandization of the Russian Revolution and of Bolshevik ideals. They were supported by Antônio Canellas, leader of the Rio strike in 1919 and later a member of the PCB Central Committee (until his expulsion in 1924), and Roberto Morena, an anarchist leader who became a chief Communist spokesman in the labor movement. Strongly opposed to the Bolsheviks were Florentino de Carvalho, José Oiticica, Fabio Luiz, Carlos Dias, Antônio Campos, Edgard Leuenroth, Adelino Pinho, and Pedro Matera.[37] These anti-Bolsheviks expressed concern over the administrative machinery and authoritarian central policy upon which the Bolsheviks built their movement in Russia, and in the international sphere they influenced a COB decision to affiliate with the anarcho-syndicalist International Workingmen's Association, mentioned above.[38]

Formation of the PCB: 1917–1922

The Communist nucleus in Brazil was profoundly affected by external events, the most important being undoubtedly the Russian Revolution of 1917 and the founding of the Communist Third International in March 1919—though Brazilians were knowledgeable as well about revolutionary events in Mexico from 1910 to 1917.

Lenin and the Revolution had a powerful impact on radical thought, projecting an increasingly favorable image on Brazilian socialists while splitting the anarchist leadership. In January 1918 an anonymous pamphlet entitled "A revolução russa e a imprensa" was circulated to clarify the Revolution's objectives. In its February 22, 1919, issue the anarchist organ *A Plebe* also carried information on the Revolution, together with an appeal by Maxim Gorki for support on the part of workers throughout the world, and a lengthy letter from "Kessler," a Soviet agent in Brazil. In its issue of March 1 *Alba Russa,* an Italian weekly in São Paulo, published an article by Lenin on the Brest-Litovsk treaty with Germany; in August the Rio de Janeiro weekly, *Spartacus,* carried the text of the first Soviet constitution and *Vanguarda,* a São Paulo worker's daily, published in its issue of March 11, 1921, some speeches inaugurating the French Communist party in December 1920.[39]

The creation of the Comintern by Soviet leaders in Moscow placed

Table 2.1

Formation of the Partido Comunista do Brasil

Coligação Social (Anarchist, 1921)

Liga Comunista Feminina

Grupo da Clarté (Socialist, 1921)

Partido Comunista do Brasil (Rio de Janeiro Anarchist, 1919)

Liga Comunista (São Paulo)

Partido Comunista do Brasil (São Paulo Anarchist, 1919)

Grupo Comunista do Rio de Janeiro (Nov. 1921)

Other state groups (Pernambuco, Minas Gerais)

Liga Comunista de Livramento (Rio Grande do Sul, 1918)

União Maximalista (Pôrto Alegre, 1919)

Grupo Comunista de Pôrto Alegre (1921)

PCB (March 25–27, 1922)

pressures on the already disunified ranks of socialists and anarchists. Unity was undermined also by factionalism among the socialist parties of the Second International. Old and new socialist groups emerged, usually on a *pro* or *contra* Bolshevik position. Likewise, polarized anarchist groups lined up behind the International Workingmen's Association in Berlin or the Red International of Labor Unions in Moscow.

Within Brazil, anarchists and anarcho-syndicalists continued to dominate the labor movement and to lead the workers' strikes of 1917–20. For three years following the general strike of July 1917 in São Paulo, there was agitation for higher pay and better working conditions in Rio de Janeiro, São Paulo, Santos, Pôrto Alegre, Salvador, Recife, and Niterói. A third COB congress was held in 1920. Despite this activity anarchist influence was in decline at a time when Marxism-Leninism offered new ideological premises for both intellectual and worker.

There were many early attempts to establish a Communist party in Brazil.[40] Among them was a Liga Comunista de Livramento in Rio Grande do Sul in 1918; under the leadership of Santos Soares the Liga functioned until 1922, despite police persecution. In Pôrto Alegre the Centro or União Maximalista began operations in 1919, and in 1921 changed its name to Grupo Comunista de Pôrto Alegre.[41] An anarchist-inspired Partido Comunista do Brasil (PCB) was formed in Rio de Janeiro on March 9, 1919, and in June convoked the first Conferência Comunista do Brasil. On May 27 the Liga Comunista Feminina, led by Maria de Lourdes Nogueira (also in Rio), declared its support of the PCB. On June 16 anarchists in São Paulo, who earlier had organized a Liga Comunista, now constituted themselves in a Partido Comunista.[42] On November 7, 1921, a Grupo Comunista do Rio de Janeiro was formed with the objective of organizing a national Communist party as well as evaluating the twenty-one principles of the Comintern.[43] Twelve members comprised the original group, all of them laborers or merchants with the exception of Astrojildo Pereira.[44] The Grupo influenced the formation of similar groups in Recife, Juiz de Fora, Cruzeiro, São Paulo, Santos, and in Pôrto Alegre, where the União Maximalista was reorganized. From January 1922 the Grupo Comunista propagated its view through a monthly, *Movimento Comunista*.[45] (Table 2.1 clarifies this organizational formation.)

These early developments culminated in the formal establishment of the PCB and convocation of its first congress from March 25 to 27,

1922. Attending the congress were nine delegates (of a total party membership of seventy-three), representing groups from the Federal District and the states of Rio de Janeiro, São Paulo, Pernambuco, Minas Gerais, and Rio Grande do Sul (two units, from Santos and Juiz de Fora, were unable to send delegates). The delegates ranged from twenty to forty years of age and included two intellectuals (Astrojildo Pereira and Cristiano Cordeiro), two tailors (Joaquim Barbosa and Manuel Cendón), one printer (João da Costa Pimenta), one broom-maker (Luiz Pérez), one electrician (Hermogêneo Fernandes da Silva), one barber (Abílio de Nequete), and one construction worker (José Elias da Silva). With the exception of Cendón, who was a socialist, the delegates had all been active in the anarcho-syndicalist movement; [46] and all were native Brazilians except Cendón (a Spaniard) and Nequete (a Syrian). The congress examined and approved the twenty-one principles of the Comintern [47] and the party statutes, which were based in large measure on those of the Partido Comunista de la Argentina. It also elected an Executive Central Committee composed of Abílio de Nequete as secretary general, Luiz Pérez, Antônio Cruz Júnior, and Antônio Canelas.[48]

In summary the PCB sprouted from the divisions and fusions of somewhat similar ideological movements whose drift depended largely upon international developments. Recognition of this dependence helps to explain, as we indicated above, why socialism and anarchism encountered difficulty in devising alternatives tailored to the Brazilian situation. These ideologies, and the emerging Communist movement as well, concentrated on the international scene rather than on national conditions,[49] and thus remained largely marginal to Brazilian society.

3 • Evolution of the Party: 1922-1945

In this chapter and in Chapter 4 we want to trace the development of the Partido Comunista do Brasil (PCB) from its beginnings to 1972. Five periods in the party's history are identifiable: (1) from its beginnings in 1922 to its Third Congress and internal division in 1929; (2) from 1930 to 1937 and the *Estado Novo* regime of Getúlio Vargas; (3) 1937 to 1945, a period of suppression and inactivity for the party; (4) from the legalization and electoral successes of the party during the interval 1945–47 to the internal divisions commencing in 1956; and (5) from 1956 to 1972, a span marked by military intervention in 1964 and the Sixth Congress of the PCB in 1967. The present chapter deals with the first three periods.

The First Phase: 1922–1929

The emergence of the Partido Comunista do Brasil coincided with several important national events. It was during this period that the state and federal oligarchies were seriously challenged and finally overthrown by the Revolution of 1930. The Brazilian First Republic, from 1889 to 1930, was dominated by a coalition of state oligarchies from the two wealthiest and most populous states, São Paulo and Minas Gerais. The strength of federal machine politics depended on a *modus vivendi* whereby these two states took turns supplying the nation's President. In the special Presidential elections of April 13, 1919, Presidential candidate Rui Barbosa of Bahia challenged (unsuccessfully) the federal machine through hard campaigning. Moreover, during the 1920's the

Partido Republicano Riograndense refused to support the Republican parties dominating Minas and São Paulo, and challenged their choices of Artur Bernardes (the governor of Minas) and Washington Luiz Pereira de Souza of São Paulo. Although these two did indeed emerge victorious, respectively in the Presidential elections of March 1, 1922, and March 1, 1926, the state of Rio Grande do Sul and its governor, Getúlio Vargas, obtained power in 1930 through revolution and a military coup that marked the demise of the "Old Republic" and the Minas-São Paulo political hegemony.[1]

The decision of Rio Grande do Sul to oppose the Presidential choice of Minas and São Paulo in 1922 set the stage for a period of turmoil. A series of crises followed the election of Bernardes, among them the abortive revolt of Fort Copacabana led by a young and ambitious lieutenant, Antônio de Siqueira Campos, in July 1922;[2] The Gaúcho Civil War of 1923; and the uprising in São Paulo during July 1924. The São Paulo uprising, for example, was in part a manifestation of the latent discontent persisting in army circles before the election of Bernardes. So too was the Fort Copacabana revolt. Instead of receiving amnesty, the *tenentes* (lieutenants) participating in the 1922 outbreak were condemned to prison. What was to emerge in consequence was a movement known as *tenentismo,* whose revolts and long forced marches eventually became identified with political and social change.[3]

The São Paulo revolt, a turning point for the tenentes, was touched off on July 5 by a group of conspirators including Siqueira Campos, who had escaped from a military hospital, Eduardo Gomes, and the brothers Joaquim and Juarez Távora, all of whom had rebelled two years earlier. Also involved were Miguel Costa, then an officer of the São Paulo state militia, and Isidoro Dias Lopes, head of the movement and a retired colonel known for his participation in an 1893 uprising.[4] Surprisingly enough, on July 8 São Paulo fell into the hands of the revolutionaries; but attacked by a large and well-reinforced federal force, the revolutionaries withdrew on July 27, and with an abundant supply of arms and munitions retreated westward, distributing issues of *O Libertador* as they proceeded. By late August this *Coluna Paulista* reached Iguaçu Falls in Paraná State, to the south, and from there João Cabanas led his "death" column through large landholdings, bringing terror to the area.[5]

Meanwhile Juarez Távora was sent to Rio Grande do Sul to join Siqueira Campos, Luiz Carlos Prestes (then a young Army engineer), and João Alberto Lins de Barros, another tenente.[6] Their revolt erupted on October 24, 1924. After encountering difficulties, Prestes, now the top commander of the revolutionaries, marched north to a point near Iguaçu Falls, where at the end of March 1925 he joined the Paulista rebels. There Miguel Costa was named general in charge of both the Rio Grande Brigade under Prestes, and of the São Paulo Brigade under Juarez Távora.[7] Then began the "long march" of fourteen thousand miles through the vast Brazilian interior, reaching Goiás in June 1925, Minas and Bahia two months later, and finally the northern states of Maranhão and Piauí, where the revolutionaries received support from anti-government politicians.

The failure of the rebels to capture Terezina, in Piauí, the capture of Juarez Távora in that state, and the harassment of battalions of Northeast *cangaceiros* (bandits) whose leaders had been appointed officers in the federal army, forced the rebels to move south. After an encounter with the Pernambuco state militia, they marked time in backland Bahia until Bernardes left the Presidency in November 1926. Then they retraced their steps and exited from Mato Grosso, Prestes with six hundred twenty men reaching Bolivia in February 1927, and Siqueira Campos entering Paraguay late in March with sixty-five men who had become separated from the main column.[8]

With the departure of the revolutionaries, President Washington Luiz Pereira de Souza peacefully took office. In Rio Grande do Sul the Republican party machine of autocratic Antônio Augusto Borges de Medeiros was rewarded for its support of Washington Luiz: Getúlio Vargas was named Finance Minister. As for the rebels, the President refused to grant them amnesty. The aging Isidoro yielded to Prestes, who had emerged during the march as a remarkable leader[9] and officially became supreme commander of the revolutionary movement in 1927. By that time Prestes was caring for the four hundred veterans remaining in southeastern Bolivia. He remained there for a year following his promotion and then moved to Buenos Aires, where he came into contact with Rodolfo Ghioldi and other Argentine Communists.

The government reaction to these crises was to suppress the activities of the PCB, which at the time was not important enough to be the target of special legislation or police action. The party seems not to have been directly involved in the main issues of the period but rather was concentrating its resources on achieving status within the interna-

tional Communist movement and consolidating the internal party organization, and in addition was concerned to eliminate anarchist remnants and to organize the working class. Its demands differed substantially from those of disenchanted mainstream elements insisting upon
representative government. In June 1923 the Rio police confiscated the
PCB's printing press and files; and during a state of siege prevailing
from July 5, 1924, to December 31, 1926, the party was banned; [10]
then it enjoyed a brief period of legality from January to August 1927.
During its initial phase the PCB set up the Juventude Comunista
(January 1924), held two party congresses (1925 and 1929), published two important periodicals (*A Classe Operária* and *A Nação*),
and achieved its first electoral success.

The PCB's Second Congress (May 16–18, 1925) followed a meeting in February of some hundred fifty delegates from the Rio de Janeiro,
Niterói, Recife, São Paulo, and Santos groups, representing roughly half
the estimated total membership. The Congress discussed and approved
policy, especially the resolutions to recruit new members through the development of cells in one hundred large business firms before June 30,
1925, and to publish a new weekly. Serious attention was given also to
modifying the party statutes, reorganizing cells and regional committees,
agitation and propaganda, and representation on the Central Committee.
Debated were such issues as English imperialism(agrarian) and American
imperialism(industrial); adaptation of the party statutes to a model of the
Comintern; "the character and direction of proletarian policy;" and
"dualism" in Brazilian society between "semifeudal agrarian capitalism
and modern industrial capitalism." [11]

Between the second and third party congresses, the PCB disseminated propaganda through two periodicals and adopted a policy of political and electoral participation through a unified workers' movement.[12] In its initial phase, *A Classe Operária* was published in
twelve issues over a three-month period from May 1, 1925; it reappeared in 1928 and continued until mid-1929, when it was repressed
by the government; and it appeared clandestinely thereafter, briefly in
1935 and after 1945 until the early 1950's. Between January 3 and
August 11, 1927, the publication of *A Nação* (edited by Leônidas
de Resende), coincided with the PCB's brief period of legality.[13] *A
Nação*, which carried the bulk of PCB propaganda, called for unity
of workers, defended the Russian Revolution, and focused on the writings of Marx and Lenin. Two days after its reappearance, *A Nação*
published the PCB's thirteen-point document on the formation of a Bloco

Operário (workers' bloc) with the objective of building a proletarian front for the February parliamentary elections.[14] The Bloco's platform called for maintenance of an independent working-class policy, criticism of the "plutocracy," struggle against "imperialism," recognition of the Soviet Union, amnesty for political prisoners, autonomy for the Federal District, social legislation, the right to free association and opinion, reform of the tax and monetary system, housing for workers, expansion of education, and suffrage for all citizens.

Under the banner of the Bloco Operário the PCB succeeded in electing João Batista de Azevedo Lima, one of two parliamentary candidates and future president of the BOC. During the October 1928 contest, after the name had been changed to Bloco Operário e Camponês, two members won seats on the Rio municipal council (Octávio Brandão and Minervino de Oliveira).[15] From then on, the BOC's success and failures (i.e., to aggregate the working masses) became the focus of internal debate. After boldly presenting Presidential, Vice Presidential, and other candidates and suffering a disastrous defeat in the March 1930 elections, the BOC was dissolved a few months later. The PCB policy of maintaining front organizations of workers was quickly revived, however; indeed the policy was later adopted by the Comintern itself.

The internal debate intensified just prior to the PCB's Third Congress held in Niterói between December 29, 1928, and January 4, 1929. The debate, provoked in mid-1928 by Joaquim Barbosa, PCB's trade-union secretary and member of the Executive Central Commission, was carried in the party magazine, *Auto-Crítica,* and dealt with such issues as Communist activity in labor unions, the PCB's political line and tactics in the BOC, the peasant problem, relations between the Juventude Comunista and the PCB, the character of the Brazilian revolution, the struggle against anarcho-syndicalism, and Comintern policy.[16] Barbosa and another labor leader, João da Costa Pimenta (the unsuccessful BOC candidate for Parliament who had received three thousand votes), aggregated their followers into the Oposição Sindical, the first factionalist group to disrupt the PCB.[17] Their dissent was directly opposed to the ultra-left line of the "Third Period." This line, adopted by the Comintern at its Sixth Congress in 1928, was of uncompromising hostility to democratic and reformist movements and thus brought the PCB into conflict with trade unionists with whom its leaders had worked closely to form the BOC. Eventually the Oposição Sindical was expelled by the PCB's Third Congress.[18]

Comintern policy and dissent in international as well as in national

Communist circles contributed to the second major split in the PCB. Soviet and international Communism were divided over the stand of the Trotskyist opposition, which in 1927 had attacked the "petty bourgeois" compromises of the Stalinist leadership. This resulted not only in the expulsion of Trotsky and suppression of the opposition but also in the tightening of Russian control over the Comintern, whose Trotskyist dissidents were forthwith ordered to be disciplined. Trotskyist sympathizers in Brazil—associated largely with the Juventude Comunista—included Mário Pedrosa, Livio Xavier, Rodolfo Coutinho, Arístedes Lobo, and Hilcar Leite. In 1929 these Trotskyists withdrew to form the Grupo Comunista Lenino, which two years later they reorganized as the Legião dos Comunistas.[19]

The PCB's Third Congress reflected the differences and disagreements manifested by these two factions as well as by the international movement; it also marked the close of the first phase in the party's evolution. Thirty-one delegates attended, including ten from the old party leadership and thirteen from six regional organizations (Pernambuco, Espírito Santo, Rio de Janeiro, São Paulo, Rio Grande do Sul, and the Federal District). Of these delegates, sixteen were workers, six were intellectuals, and six were bureaucrats. The agenda emphasized such issues as the national political situation and the position of the PCB, the struggle against imperialism and the danger of war, the work of the party in the labor unions, the peasant question, the BOC, and the struggle against fascism. These broader themes were examined in a number of theses grouped under the following heads: (1) "the semifeudal, semicolonial agrarian economy" and the influence of foreign capital in public and private sectors,[20] the class forces that confront imperialism, the "third revolutionary explosion" (represented by the Prestes Column as the successor to the movements of 1922 and 1924), and the tasks (such as organization and propaganda) of the party; (2) the struggle against imperialism and the dangers of war; (3) the labor movement, attacked for its errors, especially for its disorganized strikes, corporativism, anarchist tradition, organizational disorder, exclusion of revolutionary unions, and bureaucratic administration; (4) the peasant question, the problems of the unemployed masses, and agrarian reform; (5) the BOC and its threat to the PCB—of losing political control over its legal front organization as well as, of losing self-identification as a party; (6) fascism, "the weapon of internal reaction and imperialist penetration"; (7) the promulgation of propaganda among immigrant workers. Of special importance was a resolution on party organization, outlining nine tasks and urging that the party statutes of 1925 be adapted to Brazilian conditions. A resolution on the Juventude Comunista acknowledged difficulties in the early phase but noted recent increases in membership and improvements in organization, and outlined specific tasks for the future. The congress resolved to study the PCB's relations not only with the BOC in São Paulo but also with other organizations, including the Liga Anti-imperialista and the Liga Anti-fascista.

In evaluating this first phase of the PCB's evolution, Astrojildo Pereira offered self-criticism of his activity as secretary general and characterized the 1922–29 period as a struggle hampered by "administrative deficiencies and errors." The revolutionary objectives of the PCB, he asserted, were undermined by the social, legalistic, and parliamentary reformism of the 1920's as well as by anarcho-syndicalism. Moreover, he said, the weakness of the PCB included ideological and theoretical deficiencies, especially concerning the character of the "Brazilian revolution," the inability of the party leadership to analyze, from a Marxian perspective, the reality of Brazilian history and economic and social structure, and to comprehend the basic nature of class conflict; the failure to assess the dialectics of Brazilian developments; and the difficulties involved in tying revolutionary action to revolutionary theory, with consequence "in a permanent oscillation between the revolutionary verbiage of the left [in theory] and the opportunism of the right in practice." [21]

Ideological Polarization: 1930–1937

The election of Washington Luiz Pereira de Souza of São Paulo as President of Brazil did not bring an end to dissension within the federal machine. Under the impact of the depression of 1929, President Washington Luiz indicated Júlio Prestes de Albuquerque, another *paulista* (and no relation to Luiz Carlos), as his successor—to the detriment of Minas Gerais. Widespread dissatisfaction with economic and political conditions rapidly led to the formation of a broad oppositionist front, the Aliança Liberal, composed of young military officers and the disaffected oligarchies of Minas Gerais, Rio Grande do Sul, and Paraíba.

Several periods of conflict among ideological forces overshadowed the PCB's evolution from 1930 through 1937. The first, initiated by

the Aliança Liberal in early January 1930 with the Presidential candidacy of Rio Grande do Sul's Governor Getúlio Vargas, spanned the
elections of March 1, 1930 (won by Vargas' rival Júlio Prestes de
Albuquerque of São Paulo), the assassination on July 26 of João
Pessoa (Vargas' Aliança Liberal running mate from Paraíba), and
the outbreak of revolution on October 3 against the Washington Luiz
administration. The second period covered the overthrow of Washington
Luiz on October 24, the coming to power of Getúlio Vargas as head
of the provisional government on November 3, and the unsuccessful
constitucionalista revolution in São Paulo occurring from July 9 to October 2, 1932, against Vargas. During the third period, members were
elected to the Constituent Assembly on May 3, 1933; a constitution was
being drawn up from November 15, 1933, to July 16, 1934; and Congressional elections were held on October 14, 1934. During the fourth
period a popular front was developed, and the (aborted) rebellions of
November 23–27, 1935, were staged in Natal, Recife, and Rio de
Janeiro—with an aftermath of martial law and suppression of the PCB.
The Presidential campaign took place in 1937, and the Estado Novo
was promulgated by Vargas on November 10, 1937.

During the first period, while the PCB was beset by its internal ideological divisions, indecisive policy, and errors in tactics and strategy
attributed partially to its allegiance to the political line of the Comintern,[22] in addition it was caught up in rapid economic and political
changes that gripped Brazil (and indeed the world). By 1930 São
Paulo emerged as an industrial center that had survived the delayed
effects of the ending of the First World War, at which point small industry had been disrupted by the competition of cheap imported foreign manufactured goods purchased with the abundant exchange from
coffee exports and other goods.[23] At the same time the anti-inflationary
policy of the Bernardes regime in 1924 encouraged foreign capital investment. As a consequence the world financial crisis of 1929 had
profound impact on Brazil, and triggered the collapse of coffee prices.
Economic decline brought disaffection in the oligarchies of Minas
Gerais, São Paulo, and Rio Grande do Sul, encouraged plots and con-
spiracies among middle-class politicians and military officers, and resulted in large-scale unemployment and widespread dissatisfaction in
the labor movement, which after 1924 had been weakening under the
decline of militant activity (even though labor came increasingly under
Communist control).

The ambiguous position assumed by the PCB in 1930 may be explained, first, by the party's sectarian hostility to democratic and reformist movements, which brought it into conflict with the aims of its front organization, the BOC. Despite the expulsion of the Oposição Sindical and many BOC leaders, the PCB continued to wield influence in the labor movement, especially among unions of the printers, cabinet makers, and seamen; and after its Third Congress the party concentrated on the two central organizations, the Federação Sindical Regional do Rio de Janeiro and the União Geral dos Trabalhadores in Pernambuco.[24] Thus, the party's decision in 1930 to run Rio municipal councilman Minervino de Oliveira as its Presidential candidate under the BOC banner appeared to contradict its earlier policy stand.

Then again, the Central Committee had resolved as early as 1927 to send Astrojildo Pereira to Bolivia to discuss with Luiz Carlos Prestes the possibility of Prestes' leading an alliance between the PCB and the petty bourgeoisie. Such an alliance, it was believed, would be the catalyst for the impending revolution. While approved in the PCB's Third Congress, this resolution caused dissension in the party ranks, especially after Pereira's meeting with Prestes in December 1927 at Puerto Suárez, Bolivia.[25] In July 1929, one month after the PCB had invited Prestes to be its Presidential candidate and had accepted a united-front program, Leôncio Basbaum, the party representative, met three times with Prestes, Siqueira Campos, and Juarez Távora. The seven-point program called for nationalization of land and division of latifundios, nationalization of industrial firms and "imperialist" banks, abolition of the external debt, freedom of organization and press, right to strike, legality for the PCB, an eight-hour work day, holidays, wage increases, and other workers' benefits.[26] Juarez Távora objected to an exchange of ideas with the PCB, Siqueira Campos was against electoral participation, and Prestes refused the candidacy on the ground that the PCB program was too extreme. At the same time he proposed his own united front program, calling for the secret vote, literacy, justice, freedom of press and organization, and workers' benefits. The PCB rejected Prestes' counter proposal, but continued negotiations with the tenentes through the South American Bureau of the Comintern and a Comitê Militar Revolucionário.[27]

The Communist position was further complicated by the radicalization of the Aliança Liberal after Vargas' defeat in March 1930. The broad-based Aliança comprised the disaffected oligarchies mentioned above, of Minas Gerais, Rio Grande do Sul, and Paraíba, as well as many of the tenente militants of the 1922 and 1924 revolts and the Prestes Column, and middle-class radical figures, among them Joaquim Pimenta and Maurício de Lacerda. This coalition had supported the moderate platform outlined in Getúlio Vargas' speech of January 2, 1930, in which he appealed for social justice; a labor code for urban and rural workers; protection for the aged, women, and children, and extended social security benefits.[28] Many Aliança leaders, apparently apprehensive over the possibility of revolution,[29] complacently accepted Vargas' defeat in the March elections, although certain moderates became worried when elected Aliança candidates were not seated in Minas Gerais and Paraíba.[30] After the new Congress had declared Júlio Prestes the victor on May 31, Vargas commented that political changes would be forthcoming and that the people would "show whether or not they are in accord with the result." [31]

Aliança politicians had become attracted to the idea of revolt, but they were also confused and upset by Luiz Carlos Prestes, who in his May manifesto viewed an Aliança uprising as a traditional power struggle.[32] Popular interests had been sacrificed by the farcical election, he declared, nor could the Brazilian revolution be achieved with the Aliança's program, which signified only "a simple change of men, a secret vote . . . and other panaceas which could not interest the majority of people without whose support a revolution would be nothing more than a simple struggle between the dominant oligarchies." Therefore the insurrection and the future government must be supported by "the mass of workers in the cities and hinterland." This government would guarantee social legislation such as limited work hours, protection for working women and children, social insurance (for accidents, unemployment, old age, sickness), and the right to strike, to assemble, and to organize. Further, the revolution would be agrarian and anti-imperialist: the government would nationalize land, which would be distributed freely to workers, and would expropriate communication media, public services, mines, and banks, and cancel the foreign debt.[33]

The Prestes manifesto shocked most of the Aliança revolutionaries. Carlos de Lima Cavalcanti, a wealthy newspaper publisher named by Prestes in 1928 to represent the revolution in Pernambuco, refused to publish it.[34] Juarez Távora in a telegram and Isidoro Dias Lopes in a lengthy letter offered rebuttals.[35] And Antônio Carlos, the political patriarch of Minas, suspicious that his tenente collaborators had turned

Communist, attempted to sabotage an Aliança revolt.[36] The PCB on the other hand, was dissatisfied with Prestes' failure to mention Communism and uneasy over his August 2 announcement that *Prestismo* would be the basis of a new political movement to be designated the Liga de Ação Revolucionária (LAR), and in August 1930 declared its opposition to the Liga and urged Prestes to ally with the PCB.[37] Prestes' declaration resulted in a definitive break with the rank and file soldiers of the Column, who now turned to Vargas' "revolution"; moreover, the transfer of Prestismo from the Column to the LAR established a pattern of personalism and individual mystique that would later characterize Prestes' domination over the PCB; and, finally, Prestes' rejection of the Aliança tended to weaken the "populism" of the 1930 Revolution.[38]

As another consequence, in late September 1930 party leaders requested five thousand revolvers to arm the Communist rank and file so that they could participate in the revolt, and this complicated the PCB position. While at first the PCB appeared to have joined Prestes and perhaps even influenced him to oppose the Aliança, it now attempted to join the revolt. These moves may have been attributed to apprehensions, especially of older party leaders, that the personalism of Prestes would dominate the PCB, and to the belated realization that the Aliança's conspiracy and the tenentes' third uprising would indeed be successful. The conspirators were so alarmed by the PCB's arms request, however, that not only was the request denied but then, upon assuming power in November, they decided to suppress Communist activity and to deport PCB leaders.[39]

During the first two years of the provisional Vargas government, the PCB maintained a generally negative attitude toward the 1930 Revolution.[40] There was confusion, however, in Santos, São Paulo state, where a small nucleus of Communists dominated by Plínio Mello, Josias Carneiro Leão, and Luiz de Barros organized a regional party and obtained authorization from the revolutionary intervener in São Paulo, João Alberto Lins de Barros, brother of Luiz.[41] When their party attempted to bring together all the working-class groups in São Paulo, including Trotskyists and anarchists, they were repudiated by the anarchists, in particular, and eventually Mello and others were expelled from the PCB, which was assuming an increasingly Stalinist position, opposed to the provisional government. Thereafter many of the old founders and leaders of the PCB, especially those who had come from the anarchist movement, were replaced in leadership positions by Stalinists.[42]

Having been courted by both Communists and Trotskyists, Prestes finally declared himself a Communist in his "open letter" of March 12, 1931, denounced the Trotskyists, admitted his error in having formed the LAR, and attacked his former tenente associates as agents of imperialism. He called for an "agrarian and anti-imperialist revolution" under the aegis of the PCB, and for the organization of "a government under councils of workers and peasants, soldiers and sailors." According to his associate Abguar Bastos, Prestes believed that such a government would evolve through a three-stage process: from anti-oligarchic democracy to anti-latifundism and anti-imperialism with leadership divided between the petty bourgeoisie and the proletariat, and finally to a dictatorship of the proletariat.[43] Before departing on a four-year visit to the Soviet Union, Prestes reaffirmed his allegiance to the PCB in a letter of March 20 of 1931.[44] Later, commenting on the 1932 rebellion in São Paulo, he attacked Prestismo as a "petty bourgeois" obstacle and accused certain elements of using his name in a struggle he characterized as between "bourgeois groups of landowners and financiers at the service" of English and North American "imperialism." [45]

In August 1932, seventy-three PCB leaders were imprisoned in the penal colony on the Ilha Grande, allegedly for their involvement in the São Paulo uprising.[46] In November a party meeting was held to reconstitute the then decimated Central Committee. Joining the party at this time was Antônio Maciel Bomfim, who had been active in the LAR and would become secretary general of the party at its First National Conference in 1934, thus assuring the dominance of Prestismo over the old leadership.[47]

The final years of the provisional government were given over to drafting of a constitution, and the Paulista uprising spurred the drafting commission to finish its work. Among the rash of parties that emerged to participate in the May 3, 1933, election of a Constituent Assembly was the Partido Socialista de São Paulo, founded by tenente leader Miguel Costa. Although the authorities refused to recognize the PCB, in the 1934 state legislative elections the party supported six hundred forty-two "proletarian" candidates (including eighty-five women), and backed the União Operária e Camponesa, a legal organization in the Federal District and in several states.[48] A particular concern of the Communists was Plínio Salgado's fascist party, the Ação Integralista

Brasileira, and accordingly the PCB worked through the Frente Unica de Luta contra a Reação e o Fascismo, in Rio.[49] The elections were a near-disaster for the tenentes, who lost their hold on the Northeast while managing victories in the Federal District and Bahia. The pro-Vargas forces, however, won an overwhelming majority of deputy seats (the Constituent Assembly had elected Vargas President in July 1934).[50]

Using a false passport, Prestes returned to Brazil as a member of the PCB's Political Bureau and Central Committee as well as of the Executive Committee of the Comintern. This was in April 1935, a year after the party's adoption of a popular-front policy involving the unification of the labor movement under Communist leadership and the formation of the Aliança Nacional Libertadora (ANL).[51] During 1934 the PCB had organized local trade union conventions in an effort to detach labor from government influence and to prepare for the unity congress, which was held a year from that May and which established the Confederação Sindical Unitária do Brasil.[52] The ANL was organized in Rio de Janeiro in March 1935 as a broad coalition of groups and individuals, both Communists and tenentes, opposed to *integralismo* and to the suppressive measures enacted by the Vargas regime.[53] Among the founders were radical tenentes many of whom had once supported the 1930 Revolution but now opposed Vargas. Miguel Costa, who headed the ANL in the state of São Paulo; Hercolino Cascardo, who had led a naval mutiny during the 1924 uprising; João Cabanas, a socialist who was later suspected of being a police informer; and Carlos da Costa Leite, an officer who had participated in the Prestes Column.[54] Two tenentes, André Trifino Corêa and Agildo da Gama Barata Ribeiro, were Communists; another, Roberto Faller Sissón, a naval officer of wealthy background, was involved in preliminary organizational efforts and coordination with the PCB. Other founders were Benjamín Soares Cabello, a journalist from Rio Grande do Sul; Ivan Pedro Martins, a law student; Abguar Bastos, the radical deputy from Goías quoted above; and Rubem Braga, a young journalist.

The ANL National Executive Committee met for the first time on March 12, 1935, and the first public rally was held in Rio on March 30 (the day on which Congress pushed through a National Security Law). Prestes was nominated for the honorary presidency by Carlos Lacerda, then a young radical and (although he denies it today) a member of the PCB.[55] Others selected were Hercolino Cascardo, president, and Sissón, secretary general. The ANL five-point program demanded an end to payments on the foreign debt, nationalization of all "imperialistic" companies, protection of small and medium-sized farms and division of large properties among those who work them, full "popular" liberties, and popular government established in the interests of the Brazilian people.[56]

ANL organization consisted of a hierarchy of municipal, regional, and national secretariats and of cells of ten or more members, organized either by locale or by occupation. Membership was claimed by the ANL to total several hundred thousand three months after its founding, and was basically urban, with a predominance of middle- and lower-class elements.[57] Front organizations of the ANL included the União Feminina do Brasil (UFB), the Aliança Popular por Pão, Terra e Liberdade, and the Frente Popular para a Luta contra o Fascismo e Guerra. Propaganda was carried in the official ANL organ, *Libertador; Solidaridade,* an irregular publication of workers organized by the ANL in Pernambuco; *Movimento,* the journal of the ANL's Modern Culture Club of Rio, whose editorial board included writers Jorge Amado and José Lins do Rêgo; *A Platéia,* an ANL daily in São Paulo. ANL news appeared in *Marcha* of Rio, edited by Francisco Mangabeira and his associates Rubem Braga, Newton Freitas, and Carlos Lacerda; in *O Jovem Proletário,* organ of the Juventude Comunista; and in two Communist-owned dailies, *A Manhã* of Rio, edited by Pedro Motta Lima, and *Fôlha do Povo* of Recife, edited first by Osório Lima and after August 28 by José Cavalcanti.

On July 5, the anniversary of the rebellions of 1922 and 1924, Prestes published an "open letter," calling upon the masses to assault the government. "The idea of assault ripens in the conscience of the masses," he declared; the national liberation of Brazil and establishment of a popular revolutionary government would be achieved through the defeat of "fascism" and "the odious Vargas regime." Prestes outlined a nine-point program, calling for an end to the foreign debt; denunciation of "anti-national" treaties; nationalization of public services; workers' benefits including an eight-hour day, social security, and a guaranteed minimum salary; struggle against slavelike and feudal conditions of work; land distribution for the poor population; return of land to Indians; establishment of "popular liberties;" and fight against all "imperialist" wars.[58] Prestes' pronouncement violated the new National Security Law, and a decree signed by Vargas in July "ordered" the closing of the ANL. Inevitably, tension grew thereafter between the outlawed movement and the government when the ANL supported a rapidly spreading walkout on the Great Western Railway in October 1935. Such developments prompted the implementation of the plans for a rebellion that had been worked out many months earlier in Rio de Janeiro by the party and in the Northeast, by Silo Soares Furtado de Meireles, a member of the PCB's Central Committee and Prestes' companion in Russia.[59]

The uprising began on November 23 with a barracks' revolt in Natal, the capital of Rio Grande do Norte. Rebel soldiers were joined later by workers, many of them unemployed; and together they occupied strategic parts of the city, seized the headquarters of the military police, and arrested state police chief, João Medeiros Filho.[60] On November 25 the Comitê Popular Revolucionário was formed; [61] it ordered a reduction in streetcar fares and bread prices, requested all merchants to open their businesses, and closed the local Integralista headquarters. On November 27 the revolt collapsed—simultaneously with an outbreak in Rio, but after rebels in Recife had been overcome.

The Recife uprising began during the early morning of November 24, when a suburban military barracks was occupied. By mid-morning a column of four hundred enlisted men set out for downtown Recife under the command of Octacílio Alves de Lima, an anti-Vargas officer allegedly involved in an earlier military conspiracy, two lieutenants, and Gregório Lourenço Bezerra, a local Communist leader. A makeshift force of police and military units from Recife and Olinda led by police captain Malvino Reis Neto clashed with the column as it marched through an industrial zone.[62] The failure to attack strategic communications centers and military arsenals, the fact that only a handful of Communists and a few dozen civilians (mostly factory workers) joined the revolt, and the arrival of loyalist reinforcements forced rebel commanders to order a full retreat on November 25, and the rebellion collapsed.[63]

On November 24, following the outbreak of the Natal and Recife revolts, Rio police arrested about one hundred fifty persons, including most members of the ANL Executive Committee. During the previous night PCB leaders had decided upon a second wave of uprisings in Espírito Santo, Minas Gerais, and to the south. Prestes gave orders to followers in the Third Infantry Regiment at Praia Vermelha (a section of Rio de Janeiro) to seize their barracks in the early morning of November 27, and then to march on the presidential palace.[64]

According to schedule, the Praia Vermelha garrison was seized by the junior officers, led by Captains Alvaro Francisco de Souza and Agildo Barata, who as vice president of the ANL in Rio Grande do Sul had been responsible for the recruiting of military personnel.[65] A Comitê Revolucionário dos Soldados formed, and two-thirds of the regiment immediately joined the rebels. At about the same time another band of rebels, for the most part sergeants but led by Lieutenants Ginardo Reis and Carlos França, seized the School of Military Aviation at Campo dos Afonsos. After four hours the school was freed by government troops, who later in the day also overcame the Praia Vermelha resistance with the assistance of bombing by three planes and shelling by two ships. Some fifty rebels were dead, and the garrison lay in ruins.

There had been considerable speculation on the questions of timing and whether the rebels acted on their own, according to plan, or by mistake. Most writers agree that Moscow was involved through the dispatch of important Comintern agents to Brazil, and that the PCB and the Vargas police were both aware of preliminary instructions for the uprising.[66] Since the date originally set for the revolt—December 5—was known to the police through its "Communist agent," Rio police were able to mislead the Natal rebels by sending them a coded message ordering the revolt to commence on November 23 [67] —whence the dominant view, that the Natal revolt was precipitated by government provocation and touched off the uprisings in Recife and, after hasty action by Prestes and his aides, also in Rio.[68] According to this view, the Natal revolt probably caught the Recife and Rio rebels by surprise and facilitated police and military punishment of the ANL and the PCB. Acting on misinformation, the Natal rebels were unable to coordinate their efforts with the revolutionaries in Recife and Rio. Another view suggests that the uprisings were a culmination of an evolving political confrontation between the Vargas government, on the one hand, and the ANL and labor, on the other, and that the ANL with its military supporters initiated the revolts.[69] A variant theory is that the individual revolts corresponded closely to local conditions, and that the decision to revolt in Natal came directly from the military leaders there.[70] Despite these varying interpretations, most writers agree that the revolts served Vargas with a pretext not only for crushing the PCB but also for providing himself with extraordinary emergency powers.

In the aftermath of the revolts, Vargas moved to crush Communist activity altogether and to ensure the continuity of his own government.

On four successive occasions he pressured Congress successfully to extend the ninety-day state of siege declared originally on November 20. During this interval, officers were allowed to apply press controls, search homes, and prohibit public meetings. Several thousand prisoners were jailed in Rio, including the city's mayor, Pedro Ernesto; ANL officials such as its president, Cascardo; one senator (Abel Chermont) and four deputies (Abguar Bastos, Domingos Velasco, João Mangabeira, and Octávio de Silveira, whose immunity was revoked by the Chamber); and foreign agents, among them Harry Berger (who went insane under severe torture) and Rodolfo Ghioldi. Prestes was found on March 5, 1936, and his pregnant wife, the German Communist Olga Benário Prestes, was deported to Hitler's Germany, to die there soon after.[71] Vargas was successful also in persuading Congress to establish (in July 1936) a National Security Tribunal to punish subversives.[72]

In the midst of the investigation of Communists and left-wing subversion, politicians began preparing for the presidential elections of January 1938. Green-shirted integralistas stepped up radio and newspaper propaganda and paraded in behalf of their candidate, Plínio Salgado, and in June of 1937 nominated him. In an attempt to block Vargas from succeeding himself, Governors Juracy Magalhães of Bahia and Carlos Lima Cavalcanti of Pernambuco joined governors from all the states except Rio Grande do Sul and São Paulo in nominating as a candidate José Américo de Almeida, an ex-tenente and writer from Paraíba and former Minister of Communications and Public Works under Vargas. Américo, who appealed for working-class support, appeared to be the official candidate, although without the endorsement of Vargas, who refused to support anyone. The other leading candidate was Armando de Salles Oliveira, the successful governor of São Paulo supported by Rio Grande do Sul's Governor Flores da Cunha.

Despite the campaign, Vargas began preparations for a coup. In interventions in Mato Grosso, Maranhão, and the Federal District the elected leadership was supplanted with Vargas supporters. In April 1937 a state of siege was declared in Rio Grande do Sul, to the end of aiding opponents of Governor Flores da Cunha, whose large state militia Vargas feared. Vargas also transferred trusted army commanders to doubtful states to neutralize and isolate opposition and, if necessary, to seize control of the state militia and local police. In September an army general staff, impatient for action, revealed a forged document outlining a plan for a Communist revolt. Known as the "Cohen Plan," and drawn up by integralistas, possibly as part of an army contingency plan in anticipation of some Communist revolt, the document became the pretext for a coup. On September 30 the alleged Communist plot was denounced and on the next day Congress suspended constitutional rights.[73] Nearly six weeks later, on November 10, the coup materialized, and Vargas announced that his new dictatorship could not accommodate Congress and political parties, and that, moreover, all interest and amortization payments of the nation's foreign debt would be suspended. Congress was abruptly closed on the same day, and on December 2 all political parties were banned, including the integralistas. The new constitution, which was modeled on European corporatist and fascistic experiments, especially in Portugal and Italy, granted Vargas authoritarian powers.[74]

The Estado Novo: 1937–1945

The entrenchment of the Estado Novo—as the regime was called—changed the direction of Brazilian politics. No longer would Vargas tolerate experimentation with new political forms in any attempt to discard the old. No longer would national politics consist of uneasy compromises between liberal constitutionalists and authoritarian nationalists. Political opportunists or idealists, often representing the old-line state oligarchies and other traditional forces, would be isolated by the new authoritarian tutelage, and thus would be ended seven years of improvisation that included a regionalist revolt in São Paulo, the 1934 constitution, a popular front, a fascist movement, and an abortive coup by the left. Exhausted by violence from right and left, Brazil would pursue the goals of social welfare and economic nationalism. Oriented toward the authoritarian development of industry, the technological corporative state would resolve social tensions while containing the conservative and powerful traditional elites.

From 1938 until late 1944 the armed forces and the Vargas police provided the bulk of support to his regime, although the labor movement was a strong supporter as well. Unlike similar regimes elsewhere, the Estado Novo was not based on a party or single movement. It was in fact highly personalist in orientation, without any consistent ideology, and not dependent on widespread popular support. Because of this, Vargas was able to suppress even the integralistas, whose demise became a certainty after a small band of militants launched an abortive attack upon the Presidential palace in May 1938.[75] At the same time the federal government was strengthened by means of governmental institutes and agencies created to control production and marketing, and through federal ownership in such national industries as railways and shipping, the expansion of activity into social welfare and labor union organization through the doctrine of *trabalhismo,* and growth in governmental bureaucracy.[76]

Throughout this period the left remained suppressed as the government fired bureaucrats, professors, journalists, and others with Communist or pro-Communist ties. Leaders of Marxist groups were jailed, exiled, or driven into inactivity. A labor bureaucracy, constituting the Labor Ministry and the labor union leadership, manipulated mass labor support through the provision of workers' benefits in exchange for government control over union activities. Workers and unions were not allowed collective bargaining rights, and strikes and lockouts were prohibited. Thus would the Estado Novo depend upon the tacit support of union organizations.[77]

These conditions resulted in drastic curtailment of Communist activities. During the Presidential campaign of 1937 the PCB had suffered another split when a minority faction headed by Lauro Reginaldo da Rocha ("Bangu") backed the Américo candidacy and received support from the Comintern. The majority, suddenly turned minority, had proposed the symbolic candidacy of Prestes, and it continued to control the São Paulo Regional Committee of the party as well as the Communist organization in Paraná and fragments of the state apparatus in Minas Gerais, Rio Grande do Sul, and Pernambuco. Eventually the dissident group broke with the PCB altogether and was subject to attack from the party's propaganda apparatus. The dissidents, reduced to less than a hundred followers, joined the Trotskyist movement and formed the Partido Socialista Revolucionário (PSR); during 1937 they published a semi-legal newspaper, *Orientação Socialista* and thereafter an illegal organ, *Luta de Classes.*[78]

The Trotskyist movement included also the older group led by Mário Pedrosa, Hilcar Leite, Lívio Xavier, and other former Communists such as Agusto Besouchet and Febus Gikovate. This group had evolved from the 1929 split in the PCB and now called itself the Partido Operário Leninista; it consisted of some hundred thirty activists and distributed various periodicals.[79] The older group and the PSR joined the Fourth International, which was formally organized in

1938, and Pedrosa was present at the founding congress; the PSR, however, later became the dominant Trotskyist group in Brazil and the official representative of the Fourth International.[80]

Meanwhile, the PCB continued to advocate a national front policy and the unification of the government with the people to meet the integralista challenge.[81] By 1939—and coincidentally with the Nazi-Soviet nonaggression pact of that August—the party was supporting Vargas, whom they then considered an anti-fascist. With the outbreak of World War II, the PCB called upon the Brazilian left to hold a congress at war's end and to organize a new party.[82] In any event, the the PCB's passive stance involved it in further troubles as police in Rio de Janeiro, discounting Allied reports of Nazi penetration in Brazil and still fearful of people suspected of desiring to overthrow the regime, again moved against the Communists. One hundred were arrested in December 1939, another fifty in April 1940, and in November Prestes went on trial, with five others accused of the brutal 1936 slaying of Elza Fernandes, apparently by a police informer; thirty years were added to Prestes' original prison sentence.[83]

With its leadership and much of its rank and file in prison, the PCB was without direction. Attempts to reorganize the party in 1941 and 1942 were opposed by some of the old militants who were unable to reconcile their anti-capitalist views with a revised Communist policy that now tolerated an Anglo-Soviet-American coalition against European fascism.[84] On the other hand, with Brazilian support of the Allies police suppression of Communist activities was relaxed. Three Communist groups were distinguishable. One, in São Paulo, was comprised of old militants who distrusted Prestes and desired to resurrect the party along traditional party lines and independent policy. A seeond group, also in São Paulo, included Communist fugitives from Bahia—"opportunists and rightists who hoped to dominate a new Central Committee." A third group, the Comissão Nacional de Organização Provisória (CNOP), was composed of new and old Communists in Rio de Janeiro. While the first group sought only advice from Prestes, the other two sought his leadership over their movements. The latter two groups convoked the Second National Conference of the PCB, known as the Conference of Mantiqueira (named after the Serra da Mantiqueira, where the meeting took place), on August 27, 1943. The delegations were from the Federal District and Pará, Bahia, Rio de Janeiro, São Paulo, Paraná, Rio Grande do Sul, Minas Gerais, and other states, and focused on three matters: policy, organization, and selection of a new Central Committee. Approved was a policy of national unification in support of the government against Nazi fascism. Along with reorganization, the party approved efforts toward its own legalization; amnesty for political prisoners, including Prestes; and increased activity and influence in the labor movement. Prestes was elected secretary general.[85]

The PCB launched a propaganda campaign in favor of the opening of a second Allied front (once Hitler had invaded the Soviet Union), the sending of Brazilian military forces to fight with the Soviet ally, and a general amnesty for political prisoners. These PCB demands were issued through the Liga de Defesa Nacional, a legal and patriotic entity founded by Olavo Bilac and others.

Although still in prison, Prestes as secretary general set forth details of the PCB policy. On March 14 he took issue with "a leftist and sectarian Aliancista document" that had appeared in late 1943, attacking the Vargas government. Prestes called for national unity in the struggle against fascism. The ANL, he declared, should support the war policy of the government and at the same time exercise pressure for popular liberties, amnesty for political prisoners, and measures against hunger, sickness, and the high cost of living.[86] In April, Prestes reaffirmed support for the government's war effort, while calling also for such freedoms of assembly, of thought, and of the press, as well as of organization (to include the PCB and ANL). At the same time, he called upon political bosses, peasants' and workers' organizations, labor leaders, non-ANL tenentes, revolutionaries of 1922, 1924, and 1930 (specifically Isidoro Dias Lopez, Juarez Távora, Eduardo Gomes, Juracy Magalhães, and José Américo de Almeida),friends such as Pedro Ernesto, the União Nacional dos Estudantes, religious organizations (including the Ação Católica Brasileira), and former Congressmen to join with the PCB and ANL in the formation of the União Democrática Nacional (UDN) in support of Vargas. The eight-point program of the UDN called for resistance to facism; respect for all political opinion, religious creed, philosophy, and the like; democratic and representative government; unconditional support for the government in order to achieve total victory over Nazism; collaboration with the authorities to ameliorate high living costs; order and discipline within a milieu of freedom guaranteed by the government; establishment of democratic and representative institutions; and the elimination of reactionaries unable to adapt to these liberties.[87]

In early 1945, as the war was ending, opposition to Vargas began to intensify. A change appeared imminent, and as early as November 1944 constitutional architect Francisco Campos suggested calling a Constituent Assembly.[88] Almost immediately Juracy Magalhães and Juarez Távora began to rally support around Brigadier General Eduardo Gomes, the single remaining officer of the "eighteen" heroes who had defended the Copacabana garrison in 1922. On January 22, 1945, the First Congress of Brazilian Writers, which included many Communist intellectuals, met for a week in São Paulo, and after approving basic principles, called for a government democratically elected by the universal, direct, and secret vote of the people.[89] A month later, on February 22 in an interview published in Rio's *Correio da Manhã,* José Américo advocated presidential elections without Vargas as a candidate. Six days later the government issued an "Additional Act" affirming that an election date would be set within ninety days; yet at a news conference in early March Vargas was evasive about running, and defended the 1937 constitution. This touched off student demonstrations in Rio de Janeiro and Recife, and those in turn prompted Vargas to announce that he would not be a candidate; a movement to nominate his War Minister, General Eurico Gaspar Dutra, was initiated a day later. Further evidence of the growing strength of the opposition and the relaxation of government controls was apparent on March 15 with the publication of a mild statement by Prestes, his first public pronouncement since imprisonment nine years earlier.[90] A month later the government announced a political amnesty and released hundreds of prisoners, including Prestes and other Communist leaders.

4 • Resurgence and Decline: 1945-1972

The amnesty of April 1945 and the new electoral code of May 28 provided the legal framework for the re-emergence of the PCB as a political force. The ever-popular Prestes rallied his supporters to uphold a "victorious" Russian people who not only had repelled the Nazi advance in Europe but had been allied with Brazilians in the triumph over fascism. The party and its candidates found wide receptivity, especially among intellectuals and the younger generation, which had known only the closed politics of the Estado Novo. After World War II the PCB's revival progressed in three stages: "peaceful development" and a legal existence from 1945 until 1947, when the party was banned; anti-imperialism, from 1947 to an "extreme left" position in August 1950; and the "new orientation" beginning in 1950.[1] The party's decline was precipitated by divisions in 1956 and 1957, by the party's Fifth and Sixth Congresses, and by the military coup in 1964.

The Party as a Legal Entity: 1945–1947

During March and April 1945, leftist intellectuals in São Paulo, including both Communists and socialists, organized the União Democrática Nacional (UDN) as a political party. Their platform was based on the declaration of principles of the First Congress of Brazilian Writers, comprising leftist writers who had met in São Paulo during January 1945, as recounted in the previous chapter. Quickly aligning themselves with the UDN were members of the upper-class opposition to the Estado Novo, along with elements of the "new industrial and financial bourgeoise," a group that favored mildly liberal reforms and included Osvaldo Aranha (who had resigned as Foreign Minister in February to support the candidacy of Eduardo Gomes), Júlio Prestes (the President-elect in 1930), Assis Chateaubriand (who controlled the largest chain of newspapers), and Francisco Campos (author of the 1937 Constitution). Thus this heterogenous UDN resembled its namesake proposed by Luiz Carlos Prestes in April 1944. After the release of Prestes, however, the Communist faction left the UDN in late May or early June.[2] The socialists, meanwhile, formed the Esquerda Democrática, known as the *ala moça* (youth wing) of the UDN.[3]

In what was probably a stroke of political genius, Vargas proposed the formation of two national political parties, one to represent the bureaucratic organization established by the Estado Novo throughout the states, and the other to represent labor and apparently to undermine Communist influence in the working classes.[4] On May 9 politicians and military leaders still closely associated with the regime formally organized the Partido Social Democrático (PSD), and on July 1, at its first national convention, the party endorsed Dutra for President. José de Segadas Viana and other high officials of the Ministry of Labor organized the Partido Trabalhista Brasileiro (PTB) and joined Communists in support of Vargas, organizing mass rallies and shouting the slogan *Queremos Getúlio* ("We want Getúlio"). Expressing dissatisfaction with the military candidates of other parties, these supporters of the dictator, known as *Queremistas,* demanded postponement of Presidential elections and creation of a Constituent Assembly that would work with Vargas.[5]

Communist support of Vargas surprised many supporters and provoked dissension between two rival factions: The CNOP group in Rio de Janeiro, which favored Vargas, and the Comitê de Ação (CA), which advocated open struggle against the "dictatorship" and the "fascism" of the Estado Novo. The CNOP was to dominate the party because its position paralleled that of the charismatic Prestes.[6] Evidence cited by participants and observers alike suggests that Prestes had made a deal with Vargas: i.e., in return for his freedom, Prestes would support Vargas' continuation in office.[7] Prestes clarified his position in his first public speech after release from prison. On May 23, 1945, before seventy thousand people, he stated that Vargas' departure would bring "civil war" and chaos "and give new hope to fascists and reactionaries." Recommending "a Constituent Assembly" and postponement of the Presidential election, Prestes urged the formation of a União Nacional. Seemingly biding time to allow the reorganization and growth of the PCB, Prestes appealed to the worker to join the party's labor front, the Movimento Unificador dos Trabalhadores (MUT).[8]

Then, after leading a series of strikes between May and August, Communists attempted to turn labor discontent into support for Vargas and opposition to conservatives who might oust him. Meanwhile, the MUT sponsored state labor congresses of official unions in Ceará, Bahia, São Paulo, and the Federal District. Fearful of the apparent *modus vivendi* between Vargas and the Communists, fearful too that, like Juan Domingo Perón in Argentina, Vargas might rally labor support to retain him in office, the forces around Gomes and Dutra pressured for the dictator's removal. Finally on October 29 the army deposed Vargas, after his attempt to appoint his brother chief of the federal police.[9]

While the coup and the subsequent brief crackdown on Communists (including the suspension of the party newspaper, *Tribuna Popular*) confused the PCB, on November 10 it was officially registered as a political party, and five days later nominated Yeddo Fiúza, an engineer and former mayor of Petrópolis, as its "unity" candidate for President. In a manifesto two days later Prestes explained the PCB selection of a non-Communist candidate as a first step in the revolution of the "national bourgeoisie." Marxists, he stated, did not yet desire to establish Communism in Brazil but preferred to struggle through the União Nacional for eradication of "the misery of our people." Such had been the policy also of the Aliancistas in 1935: "They did not attempt to implant Communism." Prestes continued to urge election of a Constituent Assembly, expressing his displeasure over what he termed the "reactionary coup" of October 29.[10] His speech reiterated in general the party's minimal "electoral program of national union" of November 13, 1945,[11] and the broad program drawn up earlier (on August 21) at the first legal plenary session of the PCB National Committee.[12] These programs demanded agrarian reform and a democratic constitution as well as support for the United Nations.

The PCB continued a vigorous campaign to elect its representatives to the new Congress, and Prestes personally attracted tens of thousands of people at rallies throughout the country. Thus it was not surprising that Communists did well in the December 2 elections. The party received 9 per cent of the total votes and elected fourteen deputies and one senator. More, under the electoral system of proportional representation the PCB elected one hundred nine *suplentes* (alternates or sub-stitutes) to deputies (see Appendix A). Prestes ran for office in many states and was elected Senator in the Federal District and deputy in São Paulo, Rio de Janeiro, Pernambuco, Rio Grande do Sul, and the Federal District; he chose to sit as Senator.[13] Dutra took 55 per cent of the vote for the Presidency, with Gomes receiving 35 per cent and Fiúza 10 per cent (569,818 votes); but the PCB received the largest party vote in industrial cities and state capitals such as São Paulo, Santos, Campinas, Sorocaba, Recife, Olinda, Natal, and Aracajú.[14] The results signified a sudden and dramatic growth in PCB influence since the 1930's, a reflection partially of a changing national milieu under Vargas and a changing international situation in which capitalist and socialist nations had joined in the defeat of Nazi Germany (see Table 4.1).

President Dutra's most formidable opposition was the PCB, although elements in the PTB opposed him vigorously as well. On January 4, 1946, in a plenary session of the National Committee of the PCB, Prestes again insisted that the party would manifest its demands through the broad União Nacional. At the same time he identified two weak-nesses in the party: a lack of uniform and homogeneous political or-ganization, especially at the regional and state levels; and a failure to relate to the masses, this attributable to the "sectarianism of a large number of our comrades." These weaknesses could be resolved, he argued, through the establishment of a powerful Confederação Geral dos Trabalhadores Brasileiros (CGTB) and through the discussion and resolutions of the party's forthcoming Fourth Congress.[15]

Within the Constituent Assembly, Communists were vociferous in support of the social clauses of the new constitution while at the same time criticizing its liberal provisions.[16] They criticized also the Dutra government's efforts to attract foreign investment, and in a speech of March 26, 1946, Prestes condemned "the exploitation of foreign capi-tal," demanding that "soldiers of imperialism" abandon the country.[17] In May Prestes restated the PCB's policy "to struggle for peaceful solu-tions to national problems," but also warned the government that while fighting for peace and democracy the mobilized masses would oppose "police and fascist provocations against the legality of our party." [18]

At the party's Third National Conference during July 1946, Prestes outlined general policy. Latin America, he said, was affected by the exploitation of U.S. capital, which had disrupted the masses of organized workers and led to "political and absolute military domination." Referring to the minimal program of the União Nacional, Prestes emphasized the necessity to confront police brutality and suppression, and warned that the party must purge still existing sectarian elements and reinforce "the internal democracy" in the party ranks.[19] By way of implementing an earlier proposal, the PCB issued a formal declaration to hold a labor congress and establish the CGTB as a replacement for the MUT, which still functioned even though declared illegal in May 1946.[20] After the Ministry of Labor suddenly called a labor congress of its own, to meet in Rio between September 9 and September 23, MUT leaders decided to cooperate. The Ministry and PCB factions dominating the labor congress known as the Congresso Sindical dos Trabalhadores do Brasil soon divided over the institution of the CGTB, with result in a walkout by several hundred pro-government delegates. These dissenters reconvened in Niterói and there approved a resolution that the Minister of Labor should dissolve the Congress. Although the minister complied, pro-Communist and PTB unions were successful in establishing a Confederação dos Trabalhadores do Brasil (CTB).[21]

In the state and supplementary congressional elections of January 19, 1947, the PCB retained its fourth rank among parties, adding two deputies (Pedro Pomar and Diógenes Arruda Câmara) on the PSP ticket for São Paulo to the fourteen already in Congress; and forty-six members to fifteen state legislatures; and establishing a plurality of eighteen in the municipal council of the Federal District.[22] Prestes' popularity and the party's electoral tactic ("marching with all men and political currents that struggle against fascism . . . and unconstitutional acts") had augured well for the Communists.[23]

The Dutra government found itself confronted with growing opposition. By 1946 certain elements of the UDN, distressed at the party's minimal role in the government, went into open opposition, and in December Vargas—elected Senator a year earlier under the Dutra mainstay, the PSD—began to rally supporters around the PTB. Frequent clashes between Communists and police and ever increasing PCB criticism of government policy prompted occasional suppression of party activities. In May 1946 the government purged all known Communists in the bureaucracy,[24] and in mid-April 1947 suspended the União de Juventude Comunista.[25] Acting under a constitutional provision aimed at "anti-democratic" parties, the government filed suit in the Supreme Electoral Court and won a ruling outlawing the PCB on May 7, 1947. (It was not until January 7, 1948, however, that Congress passed a measure purging its Communist membership.[26]) The CTB was banned also, and the government intervened in one hundred forty-three of nine hundred forty-four labor unions to rid them of extremism.[27] The party daily, *Tribuna Popular,* was shut down for a day on August 30 and again on November 27, 1946.[28] This government intrusion shattered the parliamentary illusions of many Communists who had favored class collaboration rather than class struggle and had supported the Prestes position on national union. Although his position was not abandoned altogether, the PCB leadership now rejected its platform of "peaceful development" and adopted another antagonistic to foreign investment and capitalism in general. The party's militancy became closely associated with populist and nationalist appeals for unification of diverse elements in Brazil.

Table 4.1

The 1945 Presidential Elections

Total Votes Received	Eurico Dutra (PSD)	Eduardo Gomes (PTB)	Yeddo Fiúza (PCB)	Total[2] Valid Vote
Guanabara[1]	166,147	183,984	134,735	490,255
Minas Gerais	478,503	339,463	16,699	834,979
Rio Grande do Sul	447,462	110,444	50,199	608,446
São Paulo	780,546	377,613	192,867	1,353,445
Total in Four States	1,872,658 (56%)	1,011,504 (30%)	394,500 (12%)	3,287,125 (55.99%)
National Total	3,251,507 (55.3%)	2,039,341 (34.7%)	569,818 (9.7%)	5,870,667 (100%)

Source: Tribuna Superior Eleitoral, *Dados estatísticos, Eleições federal, estadual e municipal realizadas no Brasil a partir de 1945.* Rio de Janeiro: Departmento de Imprensa Nacional, 1950, p. 11.
1. Known as Federal District in 1945.
2. Including votes for other candidates.

The "Anti-Imperialist" Stance

During its legality the PCB built its membership to two hundred thousand, the largest in Latin America. This strength was undermined by the decision of the Supreme Electoral Court, and it was necessary to postpone the party's Fourth Congress, scheduled for May 23, 1947. The theses of the congress had already been published by the party's press, however, and they reflected changes generally corresponding to shifts in policy taken by Communist movements in most of the world in late 1946.[29] These shifts involved greater antagonism toward capitalist governments and militant opposition to U.S. "imperialism". The PCB, slower than most parties in effecting change, attempted through the theses to mix its anti-imperialism with peaceful proposals for economic development in Brazil. Specifically, the theses affirmed: (1) the beginning of the "peaceful development" period; (2) the military defeat of fascism; (3) the victory of socialism over fascism; (4) the substitution of U.S. imperialism for fascism as the principal international reactionary force; (5) the aggressive military character of U.S. imperialism, the result of monopoly capitalism; (6) the unlikelihood of U.S. war with the Soviet Union, on the ground that the peaceable American people would not tolerate such war; (7) basic contradictions within the imperialist camp which allow patriotic and nationalist wars by colonial and semi-colonial territories; (8) contradictions between the American people and U.S. reactionaries, between U.S. and English monopolists, and between U.S. imperialism and colonial and semi-colonial peoples; (9) the advancement of democracy and socialism while U.S. imperialism faces crisis; (10) the "growth of our party" as democracy advances; (11) favorable conditions for a broad union of forces against capitalist exploitation; (12) the implementation of an agrarian reform through the Constitution; (13) the necessity to find solutions to the problems of the "democratic-burgeois Revolution in our country;" (14) the capability of only the proletariat to lead that revolution; (15) the undermining of "peaceful development" through the violence perpetrated by anti-constitutionalists; (16) the need to organize the masses to defend the Constitution and to counter violence.[30]

The theses reflected the general confusion in the Communist world following the war. The PCB, like other parties, now returned to "the general line" of unconditional adherence to Moscow through the Cominform, thus abandoning the "independent lines" adopted by the parties after the dissolution of the Comintern. Its period of legality had been marked by broad, opportunistic appeals. While Prestes sought a national union of the party itself rather than alignment with other forces, the party generally maintained a favorable position toward the "national bourgeoisie," at the same time alienating workers because of its cautious stance on strikes.[31] In part the PCB position was based on ever-increasing government pressures. Relations between Brazil and the Soviet Union were established in 1945, but with the intensification of the Cold War the ties were broken later by the Dutra government.[32]

In early 1947 the party was accused in Congress of having received money from Moscow. Thereafter, the Communist leadership emphasized conservative aspects of their program; in March, for example, their press urged close worker-employer cooperation to ensure productivity increases and more effective competition with foreign firms. [33] Later the party's relations with labor also were strained by the split in mid-1949 in the World Federation of Trade Unions (WFTU), since the PCB was the link between Brazilian labor and the pro-Communist WFTU as well as the anti-U.S. labor Confederacíon de Trabajadores de América Latina (CTAL), headed by Vicente Lombardo Toledano in Mexico.

The ambitious, pragmatic position of the PCB is attributed also to internal Brazilian conditions. Since the end of the Estado Novo, anti-Vargas politicians attempted to reject the economic controls of the past. but the return to laissez-faire liberalism accompanied a rapid exhaustion of foreign exchange reserves, and resulted in a balance-of-payments deficit by 1947. Exchange controls were reintroduced in June 1947 and credit policy was relaxed, to the end of stimulating industrial expansion and economic gowth at the same time. The Dutra government began to coordinate public expenditures and to plan development on a regional level. A group of critical young economists, however, stressed the need to resolve structural deficiencies within the national context,[34] and they had considerable influence on economic patterns and nationalistic tendencies that reshaped Brazilian thinking during the second Vargas regime (1951–54) and thereafter. The nationalism of this period was also to affect Communist strategy and policies, as we shall see.[35]

The PCB economic policy provoked internal criticism, notably that of the party's leading theorist, intellectual, and economic historian, Caio Prado Júnior, who attacked the official Communist position on so-called "feudalism." He protested that there never had been feudalism in Brazil, where production was always oriented toward markets, and that the socio-economic structure of the plantation was unlike any form of feudalism; further, that the agrarian economy in Brazil was capitalist-based in the large enterprise, and therefore the party's position was anti-economic and reactionary.[36]

In addition the PCB found itself in frequent conflict with competitors on the left. Besides the PSB, which had broken from the UDN in April 1947, there were the União Socialista Popular, a small Marxist party founded in Rio in 1945; the Trotskyist grouping, Partido Socialista

Revolucionária, founded in 1945; and the anti-Stalinist, anti-Trotskyist União Democrática Socialista, founded in São Paulo, also in 1945 (this later became the Partido Socialista Independente). Many Trotskyists who in 1945 had broken with the Fourth International to found the publication, *Vanguarda Socialista,* joined the PSB in 1948, although some were expelled later and others voluntarily withdrew.[37] These various ideological tendencies as well as debate within the PCB undoubtedly contributed to fundamental if latent divisions that appear openly a decade later.[38]

The outlawed PCB did not cease its activities altogether. In time its newspaper, *Tribuna Popular,* which had been suppressed, reappeared briefly, and was eventually replaced by *Imprensa Popular,* a daily published in Rio de Janeiro until late 1958, when it ceased after the 1956–57 party split. Furthermore, a few Communist leaders were arrested. Although the party was successful later in electing (in other parties' slates) members to Congress and lesser legislative organizations,[39] there was a growing recognition that an alliance with Dutra or any other regime was illusory. Isolated as it was from the party system at a time when no major politician protected it and when membership was falling off rapidly and its national influence was curtailed, the PCB launched an attack on the Dutra government.[40]

Vargas had sought to dissociate the PTB from Communism during the government's campaign to suppress the PCB. To fill the vacuum created by its suppression and to prepare his return to power, he adopted a strategy of maintaining the loyalty of traditional political oligarchs in rural areas through the PSD while building support in urban centers through the PTB. Updating the corporatist social philosophy of the Estado Novo, Vargas advocated *"trabalhismo*—a mixture of social welfarism, working-class political activity, and economic nationalism." [41] Through skillful political maneuvers and alliances, Getúlio emerged victorious in the presidential elections of October 3, 1950, capturing almost a majority—48.7 per cent of the vote. The PCB had advised its members to cast blank ballots.[42]

From the "New" Line to Reformism: 1950–1956

The implementation of a "new" line or "extreme leftist" policy was marked by Prestes' manifesto of August 1, 1950, the culmination of a series of party responses to repressive conditions nationally and to polarizing Cold War attitudes internationally. From late 1950 until the party's Fourth Congress of November 1954, however, the PCB gradually drifted away from an initially militant and revolutionary posture toward a strategy and program of moderate social reform and short-range objectives.

The new line had evolved from the policy shifts affecting the international Communist movement as early as 1946. Such shifts were evident in party documentation, which at that time began to urge the defeat of imperialism through the expropriation of large monopolies and latifundios, establishment of state control over banks, and other such measures. The increasing repression of party activities by the Dutra government, its banning from elections, and efforts to diminish Communist influence in the labor movement contributed substantially to a hardening of PCB policy. And the establishment of the Communist Information Bureau (Cominform) in September 1947 assured closer relations between the PCB and the Communist Party of the Soviet Union. As a consequence the PCB, like other Communist parties outlawed in Latin America, replaced its bland popular-front reformism on domestic issues with revolutionary rhetoric. Moreover, it broke off political alliances with non-Communist organizations, adopting instead an independent policy toward electoral participation and the labor movement. The new policy, subsequently labeled "sectarian" by the very leaders who were pressing the militant line, was designed to prepare the party ideologically and militantly for the seizure of power. In practice, though, the party never effectively implemented the policy, and failed to build the revolutionary organization it called the "democratic front of national liberation." It was somewhat successful, however, in mobilizing popular support for "anti-imperialist" attacks upon the United States.

The party stance of the late 1940's was reaffirmed in its minimal program published in mid-1949, when the party called for the overthrow of U.S. imperialism.[43] The formalization of the party's hostility toward reformist parties and organizations, however, was clearly set forth in Prestes' manifesto of August 1950 demanding a "direct struggle for power" through the creation of a "broad popular organization" known as the Frente Democrática de Libertação Nacional (FDLN).[44] The FDLN nine-point program advocated popular democratic government; "peace against imperialist war"; nationalization of imperialist enterprise; land reform; development of the national economy; democratic liberties for the people; improvement of living standards; free compulsory education; and formation of a people's army of national liberation.[45] Although the tactics included strikes, protests, and military battles, this seemingly radical program did not decree a socialist government nor completely reject the support of "capitalist nationalism."

PCB policy statements immediately thereafter were based on the August manifesto. In February 1951 a report of a plenary session of the PCB National Committee stressed that the fundamental task was to build up the FDLN and to mobilize the masses to participate in the revolutionary struggle. Opportunistic tendencies in the PCB would be eliminated through strengthening of such mass organizations as the União da Juventude Comunista, reorganizing the CTB, and the formation of Comitês Democráticos de Libertação Nacional. The PCB resolved to oppose the Vargas government—"the enemy of the people, representatives of landed interests and the bourgeoisie, and the supporter of U.S. imperialism." [47]

Clearly, the revolutionary rhetoric of Prestes and the party had antagonized the government, for late in August 1950 a warrant was issued for Prestes' arrest on charges of "sedition" stemming from his call for a liberation army. Charges against Prestes and sixteen other party leaders were pressed until August 1954, when the case was thrown out of court. The government also exerted pressure to keep Communists off the ballot. The PCB lost numerous candidacies to other party tickets, including forty running under the Partido Social Trabalhista in São Paulo.[47] Only one Communist, labor leader Roberto Morena, was elected to office—that of federal deputy under the Partido Republicano Trabalhista in the Federal District, where after 1947 the local branch of the PRT was strongly influenced by the PCB.

The party also became deeply involved in popular national and international causes. Its nationalist appeals favored protection for petroleum, iron ore, manganese, and other natural resources. Communists joined other nationalists to attack the international petroleum companies and also the controversial parts of a Vargas proposal to establish a mixed public-private oil corporation known as Petrobrás. The controversy, ensuing into 1952 and 1953, was extended to the demand that all basic industry be managed by the state. Through the Centro de Estudos e Defesa do Petróleo e da Economia Nacional (CEDPEN), the party became a dominant force against alleged U.S. pressures on Brazilian foreign exchange, petroleum resources, and iron and steel deposits. In November 1953 Roberto Morena called for an expanded electrification program and nationalization of Canadian-owned power interests.[48] The degree of nationalist sentiment in support of these appeals nearly caught the party by surprise, but by the time Petrobrás had been formally inaugurated in October 1953, nationalist solutions for development had become popular manifestations of everyday political life, and especially so among students and the military.

In international affairs, the party's concern with war and peace was manifested through such organizations as the Movimento Nacional pela Proibição de Armas Atômicas (1950) and the Congresso do Movimento Brasileiro dos Partidários da Paz (1951), whose rallying point was Korea. From April 1951 to May 1952 the party campaigned in behalf of the World Peace Council, collecting three million signatures for appeals later presented to the United Nations General Assembly.[49]

During 1952 the party joined popular nationalists in attacking a proposed mutual-defense agreement between Brazil and the United States and alleged that such an accord would give "to American imperialism all the riches of the nation," and moreover "opens completely the doors of the country to the invasion of all kinds of Yankee agents and spies under the cloak of diplomatic immunity, and violates the laws of the country." Agitation throughout the year resulted in a delay in congressional approval of the pact, which finally was passed in February 1953 but not before the publication of an anti-pact manifesto by disgruntled military officers in January and an anti-pact petition with ninety thousand signatures.[50] The party also led a petition in support of an international congress for peace in Vienna during December 1952.[51]

In mid-1953 the PCB drive for peace and national autonomy (which had united nationalist elements against the bilateral military accord) now divided into two tendencies, one emphasizing Brazilian economic development, and the other, universal disarmament.[52] On September 1, 1953, the party launched another peace campaign and at the same time also intensified its long-standing demand for resumption of diplomatic and trade relations with the Soviet Union, mainland China, and Eastern Europe. On April 5, 1954, it brought into being the Liga da Emancipação Nacional (LEN), whose founding convention called for nationalization of foreign-owned electric power sources, an end to petroleum exploitation, and control of all mineral resources; agrarian reforms; stimulation of national cultural and scientific activity; and termination of U.S. domination.[53]

After the August 1950 manifesto, PCB prestige declined somewhat in the labor movement. As a result, by 1952 party leaders were beginning to reverse their precarious policy of non-cooperation with labor unions. The party clandestinely revived (as a paper organization) the CTB to serve as its labor central, and party members continued their activities in the leadership as well as rank and file. The greatest advances were achieved in São Paulo, where strike demands were won by the Communist-influenced textile and metallurgical workers' unions during March and April 1953.[54] In Rio Grande do Sul Communist influence was maintained among dockworkers and railway workers. PCB labor leaders were active in the successful railway workers' strikes of June 1952 and May 1954.[55] In Pernambuco, party strength lay in unions of spinners and weavers, urban transit employes, and dockworkers; in the Federal District of Rio de Janeiro there was considerable infiltration among bakers, tailors, and seamstresses. The party was active also in the National Federation of Journalists, and one party militant, Maria da Graça, serving as an officer, led a campaign against harassment of Communist newspapers.[56] Another Communist, Rio municipal councilman Eliseu Alves de Oliveira, headed the União Sindical dos Trabalhadores do Distrito Federal.[57]

In spite of considerable differences and reciprocal hostility, a taut alliance between the PCB and PTB was in effect from 1952 onward. The PCB also fostered close relations with João Goulart, who was Minister of Labor from June 1953 until his ouster by conservative military elements in February 1954.[58] Left-wing members of the PTB and followers of Goulart worked with Communists in the maritime strike of July 1953 and engaged in negotiations for the formation of an electoral alliance between the two groups. Earlier the government and Communists had joined forces over the issue of foreign control of Brazilian oil reserves, and together launched a campaign to create a government oil monopoly; and in behalf of the congressional bill to establish Petrobrás (passed in 1953), Communist and PTB leaders appealed impressively for popular support. That this alliance had become more or less official by 1954 was signified by the party's May Day proclamation, which avoided criticism of the government and of Vargas personally.[59] Through this alliance the party hoped to present candidates for the congressional elections of October 1954. With the suicide of Vargas on August 24, however, the party experienced a temporary decline, suffering defeat in the São Paulo gubernatorial elections.[60]

The party's shift to reformism had already been underway during

1954. On January 1 the PCB published a "Draft Program" calling for the overthrow of Vargas by a "democratic front of national liberation," a demand similar to that of the 1950 August manifesto. This program continued to circulate until Vargas' overthrow on August 24. Vargas' deposal as well as his suicide caught the party in an awkward position as a wave of popular sympathy for Getúlio swept the nation.[61] The party's draft program, however, became the basis for the reformist stance explicitly formalized at its Fourth Congress. The convening of the Fourth Congress took place during the interim regime of João Café Filho, the Partido Social Progressista (PSP) Vice President who took Vargas' place. From November 7 to 11 the congress discussed and approved a report by secretary general Prestes and the Central Committee, the new party program, presented by Diógenes Arruda Câmara, and the modified party statutes, presented by João Amazonas. In addition, party officials were elected at the congress.

The program concentrated on four tasks. The first was to shift from the struggle against imperialism in general to a confrontation with U.S. imperialism in particular, and specifically with U.S. monopolies that, it was alleged, control "our largest mineral resources." To end U.S. domination Brazil would have to collaborate, as the program stated, with peaceful countries in the defense of sovereignty and national independence. A second task concerned the nationalization of large landholdings through confiscation and free distribution of parcels to landless peasants. In a third task "a democratic government of national liberation" would replace the present government of latifundistas and capitalists. Such a coalition government would labor to keep Brazil from becoming a colony of the United States and would include in its program the working class, peasants, intelligentsia, petty bourgeoisie, and the national bourgeoisie. The program embodied forty-six measures on foreign policy, defense of national independence, popular democratic policy, independence of the national economy, labor reforms, and agrarian reform. In the fourth, the PCB would form a broad anti-imperialist, anti-feudal front as a transitional step in the formation of the coalition government.[62]

In many respects the program produced policy clarification by way of presenting "rigorous self-criticism" to correct "our errors and weaknesses" and to overcome "persistent sectarian and spontaneous tendencies in the ranks of the party." Struggle would be directed exclusively against U.S. imperialism, not to the world-wide variety; only large estates would be confiscated, since the program now acknowledged that small farmers and peasants with wealth should not necessarily be condemned as counter-revolutionaries; nationalization of private enterprise would be limited to firms and capital tied to "U.S. imperialists" while national firms would be protected; and finally the party favored an alliance of the working class, peasants, intelligentsia, and the petty and national bourgeoisie "controlled by the proletariat and its Communist party." [63]

The report of Prestes and the Central Committee affirmed the policies of the new party program and asserted that the lessening of international tensions through the ending of the Korean War was a consequence of pressures from the peace movement in Brazil and elsewhere; asserted also that whereas the economy was developing rapidly in the Soviet Union, China, and "other countries with popular democracy," in "the imperialist camp" it followed a line of stagnation and increasing difficulties as capitalist nations prepared to renew war. The Prestes report outlined seven specific political objectives considered necessary for the implementation of the party program: "organization of the popular struggle in defense of constitutional liberties, against fascist terror, and for the unmasking, isolation, and defeat of the government of latifundistas and wealthy capitalists who serve the United States"; intensification of "the patriotic struggle for national emancipation"; intensification of the struggle for peace; unification and organization of the working class; organization of the peasant masses in the struggle for land; greater attention to the masses of working women; and organization of the youth.[64]

That PCB policy had drifted rightward from a militant posture in 1950 to a strategy of gradual reform four years later was evident from several comparisons. For one thing, whereas in 1950 the party had demanded the indiscriminate confiscation of all "large" landholdings, in 1954 it insisted only on the redistribution of latifundist land, excluding property of those who supported the democratic front for national liberation. Then, although the national bourgeoisie was ignored in 1950, it was given a major role in the formation of an anti-imperialist front in 1954. Again, the 1954 program reflected the abandonment of revolutionary demands, a tendency particularly in effect since 1952, when PCB labor leaders began to cooperate with established trade union officials. Finally, in 1954 the PCB adopted an old line to orient itself toward participation in elections, and even went so far as to seek legal party registration through the Supreme Electoral Court.[65]

The Fourth Congress brought together a new generation of militants under the centralized control of the old leadership. Dissidence had shaken the party in 1952 and 1954 with the expulsion of José Maria

Crispim and the condemnation of Fernando Lacerda,[66] and the semblance of unity and harmony manifested in November 1954 would soon be destroyed again by subsequent events, especially the Twentieth Congress of the Soviet Communist Party. Some participants contended that the Fourth Congress was not representative of the party's rank and file, that the delegates were selected by the party leadership, and that the primary objective was "approval of a program, strangely prepared in Moscow under strict orders that it not be altered." [67] Actually the strategy of relying on all social strata from the urban proletariat to the national bourgeoisie stemmed from the Soviet Communist Party's renewed emphasis on moderate reformist movements as appropriate to all dependent societies. The Moscow line was accepted by PCB leaders early in 1952 and acknowledged by Prestes in a report to the party in February 1952.[68]

After the death of Vargas there ensued a struggle for leadership within the PTB. Certain of its leaders rallied Communists to their side and thus allowed Communist influence into the PTB and into the leadership of some trade unions, especially in São Paulo, where there had been Communist strength among textile and metal workers since 1945. There was also a split in the Vargas opposition during the presidential election campaign of October 1955. In August the PCB had announced its support of the candidacy of Juscelino Kubitschek for President and João Goulart for Vice President,[69] in the hope of committing Kubitschek to legalize the PCB if he were elected.[70] When a coup threatened to invalidate the elections, General Henrique Teixeira Lott, Minister of War under Café Filho, intervened on November 11 to ensure the accession of President-elect Kubitschek. Before Lott's move, the PCB had warned of an imminent coup,[71] and after the counter-coup the party claimed it had served as the principal catalyst. The PCB seems in fact to have played no significant role in these events.[72] The counter-coup, however, caused serious division in the armed forces, and by supporting Lott Communists were able to establish ties within his faction of the army.[73]

Division and Decline: 1956–1972

We may now move on to more recent developments, in particular the party's divisions in 1956 and 1957, its Fifth Congress in August 1960, and the role of the party before and after the military coup of 1964.

Internal Party Dissension

Juscelino Kubitschek assumed the Presidency in a period of economic achievement. His government embraced a policy of developmental nationalism, with priority to the establishment and expansion of industry. Private investors, both domestic and foreign, were granted special incentives to invest in Brazilian industry, especially in production of automobiles and electrical goods. At the same time the government undertook a program of public investment directed at correcting deficiencies in transportation and power. "Targets" or production goals were formulated. Indeed, developmental progress was recorded, as Brazil's real rate of growth reached 7 per cent annually from 1957 to 1961.[74] Kubitschek also fostered a sense of nationalistic self-confidence among Brazilians, and the symbol he chose was the new inland capital of Brasília, a project written into the 1891 constitution and quickly approved by Congress in 1956. Reinforcing the President's policies was the federally-financed Instituto Superior de Estudos Brasileiros (ISEB), whose objective was to formulate and implement an ideology of developmental nationalism through research, teaching, and the publication of several series of books.[75]

When Kubitschek came to power in January, Congress voted to extend the state of siege initiated by Lott's coup of November 11, 1955. While the President assumed a staunch anti-Communist position by ordering in June the suppression of Communist-controlled dock workers in Rio and the disbanding of the women's organization Liga de Emancipação Nacional, he also tolerated legislation allowing elected Communist labor leaders to take office without clearance from the Labor Ministry as had previously been required. While the PCB adapted to the pragmatic Kubitschek policies of development, nationalism, and anti-Communism, during the first two years of the new regime the party became increasingly critical of programs that stimulated inflation. The party was also faced with the internal problems of open debate and dissension generated by Khrushchev's denunciation of Stalin at the Twentieth Congress of the Soviet Communist Party in February 1956.

In January of 1956, in its first policy statement after the President's inauguration, the PCB called upon the new government to establish diplomatic relations with the Soviet Union and Communist China. The four-point action platform demanded democratic freedom for labor and assurances against reactionary coups; a policy of peace with all peoples; defense of petroleum and other national mineral resources; and a general upgrading of workers' conditions.[76] Not until late March, when Prestes dealt with the Twentieth Congress in vague, uncertain terms, did the PCB publish information on the Soviet denunciation of Stalin.[77] Thereafter until September the PCB restricted open party debate on the congress, and discussion was restricted to description and defense of the proceedings.[78] In October the party acknowledged that its failure to discuss the issues of the Soviet congress had been "unjustified"; that its Brazilian delegation to the congress should have returned immediately rather than remain in Moscow; and that the PCB should be democratized. The Central Committee then opened debate within the party.[79]

With the subsequent debate, divisions in the party became clearly apparent. The *núcleo dirigente,* or old-guard inner circle, known first as the *fechadistas* (opposed to public discussion of internal party issues) and later as the *conservadores* (conservatives), included Prestes, João Amazonas, Maurício Grabois, Pedro Pomar, Carlos Marighella, Diógenes Arruda Câmara, and Luiz Teles.[80] Opposed to this old guard were the *abridistas* or *renovadores,* who favored open debate. This faction included the Grupo de Barata, a small band led by Agildo Barata, "Batim," and André Vitor, and two other sympathizers—all of them members of the Central Committee.[81] Also associated with the renovadores was the Sinédrio (Sanhedrin or council), a group of intellectuals and journalists, among them António Rezende, a leader of the União da Juventude Comunista (UJC); Armando Lopes da Cunha, a member of the Commission of Agitation and Propaganda of the Central Committee; Aydano do Couto Ferraz, editor of *Voz Operária* and former editor of *Tribuna Popular;* Carlos Duarte, a former editor of *Imprensa Popular;* Demóstenes Lobo, a leader of the UJC; Ernesto Luiz Maia, a journalist; Horácio Macedo, affiliated with the PCB economic journal, *Emancipação;* João Batista de Lima e Silva, editor of *Voz Operária* and *Imprensa Popular;* Victor M. Kondor, editor of *Problemas;* Zacarias Carvalho, editor of the weekly *Democracia Popular* and a member of the Commission of Masses of the Central Committee; and Osvaldo Peralva, a writer. The renovadores claimed a majority of the party's Central Finance Commission, a strong representation of the Regional Committee of Bahia, all of the Regional Committee of Southern Bahia, a large group from Rio Grande do Sul, a group from Ceará, the leaders of the UJC, a majority of the party's Trade Union Commission and the Commission of Agitation and Propaganda.[82]

A third faction called *Pántano* (and known also as the "Grupo Baiano" because most of its members were from the state of Bahia), emerged from the PCB delegation attending the Eighth Congress of the Chinese Communist Party in September 1956. This faction adopted the tactic of supporting the conservadores to defeat the renovadores with the ultimate objective of destroying the conservadores and gaining control over the party.[83] This was achieved at a meeting of the Central Committee in August 1957, when the Presidium and Secretariat were altered to give control to the Pántano.[84]

The debate on the Twentieth Congress was carried in daily letters printed in *Voz Operária* and in *Imprensa Popular,* which published also a four-page weekly supplement of dialogue, *Boletim do Debate.* The open dialogue afforded Communist critics of the PCB an opportunity to attack the Soviet Union also for its suppression of liberal tendencies in Hungary and Poland. Ernesto Luiz Maia vehemently condemned the Soviet intervention in Hungary.[85] Writers such as Osvaldo Peralva also linked the Soviet move in Hungary to the PCB's subservience to the Soviet Communist Party.[86] In November Astrojildo Pereira acknowledged his earlier enthusiastic support of Stalin's "cult of personality" and attempted to assess both the negative and positive aspects of the Soviet dictator, while Paulo Cavalcanti urged moderation in debate for the sake of preserving party unity. Peralva, in contrast, called for vigorous discussion and publication of all debate.[87] At another meeting in the middle of the month the Central Committee approved Prestes' "guidelines" for debate. Prestes supported open debate but insisted that there be no criticism of the Soviet Union and the Soviet Communist Party.[88] The debate continued until late April, when the Central Committee resolved to shut off further discussion and called for party unity, declared "inadmissible" any criticism of Marxist-Leninist principles, and proclaimed the party to be the vanguard of the people and defender of the principles of democratic centralism and collective leadership.[89]

In large measure the Central Committee's resolution was in response to severe criticism from Agildo Barata, who on March 15 had condemned the party hierarchy for its abstention from the debates. He favored an independent course for Communist parties (including the PCB), whose Marxism, he said, should be relevant to "the concrete reality of each country." Accordingly, the PCB should elaborate a new program reflecting the collective participation of party leadership and rank and file; there should be democratization of the party in practice as well as in theory, and elimination of "dictatorial centralism; a "mass line," similar to that of China, should be pursued and also a decentralization of party organization; and bureaucracy and sectarianism should be combatted, party elections should reflect rank and file interests, and censorship should be limited to security problems.[90]

The closure of debate was preceded by the party leadership's arbitrary dismissal of the editor of *Voz Operária,* Aydanto do Couto Ferraz, on February 18, 1957. Twenty-seven of the daily's thirty-two journalists signed a letter of protest read by Agildo Barata in the April meeting of the Central Committee. This protest was of little avail, and in late April and May the conservadores published a series of articles attacking Barata, Maia, Peralva, and other renovadores.[91] According to one party observer, these attacks were representative of the anti-intellectualism manifested by the old-guard inner circle.[92]

Tensions increased between the two factions. The conservadores levied much of their criticism against Agildo Barata, who finally broke with the PCB on May 13.[93] Barata's resignation was followed by that of other renovadores, including Peralva on May 22; many other journalists left in October. Bruzzi Mendonça, the only PCB deputy in Congress, abandoned the party.[94] Thereafter the renovadora faction, known now as the Corrente Renovadora do Movimento Marxista Brasileiro, functioned as the embryo of a proposed Partido Comunista Nacional. It published a weekly entitled *O Nacional* and edited by Aydano do Couto Ferraz in its first phase and by Agildo Barata in its second. Under Peralva's editorship, the faction also published a magazine, *Novos Tempos.* Having criticized the PCB for "reactionary" tendencies, these dissidents could not agree on a common program; they discontinued their publications by May 1958, and abandoned plans to establish a party.[95] With that the renovadores became less visible in leftist Brazilian politics, although they pursued their activities through 1960, at least.

The independent Corrente Renovadora movement was able not only to evolve a political program of action and ideas but also to sharpen dialogue on Brazilian Marxism, nationalism, and development. Soon after its break with the PCB, the Corrente Renovadora proposed a united nationalist and leftist front with several objectives: a nationalist policy oriented toward the defense of Petrobrás; a labor policy to ensure a minimum wage, revise the social security system, and extend legislation to rural areas; a policy in defense of rights and freedoms guaranteed by the Constitution, and in defense of national industry.[96] In an effort to stimulate dialogue within the new movement and to formulate and synthesize a revolutionary program, Eros Martins Teixeira (one of its members) criticized the Corrente Renovador majority's tactics in support of the national bourgeoisie, participation in government, and efforts to strengthen nationalism as a progressive movement. Arguing that revolutionary prospects in Brazil are conditioned upon world revolution, he outlined and analyzed fourteen "theses on Brazilian reality": Brazil's political and economic dependence on U.S. imperialism; the latifundio's tie to imperialism; the nation's "wealth" and "people of poverty"; the precariousness of industrial development; the struggle of the national bourgeoisie against dependence on U.S. imperialism and the necessity to guide the working classes in winning the peasant; the vacillation of the national bourgeoisie; the heterogeneous composition of the Kubitschek government; the participation of the national bourgeoisie and some large landowners in the industrial and commercial development of the country; anti-imperialism and agrarianism as aspects of the revolution; the emancipation of national interests by the majority of people; the desire for peace among all Brazilians; and favorable conditions for formation of a Frente Popular Nacionalista against the posited U.S. exploitation. In promoting a nationalist movement constructed on a class basis with the bourgeoisie excluded, Teixeira identified three revolutionary stages: the revolution of national liberation against agents of U.S. imperialism and reactionary landowners; the democratic popular revolution (which he believed Brazil was then entering); and the socialist revolution.[97]

On September 7, 1957, the Corrente Renovadora do Movimento Marxista Brasileiro in São Paulo resolved to convene its members on October 13 to form a Movimento Socialista Renovador (MSR), whose program would "assure our emancipation through state monopolization of strategic sectors of basic industry and incentives to private investors in other industry." [98] Although the founding congress of the MSR took place on schedule, reservations prevailed among some former PCB members.[99] The party really never functioned, but the Marxists involved in its early deliberations effectively manifested their sentiments in favor of the loose conglomeration of groups and individuals who associated with the Brazilian "nationalist movement" of the period.[100]

The Fifth Congress

In March 1958 the courts dismissed charges against Prestes and other party members. After ten years in clandestinity he emerged to test the government ban on the party and to demonstrate the non-violent policies the PCB was then advocating. Thus he was able to function publicly as a political leader, although his popular appeal generated by the Prestes Column and the revolts of 1935 was minimal for the post-war generation. The party line, the "official" beginning of de-Staliniza-tion, was set by the Central Committee's March 1958 declaration back-ing the Communist Party of the Soviet Union and attacking U.S. "imperialism" and Brazilian latifundist interests. Advocating a democratic nationalist front, the PCB proposed to take power through "the peaceful pressure of the popular masses and all nationalist currents," through electoral victory, and through resistance of the popular mass aligned to nationalist forces in Congress.[101] The Central, Committee approved also the policy of international peaceful coexistence affirmed at the Twenty-first Congress of the Soviet Communist Party, January 27 to February 5, 1959. When dissidents in the Central Committee opposed this "rightist" tendency in policy, Prestes and the PCB majority leader-ship convoked its Fifth Congress for August 1960. This congress would also justify support of Marshal (erstwhile General) Henrique Lott, whom the party favored in the October 1960 Presidential elections. This support, the PCB believed, would assure legal status for the party and positions in the new government.[102] Although ostensibly the Congress was called to resolve differences over the elections, in fact it provided an opportunity for Prestes and other "reformists" to consolidate their hold and bring stability to the party.

The Fifth Congress formulated eight theses, an appeal for the legaliza-tion of the party, new statutes, and a program; it also reaffirmed the peaceful-coexistence policy earlier approved by the Central Committee, and reshuffled the party leadership to isolate dissidents opposed to the new policy. Further, the congress viewed with optimism the ramifica-tions of a Lott victory in the upcoming elections, in particular the prospects for legalization of the party. Serious consideration therefore was given to modifying the statutes and program to make them accepta-ble to the new government.

The eight theses as approved served to assess the party's role in in-ternational and domestic affairs. The first concerned the international situation, the progress of socialism, and the decline of capitalism, and concluded optimistically in the belief that the world situation favored the rise of socialism in Brazil. The second dealt with the national economy, which continued to be dependent on "imperialistic capital" and an archaic agrarian structure, although state capitalism in Brazil tended to assume "progressive and national forms." Despite this tendency, the thesis continued, structural weaknesses, including inflation and regional economic disequilibrium, imposed heavy sacrifices upon workers, aggravated social discontent, and increased economic dependency. The third had to do with social classes, the state, and institutions in Brazil. The social classes were the latifundists, the bourgeoisie, the urban petty bourgeoisie, the peasants, and the proletariat—the most "revolutionary." According to this thesis, Brazilian political parties were "increasingly more national," while labor unions, the Church, the armed forces, and student organizations "exercised a great influence in national life." A fourth thesis identified the two principal contradictions of Brazilian society as that between the nation and U.S. "imperialism," on the one hand, and that between the latifundists and the peasant masses, on the other. The Brazilian revolution, defined as "anti-imperialist, anti-feudal, national, and democratic," ought to be opposed primarily to U.S. "imperialism." In the fifth the party advocated the formation of the Frente Unica Nacionalista e Democrática, thus signifying the PCB's adherence to the general nationalist movement. In the sixth it favored the peaceful assumption of power and implementation of reforms through electoral victory, through pressure of the masses, and through the unification of popular elements. A seventh thesis committed the party to a "policy of nationalist and democratic solutions."

Lastly, the congress critically assessed PCB activities, and among other things condemned Prestes' manifesto of August 1950 ("sectarian leftism" and "inconsistent with Brazilian reality"), the party's failure to recognize "the presence of national forces" in the second Vargas government, and the "erroneous and sectarian" Fourth Congress. The party also had failed to analyze the basic contradictions of Brazilian society and the role of "the bourgeoisie in the revolution." The thesis acknowledged the "weakness" in PCB leadership, "exaggerated" centralism, and an "excess" of plans and goals. At the same time while "leftist" and "rightist" sectarian tendencies had prevailed in the party (as the accusation went on), the Central Committee and the Presidium were incapable of comprehending the Soviet Twentieth Congress, especially the criticism of the "cult of personality" and the "errors of the last period of Stalin's activity." [103]

In addition the Congress approved a lengthy policy resolution, which, like the theses of the party's Fourth and Fifth Congresses, emphasized "a theory of the Brazilian revolution."[104] Primary attention would be directed to salaried and semi-salaried agricultural workers in the mobilization of the masses, a perspective condemned by one party critic as a fundamental contradiction of the party's traditional "anti-feudal struggle."[105]

The turmoil of 1957 and 1958 accompanied the defection of elements led by Agildo Barata and Osvaldo Peralva and his journalist colleagues. The Fifth Congress represented a break with the Stalinists, who now rejected the Soviet policy of peaceful coexistence and turned toward Communist China. Representing this faction were party leaders Arruda, Amazonas, Grabois, and Pomar, who earlier had led the attacks on the Corrente Renovadora and other revisionists. While Arruda Câmara was now to all effects relegated to obscurty, and Prestes survived the denunciation of his earlier activities and policies, the small faction led by Amazonas, Grabois, and Pomar was expelled for "its systematic attack against the unity and discipline of the Communist movement." Also denounced for the same reason were José Duarte, Angelo Arroio, Walter Martins, Calil Chade, Carlos Danielli, and Lincoln Oeste. Although the expulsion was not announced until early January 1962, twelve of twenty-five members of the Central Committee were replaced at the party's Fifth Congress (though Pomar, Arroio, and Danielli apparently retained their positions until expelled).[106] In effect some "old guard" personalists were relegated to minor positions while "Revisionists" led by Jacob Gorender and Mário Alves gained control of the party machinery.[107] Because of his public image and caudillo popularity, Prestes remained leader and secretary general of the party.

The expulsion occurred after the PCB had approved a new program and statutes at a National Conference in September 1961. These statements, which had appeared a month earlier in the party press,[108] were oriented toward a change in the party name, which thereupon became the Partido Comunista Brasileiro (PCB). The change from the "Communist Party of Brazil" to the "Brazilian Communist Party" was designed to obtain legal electoral status and to convince the electoral court that the party was indeed nationalist in nature and not an instrument of the Soviet Union as had been asserted by the court in May 1947. One hundred dissidents protested this change in a letter to the Central Committee and criticized the conspicuous omission of references to Marxism-Leninism and revolutionary struggle.[109]

In February 1962 some of these dissidents held an Extraordinary National Conference in the name of the Partido Comunista do Brasil (PC do B), and approved resolutions in favor of maintaining the old party name and elected a new Central Committee to include eight members who had once served on the old PCB Central Committee. Reviewing the nation's difficulties, they agitated for a popular revolutionary government that would destroy imperialism and latifundists, assure liberties, and improve culture and the living standard of the masses.[110] In a summary statement the delegates alleged that since 1957 Communist revisionists had suppressed the party press, abandoned educational work, and nearly dissolved the UJC and other mass organizations.[111] In March 1962 the PC do B revived *A Classe Operária* under the editorship of Maurício Grabois and Pedro Pomar. At first a monthly, later a weekly, and published through March 1964, this organ reflected the major issues of the period and tended to support radical agitation in the student movement, the peasantry, and labor unions, and carried articles under Stalin's name as well as documents unfolding China's position in the Sino-Soviet debate.[112]

Leftist Agitation and a Reactionary Coup

As noted earlier, while the structure and policies of the Communist movements in Brazil corresponded directly to tensions in the Communist world as well as to the impact of the Cuban Revolution, party developments were shaped also by internal Brazilian conditions. By 1958 the Kubitshek administration, faced with severe inflation, received support and counsel from the International Monetary Fund (IMF). In an effort to stabilize the economy the government experimented with differential exchange rates during the early months of 1959. These moves were attacked by the left and the advocates of radical nationalism. The Communist press branded Finance Minister Lucas Lopes and Director of the National Bank for Economic Development Roberto de Oliveira Campos as "imperialist stooges" of Wall Street who were complying with an IMF "plot" to dominate Brazil. This pressure prompted the government decision of June 1959 to assume a nationalist stance, break off negotiations with the IMF, and replace Lopes and Campos.

Although this belated shift in policy temporarily mollified tensions on the left, Brazil's economy suffered from falling export prices on coffee, sugar, and cacao, and massive remissions of foreign investments. By 1960 Brazil was unable to meet payments on foreign loans. Deficit spending to spur developmental projects while avoiding tax reforms, rising food prices, and foreign exchange accelerated inflation. Although the gross national product increased by 7 per cent annually from 1959 to 1961, inflation tended to redistribute wealth from wage earner to investor, since prices and profits increased more rapidly than wages.[113] Nevertheless, the government and particularly Vice President João Goulart appeared to support labor demands by permitting agitation and guaranteeing sizeable wage increases. In addition Goulart and the Partido Trabalhista Brasileiro (PTB) distributed jobs in the labor courts and social security institutes, thus assuring PTB support of the government and permitting Kubitschek to maintain the old Vargas alliance among labor, middle class, and the industrialist and landowner sectors. Although an illegal party, Communists maintained influence in labor unions, working with the PTB and the Partido Social Democrático to oppose the armed forces and the União Democrática Nacional (UDN). Some Communist candidates even ran under the PTB, in exchange for PCB support.

The broad nationalist movement embracing the PTB, PSD, elements in the military, students, and Communists had provided the impetus for political support of Kubitschek's "developmentalism." A continuation of Kubitschek's policies was promised during the 1960 campaign by the presidential candidate of the PSD and PTB, Marshal Henrique Lott, a moderate army general who refused to promise legalization for the PCB but received its support anyway. His defeat discredited the nationalist movement as well as the Communists.

Lott's vice presidential running mate, Goulart, meanwhile won on a separate ballot,[114] and this victory was important to Prestes, who, in August 1960, had urged Goulart to lead the struggle for legalization of the PCB. The pragmatic Goulart could count on Communist support within the labor movement, and his PTB party was represented at the closing session of the PCB's Fifth Congress. Support for Goulart was further bolstered by the "Jan-Jan" campaign to split the ticket in favor of Jânio Quadros and "Jango" Goulart, a campaign organized in São Paulo by Dante Pelacani, a leader of graphics workers who had withdrawn from the PCB in 1958. In an effort to appeal to leftist voters during the campaign, Quadros had visited Cuba in the company of, among others, Francisco Julião, Marxist leader of the peasant leagues in the Northeast. Although not a member of the PCB, Julião eventually supported Lott and Goulart.[115]

In his assessment of the election returns, Caio Prado Júnior delivered a penetrating critique of national politics and especially the PCB. He compared the defeat of Lott to that of the "pseudo-popular and nationalist" Kubitschek by workers in São Paulo during the 1955 presidential elections, and attributed this trend to inflation and the drastic salary cut as well as to the rapid growth of capitalist profit. The PCB's failure to comprehend the trend, he went on, was due not only to its long isolation from the working and popular masses—the result of "many years of sterile policies of the ruling clique"—but also to "absurd and deformed conceptions in its political line," conceptions in which capitalism underlay a "progressive" system in Brazil. The "defeat of popular and nationalist politics," he argued, necessitated an end to party rule by a clique and an end to electoral maneuvers. Instead, the party should return to a grass-roots politics in defense of popular courses such as the earlier petroleum campaign. Direct contact with the people, he continued, would be made through existing and new institutions such as labor unions and class associations, by way of arousing "an expression of popular conscience" and giving the people an interpretation and solution of the problems and difficulties they so deeply feel but did not understand.[116]

As President, Jânio Quadros promised to end inflation through efficient rationalization of the government bureaucracy and through controls over profiteering politicians and businessmen. While he weakened Goulart's influence by appointing a Christian Democrat to head the Labor Ministry, he won nationalist and leftist support by advocating an independent foreign policy that sought markets in socialist countries, defended the Cuban Revolution, and affirmed Brazil's leadership role in the underdeveloped world. Quadros' reforms were, however, opposed by conservative forces favoring the status quo, and his decoration of Cuban hero Ernesto ("Ché") Guevara precipitated the August 1961 crisis that resulted in his resignation and an abrupt exit from the Brazilian political scene.[117] After his departure Brazil lapsed into a continuous "structural crisis" under the inept leadership of Goulart.[118]

Popular demand, in large measure mobilized by Leonel Brizola, Goulart's brother-in-law and at the time governor of Rio Grande do Sul, pressured the military to relinquish the Presidency to Goulart—but only after the implementation of a hastily improvised parliamentary system and the reduction of Presidential powers. Not until a plebiscite in January 1963 was Goulart able to regain full Presidential powers. The interim period was characterized by new inflation, trade deficits and foreign debts, wage demands and strikes, and crises in agriculture at a time when the President was promoting popular demonstrations and maneuvering to abolish the parliamentary system.

With Goulart as President, the last months of 1961 brought a resurgence of popular sentiment and the emergence of new leftist and nationalist forces. In the hope of assuming the leadership of popular nationalist currents, Brizola and Mauro Borges, governor of Goiás, formed the Frente de Libertação Nacional (FLN) with PCB support. During October of that year these and other nationalists approved a "declaration" demanding agrarian reform, controls over remission of profits abroad, and diplomatic relations with all countries. In November the first Congresso dos Lavradores e Camponeses sem Terra was held in Belo Horizonte. Francisco Julião emerged as national leader of the peasants and received backing for demanding immediate expropriation of large properties, although this radical position was partially offset by the São Paulo PCB rural worker's organization, the União dos Lavradores e Trabalhadores Agrícolas do Brasil (ULTAB), which was older and more moderate than Julião's Ligas Camponesas and aggregated coffee sharecroppers and some sugar workers. During this period, too, Brazil established diplomatic relations with the Soviet Union.[119]

The Prestes-led PCB joined the campaign for a plebiscite and a return of Presidential powers to Goulart. Anticipating an eventual payoff for their support, the party also demanded legalization.[120] In an October statement the PCB identified what it considered the "inconsistencies" and "contradictions" of the national bourgeoisie: thus, while "establishing diplomatic relations with socialist countries, upholding the principle of self-determination for peoples and non-interference in their affairs and moving nearer to the non-aligned countries on such issues as disarmament," this bourgeoisie was "incapable of making a clean break with the imperialist system with which it is linked by the basic interests of the exploiting classes and the fear of socialism."

A nine-point program was proposed: rejection of IMF and Alliance for Progress programs; limitations on the transfer of profits abroad, and extension of Petrobrás; nationalization of foreign-owned public utilities; radical agrarian reform providing for distribution of land to peasants and compensation in bonds to latifundists; curbs on inflation, controls on foreign trade and exchange, repeal of the national security law and restoration of legality to the PCB; electoral reform, with extension of the franchise to all adults including the military; an independent foreign policy, peaceful coexistence among countries, disarmament and world peace; and the combating of terrorist groups and military coups. These reforms would be achieved through "mass struggle" against "imperialism" and feudalism by peasants, workers, the revolutionary intellectuals, and the national bourgeoisie. At the same time, the statement continued, two tendencies would be combated: the "left" tendency, which fails to emphasize struggle against "imperialism" and ignores differences and contradictions between the pro-imperialist and national wings of the bourgeoisie; and the "right" tendency, which links "the interests of the working class and people with the interests of the bourgeoisie as represented by João Goulart" and ignores "the dual conciliatory character of the national bourgeoisie." [121]

In the campaign for a plebiscite, pro-Goulart elements in the labor movement established the Comando Geral de Greve (CGG). A national labor-union organization like the CGG had been proposed by Prestes and the PCB at the Third Congresso Sindical Nacional in August 1960. With the support of labor and segments of the PTB, Goulart had favored the Communist proposal and thus provoked a break with anti-Communist leaders in the labor movement. Thus the directors of the CGG included non-Communists working with Communists against the anti-Communist leadership of the greater number of the labor confederations. During its brief existence (from June to September 1962), the CGG was unsuccessful in organizing strikes in behalf of Goulart. After September, when it became known as the Comando Geral dos Trabalhadores (CGT), it led strikes aimed at wage increases, occasionally blocked Goulart's cabinet choices, and saw to it that Communists were given a few minor posts in the government.[122] Conscious of its power, the CGT thereafter organized for action independent of the government. During this period other leftist groups had formed, including the PTB-oriented União Sindical Trabalhista (UST) as a "third force" independent from Communists and Democráticos, and the Pacto Sindical de Unidade a Ação (PUA), a São Paulo group.[123]

Communists became deeply involved also in the organization of rural workers. The PCB favored extending urban labor legislation and protection to rural areas, and was notably successful in backing Miguel Arraes for governor of backward Pernambuco in 1962. This triumph of urban radicalism over conservative ruralism allowed Governor Arraes to promote unionization of sugar workers, with a result in large wage increases. This in turn led to personal hostility between Arraes and

Julião, whose Ligas Camponesas aggregated peasants rather than wage-earning rural workers. As a consequence Julião suffered some loss of prestige among peasants, but this could be attributed also to his personal ambition, his shifting from regional to national problems after being elected a deputy to the national congress, and his temporary isolation from the left when he formed his own Movimento Revolucionário Tiradentes (MRT).[124] Government legislation of March 1963, giving rural workers the right to organize, encouraged progressive Catholic priests to increase their efforts for legal peasant unions; and this activity also tended to undermine Julião's leadership. The Communist rural unions under the ULTAB also stepped up activities especially in the Northeast, where they competed with Julião and became influential in the federation of peasant leagues in the state of Paraíba.[125]

In the student movement, Communists joined with the left-wing Catholic Ação Popular (AP) to dominate the União Nacional dos Estudantes (UNE). Student radicals were particularly effective in demonstrating their commitment to improving Brazilian society through cultural and educational activities. Progressive priests working with peasants and slum dwellers, as well as prominent Christian Democrats like Paulo de Tarso, supported the humanistic leftist position of the AP. Frequently they supported legalization of the PCB. There also appeared about 1961 an independent Marxist revolutionary group, Política Operária, formed by radical youth from the PTB, PSB, and PCB.

In 1962 the PCB issued a series of resolutions. In the first, in August, they again described the difficulties of the Goulart government under a parliamentary system and reiterated their condemnation of "imperialist" forces (including the Alliance for Progress), and demanded profit remission controls, agrarian reform, nationalization of foreign enterprise, and legal status for the party.[126] After the October Congressional elections Prestes proclaimed that seventeen of the four hundred nine elected federal deputies were PCB members who had run on other tickets.[127] In November the PCB announced a campaign with the slogan "Plebiscite with Reform."[128] Then at a December National Conference it issued a twelve-point resolution including condemnation of the U.S. blockade of Cuba and praise for the Soviet Union's withdrawal of missiles during the crisis of October; recognition that the rise of political consciousness in Brazil among the popular masses along with increasing instability augured well for the struggle to form a democratic and na-

tionalist government; the assertion that bourgeois concessions to imperialism and latifundism offset positive foreign policies. The resolution
further asserted that reforms promised by the government would be
conciliatory to reactionary forces; that elections are a means of com-
batting reaction and imperialism; that structural reforms are essential;
that imperialist and reactionary forces must be isolated if nationalist
and democratic government is to be attained; that Communists must
mobilize to obtain the effective participation of the working masses; that
the party must pressure the masses to demand change, combat sectarian
and opportunist tendencies, vote for a return to a presidential system,
and lead the people to socialism.[129]

Labor agitation and strikes became an almost everyday occurrence,
and during 1963 the cost of living rose nearly 80 per cent. Politics
tended to polarize as conservative forces became alienated from Goulart,
even though his own inclinations and certain basic government policies
favored wealthy urban and rural interests. Not being adequately represented in the President's moderate cabinets, the left, in particular the
CGT and the Communists, as well as labor and the middle class, re-
sisted all austerity measures, including the three-year development plan
drawn up by Economic and Planning Minister Celso Furtado. The plan,
they argued, reflected an imperialist policy carried out by the bourgeoisie
through the Goulart government.[130] Still, the left, notably Communists
who viewed Goulart as potentially beneficial to their interests, enter-
tained the possibility of a broad front of populist forces under the
President's tutelage. Goulart himself may have preferred a dictatorship
supported by progressive military elements, and his request for a declaration of state of siege in October 1963 was an apparent move in that
direction.[131]

During 1963 Prestes and his party, which had supported the Cuban
Revolution, joined other leftists and nationalists to organize a Congresso
Continental de Solidariedade à Cuba to be held in Niterói from
March 28 to 30.[132] There was little doubt that the Cuban Revolution
had given revolutionary nationalists an examplar with which to illustrate their views. At the same time the military was increasingly worried
about internal subversion. In July the PCB published a political resolution expressing dissatisfaction with the newly appointed Goulart cabinet
and emphasizing the role of the Frente de Mobilização Popular
(FMP), the leftist nationalist pressure group of 1962 aggregating the
CGT, the UNE, and deputies of the Frente Parlamentar Nacionalista

(FPN).[133] In September the Supreme Court ruled against the seating in Congress of Sergeant Antônio Garcia Filho, a member of the FPM, on the ground that military personnel were not allowed to hold legislative posts. In reprisal six hundred sergeants, corporals, and enlisted men rebelled in Brasília on September 12, apparently provoked to do so by anti-Communist infiltrators.[134] In October the PCB paper *Novos Rumos* warned the government of an impending conspiracy but cautioned Goulart against declaring a state of siege. Instead he should "mobilize the masses against reactionary forces," and especially against Carlos Lacerda and Adhemar de Barros; this, the writer continued, would be accomplished through united action of workers, peasants, students, "patriotic" military, and the Brazilian people.[135]

By early 1964 Goulart faced an imminent coup on the right and popular impatience with his inaction on the left. In an apparent effort to offset leftist discontent he appeared at workers' rallies, and on March 13 he signed two Presidential decrees and promised two others giving his government the right to expropriate uncultivated land along federal roads, railroads, and waterways; to nationalize private oil refineries; to grant to illiterates the right to vote; and to lower the exorbitant rents in Rio.[136] Goulart was supported by the nationalist, reform-minded non-commissioned officers and enlisted men who had staged a revolt in Brasília on September 12, 1963, and now opposed conservative officers who were uneasy over the reform measures.[137]

In February the CGT had demanded a 100 per cent increase in the minimum wage level. On March 17 Prestes reiterated his party's support for a popular front and maintained that "peaceful" but "growing pressure on Congress" would provide workers with structural reforms within the existing system. He predicted that through a deliberate process the patriotic forces of the nation would achieve unification and a "nationalist and democratic government."[138] At a meeting on March 22 in commemoration of the party's founding, Prestes reportedly exclaimed that "the PCB is not yet the government, but it already has been in the government."[139] During March 26 and 27 the CGT supported striking marines and sailors led by José Anselmo dos Santos, a former radical student in UNE who had entered compulsory military service to mobilize "popular forces." When the Minister of Navy ordered the arrest of Anselmo dos Santos and a rebel Admiral, Cândido Aragão, Goulart named a new minister who promptly declared an amnesty for the rebels.[140] On the same day the PCB organ exhorted the President to issue decrees to control exchange, the debt, and concessions to foreign firms, expand public services, revoke labor laws, declare a general amnesty for political prisoners, and legalize the PCB.[141]

Then in late March the PCB published the theses of its prospective Sixth Congress, which was approved by the Central Committee in February and scheduled for November. The first thesis reiterated the party's opposition to U.S. imperialism in order to achieve national emancipation and political independence. The other five theses focused on what were termed the fundamental contradictions in the infrastructure of Brazilian society; on the "principal tactical objective" of achieving a nationalist and democratic government brought about through a policy of "united front with the national bourgeoisie"; the "anti-imperialist" and "anti-feudal" struggle to implement the "basic reforms" (reformas de base) in commerce, foreign investment, agriculture, and education; the "peaceful road" to the Brazilian revolution, which "in certain circumstances requires violent confrontation with reactionary forces"; and on the need to "consolidate an alliance of workers and peasants" and to establish "a hegemony of the proletariat." [142] These theses followed the political line of the party's Fifth Congress. While they were received with alarm by conservatives, they were subject to criticism also from the Marxist left.[143]

The party demands seemed to assume that the military would remain supportive or at least neutral on Goulart's policies. Conservative forces, however, moved against Goulart on March 31. An army revolt began in a Minas Gerais garrison and quickly spread to Rio. Without publicly attempting to mobilize popular support, and relying on loyal military commanders, Goulart fled from Rio to Brasília, then to his home state of Rio Grande do Sul, and finally to Uruguay. A last-minute general strike called by the CGT failed, and public opinion seemed relieved "to be rid of the corrupt mechanism of political payoffs that was Brazilian democracy," as one writer put it.[144] It was against such corruption—illicit funds, government patronage, and the like—that the military now moved. The military leaders also had little difficulty in justifying their intervention on the grounds that the Goulart government was Communist-infiltrated.[145]

The Aftermath of the Coup

The political forces that brought an end to the Goulart government were far from united. The military divided between the extremist *linha dura* or "hard line" officers who wished to end "corruption" and Communist "subversion" in Brazil, and the majority of *moderados* or "soft line" officers who tended to favor constitutionalism with some social reform. Closely identified with the coup was the "Sorbonne group" of "intellectual" generals and colonels, who were products of Escola Superior da Guerra and favored fundamental social and economic changes and an independent foreign policy.[146] When Congressional leaders balked at military demands to purge the civil service and state and federal legislatures of "subversive" (especially Communist) individuals, "hard line" officers arbitrarily established a Supreme Revolutionary Command and announced an emergency act, the Ato Institucional, which gave the executive necessary powers and authority to propose expenditure bills, declare states of siege, and suppress the political rights and cancel mandates of undesirable elected officials. Job security in the civil service was suspended for six months.[147] Two days later General Humberto Castelo Branco, chief of the Army General Staff, was "elected" President by Congress, and he soon proved to be a mediator between the military factions. Under "hard line" pressure, however, the government initiated the first of several purges, suspending the political rights of three hundred seventy-eight persons, including former Presidents Kubitschek, Quadros, and Goulart, six state governors (including Miguel Arraes), fifty-five members of Congress, and other leftist nationalist leaders in the foreign service, labor, military, civil service, and intelligentsia.[148]

Castelo Branco attempted to implement a program of economic stabilization, influenced by his Planning Minister Roberto de Oliveira Campos and the IMF, and in July 1964 agreed to a constitutional amendment extending his term until March 15, 1967, with Presidential elections set for late 1966. In July 1965 the government moved to control the electoral system, first, by barring from candidacy former ministers under Goulart and, second, through a reorganization of the political party system. When in gubernatorial elections of October 1965 the opposition won in Minas and Guanabara, the government issued a Second Institutional Act on October 27, under which all political parties were to be dissolved and future Presidents would be elected by Congress. The Third Institutional Act of February 6, 1966, replaced direct election of governors with selection by the state legislature. Two parties were allowed, the opposition Movimento Democrático Brasileiro (MDB) and the government Aliança Renovadora Nacional

(ARENA). Since the ARENA held the majority of congressional seats, the MDB boycotted the Presidential elections, and General Arthur Costa e Silva, the government candidate, won unopposed on October 3.[149]

The radical left and the Communists were quick to condemn the United States for alleged involvement in the events of April 1964 and thereafter. After the coup Brazil enjoyed full U.S. cooperation and substantial economic and financial assistance as well.[150] In return Brazil enthusiastically supported the U.S. intervention in the Dominican Republic in April 1965 and sent a military force to assist the Organization of American States peace mission there. Prestes denounced "U.S. imperialists" for "reverting to their old policy of the big stick" and compared the Dominican debacle to the military coup and the Castelo Branco regime in Brazil, which "consists of the most reactionary, anti-nationalist elements—agents of U.S. imperialism, latifundists, and capitalists linked with the American monopolies."[151]

After postponing its Sixth Congress from November 1964, the PCB reappraised its position in October of that year. The policy of supporting a united front had failed, according to a party spokesman, because the bourgeoisie dominated over an unstable union of popular forces: "The party as a whole and the leadership in particular, living in illusions, placed too much reliance on the command of the army. . . . In the same way we failed to combat the reckless adventurism of some groups of the radical wing of the Frente." [152] Clearly the PCB had miscalculated: "The events took us by surprise; we were unprepared, not only to face them but also to continue our activities safely and efficiently, in the light of new conditions in the country." Acknowledging its weaknesses, the party condemned as false the "outlook for an easy and immediate victory, which we presented to the party and to the masses at that time. Our class illusions, our *seguidismo* [tagging along] with respect to the sector of the national bourgeoisie that was in power, became evident." [153]

With the abrupt turn of events in 1964, Prestes may have temporarily lost his hold over the party. Blamed for allowing the party to be caught off guard by the coup, he reportedly reigned no longer as effective leader of the PCB. Apparently he remained a member of the Central Committee and as secretary general, but was stripped of the authority and power he traditionally had wielded over party affairs.[154]

Prestes' loss of power may be attributed to the fact that following the 1964 coup the party was divided by the strong *Fidelista* sentiment manifested by the "Cuban faction." Moreover, as internal criticism was aired over the party's pre-coup position, pro-Prestes and anti-Prestes factions emerged.[155] Prestes was especially vulnerable to criticism because on April 9, 1964, police had discovered twenty notebooks in his writing, in a search of his home in São Paulo. These notebooks, which described details of party meetings from 1961, became the basis for an extensive six-month investigation leading to indictments of seventy-four party members (of whom about sixty were tried during mid-1966 in a São Paulo military court), and to suspension of political rights for ten years for fifty-nine Communists.[156] The São Paulo investigation coincided with a general investigation of Brazilian Communism under the direction of Colonel Fernando de Carvalho, who terminated his proceedings in October 1966 with a report to the government.[157]

In the aftermath of the coup and the repression, regional dissension among Communist leaders created further difficulties for the party in São Paulo, Pernambuco, Guanabara, Paraná, and Rio Grande do Sul. Party headquarters had in effect been transferred from Rio to São Paulo, where on May 5, 1965, thirty-two members and alternates to the Central Committee attended its first meeting since the 1964 coup. A majority faction favoring Prestes urged that the PCB join an anti-government front, and a "hard line" faction, led by Mário Alves de Souza Vieira, Manoel Jover Telles, Jacob Gorender, and Neri Reis de Almeida, favored violence. The Prestes faction emerged victorious over Gorender's negative vote and five abstentions. Alves de Souza Vieira and Jover Telles were immediately dropped from the Executive Commission although they retained membership in the Central Committee.[158] The results of the May meeting were published in the form of a policy resolution. That the will of Prestes now prevailed was clearly evident in the reiteration of an old party line: "The immediate tactical objective in this struggle is to isolate and defeat the dictatorship, and to win a broadly representative government of anti-dictatorial forces." [159] The attainment of this objective was to be by means of participation in the municipal and federal elections expected a year later.

Division was evident also among party leaders in Pernambuco as early as May 1964, when David Capistrano da Costa and other state party leaders distributed a document attacking the national PCB leadership for "opportunism" and "illusions of class," and for failure to "politically prepare the proletariat and the working masses to face violent clashes." [160] In Guanabara, dissidents denounced the "opportunistic" majority of the Central Committee and expressed their reservations concerning the theses proposed for the party's Sixth Congress, now scheduled for late 1967. Communist leaders in Rio Grande do Sul expressed opposition to the "anti-Marxist" theses and condemned the top national leadership for "rightist opportunism and revisionism." Communists in Paraná urged creation of a worker and peasant party in place of the existing "petty-bourgeois" composition. [161]

During January 1966, the Central Committee met again at São Paulo to approve theses prepared for discussions preceding the Sixth Congress. In alternative propositions Alves de Souza Vieira and Jover Telles argued that the original theses did not relate to the Brazilian political reality. Even so, the Central Committee endorsed the original theses at a meeting in June. While the first thesis reviewed developments leading up to the coup of 1964, the second and third dealt respectively with present conditions in Brazil as dominated (according to the text) by a military dictatorship and U.S. imperialism and in the international scene (intensified, so read the thesis, by capitalist and imperialist aggression against revolutionary forces in Vietnam, Cuba, and Santo Domingo). A fourth thesis interpreted the present struggle as part of an anti-imperialist and anti-feudal stage leading to a second stage of "socialist transformations" which would be reached through "liberation from imperialist dominance in the economy of the country," "elimination of the latifundism and feudalism"; "independent and progressive development of the national economy"; "distribution of resources," and the guarantee of "democratic rights" to the working masses, and "a policy of political independence."

The fifth thesis outlined the party's tactics: "To mobilize, unite, and organize the working class and other patriotic and democratic forces in the struggle against the dictatorship." This objective involved the formation of a broad front of all forces, including "sectors of the dominant classes" opposed to the military government. A last thesis dealt with the party, its "weaknesses" and "false conception of the Brazilian revolution." Since party efforts to establish a united front had been assigned to the upper echelon (cúpula) rather than to the masses, the top leadership "underestimated the decisive role of the masses in the revolution." Further, the party had "deviated from the political line of the Fifth Congress," thereby undermining "the struggle against the conciliatory maneuvers of the national bourgeoisie." [162]

While acknowledging its past mistakes, the party maintained a cautious yet conciliatory position in a resolution of the Central Committee also issued during June 1966. Thus it advocated support for the opposition MDB, whose "program of struggle . . . corresponds to the demands of the democratic forces." The MDB was comprised of the unpurged former PTB congressional representation plus a minority segment of the old PSD and representatives of minor parties. The PCB thus supported a moderate opposition party.[163]

At its Sixth Congress, held in December 1967, the PCB approved the theses and additionally approved a resolution advocating a four-point minimal program: abolition of all dictatorial decrees and the restoration of democratic freedom, elections, and a democratic constitution as well as an amnesty for political prisoners; defense of the material wealth of the country through a policy of independent economic development; raising of living standards of the working people and partial implementation of the agrarian reform; and maintenance of a foreign policy affirming national sovereignty and self-determination. Further, the party would "wage a ideological struggle against the influences of the 'left' and the 'right'." [164]

One of those involved in the ideological debate that had split the party was Carlos Marighella, who had resigned in December 1966 from the Executive Commission with the declaration that he was "ready to take part in the revolutionary struggle with the masses but never to play a waiting game in bureaucratic politics pending its consideration." In his resignation statement Marighella condemned the party leadership for "turning to an anti-Marxist and anti-dialectical concept of the 'directing nucleus,' monolithic, imposed on the collectivity . . . an attempt at ideological intimidation, recourse to form of compulsion to avoid the circulation of ideas of which they are afraid." The only alternative for the party, he argued, was "through armed struggle, the revolutionary way." The era of democratic-liberal revolution long advocated by the PCB "has long since passed," and the party had become "an appendage of the bourgeois parties." [165] In September the Central Committee expelled Marighella from the party, along with Jover Telles. Gorender was suspended from voting in the Central Committee, and three other committee members were censured. The Sixth Congress ratified these decisions by formally expelling Marighella and Telles along with Gorender, Alves de Souza Vieira, Joaquim Câmara Ferreira, Apolônio de Carvalho, and Miguel Batista.[166] Gorender, Alves, and Ferreira immediately established the Partido Comunista Brasileiro Revolucionário (PCBR). The Central Committee also levied criticism at the dissident state party organizations in Guanabara, São Paulo, Rio Grande do Sul, and Rio de Janeiro.[167] The ouster of Marighella was no doubt prompted by his attendance at the conference of the Organization of Latin American Solidarity (OLAS), in Havana July 31 to August 10, 1967. The PCB (which had sent no official representative) later condemned the OLAS for its advocacy of armed struggle and described the late Ernesto ("Ché") Guevara as "an adventurer blinded by his own illusions" who sought "to revive in the new guise of guerrilla warfare a conception of revolution based on insurrectionary hotheads stirred up by adventures totally isolated from the mass movement." [168]

In response to Marighella's ouster the São Paulo State Committee of the PCB, still under his influence, released a document attacking the "bourgeois" tactics of the national leadership and emphasizing "the ideological divergence" between those dominating the Central Committee and the party rank and file. "The group that leads the party . . . has been corrupted by the influence of the reformist bourgeois ideology and has put itself at the service of capitalist development." As to an alternative, "the São Paulo Communists, as well as the Communists in other states, have in the majority already chosen the revolutionary method, while the 'masters' of the Central Committee prefer to work for capitalist reforms." The mistakes of the PCB before the 1964 coup were the result of "rightwing opportunism, submission to the bourgeoisie, 'tagging along'." In a real revolutionary situation, the leadership failed to prepare either the party or the masses, according to the document. In rebutting the thesis that Brazilian society should be transformed by peaceful means, the São Paulo group called for "mass armed struggle —long and arduous, tenacious and full of sacrifices." Further, the State Committee condemned the Central Committee for tolerating a parallel organization in São Paulo "composed of a factional group of comrades," which "tries to pit the rank and file and the militants against the municipal and state leadership." Finally, the São Paulo group rejected the decision of the Central Committee and affirmed that Marighella would remain as secretary of the São Paulo State Committee.[169]

During October the São Paulo State Committee of the PCB joined with those from Guanabara, Rio de Janeiro, Espírito Santo, Rio Grande do Sul, Ceará, and the Federal District of Brasília to issue a statement emanating from a national conference "to set up the political line of the Marxist-Leninist party of the working class." They defined the Brazilian revolution as "a popular, anti-imperialist, and anti-latifundista revolution paving the way to socialism." In mobilizing the industrial workers, agricultural wage earners, the peasantry, the students and intellectuals, and the middle class, the revolution would seek "to destroy the bureaucratic-military apparatus of the bourgeois-latifundist state and replace it with a popular revolutionary government." The taking of power would be through "armed struggle," since "conditions in Brazil indicate that guerrilla warfare is the best method. . . . The popular war should be started in the countryside."

Under "a united political-military command," the statement went on, the revolutionary forces would develop "the struggle of the working masses in the cities and the countryside." A single popular front "based on a cell of the leftist forces and headed by the Marxist-Leninist party" would be established "during the heat of the struggle." The masses would be involved in this movement by combining "immediate demands with the struggle for political power" and utilizing "legal methods with illegal methods of struggle," but fundamental would be "the organization of the revolutionary forces at the base." The Brazilian proletariat would be led by "a vanguard party committee" pledged to "a complete return to Marxist-Leninist principles," and to the attainment of "a popular revolutionary government, national liberation, and socialism." In the world Communist movement, the PCB State Committees agreed "to maintain an independent position, refusing to follow any fraternal party uncritically." [170]

That Prestes' fame and prestige continued to carry much weight was attested by the publication of his extensive analysis of the Sixth Congress. Whatever illusions some Communists may have had about the prospects for converting the party into an effective revolutionary force were shattered by the moderate theses and resolutions of the Congress and by Prestes' strict adherence to the Soviet line in his interpretation of both the contemporary conditions in Brazil and the international scene. The Congress rejected the view that the mistakes of the party "were the result of a right deviation" and that they were, on the contrary, "mistakes of a leftist, putschist and petty bourgeois character." The free discussion before the Congress, he argued "enabled the party to understand the errors of the opposition, safeguard its unity and, ultimately, to defeat the opposition." Further, the opposition's call for an immediate struggle for socialism "would go against the objective process and isolate itself from the patriotic and democratic front." The Congress disproved "the contention that a national bourgeoisie does not exist in Brazil." It took issue with the belief that "armed struggle is the sole and exclusive form of combating the dictatorship, the only way to win the revolution," and with the "non-Marxist conception" of the guerrilla *foco* (center) as advocated by French Marxist Regis Debray. Furthermore, the Congress opposed "the idea widespread in revolutionary struggle." [171]

In an interview published late in 1968 Prestes reaffirmed that while conditions in Brazil did not permit armed struggle he was not against that alternative. He recalled that his personal experience as leader of the Prestes Column "had carried [him] to Marxism." Nevertheless, he acknowledged differences between the PCB and Cuba and condemned radical revolutionary groups in Brazil "which are mistaken in calling for the armed struggle as the only and exclusive form of struggle." He was mistaken in his evaluation of the Bolivian conditions." [172]

The party's political line was maintained also in policy resolutions issued by the Central Committee in September 1968 and February 1969. In the September resolution the Central Committee reviewed optimistically the mass demonstrations by workers, students, and intellectuals since the Sixth Congress. Condemning "the ultra-left and adventurist elements" that pressed for "urban guerrilla war" in Guanabara, the party emphasized "the need to combine legal and illegal forms of struggle and organization." Such tactics would "make it possible, on the one hand, to stimulate and consolidate the mass movement and the unity of action of the anti-dictatorial forces and, on the other, to isolate the dictatorship." At the same time, "the policy of the leftist and adventurist groups narrows down the mass movement." The party attacked both the rightist "sectarian and putschist tendencies" and the leftist "petty-bourgeois subjectivism and impatience" still prevailing in its ranks.[173] Despite the dictatorship's assumption of a hard line on December 13, 1968, and the closure of the Brazilian Congress, the party would persist in its tactic of striving for unity of action among all forces opposed to the dictatorship. If possible, concluded the resolutions, the PCB would "work for mutual understanding with the left trends which are waging a mass struggle against the existing regime, although we don't accept their narrow-minded and hasty policy." [174]

The persistent line of Prestes and the PCB, the actions of the Sixth

Congress, and the expulsion of dissident leaders had brought the party full circle with its difficulties of more than a decade earlier. Moderation in the face of the military regime's increasing repression was unacceptable to a variety of leftist forces that had split from the PCB or formed spontaneously or on their own initiative during the late sixties. Thus it was not surprising that a series of confrontations during 1969 and 1970 between the regime and the radicalized elements of the left tended somewhat to isolate and obscure the cautious activities of the PCB. The closure of Congress on December 13, 1968, was prompted by the refusal of the Chamber of Deputies to permit the indictment of one of its members, Márcio Moureira Alves. Alves was the author of a book alleging the regime's use of torture, and he reiterated that charge in speeches on the floor of the Chamber.[175] Press censorship was rigorously enforced thereafter, and the Supreme Court was restructured in January, when three judges were purged. In February the government closed five state legislatures and expelled an additional eighty-three politicians, depriving them of their political rights for ten years. In late April some seventy university professors were forcibly retired.[176] In September the death penalty was imposed (the first time under the Republic) for "the crime of psychological warfare and revolutionary or subversive war." A month later, on October 17, a new constitution was promulgated, granting broader power to the President.[177] On February 11, 1970, the government decreed pre-sale police censorship of publications deemed to be pornographic.

The government repression was accompanied by right-wing terrorism and torture of political prisoners. For several years death squads believed composed of off-duty policemen and former soldiers had systematically tortured and executed hundreds of known former political prisoners. These squads probably provided the professional killers for such notorious right-wing terrorist organizations as the Comando da Caça aos Comunistas (CCC) and the Movimento Anti-Comunista (MAC), which (allegedly with government collaboration) engaged in assassination activities in an effort to combat radical resistance and a series of dramatic bank holdups and symbolic attacks on military and government buildings as well as on U.S. corporate and government offices.[178]

After the issuance of a National Security Law on March 11, 1967, which permitted the military to interpret any opposition as treason, radical resistance to the government repression became increasingly manifest, in both spontaneous and organized forms. After a clandestine congress of the União Nacional dos Estudantes (UNE) in August 1967, student demonstrations in particular were conspicuous during March, April, May, and June 1968. Student protesters were joined by Brazil's National Conference of Catholic Bishops, which condemned the government's "fascist" measures of security. At another UNE congress in the state of São Paulo in October one thousand representatives were arrested by police.

The radical protest escalated considerably after New York Governor Nelson Rockefeller's arrival in Brazil in June 1969 on an official visit for the Nixon administration. In mid-August resistance groups seized a São Paulo radio station to broadcast that an important event would soon take place.[179] On September 4, U.S. Ambassador C. Burke Elbrick was kidnapped and later exchanged for fifteen political prisoners, including Recife PCB leader Gregório Bezerra.[180] This operation was carried out by two urban guerrilla movements, the Ação Libertadora Nacional (ALN) and the Movimento Revolucionário do 8 de Outubro (MR-8), the latter named after the date of Ché Guevara's death. Two of the revolutionaries involved were ALN leader Marighella and MR-8 leader Captain Carlos Lamarca, who had deserted from the Brazilian army in March 1969, taking with him two non-commissioned officers and truckloads of arms and ammunition.

Both Marighella and Lamarca had since 1968 organized a rash of bank robberies, including fifty-two with a take of $60,000 in São Paulo and another twenty-three and $30,000 in Rio de Janeiro. The revolutionaries were assisted also by Jorge Medeiros Vale, a member of MR-8 and executive of the Banco de Brasil who before his arrest in July 1969 had transferred $2,000,000 to a special account in Switzerland.[181] In spite of these successes, the revolutionary left offered a sober assessment of the Brazilian situation: "Revolutionary war is not in progress in this country. The workers in the cities and countryside do not yet have an army of their own." The armed actions were adjudged useful, however, "as they prepare the way politically for arming the revolutionary social forces." [182]

Four revolutionary events highlighted the year 1970. In January five revolutionaries, who claimed to be associated with the Vanguarda Armada Revolucionária (VAR-Palmares) successfully hijacked a Brazilian plane to Cuba. In March the Japanese Consul General in São Paulo was kidnapped and exchanged for five political prisoners, one of them a Catholic nun.[183] In June another forty-four political prisoners

were flown to Algeria in exchange for the release of West German Ambassador Ehrenfried von Hollenben, who had been kidnapped by members
of the ALN and the Vanguarda Popular Revolucionária (VPR).[184]
And in December the Comando Juarez Guimarães de Brito (affiliated
with the VPR and named for a guerrilla leader who had died earlier
that year), launched what it called Operation Joaquim Câmara Ferreira in honor of a former Communist and ALN leader. The Comando
abducted Swiss Ambassador Giovanni Henrico Bucher, and after five
weeks of intensive bargaining with the authorities released him in exchange for another seventy imprisoned leftists.

While these events were generating sensational publicity within
Brazil and throughout the world, security forces consolidated their efforts to contain the guerrillas. The Swiss ambassador's kidnapping was
the last straw, and the regime announced that it would take a hard line
against all "terrorists." It also revealed to the press the extent of urban
warfare from 1964 through 1969, when forty-four persons had been
killed and one hundred ninety-three wounded in guerrilla operations
spread over twelve states, with assaults on three hundred forty-three
banks and $2,300,000 seized.[185] This publicity, designed to turn the
anxiety of many Brazilians, especially among the middle class, into support for the regime, was accompanied by nationalistic slogans proclaim-
ing success for the military's developmental policies. At the same time
security was tightened, guerrilla leaders' photographs were posted
throughout Brazil, and hundreds of leftists were rounded up and interrogated (with torture).[186] These measures had their effect, especially
after three important partisans were killed in confrontations with police: Carlos Marighella on November 4, 1969[187]; Câmara Ferreira,
who had assumed leadership of the ALN after Marighella's death, but
then died on October 23, 1971, after capture[188]; and Carlos Lamarca,
who was killed in a shootout with police in southern Bahia on September
17, 1971.[189]

With the splintered revolutionary groups to its left[190] now in decline,
the PCB appeared conspicuously isolated by its cautious line. But in a
series of resolutions issued by the Central Committee from 1970 through
1972, the party attacked "Brazil's growing dependence on the international monopolies and financial organizations, in particular American
imperialism," and coupled this with censure of the military's proclama-
tions of economic "success" and "miracle," arguing, for instance, that
the 9 or 10 per cent annual growth rate of the early 1970's did not

reflect the fact that "since 1964 real wages have dropped 45 per cent, 62 per cent of the working people earn less than 200 cruzeiros a month, only 1.3 per cent of the working people receive a wage exceeding one thousand cruzeiros." [191] According to the party's position, the dictatorship was pursuing a policy in the interests of "the big bourgeoisie, big landowners and foreign monopolies." The correct line of action, as affirmed in the decisions of the Sixth Congress, lay in coalescing an opposition front to the military dictatorship through which united action would defend "the working people's interests." Effort in this direction would be concentrated within the trade union movement.

The party considered prospects good for united action, since regional and national union congresses had demanded changes in governmental wage policy and called for the right to strike, for trade union freedoms and autonomy, democratic liberties, and measures against foreign monopoly exploitation.[192] In seeking this united front, the party recognized the need to work with the Catholic Church, which "is constantly protesting against torture and reprisal employed by the police"; with the parliamentary opposition which "continues its work"; and with students and intellectuals, whose protests "against censorship and other forms of pressure are also mounting." [193]

This party position was critically assessed by Márcio Moreira Alves, the exiled former deputy and leader of the Catholic left whose views were published by the prestigious Cuban literary institution, Casa de Américas, in 1972. Alves believed that while the PCB was the best organized and most experienced radical party in Brazil, it had failed to radicalize the youth. Nor did it offer a revolutionary theory "profoundly rooted in our reality," this being the consequence of "a strange adaptation to the objectives of Soviet foreign policy." At the same time he offered a negative perspective of the armed struggle, which had reached "bottom" in 1971. Thus, he claimed, the urban guerrillas failed to weaken the dictatorship, for they were "divided, shrunken, and impotent." They failed to mobilize masses, for they "could not even take advantage of the sympathy aroused by some of their actions." Further, the government repression "completely terrorized the middle classes and dried up the aid that some sectors were giving to the guerrillas," and the "counter-propaganda of the dictatorship and the lack of any serious training in the commando organizations turned public opinion against the revolutionaries." Alves concluded that the only course for Brazil was armed struggle, but within "an enormously broadened political and social base" which would be led by two forces: "the orthodox Communist party—still the best organized sector of the socialist forces in the country"—and the "young Catholic activists, with their habits of discipline, their logistical support, and their contacts with the masses." [194]

Indeed, activism at all levels of the Church had made it the major institutional force to oppose the military regime. During 1971 and 1972 the Church publicly attacked the social policies of the administration and in particular denounced police and military authorities for arbitrary and repressive actions, including torture, as well as policies allowing large business interests to exploit rural workers in the name of economic development. And by early 1973 the National Conference of Catholic Bishops had issued a strong public denunciation of discrimination and limitations of freedom in the country. [195]

While the PCB had acknowledged the importance of collaboration with the Church, it was as yet unwilling to turn to Alves' recommendation of armed struggle as a strategy in confronting the regime. Luiz Carlos Prestes made this position clear in a detailed analysis based on a close reading of Lenin's critique of ultra-leftism, and accordingly Brazilian Marxists-Leninists "opposed all leftist notions of terrorism and isolated armed actions" after the 1964 coup: "It was necessary to retreat, return to the modest, onerous, painstaking work of mass organization and propaganda." [196] The party's survival depended on this strategy, he argued, for over the past half-century the PCB had been "legal for a mere two years, semi-legal for little over five and brutally persecuted for nearly 43." After fifty years of struggle the party's stance was clear:

> The Communist Party is the only organized political party in the country. Not only does it continuously fortify its bonds with the masses, it is also the main rallying force in the battle against the dictatorship, for the people's interests, for democratic freedoms. [197]

Patterns of Evolution

Five basic patterns of action may be discerned in the PCB's development. A first pattern is yielded by the historical periods that marked the evolution of the Brazilian party and the international Communist movement. A correlation is clearly evident between the national and the international (in particular the Latin American) experience. Communism in Latin America divides into roughly eight periods. In the first, from the founding of the Comintern to the death of Lenin in 1924, anarcho-syndicalist and socialist groups were able to adhere to the International by agreeing to "twenty-one points." This connection led to the formation of the Brazilian party and, as elsewhere in Latin America, to internal ideological disagreements and disaffection. The PCB's Second Congress coincided with the second period, which was marked by the Soviet Union's transition to socialism and industrialization. It was also a period of personal rivalry rampant among Soviet Communist leaders until the third period, commencing in 1928, at which point Stalin consolidated his position of power and initiated attacks on Bukharin's right-wing supporters. Perhaps because of divisions within the Soviet party, Communist movements outside the Soviet Union were urged to isolate themselves from other political groups; in Brazil this led to the breakup of the BOC, the expulsion of the Oposição Sindical, withdrawal of a labor-oriented Trotskyist faction, and refusal to support the 1930 Revolution. In the fourth period, beginning in about 1934, a popular-front policy was pursued, and Prestes and his party were instrumental in the formation of the ANL, although this effort was countered by government suppression and the consolidation of power by the Vargas regime which may have provoked the November 1935 revolts. In 1939, the Nazi-Soviet agreement confused and briefly isolated the already weak Brazilian Communist movement, but the entry of the Soviet Union into World War II established a sixth period of collaboration with political forces opposed to fascism.

Despite continued harassment, the party began to consider Vargas an ally in the struggle against fascism. The party's National Conference in 1943 officially adopted a policy to this effect, and in the 1945 deal between Vargas and Prestes the PCB emerged as a legal entity. The party's brief electoral success terminated abruptly in 1947 with a new ban on its activities. Cautiously the party adopted the Cold War hostility to the United States that characterized the seventh period. The PCB was torn by the anti-Stalinist attacks of the Soviet Communist Party's Twentieth Congress, and the downgrading of the personality cult had severe repercussions on the Prestes leadership. During the eighth period, from 1958 to 1972, a policy of "peaceful coexistence" prevailed despite the guerrilla struggle and successful revolution of Fidel Castro and later efforts elsewhere to launch rural and urban guerrilla warfare.[198]

A second pattern is evident in the ambivalent attitude for/against change in Brazilian society. Dissatisfaction with oligarchic government expressed in the revolts of 1922, 1924, 1930, and 1935 and was shared by the labor movement, intellectuals and middle-class elements, and a disenchanted military. The forces opposing change, including the military and police, industrialists and businessmen, landowners, and foreign interests, led the constant struggle with "popular" forces, principally in 1937, 1947, 1955, 1961, and 1964. The ban on the PCB was maintained throughout its existence, except for brief periods of legality —in 1927 and in 1945–47, as we have seen.

Although in its formative years the party functioned as a small, disciplined organization, its orientation throughout the greater part of its evolution was toward a personalist-dominated and populist politics of accommodation. This orientation becomes a third pattern in the party's history. The style of discipline and action was particularly vulnerable to outside Communist pressure. The style of personalism and pragmatism was reminiscent of Vargas, indeed of Brazilian politics in general. The PCB experiment and moderate success with the BOC in the late 1920's established a tendency toward popular-front alignment thereafter. Pursuit of the international line resulted in the party's frequent isolation from popular groupings within Brazil (in 1929 and in the late 1940's). Deviation from the international line gave the party a degree of independence from the world-wide Communist movement (1945 to 1948 and perhaps during the early 1960's).

A fourth pattern is seen in the paired themes that dominated the party's perspective of Brazil and the world: nationalism and internationalism. The party's concern with nationalism began perhaps as a vague expression of Prestes' personal ambition to dominate the Brazilian revolution. His appeal was to the masses and their conscious identification with national life. Nationalism, of course, related closely to the party's anxieties over foreign capitalist penetration and domination of Brazilian economic and social life, for to the party the elimination of "imperialism" represented national salvation.

Internal party divisions and conflicts form a fifth pattern. At the outset the party's weak theoretical base contributed to varying ideological tendencies. Disagreements over national and international policy reinforced factional dissension. The prevalence of intellectuals in leadership positions and a weak mass base encouraged internal debate and factionalism. Moreover, the presence of an inner elite core of career-oriented bureaucratic leaders isolated top leadership from other echelons of party life.

Despite its divisions and weaknesses, the party survived. Stripped of its leadership in 1932, suppressed by police and military after November 1935, nearly extinct before its August 1943 conference, splintered by the debates of 1956–1957, and forced into obscurity after 1964, the PCB persistently demonstrated a capability of maintaining itself not only as a pressure force for reform but also of aggregating large segments of the working class and alienated intellectuals.

III • CONFLICT AND INTEGRATION

5 • Party Organization and the Role of Leaders and Followers

In many respects Communist parties, including the one in Brazil, are similar to political parties everywhere. Basically the political party is a social group, an identifiable social unit within the larger society. It is also a miniature political system comprising a membership with goals and tasks, and subject to a pattern of authority and distribution of power. It maintains communication channels through which policy decisions are disseminated, leaders and members recruited, goals defined, and internal conflicts resolved. Like other parties, the Communist party in Brazil has an organizational structure, comprising local, intermediary, and central bodies. It has a leadership and a rank and file, auxiliary and supportive agencies, organizational principles and functions. Like its Communist counterparts elsewhere, the Brazilian party is composed of a system of workplace cells, it claims to represent the interests of the working class, and it professes egalitarianism and belief in the masses. Its ideology is posited on a belief in civilizing technological progress.

Utilizing this concept of the political party as a social group and a miniature political system, we may now consider the primary structural properties of the Communist party in Brazil as specified in its statutes. We are concerned too with structural organization in relation to effective performance. For instance, how effective is the party in elections when legal and what is its revolutionary orientation when illegal? How does it relate to other national parties and to what extent is it influential, tolerated, contributory? To what extent are the changing aspirations and objectives of the party a reflection of general Brazilian conditions? We are interested in determining the impact of structure on the ideology, role perception, and motivations of party leaders at different hierarchical levels, and also in studying internal organization in relation to communication breakdown and weaknesses in managerial control. Another concern is with leadership perspectives—i.e., to what extent is there consensus or dissensus among interpersonal hierarchical relations? What is the effect upon the party of charismatic and bureaucratic tendencies? Is there diffusion of authority? decentralization of power?

Hierarchy and Power Structure

Many political parties tend to be hierarchical and oligarchical in nature, a characteristic emphasized by Roberto Michels' famous and controversial "iron law of oligarchy," which asserts that inevitably a minority assumes leadership and control of parties.[1] Michels' assumptions pertain to conservative and liberal styles of party life in the United States and England, where the emphasis is on recruiting outstanding people rather than on enlisting the masses,[2] and where, moreover, leadership rests with parliamentary representatives who are under pressure from groups manifesting particular interests. Although such parties may appear to presuppose a precisely ordered system of authority from the top down, there tends to be some tolerance of autonomy and local initiative, and rapport among the elite, the middle-class members, and local activists rests on mutual perspectives of electoral strategy.

The pattern delineated by Michels differs substantially from that of Communist parties, although some of his assumptions appear to be applicable. The Communist party attempts to recruit the masses in its ranks and holds to a strict scheme of individual subscriptions upon which the party depends for finances. Instead of caucuses (typically employed by American parties), the Communist party organizes wider-based and less exclusive working units whose principal function is the political education of the membership. Large membership necessitates administrative organization, and this frequently results in an ever growing number of permanent officials and a party bureaucracy. In theory, leadership becomes unimportant as authority and power are diffused throughout a complicated network of institutions. In practice, powerful individual and oligarchic tendencies emerge, usually as a result of politics rather than of the nature of the party itself. Doctrine and ideology are important within the party, as is discipline of the rank and file.

The Communist party in Brazil preserves its democratic skeleton, and it strives to become a truly representative organization, a kind of community based on a single class. Its pyramidal structure resembles that of the USSR Communist Party, any variance being accounted for in the statutes.[3] At the apex of the party's pyramidal shape is a centralized national organization. At the base are the local units or cells —subdivisions organized on geographical or occupational lines in residential areas and in places of business. The party's vertical structure consists of national, regional or territorial, state, zonal or municipal, and district divisions that generally remain intact while the number and hierarchical order of the horizontal organizations vary with the expansion and contraction of party size.

In theory, the supreme authority of the party is held by the Congress (Congresso, formerly called the Convenção Nacional) which is required to meet every three years by order of the Central Committee. The delegates to the Congress, who are usually party militants of several years' good standing, are elected by the Regional Conferences. These delegates are assigned tasks according to a plan devised by the Central Committee. Although its official responsibility is to determine the tactical line of current political issues and to revise official programs and statutes, the Congress's real function has been to hear and approve the document prepared and presented by the Central Committee. It has also the duty of electing members and alternates to the Central Committee.[4]

In actual practice the power of the Congress is somewhat limited. The six Brazilian congresses have taken place at irregular intervals— in 1922, 1925, 1928–1929, 1954, 1960, and 1967. Prior to each Congress all problems and documents are considered by the delegates and thoroughly discussed within each party echelon, so that the Congress tends to sanction decisions and actions already taken by the Central Committee or by a dominant faction of this committee. Only on occasions when there is an internal party struggle do dialogue and debate make much impression on organizational structure and policy. Dissent, however, was quickly suppressed when at the Third, Fifth, and Sixth Congresses top leadership exercised its prerogative to expel or discipline members of dissident factions.[5]

The National Conference (Conferência Nacional) serves the same purpose as the Congress, but it is convened by the Central Committee only to hear urgent matters when the Congress is not in session. It is constituted by delegates elected by the regional committees. Any decisions made by the Conference have to be ratified by the Central Committee.[6] Conferences convoked in 1934, 1943, 1961, and 1962 brought about a reshuffle of party leadership and the strengthening of the dominant faction's control over party decisions and policy. In 1934, for example, the Conference produced a new Central Committee and a party line favoring Prestismo and a popular-front government, thereby resolving the crisis caused by the imprisonment of top party leadership in 1932. The 1943 Conference of Mantiqueira allowed the Comissão Nacional de Organização Provisória to emerge as the dominant one of three rival factions and to affirm a policy position in favor of a party struggle for legality. The 1961 Conference gave a new name to the party in its quest for legal electoral status, and a Conference a year later reaffirmed that decision in the face of the newly created PC do B, which in February 1962 had held its own National Conference.

The Central Committee (Comitê Central and formerly known as the Directório Nacional and Comitê Nacional) comprises the top party leadership, those with high organizational abilities and other specialized skills and competence in a specific Communist activity. The usual number of members (about twenty-five in recent years) is roughly equivalent to the number of subordinate administrative committees. A minimum party membership (usually five years) is required for election to the Central Committee, and candidates normally support the current line of top leadership. Alternate members of the Central Committee (usually twenty to twenty-five in recent years) include promising youth, demoted leaders, and occasionally mediocre but loyal members with lengthy service. It is common for the leader of the party's youth branch to be a member. The Central Committee meets at least twice a year, as dictated by the statutes, or more frequently if convoked by a majority of the members. The Committee's many functions include carrying out the policies sanctioned by the Congress and enforcing the existing programs and statutes. The Committee supervises the party's finances, fixes the number of subordinate committees, and chooses delegates who participate in general elections; it also controls the press and propaganda media.[7] Power struggles usually occur within the Central Committee, the most notable of such being those of labor leaders, Trotskyists in 1927 to 1929, anti-Stalinists in 1956 to 1957, Stalinists in 1961 and 1962, and advocates of armed struggle after 1964.

The power ostensibly held by the Central Committee is actually exercised by the Executive Commission (Comissão Executiva, formerly known as the Presidium or Comissão Central Executiva), whose members (usually about ten) are elected by the Central Committee and who usually are older militants with at least six years of continuous service to the party and trusted supporters of the Secretary General. This Commission directs party activity between meetings of the Central Committee, but must be responsible for its actions and must report to the Central Committee. The Executive Commission makes most of the important decisions and actually dominates the larger Central Committee in cooperation with the latter committee's Secretariat, as well as producing most of the documents issued by the Central Committee. The Executive Commission has *de facto* power to decide when the Congress should be held, to prepare agenda, and to preside over sessions of the Congress. It also has power, with approval of the Congress, to dissolve or substitute committees.[8]

Supreme authority is held by the Secretariat, composed of the Secretary General and at least two of his important aides. These members are usually drawn from the Executive Commission by election. Besides being responsible for the administration of daily routine, party operations, and communication of decisions to the Executive Commission, the Secretariat also has the authority to shift party policy and to replace party members. The Secretariat is, however, accountable to the Central Committee for its actions.[9]

The Secretary General is the highest elected official and usually the dominant personality of the party. His powers are not specifically defined in the statutes; rather they stem from the confidence manifested by the international Communist leadership, and consequently he may maintain his power as long as he agrees with the Soviet designs on Latin America. This post was occupied by Astrojildo Pereira from the party's founding in 1922 to its Third Congress in 1929, and by Luiz Carlos Prestes from the Second National Conference in 1943 through the Sixth Congress in 1967.[10]

The Sub-Structure of Auxiliary and Supportive Organization

Political parties function as intermediaries representing and exploiting social and economic interests to achieve power and control over society. These interests may well be competitive within party structure, but they are supportive only so long as parties mediate and stabilize conflict and tension that may exist because of intraparty rivalries threatening a party's grand design for power. The Communist party in Brazil is no exception. Like other parties it maintains an alliance of social groupings —a substructure or subcoalition—based on geographical boundaries and demographic and social categories.

At the national level the Central Committee coordinates this substructure through a Comissão Central de Contrôle, constituted of members with a record of at least ten years of service. The Comissão reviews charges against individual party members, the public conduct of members of the Central Committee, and candidates for membership on committees at all levels; and also through a Comissão Central de Finanças it coordinates and controls the party's finances. In addition the Central Committee coordinates ten auxiliary Sections of the party. Each section is administered by a member of the Central Committee together with three or more party members. In coordination with the Central Committee, each section is responsible for planning its own activities and holding two monthly meetings at which issues are resolved by majority decision or, if that is not possible, submitted to the Executive Commission for arbitration. The sections of the Central Committee are: Seção de Organização (SO) for organization of party meetings and control of membership; Seção Sindical (SS) for labor; Seção de Campo (SC) for the peasantry; Seção de Educação e Propaganda (SEP) for education and information, including the party press; Seção de Masas (SM); Seção Juvenil (SJ) for youth; Seção Parlamentar e Eleitoral (SPE); Seção de Finanças (SF); Seção de Estudos Econômicos (SEE); and Seção de Relações com o Exterior (SRE).[11]

Through these sections or commissions the Central Committee coordinates intermediate echelons at state, municipal, and local levels through the State or Territorial Committee (Comitê [formerly Directório] Estadual or Territorial [formerly Regional]); the Municipal or District Committee (Comitê [Directório] Municipal [Zonas] or Distrital); and the Base Organization (Organização de Base [Célula or Cell]). At each level problems and policies submitted by the respective authorities are discussed and resolved by special Conventions or Congresses held every eighteen months. Their chief business is to transmit the directives from above and manage other party business within their respective areas of jurisdiction. District Municipal, and Territorial Committees are composed of from seven to fifteen members and three to seven alternates; State Committees, of twenty-seven members and seven alternates. These committees meet every three months.[12] The most effective state organizations have been those in the capital cities of São Paulo, Rio Grande do Sul, Pernambuco, Guanabara, Rio de Janeiro, and Minas Gerais.

Every Brazilian Communist is ordinarily required to belong to a base organization or cell—the grass roots of the party. The membership of each base organization must be a minimum of three persons in each working place (business office, factory, mine, sugar mill, school, and the like). These local cells may be created anywhere by the supervising committee having immediate control over it. The base organization functions primarily as a recruiting facility, providing contact with new members and party sympathizers. It meets frequently to collect financial contributions from the members and to discuss Marxism-Leninism. Subdivisions may occur within a base organization, which also may split into two equal and distinct base organizations. Various cells are important because of their strategic position, for example in a factory to recruit urban workers.

The cell is especially useful to the party oriented toward the working class, since factory problems, working conditions, and wages provide a basis for social education—although there is always the danger that the cell might become entirely taken up with vocational demands to the exclusion of political questions. The cell is also perfectly suited to clandestine action; indeed, it becomes the instrument of agitation and propaganda. Designed for action at the workplace, however, it is not particularly suitable for contesting an election. It has been especially important to the Communist party in Brazil, which has been subjected to illegal status throughout most of its existence. Each cell has a Conference or Assembly, which includes its entire membership and meets at weekly or biweekly intervals, and an executive Secretariat of three persons.[13]

Party members are expected to participate also in Fractions—organizations within the party with a function quite like that of the cells. The chief purpose is to infiltrate the masses in order to disseminate the party line and attract new members. Fractions are formed in an appropriate trade union, peasant organization, professional association, front group, women's or youth organization. Each fraction has its own secretariat and a minimum of three members.[14]

Traditionally there have been auxiliary organizations technically separate from the party but in fact serving as adjuncts to it. The youth auxiliary (Juventude Comunista), for example, is separate from the party yet resembles the party in structure. Its chief function is to mobilize "progressive" youth and spread the Communist line. Young people reinforce the party by attending functions and protest meetings and acting as the vanguard of the broad youth movement. They are encouraged to transfer to the party at age eighteen, since membership in the Juventude Comunista usually precludes simultaneous membership in the party. In some instances, however, youth officers at intermediate and higher levels serve as alternates or ex-officio members of the party committees. The Juventude Comunista do Brasil was established in January 1924 [15] and known thereafter as the União or Federação de Juventude Comunista. Also organized by the Communists were a woman's affiliate (the Federação Feminina do Brasil), various labor organizations, and peasant leagues.[16]

Organizational Principles: Democracy versus Centralization

In Brazil the non-ruling Communist party is grounded on disciplined organization. The power structure, or policy-making body of the party, must of course maintain discipline within the party to avoid fragmentation. Flexibility is most important in the base organizations, in which efficient penetration and mobilization of the masses is the principal function. Theoretically, it is from these grass-roots branches that the policy-making body receives the sustenance for its power. The base organizations are vast dynamic organisms directed by elected representatives whose responsibility it is to maintain the policy machine in abeyance with the needs and directives of the people.

The vertical party organization allows compartmentalization in order to prevent communication among groups at the same level. Units may be sealed off both vertically and horizontally from relations and information that the party command considers unnecessary or harmful. Centralization strengthens the downward flow of command, surveillance, and pressure. Obedience is generated upward as each delegate of a lower body keeps his superiors informed of disaffection within his group. Thus the center at each level has considerable power and is responsible for checking the party machinery and nominating officials, and of intervening quickly and effectively to correct any apparent organizational weakness and maintain party unity and homogeneity.

According to the party statutes, communication between the masses and their representatives is supposed to be facilitated by the principles of "democratic centralism" and "collective leadership." [17] Democratic centralism guarantees free and open debates at all levels of the party. Policies and directives to be advanced are selected by majority rule. Collective leadership, based on the policy of a majority of elected officers, determines executive and administrative action. Thus, theoretically, the party is an autonomous cohesive unit directed by committees whose desire is to keep in touch with the rank and file, thus ensuring that decisions taken by the center are applied strictly at all levels but with the understanding and agreement of the rank and file. The system is *centralized,* since with decisions are made at the top, and *democratic,* since they are based on consensual opinion at the bottom. This presupposes that free discussion takes place at the base before decisions are made, but that strict discipline is observed after the decision is made.[18]

In the Brazilian party, however, as in all Latin American non-ruling Communist parties, the principles of collective leadership and democratic centralism have not been effective. Consequently, the flow of communication from the masses upward has been abortive, with a result in recurrent factionalism within the party. This suggests that the highly centralized hierarchy prevents the membership at large from determining basic principles. In most cases party policy is heavily influenced, directly and indirectly, by the trends of international Communist policy. This certainly was true during the party debates of 1956 and 1957 after the Khrushchev denunciation of Stalinism. As we have recounted earlier, external and internal pressures at that time forced the party to tolerate public debate of many long-suppressed issues. The manifestation of widespread but formerly latent discontent and criticism eventually brought sharp rebuke and an abrupt suppression of dialogue from the older, dominant leadership. The result was a massive exodus of leaders and rank and file—a crippling blow to a party already in decline and in need of revitalization. The formation of the PC do B in 1962 was of course a direct response to Stalinist inclinations and to the Sino-Soviet dispute, but other defections and expulsions of party leaders and members in the 1960's seem more closely attributable to the rigid, autocratic, decision- and policy-making top echelon of the party and especially to the continued personalist and authoritarian style of Prestes himself.

Styles of Party Behavior: Three Roles

A political party is clientele-oriented, an organization greedy for new members and, according to Michels, willing, for the sake of that objective, to enter "into promiscuous relationships with the most heterogeneous political elements." [19] A party tends to be open at its base to new recruits and supporters. At its apex it is "permeable and adaptive," reflecting "an inherent tendency toward joint advantage," and is thus "a mutually exploitative relationship—it is joined by those who would use it, it mobilizes for the sake of power those who would join it." [20] These generalizations about parties are applicable to non-ruling Communist parties in developed and less developed nations alike.[21] Beyond that, however, Communist parties adopt a variety of behavioral styles— electoral, sub-cultural, and revolutionary. The Communist party in Brazil has exhibited all three styles. It may be instructive to describe these styles in the light of certain classic assumptions about the role of the Communist party in general.[22]

First, it is assumed that when the non-ruling parties "have gone beyond the confines of social protest and assumed political responsibility, their deviant and revolutionary character tends to be replaced by legitimacy and social plausibility and their difference from other political parties tends to be reduced. . . ." [23] In the case of the Brazilian Communist party, the desire for legitimacy was a response to popular-front policies of the international Communist movement, and to a tendency toward becoming a pragmatic force within an ever-hostile system in which heretical Communism was viewed with suspicion and subject to devastating suppression. When granted legality, the Communist party in Brazil has demonstrated moderate electoral success, similar to that of the Communist parties in France and Italy as well as in Latin American counterparts Venezuela and Chile.

As we saw earlier, the Brazilian party has had two periods of legality. The first, from January to August 1927, enabled the party to propagate its views through *A Nação* and to build an organizational base in the labor movement. Thus, through a front organization, the Bloco Operário e Camponês, a Communist-backed candidate was elected a deputy to the national Congress and two party members won seats in the Rio municipal council. During the second period, from 1945 to 1947, the party nominated Yeddo Fiúza, a non-Communist candidate for the 1945 presidential election. Table 4.1 gives Fiúza's vote total, nationally and in each of four major states. Although General Eurico Dutra, the PSD candidate with the support of Getúlio Vargas, received more than 55 per cent of the vote and a margin of 20 per cent over his nearest rival, Fiúza received a surprising 9.7 per cent of the total and 12 per cent of the combined total of Guanabara, Minas Gerais, Rio Grande do Sul, and São Paulo states. Luiz Carlos Prestes was the chief Communist attraction, however, and was elected deputy in the Federal District and in the states of Pernambuco and Rio Grande do Sul, and *suplente* (alternate) in the states of Bahia, Rio Grande do Sul, and São Paulo. His campaign speeches and personal popularity undoubtedly contributed to the PCB's capture of fourteen deputy seats in the Constituent Assembly.

In the January 1947 elections the PCB retained fourth rank among parties, added two deputies (under the PSP party) to Congress and gained a considerable number of state deputy seats in São Paulo and other large states, scoring heavily in industrial cities and state capitals (see Appendix A). Thereafter the party was banned from electoral participation, although its members continued to be elected on non-Communist tickets. At least one Communist was elected to Congress in 1950 and one in October 1954 (he defected from the party in May 1957). Communists backed the winning Kubitschek and Goulart slate in 1955 and moreover elected several candidates in the October 1958 elections. They supported a losing candidate, Marshal Henrique Lott, in the 1960 presidential elections; yet they or their sympathizers may have won as many as seventeen Congressional seats in October 1962. (See Appendix A for statistics.[24])

A brief review of electoral patterns in Brazil may account for the party's persistent attempts to remain within the electoral system. The traditional PCB's strategy of coalition with popular and progressive forces was indeed a prevailing conception in party circles. Had the party been able to participate in the elections of 1950, 1955, and 1960, its fortunes might well have improved. Only in 1945, before the multi-party system was fully operative, was a presidential candidate able to win a majority of the vote. Popular candidates Vargas and Quadros won by less than a majority vote and Kubitschek with less than 36 per cent. Further, party alliances were important in Brazilian electoral politics, and a high percentage of candidates for national, state, and local offices were elected with the support of such alliances. These alliances usually were short-lived and based upon the personal popularity of candidates. Prestes, never a presidential nominee, was the popular figure who might have greatly enhanced the PCB's electoral prestige had the party not been ostracized by the dominant conservative forces; indeed, it is remarkable that the pragmatic Prestes moved leftward so quickly and early after his column's retreat to Bolivia, for he seemed destined to assume, as did many of his fellow tenentes, a significant role in main-stream politics. Another characteristic of Brazilian politics favorable to a legalized PCB was the concentration of vote in populous areas where the party derived much of its strength. In the four Presidential elections from 1945 to 1960 some 50 to 60 per cent of all votes were cast in Guanabara, Rio Grande do Sul, São Paulo, and Minas Gerais; and this combined vote was decisive in determining the winning candidate.[25]

The Communist party in Brazil has utilized a second style—sub-cultural behavior—familiar to non-ruling Communist parties in societies where some segments of the population are not integrated into political and social life. In such societies the Communist party may attract alienated persons and groups, integrating them and using them to articulate dissatisfaction and protest. Usually the party is prohibited from electoral participation and therefore tends to function more as a social-protest movement than a political party. When once allowed participation in elections, these parties may encounter difficulty in casting off their traditional view of parliament as a useful forum for polemics, and so assume a role of responsibility in competitive party politics and in government itself.[26]

The Brazilian party demonstrated its subcultural capabilities most effectively perhaps between its Second and Third Congresses during the period 1925 to 1929, when it organized the Communist youth, became a strong influence in the organized labor movement in urban centers, and through its press propagated its views to workers and intellectuals alike. The party's appeal to alienated segments of the population was temporarily offset by the 1930 revolution and Vargas' coming to power, but in 1935 with Prestes as leader and the ANL front activated, dis-contented elements were effectively organized. The party was involved in organizing youth, women, labor, and peasants to participate in protest movements during the early sixties, even when such activity was not necessarily led by the party. Indeed, the party found itself belatedly and hesitantly pulled by the nationalist and revolutionary activism of the times.

At one point in its evolution the Communist party in Brazil adopted a third style—revolutionary behavior—which was characteristic of some non-ruling Communist parties in underdeveloped areas. Another of the assumptions cited by Triska is that revolutionary Communist parties are dynamic forces in a non-politicized society, that they "perform, in addition to their own objectives, the role of socializers toward modernity," and that they bring into the party "those wishing to transform their societies rapidly and make them part of the modern world." [27] Although some decisions in the international Communist movement may have provoked the party to action, Communist participation in the revolt of 1935 was indicative of the party's revolutionary stance in the face of suppression and isolation by the Vargas government. The revolt failed, however, to enlist widespread popular support in Natal, Recife, and Rio de Janeiro. Moreover, it was crushed quickly, so that there was little time and opportunity to disseminate political views and socialize the disenchanted toward solutions to societal problems. While the party ranks undoubtedly swelled during the ANL activities prior to the November revolts, the military and police crackdown involving mass arrest of party leaders and members thereafter placed the Communist movement in an awkward position of inactivity and almost total obscurity.

Status

Several types of status may be identified among non-ruling Communist parties. These are determined by the degree of influence the party may exert upon politics and society; the degree of militancy exercised by the party and the consequences in the political process; and society's degree of toleration of party activity.[28] As is apparent in Table 5.1, over the years the Brazilian party's status has changed from one type to another in varying degrees within and between historical phases of the party's evolution. The party's status is in constant flux, the result of leadership aspirations and activity as well as perspective on party potentiality during changing times of stress (military intervention and police suppression, for example) and of relaxation (constitutional stability and Brazilian democracy).

During its early phase, the party was committed to organization and involvement in the affairs of the Comintern. The effort on the domestic scene was as much that of resolving conflict among radicalized (especially anarchist and anarco-syndicalist) segments of Brazilian society as of struggling against the ruling oligarchic forces of the Old Republic. Although not an active participant in the revolts of 1922 and 1924, the party viewed these events with interest. At the same time the conservative Brazilian political systems outlawed the party as a subversive and militant force.[29] In the aftermath of the São Paulo revolt of 1924 the party acknowledged the significance of Prestes and his column, and during a brief period of legality in 1927 was able to reconcile its differences and initiate dialogue with the man who would later dominate its activities for more than a generation. During this phase, party influence was relatively weak in traditional political circles, and its militant image was viewed with considerable alarm. Party prestige within organized urban labor, however, was growing—despite the serious dif-

Table 5.1

PCB Status
(Brazilian Images of the Party)

	Influence	*Militancy*	*Toleration*
First Phase 1922–29	Weak (Increasingly strong in labor)	Medium	Weak (Legalized in 1927)
Second Phase 1929–37	Medium	Strong	Weak (Strong in 1935)
Third Phase 1937–45	Weak	Medium	Weak
Fourth Phase 1945–56	Strong–Medium	Weak–Medium	Strong–Medium (Legalized 1945–47)
Fifth Phase 1956–60	Medium	Medium	Medium
1961–64	Medium	Medium	Strong
1964–72	Weak	Strong	Weak

ferences that surfaced between Communist and other labor leaders in 1928 and 1929.

During the second phase of its evolution, party influence increased once Prestes declared himself a Communist in 1931; and while respect for Communist leadership in the labor movement continued, the party succeeded in joining the ANL coalition in 1935 (Prestes, as we know, became its honorary president).[30] Throughout the period, however, the image of Communist militancy grew more threatening, especially after the São Paulo revolt of 1932 (although Communists apparently were not officially involved, they, like the Constitutionalistas, opposed Vargas, and subsequent government anxiety brought a suppression of party activities) and the November 1935 uprisings in Natal, Recife, and Rio. Thus, natually, there was little toleration for Communism in Brazil.

During its third phase, from 1937 to 1945, the party remained underground, its leadership in prison or exile. Influence declined even in the working class as the *Estado Novo* enacted new labor legislation. The public image of Communism as a militant force continued relatively strong despite the party's ineffectiveness and cautious stance during the latter years of the Vargas dictatorship.

Once a rapproachement had been reached with Vargas in 1945, the PCB regained its legality and assumed an electoral role alongside rival political parties. Suddenly Communism became respectable for large segments of labor and the intelligentsia. That the party's influence was substantially enhanced was attested by the electoral results of late 1945. Toleration of party activities continued relatively strong, even after the new outlawing in May 1947 and the purging of Communist members from Congress in January 1948. The party's pragmatism and its new image as a non-heretical political entity tended to dispel the general view of Communism in Brazil as a revolutionary force.

These images of party status seemed to remain unchanged until about 1961, when toleration of Communist activities accompanied the successes of organized labor (to win benefits and increases in salary), of peasants (to organize and improve rural working conditions), and of students (to awaken many Brazilians to basic problems). In the face of inflation and financial troubles, the moderate Goulart government appeared to turn leftward in early 1964. After the April 1 coup, however, when the military intervened in organized labor and peasant leagues, universities and the student movement—indeed in every aspect of Brazilian life allegedly associated with the Communist "conspiracy" —low influence and toleration levels resulted, and the party was recast into its traditional image as a militant and dangerous political force.

Membership

Communist parties are generally conceived as mass parties, centralized but officially egalitarian and firmly knit, with strict supervision over recruitment. Marx's emphasis on a dialectic of progress in which progress triumphs over reaction, as well as on the inevitability of historical process, relates closely to his conception of the party as being not sharply differentiated from the proletariat. Thus, according to the Marx formula, the vanguard would guide the proletariat in its rapid awakening to class consciousness; and upon seizure of power, the proletariat would join its leadership or the party in a common consciousness of goals. In the words of Marx and Engels, "The immediate aim of the Communists is the same as that of all the other proletarian parties: formation of the proletariat into a class, overthrow of the bourgeois supremacy, conquest of political power by the proletariat." [31] In the Leninist conception, on the other hand, the party should not include the entire working class but only the advanced guard or "enlightened" segment of the proletariat during the era of the bourgeois dictatorship. Thus the party becomes a kind of elite rather than a class, possessed of knowledge not assimilable by the average proletarian, and explicitly organized in a highly disciplined and centralized framework for the coordination and control of the proletariat.[32] For Lenin, then, the party will become "an invincible force only when its ideological unification by the principles of Marxism is consolidated by the material unity of an organization which will weld millions of toilers into an army of the working class." [33]

The conception of the Communist party as a mass organization is distorted also by periodical internal purges that seek to ban the passive and the suspect. The strict supervision of recruitment reflects emphasis on quality rather than quantity of membership.[34] In Brazil as elsewhere candidates for membership require the sponsorship of one party member who must accept responsibility for evaluation of the political and moral qualities of the candidate in a signed statement. Membership is limited to individuals of eighteen years and older and to persons who accept the party statutes and program, work in a party organization, abide by party decisions, and contribute dues. A member's rights include participation in meetings, election of leaders, criticism of organization or members, and submission of proposals and suggestions to correct weaknesses in the party work.[35]

Analysis of party membership could be particularly revealing, but unfortunately, by reason of its clandestine and illegal status, the PCB does not publish membership figures. Indeed, one might assume that at critical times in the party's history precise figures were unknown even to the membership because of their slackness in keeping records and collecting dues. Thus, specific data on age, sex, race, education, and general socio-economic indices are either unavailable or unreliable (a

**Membership and Support
of the PCB, 1922–1966***

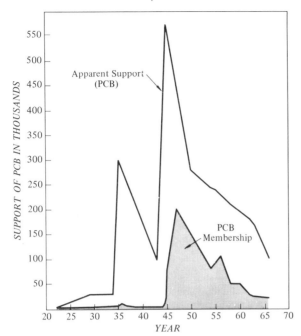

* *Membership estimate:* 1922, First Congress (73); 1925, Second Congress (300); 1928–29, Third Congress (1,000); 1934, First National Conference (500 to 1,000); 1935 (5,000 to 10,000); 1943, Second National Congress (800 to 900); April 1945 (3,100); August 1945 (25,000); December 1945 (82,000); August 1946 (130,000); December 1946 (180,000); May 1947, PCB banned (200,000); 1953–54, Fourth Congress (80,000 to 100,000); 1956 (100,000 to 130,000); 1957 (between 100,000 and 130,000); 1958 (50,000); 1959 (50,000); 1960, Fifth Congress (50,000); 1961 (40,000 to 50,000); 1962 (30,000 to 40,000); 1963 (25,000 to 35,000); 1964 (30,000); 1965 (30,000); 1966 (20,000).

These figures are drawn from the following sources: 1922, Pereira, *Formação do PCB,* p. 46; 1925, Pereira, *op. cit.,* p. 63; 1928–29, Basbaum, *História sincera da república,* Vol. II, p. 315; 1934, personal estimate; 1935, Marques, "The Seventh World Congress of the Communist International," *International Press Correspondence,* XV, 41 (August 25, 1935), 1068–69 estimated 4,000 at end of 1934 and 8,000–10,000 members by mid-1935; 1943, Alexander, "Brazil's C.P. A Case Study in Latin American Communism," *Problems of Communism,* IV (September–October, 1955), p. 18; 1945, Alexander, *op. cit.,* p. 18; 1946 (August), Alexander, *Communism in Latin America,* p. 118, based on an interview with Prestes on August 27, 1946; 1946 (December), Basbaum, *História . . . ,* III, p. 221; 1947 (May), André Silva Paraguassu, "A luta dos trabalhadores do Brasil contra o jogo do imperialismo dos Estados Unidos, pela independência nacional e pela paz," *Problemas,* 43 (November–December 1952), 27; 1953–54, Alexander, *Communism . . . ,* based on interview with Maria de Graça on June 10, 1953;

tentative assessment of class relations is offered later in this chapter). We can, however, approximate membership figures, relating yearly totals to total population and noting changes over the years. In the accompanying graph, increases and decreases in membership correlate with the party's electoral status during specific periods. Membership appears highest at times when the party is a legal entity, is operating in coalition with other political forces, and is influential among the working class. Membership totals are correspondingly low during periods of suppression, isolation, and leadership imprisonment. In this way we can tentatively chart high and low membership in relation to the evolution of the party and to political and economic events.

Leaders and Followers

In our earlier description of party hierarchy and power structure we observed that the PCB, like ruling Communist parties in general, tends to constitute a rigid order with an elite at the top, beneath which is a rank and file recruited to fit the appropriate party order and denied full participation in decision-making. Our observations suggest that party leaders constitute a collective unit developing its own pattern of communication, interest orientations, and goals, and techniques for self-perpetuation and for indoctrination of new recruits. This single self-conscious group thus exhorts the rank and file to maintain party harmony.[36] The characterization of party leadership as "collective" and "harmonious," however, warrants qualification.

As we have seen, two leaders, Astrojildo Pereira and Luiz Carlos Prestes, dominated the party throughout its history. Pereira (born in Rio Bonito in the state of Rio de Janeiro on October 8, 1890) was one of the nine founders of the PCB and served as its secretary general until 1929. The decision to establish contact with Prestes resulted in a serious party split and considerable criticism of Pereira, who had met with Prestes in Bolivia during 1927. The outcome was Pereira's ouster as secretary general, and his withdrawal from the party until the mid-

---

1956 to 1966, U.S. Department of State, Intelligence and Research Bureau, *World Strength of Communist Party Organizations,* annual eds. 1956–66.

Support estimate: 1922 (1,800 circulation of *Movimento Comunista*); 1925 (9,500 circulation of *Classe Operária*); 1928–29 (30,000 circulation of *Class Operária*); 1935 (300,000, estimated membership of ANL); 1945 (570,000 voters in presidential elections); 1947 (479,000 voters in legislative elections); 1964–65 (150,000 to 200,000 sympathizers); 1966 (100,000 sympathizers).

1940's, when he became an alternate member of the Central Committee; later he was named a member of the Committee, a position he retained until his death in 1965. While he did not complete his secondary schooling, and his early working years were spent as a printer with anarchist leanings, he quickly distinguished himself as a journalist, writer, and literary critic. In this capacity he perhaps best served the party; he even contributed a history of the Communist movement in Brazil during the formative years from 1922 to 1929.[37] Eventually Prestes assumed Pereira's office, but during the interim, party leaders such as Leôncio Basbaum and Octávio Brandão attacked Pereira and the party's conciliatory line.[38] After many members of the Central Committee were imprisoned in São Paulo in 1932, a new leadership under Antônio Maciel Bomfim emerged to assure the dominance of Prestismo.[39]

Despite almost continuous internal struggle for control of the party leadership, since the mid-thirties the PCB has been under the influence of one strong personality, Prestes. Born January 3, 1898, in Pôrto Alegre in the state of Rio Grande do Sul, Prestes followed in the footsteps of his father, a military officer, and attended military school, specialized in engineering, and in December 1919 was promoted to the rank of lieutenant. Five years later, on October 29, 1924, he led a revolt in Rio Grande do Sul and formed the famous Prestes Column of rebels from that state and from the city of São Paulo, seized by the rebels during the previous July. (Details were recounted in Chapters 3 and 4.) Particularly significant in the career of the party's most illustrious leader, however, is that a small inner circle of close associates has assured continuous power for Prestes. This core group has been reinforced by the integrating function of intense indoctrination as well as by the *esprit de corps* based on lengthy common service and association, and through vigorous organization and vigilance it has always been able to break up threats to the party center.

Certainly the persistence of a ruling center and the integrative tendency of the Brazilian party's rank and file may be attributed to the consistent support of Moscow, but it owes much also to the leadership qualities of Prestes. Michels identifies personal qualities that contribute to the success of certain individuals.[40] These qualities, if applied to Prestes, may explain in part his absolute domination of the party.[41] For one thing, as popular hero and charismatic leader, Prestes was demonstrably successful, especially in 1935 and 1945–47, in convincing the masses that his message was in their behalf. Then, too, as a maximum leader Prestes had access to special information and probably was able to impress members of his own party. Another quality was his impressive strength of conviction, not so much in the destiny of the party or Communism but in his own ability to find solutions to national problems. Other perhaps doubtful qualities emphasized by newspapers and sympathetic biographers included a self-sufficiency, accompanied by arrogant pride, and a Christ-like aspect of goodness and well-being.[42]

Besides Prestes, the top leadership was retained by a nucleus of individuals who traditionally have obeyed the command of their leader while quietly dominating the administrative machinery of the party. To a large extent the leaders close to Prestes from 1943 to 1956 set the pattern of executive and administrative activity that prevailed as late as 1966, despite the defection of certain members. Because of their significant role, these leaders provide us with useful insights into leadership personality, attitude formation, and the general composition of the party's inner circle.

The Nucleus of Power: The Arruda Group, 1943–56

The Arruda group consisted of elements that united to reconstitute the PCB at the party's Second National Conference, the so-called Conference of Mantiqueira, during August 1943; and among its members were João Amazonas, Maurício Grabois, Carlos Marighella, and Pedro Pomar, with Diógenes Arruda Câmara at its head. The group succeeded in electing Prestes secretary general of the party.

Diógenes Arruda Câmara was born in Pernambuco about 1916, and began his career as a Communist in 1934, when he reached Bahia and there worked for the Ministry of Labor and became active in PCB university politics. In 1940 he moved to São Paulo, where he rounded up the decimated regional party organization, and with some of the old party militants formed the Comissão Nacional de Organização Provisória; then he negotiated the unification of this group with another Communist band in Rio. In January 1947 he was elected a federal deputy under the PST from São Paulo, and with the government ban imposed on the PCB during the same year he consolidated his position as head of the inner circle of militants around Prestes. During late 1949 Arruda succeeded Marighella as editor of the PCB theoretic organ, *Problemas*. During the party debates of 1956 and 1957 he clung to his Stalinist inclinations but chose to remain within the party, though subsequently relegated to obscurity until his apparent withdrawal from the PCB in mid-1960.[43]

João Amazonas de Souza Pedroso was born in Belém, Pará, in 1912 and first figured in Communist activities in about 1935. He had worked his way into the inner core of the PCB by about 1943, and in 1945 was elected a federal deputy under his party's colors from the Federal District. Of middle-class background, he was an accountant for the Sindicato da Construção Civil in Rio and a technical designer until he devoted full time to party activities. Although he was apparently unable to challenge Arruda's hegemony over the inner core, he did replace Pomar as the party's No. 3 leader.[44] Along with Arruda, Grabois, and Pomar, Amazonas attempted to restrain public discussion of internal party issues during 1956 and 1957. His persistent Stalinist orientation occasioned his removal from the Executive Commission and later from the Central Committee, whose action was confirmed by the Fifth Congress. In February 1962 he became a founder of the dissident, pro-Peking PC do B.[45]

Maurício Grabois was born in 1912 in the state of Bahia of middle-class Jewish background. Grabois began his career as a Communist in 1932 as a member of the Juventude Comunista and two years later became head of that organization. After attending a military school for a few years, he worked for a Brazilian airline until his full-time employment by the party in 1945, two years after he had been named to the Executive Commission. In 1945 he was elected federal deputy from the Federal District, and he was the leader of the Communist bench in the Chamber of Deputies. He was an editor of the PCB newspaper, *A Classe Operária,* which remained registered in his name after he had left the party in the early 1960's. Though described as an "opportunistic" member of the inner circle, one who maneuvered to retain his leadership position,[46] he too, like other members of the Arruda group, lost his rank. By 1960 he was no longer a member of the Central Committee, and in early 1962 he was expelled from the PCB. A month later he helped found the PC do B.[47]

Pedro Pomar was born in about 1915 in the state of Pará. Pomar was of middle-class background and had begun medical studies before joining the party. He served in the Executive Commission, in the Central Committee as Secretary of Education and Propaganda, and as editor of *Tribuna Popular.* In 1947 he won a seat as federal deputy under the PST from São Paulo. He was considered influential with Prestes (the No. 3 leader of the party, but replaced later by Amazonas), although his prestige declined after Prestes went into hiding in 1947. First, he was removed from the Secretariat, then from the Presidium, and in 1960 from the Central Committee. When expelled two years later, he became a founder of the PC do B.[48]

Carlos Marighella was born in Salvador (Bahia) in 1911, and became active in PCB politics in about 1932 as a student leader. He never completed his engineering course, and was imprisoned several times before 1945. He served the party as a federal deputy from Bahia, and in 1948 moved to São Paulo to direct party activities there. During the late 1940's he was an editor of the Communist journal *Problemas*. Although he served as a member of the Central Committee as early as 1943, he did not reach the Executive Commission and Secretariat until 1957, when he supported Arruda and other conservatives of the inner circle in their decision to oust Agildo Barata.[49] While his party position was Stalinist-oriented, Marighella was able to retain his leadership within the party and to all effects belonged to the Bahia group that replaced Arruda's group in 1957, thus forming the link between the two groups. Later, however, his dissatisfaction with the Party's role in the events of 1964 and with Prestes' conservative stance prompted his resignation from the Executive Commission in December 1966, his defiance of the party in attending a Havana OLAS conference in 1967, and eventually his expulsion at the Sixth Congress. As we read earlier, Marighella, who had become an advocate of armed struggle, founded the Ação Libertadora Nacional, which was responsible for the abduction of U.S. Ambassador C. Burke Elbrick in 1969. On November 4, 1969, Marighella was killed in a police ambush in the city of São Paulo.[50]

A Reconsolidation of Party Power: The Bahia Group, 1957–70
This group, so called for the reason that most of its members were from the state of Bahia, successfully challenged the hegemony of the conservative Arruda men and consolidated its control over the party at a meeting of the Central Committee during August 1957. Prominent among them were Marighella, Mário Alves de Souza Vieira, Giocondo Alves Dias, and Jacob Gorender.[51]

Mário Alves de Souza Vieira was born in Sento Sé in the state of Bahia in 1923. Alves became prominent in PCB politics during the 1960's as a member of the Executive Commission and as a writer and journalist. Alves was apparently one of the party leaders who stripped Prestes of power after the coup of April 1964. He also belonged to the minority "hard line" faction that opposed the majority recommendation that the PCB join an anti-government front during May 1965. At that meeting in São Paulo on May 5, Alves was removed from the Executive Commission. During a January 1966 meeting of the Central Committee he and Manoel Jover Telles proposed alternative theses for the party's Sixth Congress. Finally at the Sixth Congress in December 1967 Alves was expelled from the party, and immediately thereafter he became a founder of the dissident Partido Comunista Brasileiro Revolucionária (PCBR) and led it until his arrest in early 1970 (torture resulted in his death).

Giocondo Alves Dias was born in the state of Bahia in 1913, Dias became active in the PCB during 1935, when he participated as an army corporal in the revolt in Natal. In 1945 under the PCB he was elected an alternate federal deputy from the state of Bahia. Throughout the 1960's he was a member of the Executive Commission, the only one of the original Bahia group to retain his position as late as 1970. Other than Prestes, who remained a figurehead of the party, Alves Dias had undoubtedly become the most important Communist at that time.

Jacob Gorender was probably also born in Bahia. With a working-class background he became a journalist and party theoretician. First active in the PCB as early as 1956, he was elected a member of the Central Committee by 1960 and soon thereafter was added to the Executive Commission. Like Mário Alves he may have joined other leaders in seizing power after the April 1964 coup, and was aligned with the "hard line" faction opposed to the majority, which in 1965 supported the Prestes position. In September 1967 he was suspended from voting in the Central Committee, and three months later was expelled from the party. Thereafter he joined with Alves in founding the PCBR and turned to armed struggle as the way to deal with the dictatorship.

In summary, six of these eight party leaders were born between 1911 and 1916, six stemmed from the middle-class, two were of the working class, and all were from the North and Northeast. At least four were born in a large city. Only two had studied at the university level, but at least two more had reached high school. Five had served the party in the Chamber of Deputies. In general the Arruda group was conformist, entrenched behind Prestes. Stalinism exerted great impact on their thinking. They apparently remained relatively aloof from the party rank and file, and when faced with division in the international Communist world they were unable to maintain their dominant position. Long service, loyalty, and belief in the old party principles kept these men aligned with the party for many years after the break with Stalinism, although by 1968 only Arruda and Alves Dias had kept their affiliation. While Alves Dias and especially Marighella constituted a link between the Arruda and Bahia groups, Marighella as well as Mário Alves de Souza Vieira and Gorender became impatient with the conformist pattern traditionally characterizing the relations between these groups and Prestes. Only Alves de Souza Vieira and Gorender had not affiliated with the party during the 1930's.

Table 5.2

**Leadership Support and Confidence
(Frequency of Names in Prestes' Notebooks)***

	Incidence of Mention	% of Total
1. Mário Alves de Souza Vieira	152	6.6
2. Manoel Jover Telles	135	5.9
3. Carlos Marighella	133	5.8
4. Orlando Bonfim Júnior	127	5.5
5. Ramiro Luchesi	121	5.3
6. Ivan Ramos Ribeiro	118	5.2
7. Giocondo Alves Dias	115	5.0
8. Marco Dinarco Reis	106	4.6
9. Geraldo Rodrigues dos Santos	105	4.6
10. João Belini Burza	94	4.1
Others (64 members of the PCB)	1087	47.4
Total	2293	100.0

Source: Computed from the notebooks as reproduced in São Paulo State, Secretaria de Segurança Pública, Departamento de Ordem Política e Social, *Relatório: inquérito instaurado contra Luiz Carlos Prestes e outros por ocasião da revolução de Março de 1964.*

*All those listed were members of the Executive Commission at some time during the period 1960–65.

An interesting index of mutual support and confidence between Prestes and seventy-three other party leaders may be drawn from the notebooks meticulously maintained by Prestes from 1961 until their discovery by police in April 1964, as we have already unfolded in another connection. The notebooks contain impressionistic details of the functions, activities, and performance of the top party leadership. Our tentative ranking of leaders in Table 5.2 is based on a count of fellow Communist officers whose names appear repeatedly in the Prestes notebooks. Three of the four leaders of the Bahia group (Alves de Souza Vieira, Jover Telles, and Marighella) are mentioned most frequently in Prestes' notes, thus supporting our proposition that an inner core tends to develop around the top leader. Although according to the evidence this core of support and confidence extends to persons outside the Bahia group, still a ruling center does indeed appear to maintain substantial power over party decisions and policy.

Several disintegrative tendencies have been apparent in the party leadership, despite Prestes' commanding role. In the PCB power may be held either by one man and shared with a small clique, or by one man alone.[52] Dissident groups and individuals within the PCB, however, have opposed this power structure, especially since 1956. Often disintegration in Communist parties begins when the top leadership consists of clusters of powerful individuals and their trusted associates rather than of a homogeneous inner core. Since leaders develop friendships and alliances not only within the party organization but outside as well, these clusters or power groups may cut across the functional lines of the party.[53] That such groups evolved within the non-ruling Communist party was evident in 1956 and 1957.

The old-guard Stalinists, including Prestes, Grabois, Pomar, Arruda, and apparently Marighella, opposed a small revisionist group around Agildo Barata which had aligned itself with a larger group of intellectuals, for the most part journalists such as Osvaldo Peralva. The ensuing power struggle stripped the party of some dissident elements. Barata and his group were expelled, and other members, including Peralva, withdrew and attempted unsuccessfully to form a new party. In the face of anti-Stalinist pressures in both Brazil and the Soviet Union, the old-guard leadership relinquished power to a faction of leaders from Bahia. Pragmatically shifting his allegiance from the old Stalinists to the new group, Prestes managed to maintain his top position and temporarily retain his trusted associates.

Shifts in leadership are visible in the composition of the Central Committee at various periods between 1946 and 1970 (see Appendix B). Of the twenty-six members and nineteen alternates of the Central Committee in 1946, only seventeen (38 per cent) were retained on the committee in 1960; ten (22 per cent) in 1964; five (11 per cent) in 1967; and only two (Prestes and Alves Dias) remained in 1970. Of the thirty-seven members of the Central Committee in 1960, eighteen (49 per cent) were members in 1964; four (11 per cent) in 1967; and two

(5 per cent) in 1970. Only four (14 per cent) of the twenty-eight members of the 1964 committee were on the 1967 committee, only two (7 per cent) in 1970. Five of the twenty-two members of the Central Committee in 1967 had previously served on the committee (four since 1946, one in 1960), and two of these officials (Marighella and Jover Telles) were expelled in that year. These trends reflect the party splits that developed during 1956 and 1957, 1960–62, and after April 1964.

General Leadership Characteristics

Socio-economic data and description of leaders' activities are available for two significant periods in PCB history. For one period from 1945 to 1947 we have biographies of sixteen Communists who served in Congress.[54] All were men and nearly all were born in the North and Northeast (four in Bahia, three each in Pernambuco and Pará, and one each in Ceará and Paraíba), except for the two each from Rio de Janeiro and Rio Grande do Sul. While half the Congressmen had only a primary education, two had reached the secondary level, three the military school, and three the university. The average age was about forty, one being under thirty and one over fifty. At least seven of the group were of working-class background, three were journalists, and three were professional (doctor, professor, and architect).

Two of the Congressmen had joined the party during its early years, nine became members in the 1930–35 period, two in the period 1936–44, and two after the party was declared legal in 1945 (see Table 7.3). Fourteen joined through experience in issue-oriented groups supported by the party. Nine had been involved in the ANL or in the 1935 revolt; eight had participated in labor strikes, two in university strikes, fifteen in campaigns in behalf of nationalist issues such as Petrobrás; nine were active in international causes. Nearly half the Congressmen concentrated their party activity on organizational efforts in the labor movement; the rest on party administrative functions at the state and national levels. Four were members of a PCB state committee, eleven of the Central Committee, and eight of the Executive Commission.

From the biographical data available for seventy-four party leaders for the period 1961–64,[55] we learn that thirty-six had served on the Central Committee at some time during the period 1943–70. Seventy were men, only four, women. Twenty-four were born in São Paulo state, eight in Pernambuco, six in Rio Grande do Sul, five in Bahia, and four in Guanabara. Members of the Central Committee or primary leadership (only 40 per cent of them under fifty years of age) tended to be considerably older than leaders at a secondary level (about 20 per cent over fifty years). Some 62 per cent of those whose birthplace was identified in our sample were from cities of over 50,000 people, and 38 per cent from rural areas. Half the sample had only primary schooling, 31 per cent had reached secondary school, 4 per cent military school, and 15 per cent the university. Of forty-eight leaders whose year of affiliation with the party was identifiable, only three had joined

Table 5.3

**Major Occupation and Class Stratification
of Communist Leadership, 1961–1964**

Occupation	Primary Leadership	Secondary Leadership	Total	Class % of Total
Traditional Upper Class				
Medical Doctor	0	5	5	
Lawyer	0	3	3	13.5
Architect, engineer	1	1	2	
Middle Class				
Military	4	0	4	
Merchant	3	3	6	
Civil Servant	1	2	3	
Bank Clerk	2	1	3	41.9
Journalist	9	3	12	
Teacher	1	1	2	
Pharmacist	0	1	1	
Working Class	14	15	29	39.2
Not Identified or No Occupation	1	3	4	5.4
Total	36	38	74	100.0

during the 1922–29 period, twelve during the 1930–35, four during the 1936–44, eleven during the 1945–47, twelve during the 1948–55, and six thereafter. The long affiliation of so many leaders helps explain why the PCB perdures with considerable stability throughout periods of national turmoil and internal party dissension.

Occupational and class differences among party leaders are seen in Table 5.3. A majority of Central Committee members, or nearly 42 per cent of the entire leadership sample, appear to be middle class in orientation. Almost two-fifths of all leaders are working class, and this tendency is evident especially among primary leadership. An upper-class orientation is identifiable with only one primary leader, but is evident in nearly 14 per cent of the total leadership.

Obviously, class differences affect party behavior. If bourgeois elements dominate the leadership of the Communist party in Brazil, or if leadership is drawn from the proletariat as well as the bourgeoisie, this may give rise to class cleavage within the party and a disintegrating effect on the core leadership. The PCB leadership, as illustrated in Figure 5.4, has generally been drawn from the middle and working classes; the small farmers, independent artisans, and shopkeepers have provided few leaders. And the differences between bourgeois and working-class leadership may lessen through lengthy association. The middle-class leader, often an idealist, may cast off his family values and hostility toward workers. He usually makes material sacrifices in joining the Communist party and deliberately associates with the weak, the poor, and the underprivileged, for whom he seeks justice and equal opportunity.[56] Working-class leaders may inherit a Marxist tradition from their father or grandfather or may enroll in the party because of personal interest and a willingness to work for a common cause, even though such affiliation may bring hardship and material damage such as the loss of employment.[57]

In Table 5.4 the socio-economic distribution of leaders in 1922 is based on the composition of the nine delegates to the PCB's First Congress (two intellectuals, two tailors, five workers) and the first Central Committee (one tailor, three workers).[58] The 1935–36 evaluation is drawn from the leadership characteristics of the PCB's National Secretariat and the principal Communist participants in the Natal, Recife, and Rio de Janeiro uprisings of November 1935, among them some important military figures.[59] For the period 1945–47 the composition is based on the nine members of the Executive Commission, the twenty-six members of the Central Committee, and nineteen alternates to the Central Committee (see Appendix B).[60] Also considered are the sixteen PCB members of Congress during the same period. In the later decades the party leadership has been conspicuously of middle-class as well as working-class origin, whereas in the early years leadership was principally drawn from the working class (see Table 5.3). Only occasionally in the party's history and to a limited extent during the early sixties have peasants and farmers played any significant leadership role. As to each leader's major activity within the party from 1961 to 1964, 43 per cent were active in the labor or peasant sector, 20 per cent in administrative activities, 12 per cent in mass organizations not labor- or peasant-oriented, 11 per cent in relations with socialist countries, 9 per cent in parliamentary activities; the remainder were unidentified. Nearly half the leaders had been members on a state committee as well as on the Central Committee, though only nine of the leaders

Table 5.4

Socio-Economic Distribution of the
Leadership and Membership of the PCB*

	Peasant Farmer	*Worker*	*Intellectual*	*Other* [1] *Bourgeois*
National Leadership [2]				
1922	Very Weak	Very Strong	Weak	Weak
1934–36	Very Weak	Medium	Medium	Medium
1945–47	Very Weak	Medium	Medium	Strong
1961–64	Weak	Medium to Strong	Weak	Strong
National Membership [3]				
1970	Very Weak	Medium to Weak	Medium to Weak	Medium

*Tentative evaluation subject to modification. These categories are not necessarily mutually exclusive. Strength is assigned on the basis of a five-term scale: very weak, weak, medium, strong, very strong. Strength relates to numbers and importance within the party, not to the relative numerical proportion to the class in society.

1. Includes military who were active especially 1924–35. Prestes, Agildo Barata, and Gregório Bezerra were examples of military activists.

2. Refers to members and alternate members of the executive and central committees.

3. Very tentative evaluation: no memberships figures available.

had served on the Executive Commission. Only one of the leaders had participated in the 1924 revolt, one in the 1930 revolution, and fifteen in the ANL popular front and/or revolt of 1935. Nearly half the leadership had participated in a labor strike, and about one of every ten in a student strike. Nearly all were conspicuous in struggles over nationalist issues during the fifties and sixties, and about 65 per cent were actively involved in such international causes as peace, anti-imperialism, and defense of other socialist countries.

From these statistics investigators have isolated three basic types: the ideologue, the activist, and the careerist.[61] The ideologue represents the intellectual class, resents the status quo, desires social change, and is an articulate spokesman of Marxist and Leninist philosophies. Literally hundreds of Brazilian intellectuals have belonged to the PCB, many of them novelists and poets unwilling to express themselves prolifically in Communist propaganda. A notable exception was the novelist Jorge Amado, who besides writing extensively in the party press also produced a since-celebrated biography of Prestes.[62] Brazilian Communist literature is sparse in theoretical writings other than official party documents and the writings of Prestes and his inner circle. Caio Prado Júnior, a long-time critic, and by the 1960's apparently no longer a party member, is perhaps Brazil's most distinguished Marxist,[63] but he seems to have contributed little to the party's theoretical basis, probably because his unorthodox views have contrasted sharply with the established and frequently intransigent party line. The exodus of many intellectuals after 1956 was the result of differences within the old leadership itself.

Intellectuals may have been mistrusted on principle by Prestes and his inner core and by a suspicious working class as well.[64] There is evidence, for example, that Prestes despised intellectual types and surrounded himself with bureaucrats, whom he considered to be true representatives of the proletariat. One observer notes that "in converting to Marxism-Leninism, Prestes had succumbed to the mystique of the revolutionary proletariat, that is, to the belief that workers are endowed with an innate revolutionary instinct which makes them politically superior to intellectuals." [65] Osvaldo Peralva writes that the recruitment of industrial workers was given priority over that of intellectuals, and that prominent Communist intellectuals were used to sign manifestos of protest, even though their work was viewed with contempt by the party.[66] Jorge Amado, whose characters are usually taken from real life, depicts party intellectuals as "well-intentioned but vacillating, without the sure compass of class interest and class consciousness and therefore constantly in need of guidance." [67]

As is evident in Table 5.5, ideologues have frequently disrupted the Communist party by upholding a variety of conflicting beliefs—beliefs ranging from populist and nationalist sentiments to Trotskyism. The populist and nationalist ideals of Prestes and some of the leadership around him, especially in the mid-1930's, clashed with orthodox ideological currents in the party. Anarchists and anarcho-syndicalists had, as we know, constituted the party leadership in its early years; yet adherence to these ideologies led to expulsion or defection on the part of some. The Stalinists who defected in 1962 retained their old allegiance by assuming a pro-Chinese position and organizing a splinter party. Other leaders formed or participated in a variety of socialist parties, the most important being the PSB. Communists oriented toward Trotskyism were active in the labor movement in the thirties and challenged the PCB's influence among workers at that time and following World War II.[68]

The activist is another prominent type of Communist leader. Interested neither in theory nor in intellectual discussion, he is attracted to the Communist party because it provides an outlet for his organizational skills and because of the possibility of action and revolution. Agildo Barata, who led the Rio uprising in November 1935, perhaps exemplifies this type of leader, although he had moved toward a less radical course by 1957, when he was expelled from the party.[69] Gregório Bezerra, the Pernambuco leader who participated in the Recife revolt in 1935 and in the peasant movement in the sixties, is certainly a rare example of the Brazilian Communist activist whose loyalty to the party has never faltered.[70]

The third type, the careerist, is exemplified by the leader seeking personal advancement through the Communist party. This type might be a peasant or a worker for whom the party means education and status, or it might be a student or a military figure who sees the party as offering a chance to realize personal ambitions (Prestes and Barata would personify the military careerist). Whereas after 1945 the election to legislative office guaranteed prestige, status, and a forum for the articulation of personal and party views for working-class figures such as Roberto Morena and middle-class party bureaucrats such as Grabois and Amazonas.[71]

Party leadership may be differentiated in other ways, and prestige and status within the party may be the result of varying styles of activity. Thus, a generation gap between old and new, and old and young, leaders may promote tension, whereas socio-economic characteristics may account for personality conflict and like psychological problems.

A prime difference could be posited between leaders who have ac-

Table 5.5
**Disruptive Ideological Influences
in the PCB Leadership**

Trotskyist	Marxist and Leninist (including Socialist)	Stalinist	Anarchist and Syndicalist	Populist and Nationalist
João da Costa Pimenta (expelled 1929)	Manuel Cendón		Astrojildo Pereira (lost leadership, 1929; returned 1940's)	
			Octávio Brandão (elected Rio Municipal Council; demoted in PCB 1929 or 1930)	
			Antônio Canellas (expelled)	
			Roberto Morena (elected federal deputy)	
Joaquim Barbosa (expelled 1929; returned to PCB 1943)			Abílio de Nequete (expelled)	
			Everardo Dias	
Mário Pedrosa			Cristiano Cordeiro (expelled 1947)	
Rodolfo Coutinho Arístedes Lobo	Plínio Mello Josias Carneiro Leão			Luiz Carlos Prestes (head of Liga de Ação Revolucionária, ANL, and PCB secretary general since 1943)
Hilcar Leite (expelled 1929)	Luiz de Barros (expelled 1930) Fernando			
Lauro Reginaldo da Rocha (withdrew 1937)	Lacerda (critical of party 1943, 1952–54)			

Trotskyist	Marxist and Leninist (including Socialist)	Stalinist	Anarchist and Syndicalist	Populist and Nationalist
	Cristiano Cordeiro	João Amazonas		
	Silo Meireles	Pedro Pomar		
	Mota Cabral	Maurício Grabois		
	José Medina (expelled 1947)	José Duarte		
		Angelo Arroio		
	José Maria Crispim (expelled 1952)	Walter Martins		
	Agildo Barata (expelled 1957)	Calid Chade		
		Carlos Danielli		
	Osvaldo Peralva and others (withdrew 1957)	Lincoln Oeste		
		Clóvis Melo (Pernambuco) (formed PC do B 1962)		
	Leôncio Basbaum (withdrew 1957)			
	Clodomir Morais (expelled 1962)	Carlos Marighella (expelled 1967)		
	M. Alves de Souza Vieira			
	Jacob Gorender			
	Câmara Ferreira			
	M. Jover Telles			
	Apolônio de Carvalho			
	Miguel Batista (expelled 1967)			
	Rafael Martineli (expelled 1968)			

quired fame solely in the ranks of the party through long struggle, and those who associated with the masses after achieving prestige independent of party activities. Few leaders fall into either of these categories. A leader of the first type mentioned, such as Astrojildo Pereira or Octávio Brandão, would have greater familiarity and perhaps personal experience with the labor movement, and greater understanding of mass psychology, and a firmer grasp of the party program's doctrinal content. Prestes, of course, would exemplify the second type; but Carlos Marighella, for his part, became prominent as an urban guerrilla leader during the late 1960's after withdrawing from the PCB leadership. One might envision a prolonged struggle for domination between factions led by these two types of leaders, with envy and jealousy on the one hand and presumption and ambition on the other. Such was the situation in the early thirties when Brandão along with Fernando Lacerda and Leôncio Basbaum attacked Prestismo in a series of articles in the Communist press.[72]

The above conflict divided old from new leadership. The opposition of Communist leaders Joaquim Barbosa and João da Costa Pimenta during 1927 and 1928 was in part a response to a policy change in the party's relations with "reformist" labor unions, but was also linked to anxiety over the party's decision to make contact with Prestes.[73] The internal dispute also separated the old leadership from younger elements when members of the Juventude Comunista—Trotskyist sympathizers led by Mário Pedrosa—withdrew from the PCB in 1929. In 1934 the new "nationalist" leaders, influenced by Prestes, consolidated their hold over the party when a police agent, Antônio Maciel Bomfim, became secretary general.[74] Thereafter, Prestes represented the old guard, a sort of second generation leadership identifiable with the Stalin era. While the first-generation leaders are fading away (Pereira died in 1965, for example), the Prestes leadership, through the pragmatic modification of its old stereotyped style, survived challenges from the younger generation—a pattern found elsewhere among older parties in Latin America, with the exception of Cuba, where the key figures in the "new" Communist party all began their careers late in the Stalin era or thereafter.[75] The leadership of a rigid, authoritarian, personality-dominated party like the PCB might thus be expected to be inflexible, less eclectic, and less willing to experiment with new strategies than perhaps newer Communist parties in other parts of the Third World, where leadership emerged out of de-Stalinization and is relatively young.

Rank and File Participation

The behavior of the rank and file corresponds to degrees of participation in the activities of a Communist party. Three categories of participation may be distinguished.[76] First, there is the militant who holds formal membership, is an activist involved in the party's basic organization, and propagates the party's slogans. Technically, all Communists are militants in Brazil, although the degree of active or passive participation among party members would be difficult to determine.[77]

A second category embraces the supporter who declares his agreement with the doctrines of the party and sometimes lends support while not holding formal membership. This supporter may be an elector, although unlike the average elector he openly defends the party, sometimes supporting it financially and usually participating in one of its auxiliary organizations. Tables 5.2 and 5.6 give some rough degree of support for the PCB, the estimates being based on circulation of a major party organ, on the size of membership in auxiliary or front organizations, and on electoral support. Considerable support is revealed for 1935 during the brief speaking campaign of Prestes in behalf of the ANL, and for the period 1945–47, when the party as a legal entity attracted a half-million voters.

The elector constitutes a third category and, although included in the measurement of support in Figure 5.2, is distinguished from the supporter by his unwillingness to acknowledge loyalty to the party. Through the secrecy of the ballot the elector may manifest his protest vote, his disenchantment with the political system or with social and economic conditions in general. Thus, the elector may support the party under special circumstances, but there is little assurance that he will vote for the party in future elections. In contrast, the supporter may participate not only through the vote but by regular reading of party newspapers and attendance at meetings. Like the elector, the supporter may refuse to join the party because his vocation or profession does not allow him formal affiliation or perhaps because of lack of time or a distain for regimentation.

Despite these differences between supporters and electors, there is some evidence of PCB electoral stability during its legal period. Although the total number of ballots cast in favor of PCB candidates for the Chamber of Deputies in the 1947 elections was 32,278 votes less than that in the 1945 elections, the number for most other parties also declined. These parties included the PSD (a decline of 867,768 votes),

Table 5.6
PCB Members, Voters, Supporters*

Election Year	Population	Adult Population registered (%)	Population voting (%)	Population PCB members (%)	Population PCB voters (%)	Actual Vote of PCB voters (%)	Population PCB supporters (%)
1945 Presidential	46,215,000	16.1	13.4	.17	1.2	9.2	1.23
1947 Legislative	47,500,000 est.	16.2	11.5	.42	1.0	8.7	1.00
1950 Presidential	51,976,000	22.0	15.9	.29	—	—	.50
1954 Legislative	57,098,000	26.5	17.3	.14	—	—	.43
1955 Presidential	58,456,000	26.1	15.6	.15	—	—	.41
1958 Legislative	62,725,000	22.0	20.3	.08	—	—	.33
1960 Presidential	70,967,000	21.9	17.7	.07	—	—	.27
1962 Legislative	75,271,000	24.6	19.6	.04	—	—	.24
1963 Plebiscite	77,521,000	23.9	15.8	.03	—	—	.22
1966 Presidential[1]	84,679,000	26.7	22.4	.02	—	—	.12

*PCB statistics on membership, voters, and supporters based on graph on p. 117. Voting data based on statistics in Tribunal Superior Eleitoral, *Dados estatísticos: eleições federal, estadual e municipal realizadas no Brasil a partir de 1954*, Rio de Janeiro: Departamento de Imprensa Nacional, 6 vols., 1950 to 1964; Institute for Comparative Study of Political Systems, *Brazil, Election Factbook*, No. 2, 1965, p. 19 and Supplement to No. 2, November 1966. Population statistics based on Conselho Nacional de Estatística, *Anuário Estatístico do Brasil*, Rio de Janeiro, respective years.

1. Arthur Costa e Silva, receiving 255 votes of 409 members of the Chamber of Deputies and 40 votes of 66 members of the Senate, was named President on October 3, 1966, not by popular vote but by vote of Congress. The change in the electoral system resulted from the October 1965 gubernatorial elections in which 7,000,000 participated from 11 states; PSD candidates in Minas Gerais and Guanabara won widely celebrated victories. After Costa e Silva suffered a stroke in August 1969, General Emílio Garrastazú Médici, the Armed Forces designate, was elected on October 25, 1969, as President by Congress, which cast 293 votes in favor, with 76 abstentions (generally by a decimated MDB opposition).

UDN (337,863 less), PDC (30,772 less), and PL (448 less). The PCB vote actually increased in the Federal District and in ten states: Maranhão (up 481 votes), Piauí (up 23), Ceará (up 480), Rio Grande do Norte (up 229), Paraíba (up 103), Pernambuco (up 1,128), Alagoas (up 566), Espírito Santo (up 36), Santa Caterina (up 532), Mato Grosso (up 61), and the Federal District (up 8,087). The decline was substantial in Sergipe (down 2,676 votes), Bahia (down 6,111), Rio de Janeiro (down 5,600), São Paulo (down 15,768), Minas Gerais (down 4,467), Paraná (down 1,265), and Rio Grande do Sul (down 6,753).

This decrease in voter strength might be attributed in part to the absence of a presidential election in 1947, in part to a new interest in suffrage in 1945 among Brazilians whose previous participation in national elections had been limited. It was also true that the PTB, a rival to the PCB, had begun to undermine Communist influence in the labor movement, and this probably accounted for its increase of 127,408 votes from 1945 to 1947. Overall support for the PCB, however, seems to have remained strong, and the gain of two seats in the Chamber of Deputies and of a plurality of seats on the Federal District Municipal Council, in the face of increasing government repression of Communist activities, was indicative of continued support for the party.[78]

The effectiveness of the Communist party depends in large measure upon the behavior of the formal members, their agreement on objectives and loyalty to the party. The militant Communist in Brazil as elsewhere devotes himself fully to party life. He militates within his cell, discusses with fellow members the important issues in the party press, renders service to the party and its auxiliary organizations. Even his private or family life is incorporated into party life, since the party organizes not only work but also sports, amusements, leisure, and cultural pursuits. The militant Communist is provided also with a framework of ideas, a political doctrine, a total philosophy: a systematic explanation of the universe, a set of values, and a sense of faith.[79] In Brazil one might assume that many Communists had experienced frustrations and an awareness that the values of their life prior to joining the party had been unrealistic, since their system had failed to provide rewards and opportunities commensurate with expectations. Alienated from their society, these persons turn to the Communist party for a new faith, values, and a philosophy. Within the party they hope to enjoy participation in the flow of everyday events, assurance that a means can be found to achieve intended goals, and expectation that hopes will be confirmed. Any undermining of the new faith, of course, accounts for dissatisfaction and even eventual defection from party ranks.

A tentative breakdown of the party's rank and file can be suggested. Middle-class adherents probably constituted the larger membership in 1966. Throughout its history and particularly during its early years, however, the party rank and file has included a large labor element. In 1929 about 80 per cent of the members were of working-class origin.[80] In 1964, prior to the military intervention, the party controlled about 10 per cent of the country's sixteen hundred trade unions and controlled or wielded sizable influence in four of the six national labor confederations.[81] But Communist strength declines in proportion to the degree of government control over Communist participation in the labor movement. Thus both membership and the number of supporters declined after 1947, substantially so after 1964. This decline has occurred while population has increased rapidly and a once-booming economy has been subject to inflation and recession.

Organization and Performance

We might hypothesize that a strong non-ruling Communist party would be represented by a large, well-organized mass base, constituted of peasants and workers, for these are the classes that provide guerrilla and revolutionary armed forces and meaningful economic and social action. The strong party might also require a substantial intellectual elite in its membership. A military element also contributes to the revolutionary potential of such a party. In contrast, the weak or negligible party may be characterized by a very strongly intellectual thrust and no mass base and minimal military potential. Such a party may be divorced from reality and lack capacity for significant action. In the intellectual-oriented party, factionalism tends to be high. In recent years the Brazilian party could be characterized by three such elements of weakness.

First, the party organization since its inception has been based on the Soviet model, as comparison of the statutes of the Brazilian and Soviet parties will confirm. The highly centralized and hierarchical structure of the party has contributed to the dominance of a clique-styled minority over an often not fully participating majority. During periods of clandestinity this majority may be isolated from its leadership, to the effect of a decline in membership. Non-participation by the mass membership contributes substantially to ineffective party performance.

Second, the hierarchical centralization and the failure of the party leadership to facilitate and encourage mass involvement resulted in rigid control over democratic tendencies at all levels of the party organization. During times of legality this tendency was undercut by the search for support—for workers, petty bourgeois, and intellectual elements. The expansion of the rank and file membership also loosened party discipline and encouraged divisive currents. A militant course of action during illegality, however, brought severe repression upon leadership and rank and file alike, and near extinction to the party machinery.

Third, further complicating the effectiveness of party performance was the persistent domination of a single charismatic leader and the administrative core surrounding him. The charisma of Prestes aroused mass sentiment and support for the party, even though the personalist image was often tarnished by party failure. Further, in the midst of a society unable to find solutions to basic human needs, Prestes, despite his party's failure, was usually successful in arousing mass aspirations and hopes for social, economic, and political change.

Fourth, Prestes' hero image contributed to and at times intensified public toleration for Communist participation in Brazilian society. This image helped make respectable the involvement of many sympathizers in party activities and allowed the party sometimes to play a socializing role by identifying societal problems. The preoccupation with remaining within the center of Brazilian politics in order to build support for its position on vital issues, however, seems to have blinded the party leadership from recognizing many significant issues. Frequently out of touch with reality, the leadership often found itself opposed to the aspirations of the rank and file. This certainly encouraged the defection of some members. Prestes' opportunism and personal ambitions appear to have undermined party unity. Under such circumstances communication breakdown between leaders and followers could be expected frequently.

Fifth, despite disruptive tendencies within the leadership as well as communication gaps between leaders and followers, the party organization represented a means of upward mobility for working-class supporters. While the rank and file membership could often be held intact by its recognition of the historical, intellectual, technical, and even economic superiority of the party elite, it also knew that party membership signified the possibility of higher class status. Often a bourgeois dignity was assumed by the Communist labor leader through association with the predominantly middle-class party leadership. The government tendency, especially after Vargas, to co-opt the union leadership also undoubtedly compromised many Communists. Improved status often accompanied a conservative stance in the face of a threatening society, and Communist elements in labor often were content with the status quo while neglecting the demands of their rank and file.

6 • Conflict and Integration with the National Environment

Since societal influences in general affect the organizational and be-havioral patterns of political parties, it is especially important for us to observe the interaction of these parties with their national environment. At the same time we should test Neumann's proposition that in under-taking to modernize society a political party of individual representation tends to transform to a party of integration.[1] And this we shall do in the light of past and current strategies of action, with particular atten-tion to forms of violence and association with popular causes as well as to interaction with competing associations and ideologies.

Past Strategies

Lenin established the tactics and organizational principles upon which the ruling and non-ruling Communist parties are generally based. In his April "theses" he called for the passing of power from the government to the proletariat and the complete break "with all capital interests." Maintaining that the masses were "being deceived by the bourgeoisie," he argued that world struggle could not be ended "by a truly demo-cratic, non-coercive peace without the overthrow of capital." Even though, because of the insufficient class-consciousness of the proletariat (as he believed), power was controlled by the bourgeoisie in the first stage of the Russian Revolution, in the second stage power would rest with "the proletariat and the poorest strata of the peasantry." This transition in power would be brought about, he predicted, by the party whose task was to expose the "imperialist" government of "capitalists" and systematically explain "the errors of their tactic." A return to a parliamentary republic would be prevented, the police, army, and bureaucracy abolished, all landed estates confiscated and nationalized, all banks amalgamated into a single national bank.[2]

Thus, Lenin proposed a variety of tactics and strategies, applicable according to specific stages through which power would be transformed by the revolutionary activity of the party. His proposals were particularly relevant to the Russian experience, and there were attempts elsewhere to implement them. In Latin America and especially in Brazil Communists found it necessary to adjust their tactics and strategy to national developments and conditions. Two general strategies were employed frequently by the Communist party in Brazil. One strategy, violent in orientation, involved open revolution, general strikes, and prolonged terrorism and sabotage. The other was oriented to peaceful association with the masses outside the party and was more representative of the Brazilian experience.

Violence and Revolution
Traditionally the Communist party had geared its activities to the Brazilian working classes in large urban centers. Since violence in the form of demonstrations and strikes had been frequently employed by the labor movement since its inception, it was not surprising that the PCB would also advocate such measures. Since in its early years both its leadership and its membership were drawn principally from the working classes, the party became involved in a variety of labor organizations in their strikes and demonstrations. As noted earlier, in recent years street demonstrations and public meetings were held to protest U.S. imperialism and private enterprise in Brazil and to support such popular causes as agrarian reform, nationalization of foreign banks, establishment of diplomatic relations with the Soviet Union and China, Petrobrás, disarmament, and solidarity with the Cuban Revolution. Through the Comando Geral dos Trabalhadores (CGT) and the Comando Geral de Greve (CGG), one hundred sixty-nine major strikes occurred from January 1961 to March 1964. Communist labor leaders were involved in most of the strikes.[3]

At one point in its past, moreover, the PCB participated in an insurrectionary struggle of some importance: the uprisings of November 1935 in Natal, Recife, and Rio de Janeiro. While these revolts were carried out in the name of the ANL, they were carefully planned by the party in collaboration with agents of the Comintern.[4] According to the party interpretation of these events, as set forth by Prestes himself in *Novos Rumos* during the early sixties, Communists constituted a vanguard that together with other popular forces mobilized the masses to oppose "fascism" at that time. "We saved our country from fascism," the account states; the 1935 revolt represented "one of the most heroic [events] of our people and our PCB." Furthermore, says Prestes, the party proved itself able to organize revolutionary forces into a "united front" with the working class, the peasant masses, and other "patriots," while avoiding "isolated movements."[5] Thus, despite its more circumspect approach in the sixties, the PCB viewed the revolts as significant for its evolution. As we have stressed earlier, however, the party had not officially participated in the revolutions of 1922, 1924, 1930, and 1932, even though Prestes, as a non-Communist, had led that long march through the backlands of Brazil after the São Paulo insurrection of 1924. Also, at the time, the 1935 revolt was one of only two major Communist-inspired uprisings to have occurred in Latin America.[6] As discussed above, it proved disastrous for the party, however, and thus, following the international Communist line, the PCB quickly and expediently returned to its traditional policy of alignment with popular non-Communist forces.

Another strategy, allegedly Communist-initiated but actually viewed with suspicion by the PCB and generally supported in principle if not in practice by the PC do B, was that of guerrilla warfare. While in fact, guerrilla movements in Brazil seem to have been only rarely inspired by the example of the Communist party, efforts to activate a viable guerrilla movement gradually intensified throughout the sixties. During 1961 and 1962 Cuba reportedly supported a program to convert Brazilian peasants to guerrillas under Francisco Julião's leadership. Twelve Brazilians were trained in Cuba during August 1961, and encampments were established on *fazendas* (ranches) in the states of Goiás, Maranhão, Mato Grosso, Rio de Janeiro, and Bahia. Less than fifty peasants were found at these encampments, and no guerrilla actions were actually initiated.[7]

The organization of *Grupos dos Onze* ("Groups of Eleven") was another conspicuous example of the guerrilla movement. Formally launched on October 25, 1963, with a pronouncement by Leonel Brizola, these groups were, in his words, "to serve as the principal means and the advance vanguard of the revolutionary movement that will liberate the country from international capitalist oppression and its internal allies with the objective of establishing in Brazil a government of the people, by the people, and for the people." [8] In May 1966 the Grupos chiefs issued "secret instructions" to its regional command, calling for "permanent revolution" and "a war of national liberation." These instructions described strategy and tactics for guerrilla warfare and reasons for the revolution.[9] While acknowledging the PCB as its "principal ally," the pronouncement condemned Prestes for allowing his party to splinter and for his subservience to Moscow.

After the 1964 coup, Brizola criticized the PCB for "forty years in which the frustrations, the errors, the obstinate quirks and narrow attitudes remote from Brazilian reality outweigh the successes." Its leaders, he stated, "long ago completely lost the capacity for self-criticism . . . they never make mistakes and always find a justification for their errors." [10] In May, however, the Grupos dos Onze leadership urged collaboration with dissident Communist groups not aligned with the pro-Moscow PCB.

Brizola and his movement were associated by the press with a series of guerrilla and revolutionary maneuvers that alarmed Brazilian authorities. He was allegedly behind a plot in November 1964 to seize the state governments in Rio Grande do Sul, São Paulo, Guanabara, and Goiás. Thereafter guerrilla bands appeared in different locales throughout the country. Among the more effective were: [11] Operation Pintassilgo in Rio Grande do Sul, the creation of a former aviation captain, Alfredo Ribeiro Daudt, and other ex-military men formerly associated with the Goulart government; the Mato Grosso group, consisting of both Brazilians and Paraguayans and led by Lourenzo Arrua, former colonel of the Paraguayan army (while its operations extended to São Paulo, its primary target was Paraguayan dictator Alfredo Stroessner); the Serra do Caparaó group, which began operations in March 1967 in the eastern part of Minas Gerais and was believed to be directed and financed by Brizola and to involve several former military men [12]; the Itaucu group affiliated with radical elements of the Ação Popular (AP), and one of the first to venture into the countryside; the Uberlândia group, which reportedly included elements of the PC do B; the Manaus group, believed affiliated with the AP and led by a Venezuelan Ricardo Gómez [13]; and the Barra Mansa group, identified with a French seminarian, Guy Michel Camille Thebault, and a Brazilian bishop, Dom Valdir Calheiros.

These sporadic groupings, as well as the Cuban Revolution and Ernesto "Ché" Guevara's abortive guerrilla struggle in Bolivia, undoubtedly influenced Marighella and other dissidents within the PCB to adopt a revolutionary line. As we have seen earlier, after their expulsion from the party in 1967 they formed a revolutionary movement from a variety of dissident Communist and other groups (see below) generally favorable to the armed struggle strategy advocated by Marighella as being "the only fundamental way to expel imperialism and destroy the oligarchies, thus allowing the masses to take power." Since the problem in Brazil, as he acknowledged, was the defeat suffered by popular and revolutionary forces in April 1964, it would be necessary to initiate the guerrilla offensive immediately. He envisaged three phases: preparation, launching of the struggle, and conversion to full-scale war led by the revolutionary army.[14]

Among Marighella's most sensational writings was his minimanual of the urban guerrilla, written in June 1969 and circulated widely after his death in November. "The principal task," he stated, "is to distract, to wear out, to demoralize the militarists, the military dictatorship and its repressive forces, and also to attack and destroy the wealth and property of the North Americans, the foreign managers, and the Brazilian upper class." The goal of the urban guerrilla would be the dismantling of the present Brazilian economic, political, and social system in order to assist the rural guerrilla, and to collaborate with him "in the creation of a totally new and revolutionary social and political structure, with the armed people in power." There would be two immediate objectives: "the physical liquidation of the chiefs and assistants of the armed forces and of the police," and "the expropriation of government resources and those belonging to the big capitalists, latifundists, and imperialists."

Marighella's minimanual included a detailed description of the urban guerrilla's techniques of offensive and retreat to "demoralize and distract the enemy forces, permitting the emergence and survival of rural guerrilla warfare which is designed to play the decisive role in the revolutionary war." The guerrilla would benefit by the elements of surprise, knowledge of the terrain, mobility and speed, and communications. Action would involve "assaults, raids and penetrations, occupations, ambush, street tactics, strikes and work interruptions, desertions, diversions, seizures, expropriations of arms, ammunition, explosives, liberation of prisoners, executions, kidnappings, sabotage, terrorism, armed propaganda, and war of nerves." The minimanual also proposed guidelines for guerrilla security and warned against "seven sins": inexperience, boastfulness, vanity, exaggeration, precipitous action, attacks against an angry enemy, and failure to plan and improvise. Popular support is won by the urban guerrilla's "persistence in public questions." For, "As soon as a reasonable section of the population begins to take seriously the action of the urban guerrilla, his success is guaranteed." [15]

Mass Association

A familiar strategy has been that of peaceful association with the mass outside the party for the purpose of promoting favorable or tolerant attitudes toward Communism and influencing opinion-molding segments of the population. Since its inception the PCB has been concerned to establish or penetrate mass groups. By organizing labor unions, student societies, and a women's federation, by creating a variety of front groups, and by participating in institutions influencing public opinion, Communists were able to make use of their organizational skills. The party's effectiveness in interacting with national society depends largely on interlocking front groups and Communist-led mass organizations that allow for involvement in professional societies, cultural associations, ethnic groups, and other special-interest bodies in the national society. We shall review Communist association, first, with peripheral groups such as the military, trade unions, peasant associations, student and women organizations, specific interest societies, and electoral fronts; and, second, with ideological tendencies that fuse or compete with the party.

Military

It is probable that Brazilian Communist strategists have been directing their attention to the military since the 1920's, for rebellious officers participated in the revolts of 1922 and 1924 and in the Prestes Column of 1924 to 1927. Military officers were also deeply involved in the 1930 revolution and in the 1932 regionalist rising in São Paulo. Although the PCB was not conspicuous during these events, the party attempted to capitalize on weaknesses and divisions within the armed forces during the mid-thirties. Prestes' own military experience undoubtedly contributed to the belief that the military was vulnerable, that it could be mobilized to neutralize the government and bring about a revolution. The army was "demoralized from the top to the bottom" and suffered from "bad discipline," as one rebel of 1922 recalls; yet it "has behind it traditions of revolutionary struggle." [16] Whence the attempt to put their belief into practice in the form of the abortive revolt of November 1935.[17]

The Communist effort to gain military supporters was initiated by the Central Committee's decision to send Astrojildo Pereira to Bolivia in 1927 to try to convert Prestes. In about 1930 the party put together a revolutionary military committee with the objective of "maintaining

Table 6.1

Communist and Military Participation in Revolt of November 27, 1935 (Federal District)

	Revolt Leaders	ANL Organizers	Revolt Supporters	Other Participants	Total	% of Total
PCB Affiliation						
Member	7	6	18	5	36	15.1
Probable Member	1	2	17	0	20	8.4
No Affiliation	0	21	44	117	182	76.5
Total	8	29	79 [1]	122	238	100.0
Military Affiliation						
Officer [2]	2	17	16	6	41	17.2
Other Military	0	1	18	116	135	56.7
Other Occupation	4 [3]	7 [4]	12 [5]	0	23	9.7
Not Identified	2	4	33	0	39	16.4
Total	8	29	79	122	238	100.0

Source: Eurico Bellens Porto, *A insurreição de 27 de Novembro. Relatório.* Data based on content analysis of this report. Known Communists who were interrogated generally acknowledged their affiliation; some were identified by this writer. The number of Communists is conservatively estimated and probably low but difficult to verify. Military affiliation is reasonably accurate.

1. Excludes 13 persons dismissed in report, including wives of Berger, Prestes, Ghioldi, and Meireles, all of whom were probably Communists.

2. Includes one colonel, two majors, 13 captains, 25 lieutenants.

3. Includes two journalists, one medical doctor, one labor leader.

4. Includes four federal deputies, two medical doctors, one senator.

5. Includes five labor leaders, two journalists, two engineers, one lawyer, one medical doctor, one civil servant.

ties and conspiring with the old leaders of the Column." [18] Thereafter, according to sporadic reports, Communists attempted to penetrate the military. During February 1930 five alleged Communists were arrested for fomenting disorder among Brazilian troops in the state of Rio Grande do Sul. In August Communists were believed to have agitated within the Pernambucan police force. During March 1934, twenty-four sailors were jailed for "undermining" the morale of the navy with Communist propaganda.[19]

A link between Communists and military men was clearly evident in the 1935 revolt, as revealed in Table 6.1. Of two hundred thirty-eight persons charged with involvement in the revolt, nearly a quarter were identifiable as members or probable members of the PCB.[20] All eight of the rebel leaders were probably affiliated with the party, and two of the leaders had been military officers. In contrast, only eight of the ANL organizers charged in the plot were Communists, while seventeen were military officers. Of seventy-nine supporters of the revolt, nearly half (or 35) were probably members of the PCB and thirty-four had a military affiliation. The other one hundred twenty-two participants were military men, five Communists among them. Nearly 75 per cent of the total was military—and interestingly enough, ten of the total were to serve on the PCB Central Committee after 1945.[21]

After 1935 and conspicuously after 1945 ties were apparently strong between the party and the military.[22] After Prestes was released from prison, there was an unsuccessful attempt to have him reinstated in the army. The Movimento Militar Constitucionalista, led by General Zenóbio da Costa and alleged to have connections with the PCB, defended Kubitschek and Goulart against anti-Communist opposition during 1955.[23] The sailors' mutiny of March 25–27, 1964, had the strong backing of the Communist-influenced Comando Geral dos Trabalhadores.[24] That the party had lost contact with military supporters after the 1964 coup was evident in the list of Central Committee members, none of whom in June of that year had responsibility for the military sector.

Labor

In its formative years the PCB drew most of its leadership and membership from organized urban labor, and throughout its evolution the party concentrated on maintaining its influence in labor.[25] Apparently the first central organization under Communist dominance was the short-lived Confederação Sindicalista Cooperativista, led by Sarandy Reposo during 1924.[26] Communists were influential also in the Federação dos Trabalhadores do Rio de Janeiro, founded in April 1929, and in the Confederação Geral do Trabalho do Brasil (CGTB) founded in April 1929.[27] In the late twenties the PCB attempted to mobilize worker support through the BOC while controlling graphic-arts workers and hotel and restaurant employees in São Paulo and a majority of unions in Recife, which had a base of sixty committees organized in the unions, factories, and workers' districts.[28] Policy changes confirmed at the party's Third Congress, however, resulted in the expulsion or withdrawal (as the case might be) of labor and Trotskyist elements, and eventually in the demise of the BOC.

The Vargas government of 1930 recognized the legality of labor unions by means of legislation opposed by anarchists and Communists, who declared the measure a "fascist" attempt to undermine labor organizations. There ensued a struggle between the new Vargas-sponsored unions and the older Communist and anarchist unions. Then in May 1935, the PCB under its popular-front policy called a unity conference to organize the Confederação Sindical Unitária do Brasil, which apparently absorbed the membership of the União Operária e Camponesa (known to exist during 1933 and 1934 [29]) and attempted to coalesce dissident unions in the labor movement.

Under the *Estado Novo,* proclaimed in late 1937, trade unions were affiliated to state federations; and where there were more than three such federations, a confederation was set up. Seven workers' confederations were to prevail over this pyramidal structure.[30] After the *Estado Novo,* the industrial Confederação Nacional dos Trabalhadores na Indústria (CNTI), was constituted in October 1946; the commercial Confederação Nacional dos Trabalhadores no Comércio (CNTC), in November 1946; and the land transport Confederação Nacional dos Trabalhadores em Transportes Terrestres (CNTTT), in February 1953. The credit institution Confederação Nacional dos Trabalhadores em Emprêsas de Crédito (CONTEC) was constituted in August 1949; the Confederação Nacional dos Trabalhadores em Transportes Marítimos, Fluviais e Aéreos (CNTTMFA), in June 1960; and two confederations—for workers in communications and publicity, and those in education and cultural institutions—have not yet materialized. The Vargas system allowed for government arbitration between capital and labor, and maintained control through a paternalistic labor code and a vast program of social welfare.

The end of the Vargas dictatorship in 1945 did not free labor from

official control. The corporativist organization remained intact, and the
Labor Ministry continued to control labor through the union tax and
the threat of intervention. After the PTB had been instituted by the officials, Communists adopted the tactic of working within the government-
sponsored unions rather than of forming a rival organization. Thus,
as we saw earlier, the PCB operated via the MUT, which in 1946
called for the establishment of a central labor confederation. When the
MUT was declared illegal, Communists and Labor Ministry officials divided over the issue of forming a confederation. Yet, as we know, pro-
Communist and PTB unions did establish the CTB. Repression of
Communists and strong controls over labor unions were continued by
the Dutra government until the return of Vargas as President in 1950.

Under Vargas, during the 1950's, union elections were tolerated, and
Communists gained some support despite harassment of PCB leadership and the increasing recognition by workers that Communist loyalties
lay in large measure outside the working class. Just before Vargas' suicide in 1954, his Minister of Labor, Goulart, sided with Communists
to resolve a national maritime strike, and this brought him prestige
among workers. After Vargas' death Communists began to work within
the PTB.[31] In return for this needed support, the PTB allowed some
Communist candidates to run under the PTB label. Meanwhile, until
Goulart's forced resignation in 1954, he and the PTB co-opted the labor
movement through the distribution of government jobs in the labor
courts and in social security institutes, and thus, according to one writer,
made "it possible for labor leaders to live in the middle class from
which a great many had come." [32]

Under President Kubitschek and his Vice President, Goulart, government control over the trade unions relaxed somewhat: thus, the administration adopted a cautious policy of generous wage settlements, and
Goulart restored his links with the Labor Ministry. Meanwhile nationalist
issues, like the defense of Petrobrás, unified the worker with student,
intellectual, and other social elements. Likewise, such issues as the right
to strike and increased social welfare encouraged radicalization of the
labor masses.[33] Toward the end of Kubitschek's term a new leadership,
in general anti-Communist and less concerned with nationalism than
with wage demands, challenged the hegemony of PCB and Communist
labor leaders. The position of this leadership was temporarily reinforced
by Quadros' election in 1960.

The new leaders, known as "renovating" or "democratic," and in-

cluding Quadros supporters and "opportunists" opposed to the concilia-
tion of nationalists with Communists, promoted their cause at the third
Congresso Sindical Nacional, held in Rio in 1960. Their program called
for depolitization of the labor movement, trade unionism based on collective contracts, and elimination of the labor tax. The Congress was
attended also by a majority faction composed of a united front of nationalists and Communists who advocated the labor movement's political participation in the struggle for nationalism and for a Central Sindical
Nacional. This current was labeled *pelegos vermelhos*—i.e., "red"
labor leaders who cooperated with the Ministry of Labor.[34] A third current, called *pelegos amarelos* (older "official" labor leaders), was dependent on labor funds and political ties with the government. Because
of ideological differences, the "official" leaders were unable to maintain
their shaky alliance with the majority current, and eventually formed
an anti-Communist organization known as the Movimento Sindical
Democrático, which quickly established relations with the AFL-CIO-
supported Organización Regional Interamericana de Trabajadores
(ORIT) and the International Confederation of Free Trade Unions.[35]

Under Quadros the Communist-nationalist coalition was weakened
temporarily when control of the Labor Ministry was turned over to a
Christian Democrat. Quadros resigned in August 1961, however, and
Goulart's assumption of power brought a realignment of the PTB and
Communist forces; but in the labor split coinciding with Quadros' election union leaders became somewhat independent of Goulart, who had
regained his leadership role in labor through concessions to union bosses.
In consequence, Communist, PTB, and some former pro-Quadros
union leaders formed the unofficial but powerful CGT in late 1961, and
through this organization won government concessions, including substantial wage increases, for every strike they initiated and supported.
These wage increases, together with rapid inflation and increasing
anxiety on the part of conservatives about Goulart's liaison with labor,
tended to polarize left and right political forces, and this occasioned military intervention in 1964.[36]

Historically the bond between Communism and the labor movement
is readily identifiable, for information and analysis are available in
conservative and anti-Communist as well as radical sources. From this
material we concluded in Chapter 5 that a large segment of party membership and leadership was drawn from the working classes (Tables 5.3
and 5.4). We saw too that Communist electoral strength is found in the

labor movement. In the late twenties labor support developed within the BOC, and in 1933 a small vote was cast for the Communist-dominated União Operária e Camponesa[37]; moreover, in the 1945 São Paulo elections the majority of workers cast their vote for the PCB and PTB.[38] Again, it may be demonstrated that Communist influence in labor organization has been evident since the party's beginning. During the early sixties there was some degree of Communist leadership in all the official confederations, as indicated in Table 6.2.

While we do not want to overstate the PCB role in the labor movement, still it is clear that the movement was headed, especially at top levels, by many able and conscientious figures who also were affiliated with the party. After an internal struggle in December 1961, Communists and radical elements of the PTB gained control of the industrial workers' CNTI, the largest and most powerful confederation, with a membership of one million. Elected in early 1964 were pro-Communist Clodsmidt Riani (President), former Communist Dante Pelacani[39] of the graphic-arts workers (Secretary General), São Paulo Communist leader Luís de Tenório Lima of the food packaging workers (Secretary for Organization), and Communist sympathizer deputy Benedito Cerqueira[40] of the Guanabara metallurgical workers (Secretary for Social Security). Within the CNTI Communist strength existed in unions of carpenters (Roberto Morena),[41] textile workers (Hércules Correia dos Reis), printers and metallurgical, petroleum, and electrical workers.[42] Communists controlled Brazil's largest union, the twenty-five thousand-member São Paulo city metalworkers' Sindicato dos Trabalhadores nas Indústrias Metalúrgicas, Mecânicas e de Material Elétrico de São Paulo.

Developments in the CNTI strengthened the position of pro-Communist and Communist elements also in the CNTC—the commerce confederation, second largest in Brazil. During the early sixties the CNTC had been identified with the "democratic" bloc opposed in general to the Communist-influenced confederations and other labor organizations. But when one-half (ten) of the CNTC federations came out in favor of a slate of pro-Communist leaders, and no electoral decision could be reached, the Labor Ministry took temporary control of the confederation early in 1964. The CONTEC, with about forty thousand members, was from the start under Communist influence, with leaders such as Armando Ziller, a member of the PCB Central Committee during the early sixties. The CNTTMFA, with one hundred thirty-five thousand members, contained pro-Communist segments, noticeably in the stevedore's federation headed by PCB Central Committee member Osvaldo Pacheco da Silva, and in the federations of dock, maritime, and aviation workers. The land transport confederation, the CNTTT, was controlled by four anti-Communist federations, although its federation of railroad workers was led by Communist Rafael Martineli.

Communists were prominent in unofficial "horizontal" labor organizations that embraced workers from different occupational categories and had no affiliation with the confederations erected by labor legislation. The Comando Geral de Greve (CGG), which existed briefly in mid-1962 with the immediate purpose of calling general strikes and was known thereafter as the Comando Geral dos Trabalhadores (CGT), was led by Communists such as Pacheco da Silva (Secretary General) and Martineli (Treasurer), Moreno, and Correia dos Reis, as well as Communist sympathizers Riani (President) and Pelacani. Just before the 1964 coup the GCT was effectively putting pressure on Goulart, conspicuously in the sailors' meeting of late March. The Comissão Permanente de Organizações Sindicais (CPOS), a united labor front of industrial workers emerging during the Kubitschek Presidency in the city of Rio de Janeiro, was also under Communist leadership—that of Morena, Correia dos Reis, and sympathizer Cerqueira, though one of its founders, Ari Campista, was a non-Communist. Two other organizations came under Communist domination: the Pacto de Unidade e Ação (PUA) representing maritime and railroad workers, which had also come into being under Kubitschek's reign and was led by Pacheco da Silva; and the Forum Sindical de Debates (FSD) of Santos. The Movimento Sindical Democrático (MSD) was an anti-Communist, unofficial organization established in São Paulo during June 1961, and the União Sindical dos Trabalhadores (UST) represented a third position between the MSD and the CPOS.[43]

The apparent success of Communists in penetrating the labor movement in the late fifties and early sixties was due in large measure to the government's temporary loss of control over union activities.[44] In fact, the pragmatic leadership of Goulart in the midst of rapid inflation and other economic problems helped open up the Brazilian system, so that the prudent PCB was able to align itself with more radical and revolutionary popular forces. The PCB objective was "a coalition of workers of Communist, PTB, socialist, Catholic orientation" to work toward containing the high cost of living, toward a readjustment of sal-

Table 6.2

**Communist Leadership and Influence in
Brazilian Labor (January–March 1964)**

Organization	Leadership	Degree of PCB Influence
Official Confederations		
CNTC	Labor Ministry Control, Anti-Communist Leadership Isolated	Moderate with half federations pro-Communist
CNTI	(Riani, Pelacani, Tenório de Lima, Cerqueira)	Strong (São Paulo metal-workers)
CNTTMFA	Pro-Communist Segments (Osvaldo Pacheco da Silva)	Moderate
CNTTT	Anti-Communist in 4 of 5 federations (Rafael Martineli)	Strong in federation of railroad workers
CONTAG	Pro-Communist (Lindolfo Silva, Bezerra da Costa, Nestor Vera)	ULTAB and one-third of federations
CONTEC	Pro-Communist (Armando Ziller)	Moderate
Unofficial		
CGG and CGC	(Pelacani, Riani, Martineli, Pacheco da Silva, Correia dos Reis, Morena)	Strong
CPOS	Pro-Communist (Morena, Correia dos Reis)	Strong
FSD	Pro-Communist	Strong
MSD	Anti-Communist	None
PUA	Pro-Communist (Pacheco da Silva)	Strong
UST	Third Force (José Maria Crispim)	None

aries, toward social welfare legislation and labor reorganization.[45] With its cadres already entrenched in the labor movement, the PCB held a distinct advantage over its rivals on the left, as the only Marxist-Leninist entity to have worked within trade unions to form cells and exert influence in an organized fashion. Further, the stress on the training and indoctrination of its members meant that the party could expect disciplined and loyal Communist activity in the unions.[46] Other PCB strengths might be seen in their effectiveness in dealing directly with employers and their increasing criticism of the high echelon trade union leaders who were indebted for their position to the Ministry of Labor rather than to the rank and file.[47] And then their press and propaganda media, unlike non-Communist counterparts in the large cities, were visibly dedicated to the cause of the labor movement.

Communist strength and success in the trade unions correlate in general with the lack of an effective labor opposition. The anxiety of employers and even government over the activities of organized labor often resulted in the labeling of any militant trade unionist as a "Communist," thereby enhancing the PCB image as dominant among workers. This situation, as well as the awareness that their labor position remained tenuous in the face of government or military suppression will in part explain the party's over-cautious stance on strikes and agitation. During the early sixties, indeed, the party tended to assume an activist role only after its leftist competitors demonstrated success in winning demands. Thus, it seems that the party's role in the chaotic events leading to the coup of 1964 was greatly exaggerated by the right-wing opposition.

Peasant Associations

Traditionally peasants have been tied to the conservative landowners upon whom they are dependent. A paternalistic relation between landowner and peasant developed within the slave system, which after 1888 gave way to a variety of new patterns such as sharecropping and renting. The *fazendas* (large agricultural farms and plantations) occupy nearly 80 per cent of all cultivated land in Brazil. On the fazenda—often isolated by poor roads and lack of communications—there are usually food and supply stores, a school, a chapel, and sometimes an armed force. Peasants usually chose to live on the fazenda rather than in a neighboring village, often because the owner provided them with a small piece of land to grow their own food. Upward mobility depended upon winning the confidence of the landowner or on farming unoccupied land. The piece of land that the worker could cultivate signified a favor, not a right.[48] At the same time local political life consisted of alliances and hostilities between big landowners, each with his following of small farmers, tenants, sharecroppers, and laborers. The landowner thus could control the peasant vote as well as the existing political order. Occasionally those peasants, unable to fit the prevailing institutional patterns or to maintain even a subsistence existence, expressed their discontent through religious, often messianic, movements led by charismatic leaders.[49]

Since the thirties, several changes have modified the landowner-peasant relationship.[50] For one thing, large numbers of landowners left the fazenda for urban life; and if the city was at a distance from the fazenda, he frequently became an absentee owner. The bonds between owner and his peasants loosened, and the overseer left in charge often was restricted in decision-making and expenditures. Moreover, the prospect of higher wages and a better life lured many peasants to the cities and newly developed areas. In some areas the availability of migratory labor at necessary times weakened the tie of landowner to peasant, since the owner felt no obligation to migrants. Again, agriculture became increasingly commercialized and regional monopolies developed because of poor communications and difficulties in the transportation and storage of goods. As a consequence producers and wholesalers sometimes limited distribution of their produce, and the increase in demand led to rapid increases in price and, of course, substantial profit; during the sixties such a situation provoked occasional food riots and raids on warehouses.

Another factor was that industrialization in the growing towns and cities benefited from the export of commercial agricultural products, for commercial agriculture provided exchange earnings and capital for urban industry and commerce.[51] The result was a widening gap between rural and urban Brazil, as inflation isolated the peasant from the national market, and rural workers were not allowed to organize unions or to receive social security benefits. Where paternalism broke down, conflict intensified between landowner and peasant, and peasant organizations emerged, usually in frontier areas and in marginal fazendas that had encountered difficulties in competing with commercial agriculture, as well as near cities and in frontier areas where commercial farmers seized land from squatters.

Communists were the first to attempt to organize dissident peasants. The Communist-backed BOC included "peasants" in its name as did the União Operária e Camponesa. One of the early Communist efforts to organize a peasant league occurred in about 1928 in São Paulo in the zones of Sertãozinho and Ribeirão Prêto, where farm workers under the leadership of Teotônio de Sousa Lima marched in protest on the large coffee plantations.[52] The Pernambuco branch of the party actively organized commercial agricultural workers into leagues during 1946 to 1948.[53] In about 1954 the PCB formed a rural workers' organization known as the União dos Lavradores e Trabalhadores Agrícolas do Brasil (ULTAB), which aggregated sharecroppers on coffee plantations, and some sugar workers in São Paulo state. ULTAB engaged in collective bargaining, pushing for trade-union-type legislation for workers in the countryside.[54]

In 1955 rival organizations known as *ligas camponesas* (peasant leagues) appeared in the Northeast on the occasion when Francisco Julião, a lawyer and state deputy in the Pernambuco assembly, defended in court a group of peasants of the Galiléia plantation, located near Vitória de Santo Antão in the transitional *agreste* zone between the wet coastal sugar lands (*mata* zone) and the dry cattle interior lands (*sertão* zone). As tenant farmers on the plantation, these peasants had formed an association (apparently with the owner's consent) to assure rental payments. The owner's son, however, opposed the peasant association and, with the assistance of police, expelled the peasants from the land, which he desired for cattle raising. Julião fought the case in behalf of the peasants and eventually prevailed upon the state governor to expropriate the property, which in 1959 became a cooperative.[55] The Galiléia association thus became the first such Liga, and thereafter Julião organized peasant leagues in other municipalities, generally west of the populous sugar lands in the states of Pernambuco and Paraíba. The movement eventually spread to other states.[56] At first Julião favored peaceful means to defend the peasant and improve his condition. In particular, the Ligas directed attention to the prevention of rising rents, the abolition of the *cambão* (the obligation of sharecroppers and tenants to work for a certain period without pay), the enforcement of existing legislation, and implementation of land reform.[57]

Later, Julião called for radical and revolutionary changes. There is no doubt that his image as a revolutionary was exaggerated by the foreign press, and it is doubtful that he desired to overturn the system he vigorously opposed (even though he was the son of a large plantation owner).[58] Julião classified the rural population as in part a proletariat of rural wage earners and in part a peasantry of those with some control over the land (sharecroppers, squatters, renters, or small property owners), and he appealed to the peasantry as the largest segment of the rural population.[59] His primary objective was to build a firm electoral base. In 1962 under the PSB he was elected deputy to the national Congress, and in 1963 he tried to form his own leftist Movimento Revolucionário Tiradentes (MRT), with the Ligas as its foundation.[60] He also promoted a popular front named the Movimento Unificado da Revolução Brasileira (MURB).[61]

Julião's personal ambitions, however, isolated him from some of the Ligas. Eventually he broke with Assis Lemos, head of the large Sapé league in Paráiba. In addition, leftists criticized him for superficiality and vagueness, and he declined as a national figure; he was condemned for false promises, for excessive mysticism, and for a lack of any clearly defined ideological position.[62] Julião found himself competing with Miguel Arraes, who in 1962 was elected governor of Pernambuco in a victory over the conservative rural oligarchy. As governor, Arraes encouraged the unionization of sugar workers in accordance with a new rural labor law, passed in March 1963, which gave rural workers most of the same rights as urban workers.[63] Inevitably, differences developed between the Julião and Arraes constituencies.[64]

Julião encountered serious differences with the PCB also, even though the party and the peasant leagues had something in common.[65] According to at least one account (which cannot be adequately substantiated), the leagues of the fifties were founded with the assistance of Communists.[66] Both movements demanded rural legislation for workers as well as agrarian reform, and their emphasis was on the implementation and extension of existing legislation, aid, schools, and the like. One source of conflict may have been that Julião demanded thorough agrarian reform, while Communists emphasized minimal demands.[67] The PCB was suspicious of Julião's political ambitions and the autonomy of the leagues, and considered him to be too radical. Julião's appeals to the peasantry for radical change were undoubtedly viewed as potentially detrimental to the slow gains Communists sought through legislation.[68]

The Communist effort focused on the rural proletariat rather than on the peasantry, and thus the PCB's chief competition was with the progressive Catholics of Ação Popular and the Church, which in the early sixties initiated efforts to organize these rural workers. The Church-supported rural unions had their origin in the state of Rio Grande do Norte under Bishop Eugênio Sales de Araújo. In 1961 the younger priests, inspired by Bishop Sales' work, initiated a training program in Pernambuco and formed legally recognized rural unions. By 1963 there were forty-eight legal rural unions in Rio Grande do Norte, apparently all Church-sponsored, and sixty-two unions in Pernambuco of which all but one were Church-sponsored.[69] The Church also was particularly aggressive in organizing rural unions in São Paulo, with lesser activity in Minas Gerais and the southern states of Paraná, Santa Catarina, and Rio Grande do Sul. The effort was led by two parish priests, Padres Antônio Melo and Antônio Crespo, respectively of Cabo and of Jaboatão, two municipalities in the depressed sugar belt around Recife. In 1963 Melo led a strike that brought an 80 per cent salary increase for two hundred thousand collective workers. The campaign for a bonus of an annual extra month's pay, however, encountered resistance from recalcitrant landowners as well as from the Communist and other leftist rural organizations competing with the official Church-sponsored unions.[70]

With the creation of over two thousand rural unions between 1962 and 1964, federations were also established for wage earners, small property owners, and those with leased land.[71] Among the twenty-seven federations, the ULTAB had nine as well as the greatest number of unions, the AP had nine, and Catholics not affiliated with AP had nine also. In December 1963 a confederation of agricultural workers was set up in Rio and named Confederação Nacional dos Trabalhadores na Agricultura (CONTAG). An agreement between the AP and the Communist leadership gave most of the top posts to Communists, as Communists Lindolfo Silva, José Leandro Bezerra da Costa, and Nestor Vera were elected respectively President, Second Vice President, and Treasurer of the new confederation (see Table 6.2).[72]

With the military coup of 1964, the peasant leagues, the Communist unions, along with other unofficial organizations, were banned and their leadership imprisoned or exiled. The official rural unions were allowed to continue, although in many cases they were intervened by government officials. With their competitors eliminated, Padres Melo and Crespo moved to strengthen their unions, but their efforts to improve the lot of the workers met with only moderate success in the face of a conservative government.[73] The Church, however, was effective in vividly describing and analyzing with statistics the plight of the rural workers.[74]

Besides the ULTAB in São Paulo,[75] PCB influence developed elsewhere; it was particularly strong in the peasant leagues of Paráiba, for example, and apparently controlled the Movimento dos Agricultores Sem Terra (MASTER), a peasant organization in Rio Grande do Sul.[76]

Communists became involved in the defense of squatters and home-
steaders who through fraud or force had relinquished their land to spec-
ulators. The defense associations originated at Amaro Leite [77] and
Formoso [78] in the state of Goiás during 1954 and 1955. Similar peasant organizations sprang up around Brasília, the new capital, where
land values inflated rapidly. Other organizations were formed also in
Maranhão in northern and western Paraná, and in the state of Rio
de Janeiro. [79]

The PCB encountered difficulty in the attempt to organize peasants.
Communist militants sent to rural areas were frequently of middle- and
working-class background and from urban areas, and inevitably they
were unable to identify with the peasant, whose mysticism made him
suspicious of the Marxist-Leninist. [80] Some Communists, however,
worked effectively with the rural proletariat, as for example at Palmares,
situated in the sugar zone of Pernambuco. The "independent" rural
union, based on a workers' association formed in 1953, was organized
here in 1961 and officially recognized in January 1963. The union, extending to twenty-one municipalities and thirty-thousand members, was
able to provide such services as legal aid, dental care, and schooling.
The influential Communist at Palmares was Gregório Bezerra, ex-
federal deputy, a leader of the Recife uprising in November 1935, and,
unlike most of the current PCB leadership, the son of a poor peasant
family. [81]

Among the various groups competing for the allegiance of the peasantry, the PCB assumed a relatively conservative position. [82] At the
first Congresso Nacional dos Lavradores e Trabalhadores Agrícolas,
the meeting of peasant organizations at Belo Horizonte in November
1961, the Communist rural workers' organization, ULTAB, pushed
for resolutions extending urban labor legislation to the countryside; its
demands conflicted with those of the majority of delegates at the meeting who favored Julião's call for expropriation of large landholdings.
Both demands finally were incorporated in a declaration issued by the
congress. [83]

Students

As recounted earlier, since its early years the PCB has maintained a
youth affiliate. [84] The Juventude Comunista do Brasil, founded in January 1924, enlisted its first fourteen members in 1925 and another thirteen a year later, although only eight remained in 1927. After a reorganization, the Juventude membership increased to some two hundred

fifty members by December 1928.[85] In January 1929, its first Congress was held, but a split during the same year resulted in the withdrawal of a Trotskyist contingent. Thereafter the affiliate languished, more or less disappeared after 1935, and then revived on March 28, 1947, as a legal entity known as the União da Juventude Comunista (UJC).[86] Shortly later it was declared illegal—to reappear on August 1, 1950, as an organization independent of the PCB.[87]

During the sixties, as in the past, the UJC pursued a policy of coalescing with other student groups to support popular causes. Before 1964, middle-class student radicals assumed a vanguard position to protest the injustices of Brazilian society. Their dissent was manifested through the União Nacional dos Estudantes (UNE), which was controlled by a coalition of Communists and Ação Popular (AP), the left-wing Catholic group whose radicalism was based on the philosophy of Christian Democracy and whose work was carried on by young priests serving the peasants and slum dwellers. The PCB organized its youth sector under Zuleika Alambert to work both within and parallel to the UNE; Marcos Jaimovith, Homero Nepomuceno, and others worked within the UNE.[88] A third element in the student movement was the Marxist, revolutionary Política Operária (POLOP) comprising dissident radical youth from the PTB, PSB, and the PCB as well as independent Marxists influenced by Fidelismo. This group unrelentingly attacked Goulart and his reform proposals and thus estranged itself from the more pragmatic PCB.[89]

With the support of the Ministry of Education and Culture the UNE participated vigorously in the national literacy campaign, the adult literacy campaign, the campaign for student aid, and the Movimento de Cultura Popular. The UNE sponsored a seminar of students of the underdeveloped world, held in Salvador during July 1963, and organized Centros Populares de Cultura, designed to politicize students through periodical literature, film, theater, and other cultural forms.[90]

When the UNE was suppressed after the military coup of 1964, political forces within the student movement were realigned in a coalition of the AP, dissident Communist youth, and the POC, which fused several dissident PCB groups with the POLOP.[91] While the UNE held its annual congress every year from 1965 to 1968 the PCB, suffering from internal division and a decline in its influence and strength, found itself outflanked by the student left. The UNE congress in São Paulo during 1965, attended by three hundred delegates from fifteen states, resolved to work for the formation of a union of Latin American students, support workers against capitalism, to denounce U.S. technicians in Brazil, and to maintain close ties with the International Union of Students (IUS), a Soviet-backed organization. Subsequent congresses demanded cancellation of a controversial agreement between the U.S.-financed Agency for International Development and the Ministry of Education and Culture, as well as free education at all levels, legal status for UNE, and an end to the dictatorship and "imperialism." [92]

The apparent unity of the AP and the PCB within the UNE was undermined when the PCB instructed its followers to vote for certain candidates in the November 15, 1966, elections; the AP ordered its followers to cast blank ballots. At the UNE Congress in São Paulo during July 1967, AP members were elected to four of the ten UNE executive positions, and the POLOP won three positions. The Prestes wing of the PCB was ignored altogether, and three members of the Marighella wing filled the remaining positions. Further, the UNE refused to consider a PCB program for students, and disaffiliated itself from the IUS. The traditional UNE was effectively decimated in 1968 by the arrest of some eight hundred to a thousand students attending the organization's thirtieth Congress, at Ibiuna in the state of São Paulo. Among those seized were José Dirceu, leader of the students in the state of São Paulo, and Waldimir Palmeiras, leader in Guanabara. Thereafter a new UNE emerged, with close ties to the Havana-based Organización Continental Latinoamericana de Estudiantes (OCLAE), and a political line favoring armed revolution—and this at a time when the cautious remnants of the PCB exerted very little influence. [93]

Women

The PCB effort to organize women has been carried out through an affiliate known variously as the União Feminina do Brasil (UFB) [94] and the Federação de Mulheres do Brasil (FMB). [95] The women's affiliate sponsored national conferences and a monthly magazine through which it disseminated its views. [96] In January 1963 the FMB participated in a congress of women in Havana, with a delegation headed by Bertina Blum and representatives of the Federação de Mulheres de São Paulo, the Comissão Feminina de Intercâmbio e Amistade, and the Liga Feminina do Estado de Guanabara. [97]

Electoral Fronts

During both times of legality and times of illegality the PCB has been moderately successful in its tactic of allying with other parties and organizations to contest elections and issues. Three types of alliance have evolved. One consisted of a united front of leftist and popular forces in which the PCB was influential but not necessarily the principal force. The ANL, for example, provided the party ample exposure, as we have seen. After 1945, electoral alliances with the PTB and even the PSD allowed Communists to run and occasionally win Congressional seats and lesser offices.

Another type involved a union of forces dominated by the PCB. An early example—from the late twenties—was the BOC, which allowed the party a degree of recognition and the victory of several candidates. As early as 1944 Prestes was agitating for a União Democrática Nacional, and in August 1950 he adopted an "extreme" leftist position by calling for direct struggle for power through the creation of the Frente Democrática de Libertação Nacional (FDLA). The FDLA was to be composed of Comitês Democráticos de Libertação Nacional and a military Exército de Libertação Nacional, and its objective was to inaugurate immediately "a radical revolutionary program." By 1960 at the PCB's Fifth Congress, however, the FDLA was censured as "adventurous" and "ultra leftist."

A third type of alliance involved a national liberation front similar to radical left movements in other Latin American countries and in Africa. Because of its revolutionary overtures this type tended not to be dominated by the PCB. Thus the Frente de Libertação Nacional was founded in Goiânia in October 1961 under the conspicuously non-Communist leadership of Leonel Brizola, Mauro Borges, Miguel Arraes, and others, but allegedly received support from the PCB in time.[98] A similar organization was the Frente de Mobilização Popular (FMP), created in 1962 to demand agrarian, urban, and tax reform, and led by Brizola and non-Communists as well as PCB members, including Nestor Vera and Lindolfo Silva.[99] In addition there may have been some Communist influence by way of the Frente Parlamentar Nacionalista, which claimed national deputies from several political parties among its members. In January 1964 President Goulart proposed a popular or progressive front of political parties, including the PCB.[100]

Specific-Issue Societies

As influenced by the Soviet pattern, Communist party strategy generally requires its organizations to attend to specific national and international issues. Thus, during the 1920's the PCB—no exception to this practice —was concerned with war, with imperialism, and with the USSR, and expressed those concerns through, respectively, the Liga contra a Guerra, the Liga contra o Imperialismo, and the Sociedade dos Amigos da URSS. In the thirties the PCB rallied its forces to oppose fascism through the Frente Unica de Luta Contra a Reação e o Fascismo and the Frente Popular para a Luta contra o Fascismo e Guerra, and to oppose exploitation and hunger through the Alliança Popular por Pão, Terra e Liberdade. During the forties and fifties the party joined nationalists to attack the international petroleum companies in Brazil. At the same time the PCB manifested its concern with war and peace through the Liga de Defesa Nacional, the Movimento Nacional pela Proibição de Armas Atômicas, and the Congresso do Movimento Brasileiro dos Partidários da Paz. A Liga de Emancipação Nacional was formed in 1954. There was a proliferation of similar movements in the early sixties, among them Sociedades Sino-Brasileiras, Institutos Brasil-URSS, the Sociedade dos Amigos de Cuba, and others. Valério Kondor, a Communist, headed the peace Movimento Brasileiro de Partidários da Paz.

These and other organizations brought together both the Communist and the non-Communist intelligentsia. For example, the Comando de Trabalhadores Intelectuais, allegedly PCB-controlled, included writers Jorge Amado, Astrojildo Pereira, Caio Prado Júnior, Nelson Werneck Sodré, Alberto Passos Guimarães, Leandro Kondor; artists Di Cavalcanti and Armando Estrêla; and the architect Oscar Niemeyer.[101] Cultural exchange institutes with Bulgaria, Hungary, China, and other socialist countries were established.[102]

Competition with the Ideological Periphery
Both Marxism and Marxism-Leninism gave promise of progressiveness for the vanguard of intellectuals as well as for others who seek changes in the traditional system. Sometimes the Marxism and Leninism manifest a profound commitment to the concept of democracy and the ideas of freedom, equality, and participation. As ideology, Marxism and Leninism provide impetus for national and orderly nation-building, and suggest an ideal society achieved through progressive stages of development. While these beliefs apply to the thought and action of the PCB, they may be espoused on occasion by certain rival Marxist and even non-Marxist revolutionary parties, movements, groups, and individuals, with a result in intense competition and differences among those advocating anarchism, socialism, Communism, and nationalism.

Earlier we traced the evolution of anarchism and anarcho-sindicalism and discussed how and why Communism was able to supplant the older ideologies. We also described socialism in its incipient forms as an unimportant organized force, even though it had contributed significantly to the thinking of Brazilian intellectuals: indeed, from 1947, when it was reconstituted, to the coup of 1964 the PSB maintained some influence and Congressional representation. Communist movements were divided, as we have seen, among Marxist, Marxist-Leninist, Stalinist, and Trotskyist orientations—the PC do B offering a particularly formidable threat to the PCB. Nationalist currents emerged within the fascism of the thirties, in military tenentismo and Prestismo, and later in Communist thought. Now to discuss briefly some of the PCB's revolutionary competitors and assess their successes and failures in relation to current PCB strategy.

Marxist Competitors

Table 6.3 delineates the relations between mainstream and radical Marxist tendencies. Thus we see the PCB representing a stabilizing and persistent current during the decade of the sixties, and radical groups splintering from the party after 1964. In fact, one may note a correlation between the radical left splintering and leftist advocacy of armed struggle, on the one hand, and the increase of government repression, on the other.

Like the PCB, the PSB suffered from the defection of radical elements as it remained in the center of Marxist politics, relegated to obscurity by the late sixties. After the Second World War the PSB had re-emerged from clandestinity as an amalgamation of disparate elements, including moderate Marxists and revolutionary radicals. Its Presidential candidate in 1950 (João Mangabeira) received less than ten thousand votes. The party won about 1 per cent of the vote in 1954, 3 per cent in 1958 and 1962. With its constituency of intellectuals, the PSB depended on electoral alliances to maintain its small representation in Congress (five seats after the 1962 elections). Its leadership included Francisco Julião, who after 1962 was censured by the PCB.[103] Its organization was similar to that of the PCB although it had no cells.[104]

Another competitive current, the Trotskyist, was represented variously by dissident Communists in the Grupo Comunista Lenino, the Legião dos Comunistas, and the Partido Operário Leninista during the thirties; during the forties, by the Partido Socialista Revolucionário (PSR) and the Vanguarda Socialista, a dissident group that withdrew from the Fourth International in 1945;[105] and by the Partido Operário

Revolucionário Trotskista (PORT) in the sixties. The PORT, an affiliate of the Latin American Bureau, emerged in 1961 and held its first national congress in São Paulo during February 1963.[106] Its Central Committee held forth in São Paulo, and a branch was located in Recife. After the 1964 coup, government investigators exaggerated the importance of the PORT, for it was alleged that thirty-five military men in the São Paulo area, many of them sergeants, had been influenced by the PORT and before April 1964 had been planning to revolt. Under the leadership of Pedro Makovsck Clemachuk, PORT's secretary for the Northeast, the state committees of Pernambuco and Paraíba had been reorganized, and the PORT reportedly had some success in attracting members of the air force sergeants' club in Recife.[107] The PORT also met with Brizola and other exiles in Uruguay, and this apparently issued in the formation of a Frente Popular de Libertação in Montevideo in January 1965.[108] It was a tenuous alliance, however, and did not preclude PORT criticism of the PCB and PC do B.[109]

A Stalinist, pro-Chinese position divided the PCB throughout the late fifties and until the PC do B was formed in February 1962. The new party attacked the PCB for its conciliatory attitude toward the government and for abandoning the work of educating the masses in Marxism, suppressing the party press, and allowing its youth and women's affiliates to become inactive. The PC do B managed to remain active after the 1964 coup. In late May 1965 at a Central Committee meeting in the city of São Paulo, one absent member was expelled for "inefficiency," and it was resolved to increase the size of the Central Committee from twelve to twenty members. During June 1966 the PC do B held its Sixth National Conference (to correspond with the Sixth Congress of the PCB) and approved new statutes and a policy resolution calling for "a union of Brazilians to free the nation from the crisis, the dictatorship, and neocolonialist threat." [110] Later the PC do B was implicated in the Uberlandia guerrilla movement (as described above), and was reportedly active also in Goiás under the leadership of Tarzan de Castro, who had once been affiliated with the PCB and, before breaking with Francisco Julião, had headed the training of guerrillas during the early sixties. Castro and Gerson Alves Parreira, (reportedly trained in China), were seized by authorities upon their return to Brazil, but escaped to asylum in the Uruguayan Embassy and were eventually exiled to Uruguay.[111]

In August 1968 the PC do B was bolstered by the support of the Comitê Estudual da Maioria Revolucionária, the dissident majority faction of the PCB Guanabara State Committee. The PC do B, these partisans declared, "is the most coherent, most aware, and most important leftist organization in the country." [112] The Guanabara faction's desertion was prompted by the continued advocacy of revisionism by the Prestes majority in the PCB. Early in 1970 the PC do B attacked this revisionism, linking PCB's tendency to support a military solution in Brazil to that of military regimes in Peru and Bolivia, which had respectively nationalized the holdings of subsidiaries of Standard Oil and Gulf Oil. Also denounced was Fidel Castro's support of the Peruvian regime. The Peruvian solution would be "detrimental to Brazil," declared the PC do B; instead Brazilians must wage "an armed struggle, a people's war," for "the solution lies in revolution, not in reforms." [113]

The Política Operária (POLOP) emerged in February 1961 partly in response to the Cuban Revolution and partly in the hope of coalescing splintered leftist forces in Brazil. Its founders, radical leftists from Rio, São Paulo, and Belo Horizonte, represented the Juventude Socialista of Rio de Janeiro and Salvador as well as segments from São Paulo, the Liga Socialista, and the Marxist wing of the Juventudes Trabalhistas y Socialistas of Minas Gerais. Its ranks included Communist dissidents although it advocated independent Marxism. According to one of its sympathizers, POLOP was a product of "a period of schisms and revolutionary regrouping," and criticized nationalism as "an instrument of control of the Brazilian proletariat." Marxism-Leninism was "its basic instrument of interpretation of the social reality and of the orientation of political struggle." [114] To resolve national issues the POLOP advocated a Frente de Esquerda Revolucionária (FER), "led by the working class and aggregating all exploited classes . . . to eliminate the bourgeois-latifundista domination in Brazil." The POLOP was especially critical of the PCB for its "nationalist and democratic" policy uniting the proletariat and the bourgeoisie in the struggle against latifundism and imperialism; such a policy, said POLOP, subordinated proletarian interests to those of the bourgeoisie.[115]

POLOP survived the 1964 coup, and in July 1967 three members were elected to the ten-man UNE executive committee. At its Fourth National Congress that September, POLOP advocated guerrilla struggle in the interior and proletarian uprisings in the cities.[116] By now, however, internal division had already affected POLOP and later would bring about its demise. In 1967 one of its former Trotskyist leaders, Luís Alberto Moniz Bandeira, pronounced the organization "dead." [117] A year later POLOP factions joined various organizations (see below), and with that it apparently ceased to have an independent existence.[118]

The Ação Popular (AP) was another radical organization active before the military intervention in 1964. Like the POLOP it too was in decline by the late sixties. Organized on May 1, 1962, at a meeting held at the University of Minas Gerais, AP fostered radicalization of Catholic Action organizations such as the Juventude Estudantil Católica (JEC), the Juventude Operária Católica (JOC), and the Juventude Universitária Católica (JUC).[119] AP philosophy was based on the writings of French philosopher Emmanuel Mounier and others, and during the early sixties it appealed to progressive politicians such as Paulo de Tarso. As we have recounted above, from 1962 to 1964 AP maintained a coalition with the PCB to dominate the UNE directorship, but after the 1964 coup and the military repression of the student movement, AP assumed a Christian-Marxist stance in opposition to the PCB. It recovered from the 1964 events by rearranging its leadership. With perhaps from twelve to fifteen hundred members divided into cells of five or less, AP denounced both segments of the Brazilian Communist movement: the PCB, for its popular frontism and non-violent strategy, the PC do B, for its alleged domination by "old" Communists such as Amazonas and Grabois. In 1967 it aligned with POLOP and the Marighella wing of the PCB to control the UNE.

By this time AP had declared itself Marxist [120] and proposed an "action plan" in which the primary "strategic objective" was "the radicalization of the institutional struggle" and "a popular constituency." The Marxist stance obviously alienated non-Marxist elements within its ranks, and, further, led to disintegration of the movement itself. In June 1968 one faction aligned itself with the PCBR and another with the POC, the two groupings lately constituted by PCB dissidents.[121]

The Frente de Libertação Nacional (FLN), the organization of Leonel Brizola discussed earlier in this chapter, proclaimed itself still active in mid-1970, as "a movement which by gathering together people of every political, religious, and philosophical leaning is prepared to orient and lead the armed struggle against the gorilla-militaristic regime, and which, once the latter is overthrown, plans to set up a Revolutionary Popular Government that will finally free the nation from the clutches of American imperialism." The most important element in the FLN was its national liberation army, which commanded "military actions" and also guided "FLN political activity." The organization claimed to have engaged in joint action with other revolutionary groups, such as the ALN, PCBR, and the VPR.[122]

After the military intervention in 1964 and the subsequent repression of the left, the PCB suffered severe factionalization among elements advocating armed struggle as the effective means of combating the dictatorship. Four of these factions became revolutionary movements independent of the PCB, and came to dominate the urban guerrilla warfare launched in major Brazilian cities during the late sixties.

One of the most prominent of these movements was the Ação Libertadora Nacional (ALN), led by Carlos Marighella, whose career and philosophy we have already described. The ALN evolved from the dissident PCB São Paulo State Committee which Marighella had headed despite disagreements with the Prestes-influenced national leadership. That segment of the São Paulo State Committee, which eventually withdrew from the PCB, was known first as the Agrupação Comunista de São Paulo, but by 1969, when it was engaged in bank robberies and the kidnapping of foreign diplomats, it was identifiable as the ALN. Marighella attempted to align his movement with other revolutionary movements, especially those in the VAR-Palmares coalition described below. Under his leadership a loose coalition of such movements apparently grew up, only to disappear after his death early in November 1969. The ALN leadership passed to another former PCB member, Joaquim Câmara Ferreira.[123]

A second major movement clustered around the Vanguarda Armada Revolucionária Palmares (VAR-Palmares), which had formed in July 1969 as a coalition of several currents and stemmed from the Vanguardia Popular Revolucionária (VPR), which had undertaken the assassination during 1968 of an American army captain attached to the U. S. military mission in Brazil. At that time a Brazilian army captain, Carlos Lamarca, organized a cell of the VPR and in January 1969 defected with several comrades and a supply of ammunition.[124] A phase of disorganization ensued during which Lamarca and VPR elements came temporarily under the influence of Marighella and the ALN. A second phase was marked by a congress held in Monguagua (along the southern coast of São Paulo) under the aegis of VPR leader José Raimundo da Costa, to discuss the creation of guerrilla columns as the nucleus of its activities.[125] During a third phase the VAR-Palmares was formally instituted in July 1969 as a coalition of the VPR and the Comando de Libertação Nacional (COLINA), a revolutionary organization based in Minas Gerais. Leadership of the VAR-Palmares was in the hands of Carlos Lamarca, Claudio Souza Ribeiro, and Antônio Roberto Espinosa for the VPR, and Carlos Franklin Paixão de Araújo, Maria de Carmo Brito, and Juárez Guimarães de Brito for COLINA. During the twenty-five-day congress constituting the fourth phase there was a split, and Carlos Lamarca together with six others formed a dissident combination called Racha but later apparently resuming the VPR tag.

Two other groups split from the PCB after 1964. One was the Partido Comunista Brasileiro Revolucionário (PCBR) led by Mário Alves de Souza Vieira, Jacob Gorender, and Apolônio Pinto de Carvalho, all of whom had been expelled from the PCB late in 1967. Its objective was to regroup working-class elements "that have become alienated from the PCB because of their high degree of revolutionary conscience." In disagreement with French Marxist Regis Debray, the PCBR did not "accept the argument that the Communist party will grow out of the guerrilla operations. It does not accept the idea that the party should advocate armed struggle." [126] Even though Manoel Jover Telles, who as we know had also been expelled from the PCB in 1967, helped organize the PCBR and became head of its Guanabara State Committee, upon assuming that post he accused other PCBR leaders of taking a middle position between revisionism and Marxist-Leninism, and defected to the PC do B along with a majority of the Guanabara committee.[127]

The other group was the Partido Operária Comunista (POC), comprised of factions of the POLOP and AP as well as of the Comitê Estadual da Dissidência do Rio Grande do Sul.[128] In an effort to coalesce the leftist groups, the POC had earlier promoted the Frente de Esquerda Revolucionária (FER) which brought together the National Committee of POLOP, the Comitê Estadual da Dissidência do Rio Grande do Sul, the Comitê Municipal (Leninista) do Rio Grande do Sul, and the Comitê Secundarista da Guanabara.[129]

Non-Marxist Competitors

The PCB's interaction with the major Brazilian parties was clearly evident in the period from 1945 to 1964. Until it was legalized, the PCB maneuvered through the UDN during 1945, and thereafter its support of Vargas facilitated alliances with the PTB and the PSD. None of these parties gained a majority in the elections after 1945. The character of each was shaped more by historical, regional, and personality traits than by ideological differences. All were pragmatic in outlook, and lacked tight internal discipline. As a rule they could not claim the adherence of their own leaders, and hard-core memberships hardly existed. In these respects they differed considerably from the highly centralized and disciplined PCB—though of course the cult of personality pervaded the PCB as well as the major parties. While the legendary Prestes was assured leadership and a caudillo-like pre-eminence in the PCB, Jânio Quadros allowed his name to be endorsed by the UDN and João Goulart, a latifundista, headed the PTB ticket to ensure widespread labor support.

Although conservative critics alleged Communist influence in the progressive Catholic movement in Brazil, the Partido Democrata Cristão (PDC), founded in 1948, assumed a generally anti-Communist position to the left of the PTB during the sixties. Its radical position on social and political issues, often inspired by personalities such as Paulo de Tarso, Education Minister under Goulart, received support from professional and intellectual circles as well as from members of the Church-sponsored labor movements. The AP, not formally a part of the PDC, attempted to sway the PDC with its radicalism, such as when it advocated socialist revolution and tolerated alliances with the PCB in the student movement. The AP and other Catholic Action organizations combined with Communist elements to support the Movimento de Cultura Popular, which utilized the teaching methods of a young Catholic radical, Paulo Freire, to educate and politicize illiterate adults.

Although Prestes had aligned himself with the PCB, and his fellow tenentes turned to other organizations, they shared certain nationalist goals. The convergence of the PCB and some military leaders on the matter of the nationalism of the fifties and sixties was cause for dialogue in the radical nationalist and Marxist intellectual journal, *Revista Brasiliense,* owned by Communist Caio Prado Júnior. Prestes took issue with the first number of this journal published in September-October 1955, accusing its editor Elias Chaves Neto (also a Communist, and related to Caio Prado Júnior), of taking a reformist nationalist position. Although critical in his rejoinder to Prestes, Chaves Neto later called for dismissal of court charges against Prestes and other party leaders, and for legalization of the PCB.[130]

The nationalist movement around the *Revista* in São Paulo spoke to the failure of the left to find adequate and satisfactory programs for solving problems of underdevelopment. It was also a sophisticated response to inept and dishonest politicians, structural deficiences in the economy and foreign domination over industry and markets. The Rio nationalist movement, institutionalized into the ISEB, manifested similar responses.

With the unfolding of events in the early sixties, the nationalist movements achieved some visibility. Although they were eliminated by the 1964 coup, they shared demands and ideals with the PCB. No single nationalist ideology emerged, however, and there are many indications that the Rio and São Paulo groups developed weaknesses similar to those of the PCB. Like the PCB, the São Paulo group consisted of Marxists and Leninists, and the Rio group included many former integralista sympathizers as well as progressive Catholics and Marxists. Unlike the PCB in the sixties, the Rio and São Paulo groups were constituted primarily by intellectuals. Like the PCB, the ISEB experienced several ideological crises that resulted in the expulsion or defection of some members; both groups had also to confront ideologies of nationalism and Marxism. Both tended to advocate peaceful, non-revolutionary change; yet both were militantly radical by 1963.[131]

Past and Current Strategy Assessed

If we wish to place the PCB and its competitors in a critical perspective, we must do so within a frame of *effective ideology,* since ideology is a pattern of belief and ideas that purport to explain complex social phenomena and to direct and simplify socio-political choices facing individuals and groups. As we have defined it in another place, effective ideology offers a critique of the existing social, economic, political, and cultural order; provides alternatives and desirable substitutes, if necessary for that order; does not remain isolated from practical life; consists of an abstract set of principles for action and as such promotes volition and motivation to implement and maintain the principles; and is linked to organization; although rather than creating organization, ideology tends to reinforce and broaden the process of organization by clarifying causes and aims.[132]

The personalist nature of Brazilian politics suggests that ideological forces tend not to offer solutions to the existing order. Anarchism, socialism, Marxism, Leninism, Stalinism, even nationalism all were alien in origin and ideals. PCB strategy related closely to that of the international Communist movement. Frequently, too, the beliefs and ideals of the Communist party, like its revolutionary competitors, were so closely tied to the prevailing oligarchs or bourgeois-dominated system that few alternatives were available to confront ever-changing national and international conditions. The inflexibility of the PCB allowed it to be outflanked during the sixties by a more radical student vanguard and by progressive Catholic movements. Indeed, the demands and ideals of many of the small, isolated Marxist revolutionary groups seemed more meaningful to underdeveloped Brazil. Like anarchism and socialism, Communism quickly became irrelevant and divorced from everyday Brazilian life. Although nationalism represented revolutionary potential, it too remained vague in content and undermined by vested interests, and was never fully implemented. The irrelevancy of these revolutionary movements could be laid also to the subservience to some foreign model, the splintering of forces on the left in response to suppression and manipulation by those in power, and to leadership that maintained commitments to class or peer group and ignored the rank and file mass.

Although the PCB and other revolutionary movements professed a doctrine and principles for action, these were useless without power. When the PCB was stripped of its legality, its effectiveness was limited to its desire to participate in electoral, mainstream politics; and consequently it tended to ignore its constituency, especially the urban working class but also the rural proletariat, in which it showed little interest. More radical competitors generally lacked both the charismatic leadership and the mobilizing potential of the PCB. The party and its competitors were largely ineffectual also because of the dominance of personalities who were able to co-opt opposition elements to support the status quo and stability while being unable either to direct or rationalize the course of societal events.[133] Organizationally, the PCB was unique in its discipline and centralization; but without an ideology responsive to the demands of Brazilian society—to human needs in particular—it inevitably declined and lost prestige.

These problems and the persistence of the Prestes leadership in the face of worsening economic conditions and military dictatorship accounted in part for the regroupment of radical forces in the late sixties. Within the suppressed but still vigorous student movement, dissident Communist youth aligned with the POC coalition of revolutionary Marxist organizations and the POLOP to organize the FER. Aligned also to the POC were segments of AP and the PC do B as well as the Partido Comunista Brasileiro Revolucionário and the Marighella group.[134] Although it would be unreasonable to suggest that the POC signified a revolutionary movement of substantial importance, it was apparent that the PCB's conservative response to events placed it out of touch with Brazilian reality. Policies adopted by the PCB at its Sixth Congress not only reaffirmed the traditional adherence to personalist leadership, alliance with the national bourgeoisie, and reluctance to become involved in revolutionary struggle; these policies represented also retrenchment and blind adherence to the Soviet Union. In the Third World of revolutionary ferment the PCB found itself isolated and discredited. Fidel Castro's crushing indictment of the PCB was the last straw; and the party's only consolation was Fidel's simultaneous blast at the Soviet-oriented Communist parties in Bolivia, Guatemala, Venezuela, and elsewhere in Latin America.

7 • Conflict and Integration with the Local Environment

A preliminary and as yet untested assumption is that Communist party politics at the state level differs considerably from that at the national level. As might be expected, however, there is little evidence of any substantial differences in official party policy. State policy seems largely determined by the decision-making of the Central Committee at the national level, which in turn generally has followed the line of the Soviet Communist Party.

A cursory survey of party newspapers published by the national organization in Rio de Janeiro and by the state organization in Pernambuco reveals that during the period February 1959–March 1964 there was close correlation in the manifestation of the PCB position on a variety of issues. During the period fifteen major policy statements were published in the party's national weekly, *Novos Rumos,* and eleven more appeared in *Fôlha do Povo* and its successor, *A Hora,* published weekly in Recife. Curiously, all statements published in Recife were signed by the national Central Committee; eight focused on electoral politics at the national level, two on internal party affairs, and one on the Soviet Communist Party. Fourteen of the policy statements released in Rio emanated from the PCB Central Committee, and only one represented the position of the Pernambuco State Committee.[1] Of these statements, thirteen reflected the party's electoral stance, but only two related to internal party affairs. The strong influence of the national leadership on state party perspectives is evident also in the articles and speeches of Luiz Carlos Prestes carried in the party press. During the same period described above, *Fôlha do Povo* and *A Hora* published thirty-two pronouncements by Prestes, and *Novos Rumos,* forty-six.[2]

While official policy positions appear to differ little from national to state levels of the party, some differences as well as similarities are evident between the two levels. We shall consider these similarities and differences by way of assessing another dimension of party conflict and integration—that of the party with the local milieu. In the process we shall describe ideological differences among six state party organizations, outline the characteristics of PCB state leadership, and look briefly at the evolution, organization, and leadership of the party in Pernambuco.

Ideology: Regional Differentiation

Divisions in the PCB during the sixties tended to reflect dissidence at the state level of Communist organization, especially in São Paulo, Pernambuco, Guanabara, Paraná, Rio Grande do Sul, and Minas Gerais.

Table 7.1

Ideological Dissidence and Organizational Splits of the PCB State Committees

São Paulo	Comitê Estadual Agrupação Comunista do PCB————————→de São Paulo———→ALN————→ Comitê Universitário Paulista Branch of PCBR————————————————→ Paulista Branch of POC————————————————→
Pernambuco	Comitê Municipal do Recife————————→PC do B————→
Guanabara	PC do B——————————————————————→ Comitê Estadual de Maioria Revolucionária Guanabara State Committee PCBR——————————————————————————→ Comitê Secundarista da Guanabara———→POC————————→ Fração Universitária do PCB—→MR-8—→VAR-Palmares —→
Paraná	Ala Tradicional (Pacifista)——————————————→ Ala Renovadora——————————————————→
Rio Grande do Sul	Comitê Estadual da Dissidência do Rio Grande do Sul FER———→POC———→ Comitê Municipal (Leninista) do Rio Grande do Sul
Minas Gerais	MNR VPR Política Operária VAR-Palmares COLINA

(See Table 7.1.) A general perspective on the elements of the state parties opposing the PCB Central Committee's position was set forth in a joint statement during November 1967. Assuming "a revolutionary posture differing from the opportunist orientation of the Central Committee," delegates from seven states and the Federal District advocated a combination of methods—pacifist, armed, legal and illegal combat —as the means to developing their armed struggle. A united political-military command would assume the leadership of "the popular war" in the countryside and of a popular front of "industrial and agricultural workers and peasants, students, and intellectuals, parts of the middle class, progressive religious groups, members of the armed forces." The popular front would be headed by a Marxist-Leninst party based on "a complete return to Marxist-Leninist principles, which were altered or abandoned under the influence of bourgeois ideology." [3]

São Paulo   After the 1964 coup, the Communist national leadership in São Paulo divided into factions advocating and factions opposing the Prestes line that had dominated the party. While Prestes was temporarily deposed as effective party head during late 1964, the faction opposed to him, led by Mário Alves de Souza Vieira, Manoel Jover Telles, Jacob Gorender, and others attempted to modify the party line by calling for violent resistance to the military takeover. The Prestes faction emerged dominant at a May 1965 meeting of the Central Committee, however, but disenchantment with the faction's conciliatory line of a united front resulted in the radicalization of a majority of the São Paulo State Committee.

The São Paulo State Committee soon polarized into three factions. The faction on the right accused the center and the left of "leftist deviations." In a document entitled "Tema" the right faction declared itself in favor of an alliance with the national bourgeoisie and with progressive sectors of the armed forces and the police. This position was attacked by a leftist nucleus known as the Comitê Universitário, which published a counter-declaration entitled "Tema revolucionário." A centrist group was backing Prestes with the tenuous support of the leftist faction led by Carlos Marighella, who by 1966 had begun to make a name for himself.[4] During June 1966 he was elected head of the São Paulo State Committee. In December he resigned from the Executive Commission, and in September 1967 (as we know from earlier chapters) he was expelled from the party, a decision ratified three months later at the party's Sixth Congress.

The dissent leading to Marighella's ouster probably originated with elements in the São Paulo State Committee that were restive well before the 1964 coup, as is evident from the notebooks kept by Prestes from 1961 to 1964. In these notebooks he is critical of São Paulo leaders. Thus Francisco Luciano Lepera, a candidate for the São Paulo State Committee, was described as "an anarchist, undisciplined, and lacking interest in the party." [5] Prestes carefully recorded impressions by other party leaders as well. Peasant leader Moises Vinhas, for example, described the Executive Commission of the São Paulo State Committee as "weak" and "lacking organization," and as for Joaquim Câmara Ferreira, he was "inept in handling propaganda." [6] Labor leader Ramiro Luchesi stated that the weaknesses of the party in São Paulo had "national repercussions." As he admitted, "Our weaknesses are the result of our failure to assimilate the [policy] line and our ignorance of the realities in São Paulo." [7] Arlindo Alves Lucena, a member of the São Paulo Executive Committee, described the committee as "not functioning collectively." [8] Finally, Prestes noted the position of Marighella, who condemned the party leadership for maintaining "the cult of personality," and called for an immediate change in "the methods of leadership." [9]

Marighella's split with the national leadership was significant, for he was able to aggregate a majority of the São Paulo State Committee into the Agrupação Comunista de São Paulo and later into the Ação Libertadora Nacional (ALN). During 1969 Marighella was apparently unsuccessful in forming on a national level a united front of radical groups, including the Vanguarda Armada Revolucionária-Palmares (VAR-Palmares) discussed in the previous chapter.[10] Meanwhile, dissident elements of the PCB formed Paulista branches of the Partido Comunista Brasileiro Revolucionário (PCBR) and the Partido Operário Comunista (POC). Most members of the National Committee of Política Operária withdrew to join the POC and VAR-Palmares.

Several ideological differences separated the São Paulo dissidents from the PCB, one being their insistence on fighting "against the ideological influence of the bourgeoisie in the party and against the submission of the proletariat to bourgeois leadership." Another was their resistance to the PCB's advocacy of reforming society through peaceful means: "To uphold the possibility of the peaceful method today is to lie to oneself, to deceive the militants, and to create illusions among the masses—illusions that blunt their awareness and objectively help reaction and the ruling classes." Finally, the dissidents attacked the national party leadership for distributing "material through abnormal channels," dividing "the union movement," and pitting "the rank and file and the militants against the municipal and state [party] leadership." No steps were taken at headquarters to correct these tendencies "because it is in the interests of the Central Committee to create difficulties for our work and divide the party in São Paulo." [11]

Pernambuco   Division in the Pernambuco state party coincided with the formation of the PC do B in 1962, when Clóvis Melo and other Recife party leaders withdrew from the PCB. Assessing developments in Pernambuco, Mário Alves de Souza Vieira observed that "the situation of the party and of the mass movement was very weak." Again, "The party press was not functioning nor was the party active." Furthermore, "In the countryside nothing happens," he exclaimed; "the party was disorganized and unprepared to deal with events." [12] State party leader David Capistrano da Costa confirmed that the PCB Municipal Committee had split. Condemning the Municipal Committee for its "sectarian position" against then governor Miguel Arraes de Alencar, Capistrano took the part of the governor.[13] It was also Capistrano who blamed the party's national leadership for the setback resulting from the 1964 coup. If the leadership had not been guilty of opportunism and a lack of revolutionary vigilance, he argued, it would have been easy to mobilize workers and peasants to fight in behalf of Goulart and Arraes.[14]

Guanabara   During the early sixties, a number of Guanabara leaders had formed the PC do B after losing their positions on the Central Committee. As detailed above, in August 1968 the PC do B was strengthened by the support of Comitê Estadual da Maioria Revolucionária, the dissident majority faction of the PCB Guanabara State Committee opposed to the revisionism of the Prestes-dominated national leadership. Other dissidence within the Guanabara state leadership had culminated in the establishment of the PCBR by Alves do Souza Vieira, Gorender, Pinto de Carvalho, and Jover Telles after their expulsion from the PCB late in 1967. Jover Telles became head of the PCBR's Guanabara State Committee, but soon after assuming that post, he defected to the PC do B with a majority of the Guanabara committee. At about the same time the POC was organized and took in Communist dissidents who had formed the Comitê Secundarista da Guanabara. Also in Guanabara, the Fração Universitária do PCB evolved into the Movimento Revolucionário 8 de Outubro (MR-8), which in 1968 was closely affiliated with the Vanguarda Popular Revolucionário (VPR) and later with the VAR-Palmares.[15]

Paraná   After the 1964 coup, party leaders in Paraná drifted into two positions, one known as the Ala Tradicional or pacifist line, and the other, as the Ala Renovadora or renovating line. The views of the latter were to prevail, first at a conference in early 1967 of the Municipal Committee of Curitiba, which favored "armed struggle" as "the principal struggle in order to take power."[16] In the same year, the renovating wing of the party also dominated a state conference at which a resolution advocating a line of violent action was approved and the theses of the PCB Sixth Congress were rejected.[17]

Rio Grande do Sul   In the southern extreme of Brazil as well, party unity was undermined by divisive tendencies. After his expulsion from the party early in 1962, João Amazonas apparently continued to wield influence among "leftist" members of the regional party, and this at the same time that national party leaders were fearful that armed violence would sweep the countryside.[18] Differences among members of the regional party executive committee also were in evidence.[19] After the military takeover in 1964, the Comitê Regional do Rio Grande do Sul began cautiously to advocate revolutionary armed combat as "one form of mass struggle." In a policy resolution of March 1965, the regional committee proclaimed that such a strategy necessitated "the support of the masses," and that, further, "armed self-defense constituted one way to prepare for armed struggle."[20] By 1968 several factions had split the party ranks. Elements of the Comitê Estadual da Dissidência do Rio Grande do Sul joined with the Comitê Municipal (Leninista) do Rio Grande do Sul in the coalition Frente de Esquerda Revolucionária (FER), which almost immediately became the POC.[21]

Minas Gerais   Independently of the PCB several revolutionary groups emerged in Minas and soon linked up with dissident Communists elsewhere. These groups included the Movimento Nacionalista Revolucionário (MNR), which had been formed by nationalist military men with links to Leonel Brizola (brother-in-law of former President Goulart), and which had organized the abortive Caparaó guerrilla movement. As we read in the previous chapter, some members of the MNR joined dissidents of the PCB and Política Operária in establishing the Vanguarda Popular Revolucionário, and in July 1969 the VPR aligned with the Comando de Libertação Nacional (COLINA) in support of the VAR-Palmares.[22]

State Leadership Characteristics

We have synthesized biographical data on forty-nine members of PCB state committees during the period 1945–70. Our selection of these state leaders has not been systematic or comprehensive but dependent on available information.[23] In our sample forty-six persons were men, only three were women. As for geographical distribution, twenty-six were members of the São Paulo State Committee and fourteen, of the

Table 7.2

**Major Occupation and Class Stratification
Communist Leaders of State Committees
(1945–1970)**

Occupation	Number of Leaders	Class % of Total
Traditional Upper Class		
Medical Doctor	3	
Lawyer	3	14.3
Architect, Engineer	1	
Middle Class		
Military	2	
Merchant	1	
Civic Servant	0	
Bank Clerk	2	32.7
Journalist	8	
Teacher	2	
Pharmacist	1	
Working Class	23	46.9
Not Identified or No Occupation	3	6.1
Total	49	100.0

Sources: Gastão Pereira da Silva, *Constituintes de 46: dados biográficas,* Rio de Janeiro: Editôra Spinoza, 1947; Alvaro Gonçalves da Costa Lima *et al., Aspectos da atividade do comunismo em Pernambuco,* Recife: Secretaria da Segurança Pública, Delegacia Auxiliar, 1958; and São Paulo State, Secretaria de Segurança Pública, Departamento de Ordem Política e Social, *Relatório: inquérito instaurado contra Luiz Carlos Prestes e outros por ocasião da revolução de Março de 1964,* São Paulo: Serviço-Gráfico de Segurança Pública, 1964.

Pernambuco State Committee; the remainder were from state committees in Rio Grande do Sul (four), Minas Gerais (two), Guanabara (one), Paraná (one), and Rio de Janeiro (one). Their birth places, however, were scattered among fifteen states, only fifteen state leaders being from São Paulo. Eighteen leaders were from the states of the Northeast, eleven from Pernambuco. In general, age differentiations in the sample were dissimilar from those earlier identified for the national leadership. Only 18 per cent were over fifty years of age; 41 per cent were between forty and fifty; 14 per cent were in their thirties, and another 14 per cent in their twenties.[24]

Identification of the chief occupation of each leader in our sample also gives us a rough estimate of their social-class identification, as noted in Table 7.2. Thus, nearly half the state leaders were from the working class—considerably more than in the sample of national leadership in Table 5.3. About a third of the state leaders were middle-class—less than the nearly 40 per cent of our national sample. Among the state leaders whose father's occupation was identifiable, more than half had fathers of peasant or working-class background.

Class orientations may be partially attributed to levels of education attained in the Brazilian school system. About 41 per cent of the state Communist leaders had attended elementary school, 29 per cent had reached secondary school, 4 per cent military school, and 14 per cent the university.

From biographical information available, we could adduce the reasons that about a third of the state leaders in our sample had become Communists. Eight leaders joined the party through association with interest- or issue-oriented groups whose causes were supported by the PCB. Five were recruited by friends or other party members. It was possible also to identify the years in which about two-thirds of the state leaders entered the party ranks: two during the 1922–29 period; six during 1930–35; one during 1936–44; eight during 1945–47; ten during 1948–55; and four thereafter. This data closely parallels that for the national leadership sample, as is evident in Table 7.3.

Within the party about 40 per cent of the state leaders were engaged in activities in the labor and peasant sectors. Another 20 per cent of the leaders devoted their efforts largely to administrative affairs of the party, and 15 per cent worked in student, women, or other non-labor organizations affiliated with the party. Fifteen per cent spent most of their time representing the party as public officials (elected or appointed), and about 10 per cent, in relations with socialist countries.

As might be concluded from the above data, outside the party more than half the state leaders were active in labor and peasant affairs, another third in promoting the party image through the press or other communication media. Two state leaders had participated in the 1924 movement, eight, in the ANL during 1935. Nearly all the state leaders indicated involvement in nationalist causes, and three-fifths of them had participated in such international causes as peace and defense of Cuba and other socialist nations. More than half the leaders had been active in labor strikes, another 15 per cent, in student demonstrations. Many of the leaders had suffered for their party affiliation or activities: four

Table 7.3

Communist State and National Leadership
Period in Which Party Was Joined (percentage)

Period	State Leaders (N = 49)	National Leaders (N = 74)
1922–29	4	4
1930–35	16	12
1936–44	6	2
1945–47	15	16
1948–55	16	21
1956–64	8	8
Not Identified	35	37
Total	100%	100%

Source: See references cited in Table 7.2.

leaders had been imprisoned once, fifteen, from two to five times, and four, more than five times.

Two Personalities

Two Communists whose activities have been conspicuous at the regional level may be isolated from our sample. Both men were born in the Northeast. Both used weapons in the revolt of 1935. Both became national party leaders. Both were arrested after the 1964 coup, held in prison, and tortured. Both wrote autobiographical accounts and a denunciation of the military regimes in power throughout the sixties. It is from these accounts that the following details of their years as Communist militants are reproduced.[25]

Agilberto Vieira de Azevedo. Born October 19, 1906, son of lower middle-class owners of a small sugar plantation in the city of Rosário, state of Sergipe. His early education and political socialization took place within "a traditional Catholic family" in which his father, an "authentic liberal," exposed him to such Brazilian writers as Machado de Assis and Tobias Barreto. From elementary school he entered a military school, where he came into contact "with socialist ideas." His "awakening" occurred with the realization that he was the "grandson of slave owners" and part of a "paternalistic" system in which economic and social privileges prevailed. He seems to have been profoundly impressed with Brazilian politics, especially with the political maneuvering of presidential aspirants and the military movements of 1922 and 1924. "These events," he recalled, "linked with my first vivid experiences on the plantations of my parents and grandparents."

After finishing his course in military school in 1926, Agilberto matriculated in the Escola Militar do Realengo, and three years later was commissioned a second lieutenent in the aviation corps. Although his political perspectives were sharpened by the Vargas government's repression of workers, he did not participate actively in the 1930 and 1932 revolutions. In 1933 he formally joined the PCB, and figured a year later in "the great struggles of the Brazilian proletariat" and in 1935, in the organization of the ANL. As a result of his part in the revolt of November 1935, he was sentenced to twenty-seven years in prison, and served nine years and five months before his release when an amnesty was decreed in April 1945. He described his imprisonment as "a rich experience," one that strengthened his convictions to carry on with the struggle.

Five years later he was arrested in Recife and sentenced to another four years for engaging in political organization within the armed forces. About 1958 he became active in the PCB state organization in Paraná, where he collaborated on the weekly *Tribuna do Povo* and later on *Novos Rumos* and *Terra Livre*. In 1962 he ran unsuccessfully for state deputy in Paraná. On July 30, 1964, he was arrested in São Paulo and held until September 30, 1966, when released on habeas corpus appeal after twenty-six months' imprisonment without any formal charge. At the time of his release he had become famous not only as a top Communist leader, having served on the Central Committee since at least the mid-1940's, but also as a party activist who had effectively organized at the regional level. He had also spent nearly half his years as a Communist militant in prison—longer than any other party member.

Gregório Lourenço Bezerra. Soon after Agilberto's release, Bezerra established the record for total time that a Communist had been in prison. His parents, unlike Agilberto's, were "impoverished and illiterate peasants." He was born on March 13, 1901, in Panelas de Miranda in the state of Pernambuco. Bezerra's outlook on life was beclouded by several childhood traumas. First, a severe drought in 1905 forced his family from the interior to the coastal zone. Then, two years later his parents were dead, and in 1910 he was taken to Recife as "a domestic slave." In 1922 he entered the army, in which he learned to read, and four years later was promoted to sergeant. At about 1930 he began to be politicized "through the reading of books on socialism and social struggles." As he wrote later, "I found the truth, finally . . . the path which I had been seeking: the path of the liberation of the proletariat and the peasant masses." Soon thereafter he joined the PCB, considering himself "a conscientious and faithful soldier of the working class and the people."

Within the party, Bezerra was in Pernambuco as a leader of the ANL and of the November 1935 revolt, during which he was "gravely wounded, imprisoned, and brutally beaten and tortured by the political police," and then sentenced to twenty-seven and one-half years in prison. While in prison he was deeply affected by the death of his brother, a labor leader who had been tortured and beaten by police over a fourteen-day period. After his release in May, 1945 (one month after Agilberto), he returned to Recife and helped reorganize the PCB State Committee, of which he was an activist. In December 1945 he was elected federal deputy from Pernambuco, receiving more votes than any candidate from Recife. As a member of the Constituent Assembly he gave a number of speeches (twenty-two in all) to call attention to the voting rights of illiterates and the military and to the problems of the young workers of the Northeast. In 1948 he was seized by police in Rio de Janeiro and held incommunicado for ninety-one days before being acquitted.

The next nine years he spent hiding from police, but in addition speaking about agrarian reform and organizing peasants into leagues and unions, especially in Paraná and Goiás. Following his brief imprisonment in the interior of Pernambuco during 1957, he supported populist campaigns to elect Pelópidas Silveira and Miguel Arraes de Alencar successive mayors of Recife during the late fifties, and Arraes governor of the state in 1962. During the 1960's he was active chiefly in the unions of rural workers, especially in the municipality of Palmares. It was in Palmares that he was arrested after the military intervention in 1964, and he was held in prison until exchanged in late 1969 for U.S. Ambassador C. Burke Elbrick, who had been kidnapped by armed revolutionaries led by Carlos Marighella. Bezerra was flown to Mexico, and from there he moved to Cuba.

The Pernambuco State Party: A Case Study

The state of Pernambuco is a section of Northeast Brazil, an area in which "for centuries both man and earth have been martyred by adverse forces—natural and cultural," in the words of Josué de Castro, noted Brazilian diplomat and nutrition expert.[26] Like other states in the Northeast, Pernambuco is divided into an eastern coastal area, where sugar plantations are located, and a drought region of the hinterland or *sertão*. These two regions are climatically quite unlike. The green, fertile coastal strip is ideal for growing sugar cane, whereas in the gray semi-arid interior the soil is poor and baked hard by the sun. Whether stricken by drought or by the degrading effects of plantation monoculture, the people of these regions have suffered relentlessly. De Castro has characterized the Northeast as beset with "the cruel geography of hunger, a strange geography where the earth does not feed man so much as man the earth." [27]

It is in such a setting that popular-based tensions and pressures for change develop. This explains in part the success of the defrocked Padre Cícero, who mobilized the inhabitants of Juàzeiro do Norte to overthrow the Ceará state oligarchy and to defy federal troops sent to dislodge him, during the early twentieth century; not to mention the masses' respect, still prevailing today, for "social bandits" such as Antônio Silvino and Lampião as well as for the Marxist lawyer-politician, Francisco Julião, whose first peasant league was founded on the Galiléia sugar plantation in the transitional *agreste* zone near Vitória de Santo Antão. The thread of popular resistance and rebellion running through the history of the Northeast and especially of Pernambuco, also may have motivated Communist leaders to plan their 1935 revolt to start in that section of Brazil.

Evolution of the Pernambuco Party

Before 1935 the PCB elements in Pernambuco had concentrated on organizing the urban centers, and particularly Recife, where they were able to reach segments of the labor movement as well as the intelligentsia.

The party exercised some influence in the military, to conclude from the leadership of the November uprising in Recife late in November 1935. It was during that year that the party daily, *Fôlha do Povo,* was published.[28] While officially the paper focused on the activities of the Aliança Nacional Libertador, its broad appeal was "for workers of all professions, merchants, proprietors and moderate industrialists, students and soldiers, for all who suffer from the oppression of low salaries, from high taxes, and from a difficult life." [29] Featured were the activities of Prestes, the ANL, the party and its youth and women's affiliates, and organized labor in the struggle against "imperialism" and "fascism," in particular, labor disputes such as that involving the Great Western Railway in October and November.[30] Occasional articles recalled the black resistance movements of the past as well as the social banditry still very much in evidence during 1935.[31]

During the October municipal elections in Recife, the state PCB supported fifteen candidates, among whom a local party leader, Cristiano Cordeiro, was elected with the largest vote.[32] The collapse of Recife's November uprising, led by Gregório Bezerra and others, was ensured by mass arrests of the local party leadership and the imprisonment of many Communists. There was also a police raid on PCB headquarters in December 1941. These developments left the party in a weakened condition and unable to mobilize support for popular causes.[33]

After 1945 the party in Pernambuco demonstrated considerable success in local and state elections. Three Communists were elected federal deputies in December 1945 (see Appendix A). In January 1947 nine party candidates won seats in the State Assembly, and in the Recife municipal elections during the same year thirteen of the twenty-five council seats went to Communists; a party candidate was elected mayor of the nearby municipality of Jaboatão. Among all parties contesting these elections from 1945 to 1947, the PCB consistently ranked third behind the PSD and UDN. In fact PCB voting strength increased by 1,128 votes during the period.[34]

Although after 1947 the PCB was banned and its members deprived of their elected offices, the party was able to run candidates under other party names, capturing two and three state deputy seats respectively in 1950 and 1954 and two municipal council seats each in the 1951 and 1955 elections in Recife. The party also supported a popular leftist, Pelópidas Silveira, in his (successful) campaign in the 1955 election for mayor of Recife.[35]

A Conferência Regional do Partido Comunista Pró-IV Congresso in July 1954 signified the Pernambuco party's affirmation of the program of the PCB Fourth Congress. The July congress attacked the proposition that urban workers unite with rural workers in an "army of national liberation," resolving rather to intensify party efforts to organize rural workers. Partly as a consequence of this activity, Pernambuco police raided party headquarters on January 6, 1956, confiscating documents and records, and four months later claimed to have destroyed the party organization throughout Pernambuco. The police alleged also that ties between the national and state leadership were broken as a result, thereby "leaving local Communists to direct their own destiny." [36]

The Pernambuco party remained active, however, and following the line of the Central Committee, it joined with PCB supporters and sympathizers in the denunciation of U.S. military bases on Brazilian territory and in the campaign to preserve national petroleum interests. In about 1957 a nationalist movement in Pernambuco began to take shape with PCB endorsement. It was this movement that had successfully backed the Marxist Pelópidas Silveira as mayor of Recife in 1955 and as vice governor of Pernambuco in 1958.[37] The momentum of the movement also aided in the election of Miguel Arraes as mayor of Recife in 1959 and as governor in 1962.[38] While neither Silveira nor Arraes was a member of the PCB, both cooperated with the party. As mayor, Arraes included many leftists in his cabinet, though only two were Communist militants—Hiram de Lima Pereira, an old party member, and Rildo Souto Maior, who was later expelled from the party.[39] As governor Arraes developed a leftist-oriented administration that tolerated Communist activity but excluded the party from leadership roles. The Central Committee dispatched Diógenes de Arruda Câmara, former party leader and still a Stalinist, to Recife, where he condemned Arraes' policy of "reconciliation" with democratic forces.[40] The party's reprobation of Francisco Julião, leader of the Ligas Camponesas, however, paralleled that of the Arraes government.[41] This dissidence among the leftist forces in Pernambuco prevailed until the military intervention in 1964.

Organization

Party organization at the state level is similar to the national structure, as might be expected. Subordinate to but dominant over state party affairs is the Comitê Estadual de Pernambuco (sometimes called the Comitê Regional), and under that are ten commissions: for organization, finances, labor, solidarity, agitation and propaganda, rural affairs, masses, education, sugar mills, and women. Directly tied to the Comitê Estadual are six Comitês de Zona (Zone committees) representing Recife, the coastal area or *mata,* the transitional *agreste* area, Garanhuns, the North, and the hinterland (*sertão*). Attached to each zone committee are committees for districts, base organizations, and sections. Also affiliated with the Comitê Estadual are the Fração Parlamentar, active when the state assembly is in session, the União da Juventude Comunista, and the Federação das Mulheres de Pernambuco, as well as a number of front organizations.[42]

The Pernambuco Leadership

In correlating the socio-economic data of fourteen party leaders from the autobiographical material seized in the 1956 police raid, we find that among those whose backgrounds were identifiable, four were from peasant families, one from the working class, and five from the middle class. The educational average was low, one of the leaders having had no formal schooling, four attending secondary school, and only one going beyond that to university. Most of the leaders were initiated to the party through the reading of Marx, but three became involved first as sympathizers and later as members through personal contacts with party militants.[43] Excerpts from biographical accounts of two leading figures reproduced below indicate the differences in class origins and educational background.

Adalgilsa Cavalcanti was born July 28, 1907, the daughter of a small farmer in the interior of Pernambuco, and obtained only an elementary education. She was elected an alternate federal deputy from Pernambuco in 1945 and a state deputy in 1947. She modestly described her role in the party:

> In 1945 I joined the party, affiliating myself with the 13 of May Cell. A few days later I became a member of the State Committee. Of all the struggles in which I have participated, I found that sometimes I did not know how to lead the masses. . . . I was imprisoned nine times, tortured once. . . . Because of my lack of political experience, my abilities do not correspond to the confidence which the party holds for me. For this reason, I have attempted to raise my political and ideological level. . . . (Recife, June 1954)[44]

Paulo de Figueiredo Cavalcanti, the son of a state bureaucrat and a descendant of the sugar aristocracy of Cabo, was born in a Recife suburb on May 25, 1915. After receiving a law degree from the Faculty of Law in Recife, he served in several governmental capacities, and

Table 7.4

The PCB Organization in Pernambuco

	Comitê Regional or Comitê Estadual de Pernambuco	Fração Parlamentar	Frente de
UJC		Associação de Bairro	Auxílio
	Comissões (Organização, Finanças, Sindical Solidariedade, Feminina)	Comissões (Campos, Agitaçã e Propaganda, Masa Educação, Usinas)	(Front Organizations)

Comitê Zonal
de Recife

Comitês Distritais

Organizações
de Base

Comitê de Zona Mata Agreste Garanhuns	Comitê de Zona Sertão Norte

Source: Alvaro Gonçalves Costa Lima *et al., Aspectos da atividade do comunismo em Pernambuco,* Recife: Secretaria de Segurança Pública, Delegacia Auxiliar, 1958, pp. 21–24.

in 1947 was elected a first alternate state deputy. He was a distinguished writer and journalist.

> I was a sympathizer from 1943 until November 1949 when I requested membership in the party (at the time I was a deputy, having taken office in August 1948). During 1933 and 1934 I was a member of Ação Integralista Brasileira. . . . Later I became a materialist, an about-face, since earier I had been a fervent Catholic. . . . In 1950 I was elected (deputy), receiving the most votes of any candidate in the capital and third in the state. My parliamentary activity is defective, the result of

a lack of political experience and of a serious and criminal underestimation of the parliamentary front . . . what characterizes my work in the party is the illusion of class, the petty bourgeois tendency of collaboration. . . . I would like to be active in intellectual life and in the press. But I have noted that in Pernambuco the party does not understand the significance of an intellectual front. . . . My wife has been active in the party since 1953.[45]

The contrast between leaders in Pernambuco and leaders in São Paulo is evident in Tables 7.5, 7.6, and 7.7. While there appears to be a similar pattern of class affiliation for the two leadership groups, edu-

Table 7.5

Class Stratification of State Leaders
Pernambuco (1956) and São Paulo (1961–64)
(percentage)

	Pernambuco State Leaders (N = 14)	São Paulo State Leaders (N = 25)
Traditional Upper Class	14	22
Middle Class	29	26
Lower Class	57	52
Total	100%	100%

Source: See references cited in Table 7.2.

Table 7.6

Education of State Leaders
Pernambuco (1956) and São Paulo (1961–64)
(percentage)

	Pernambuco (N = 14)	São Paulo (N = 25)
Elementary	50	35
Secondary	43	35
University	7	30
Total	100%	100%

Source: See references cited in Table 7.2.

cational levels differ substantially. Thus only one Pernambuco leader
reached the university, as compared with nearly a third of São Paulo
leaders. Curiously, however, participation patterns as recorded in Table
7.7 for the two groups are somewhat similar. Roughly the same percentage of leaders from both state contingents were active in the military,
labor and peasantry, and parliamentary affairs. A higher level of education among the São Paulo leaders may account in part for their involvement in foreign affairs, specifically with socialist nations.

Table 7.7

Party Participation of State Leaders
Pernambuco (1956) and São Paulo (1961–64)
(percentage)

Sector in Which Active	Pernambuco (N = 14)	São Paulo (N = 25)
Military	3	2
Labor and Peasantry	28	25
Student Movement	10	4
Parliamentary	28	28
Press and Propaganda	24	14
Foreign Relations with Socialist Countries	7	25
Not identified		2
Total	100%	100%

Source: See references cited in Table 7.2.

In summary, our profile of Pernambuco supports the contention that
local conditions and events tend to shape and influence Communist
activity and behavior, thereby lending credence to the assumption stated
at the outset of this chapter that party politics may indeed differ from
national to state levels. While conditions may sometimes occasion the
integration of the state party apparatus with the local milieu, such integration has rarely affected the state party's relations with the national
organization. Throughout much of its history the state party has been
rejected by the local polity as an illegitimate entity; and at times (as in
Pernambuco) the resultant conflict has isolated state leadership from
national leadership. While isolation may signify autonomy for the state
leadership, a more common pattern in times of party crisis and repres-

sion has been the concerted effort of state and national leadership to find
unity through adherence to national and international Communist policy
and decision-making. In turn, this integrative effort has been accompanied by a purging or withdrawal of dissident factions opposed to the
dominant national and international Communist leadership.

8 • Conflict and Integration with the Cross-National Environment

Our concern in this chapter is to trace the interrelations between the PCB and the outside world, in particular with the ruling and non-ruling Communist parties. First, we shall look briefly at the party's relations with the ruling Communist parties, then at the impact of those parties upon Brazilian Communism in the areas of policy, leadership, and ideology. We hope to assess also the PCB's perceived position in the world Communist system, its attempts to influence the ruling parties, and its attitudes toward the Sino-Soviet dispute, the Cuban Revolution, and the other Communist parties in Latin America.

Relations with the Ruling Parties, Past and Present

One American historian has observed that "the parties in Latin America have always conformed to current Soviet foreign policies, and those occasional conflicts between Soviet and Latin American party interests have invariably been resolved in favor of the Soviet Union." [1] From a slightly different perspective a leftist Brazilian social scientist agrees: "The PCB never became an organization capable of elaborating a Marxist vision of Brazilian reality," he states. "Instead it has relied heavily upon Soviet documents." [2]

To review the history of this relation . . . In about 1921, militant revolutionaries led by Astrojildo Pereira began to divert their attention from anarchism to the establishment of a party in accordance with the principles of the Third International. Probably during that same year the South American Secretariat of the Comintern contacted the União

Maximalista of Pôrto Alegre and the Grupo Comunista of Rio. Because of its proximity to Montevideo the União Maximalista maintained close ties with the Communist movement in Uruguay, and the União's leader, Abílio de Nequete, probably represented the Secretariat at the Third Congress of the Comintern held in Moscow from June 22 to July 12 of 1921.[3] Late in the year the English Communist agent Ramison contacted Pereira and others in Rio.[4] These early overtures led to the formation of the PCB in March 1922. Representatives at the party's founding congress discussed and approved the twenty-one principles of the Comintern.[5]

Once set in motion, the PCB was represented at every Comintern congress. Thus Antônio Bernardo Canellas, a printer originally in the anarchist movement, represented the PCB at the Fourth Congress of the Comintern in Petrograd and Moscow during November and December 1922. Since, however, Canellas, appeared too anarchistic in tone to leaders in Moscow, the Comintern withheld its recognition of the PCB, stating that the party "conserved traces of bourgeois ideology, sustained by the presence of Masonry and influenced by anarchist preconceptions." [6] At its Fifth Congress, in Moscow from June 17 to July 8, 1924, the Comintern recognized the PCB. The Brazilian party was represented by Astrojildo Pereira, and Leôncio Basbaum served as a delegate to the youth branch of the Comintern.[7] Brazilian delegates to the Comintern's Sixth Congress, in Moscow from July 17 to September 1, 1928, were Fernando Lacerda, Heitor Ferreira Lima, and Basbaum. Lacerda was elected to the Executive Committee of the Comintern to represent the South American parties.[8] During his years in the Soviet Union and before formally joining the PCB, Prestes became a member of the Executive Committee of the Comintern. The Comintern's Seventh Congress (Moscow, July 25 to August 21, 1935) was attended by Lacerda and other Brazilian delegates.

In accordance with the popular-front policy of the Seventh Congress, many of the international Communist organizations were dissolved in order to ensure harmony with socialist and reformist groups with whom collaboration might be possible. In the light of the failure of the 1935 revolt in Brazil, dissolution of the Comintern was discussed at a conference of Latin American Communist parties in Moscow during 1938. For several years thereafter there were no large international meetings to attract Latin delegates to the Soviet Union, so that direct contact between their parties and the Kremlin was maintained through visits of individual Communists to Moscow. During World War II these communications were disrupted, and in May 1943 the Comintern was dissolved. Nevertheless the Latin American parties, including the PCB, maintained their loyalty to the Soviet Union. Besides their traditional ties, the climate was favorable for expansion of diplomatic relations between the Soviet Union and the Latin American republics, and between 1942 and 1945 thirteen Latin American countries established relations or formally recognized the Soviet government. In April of 1945 Brazil recognized the Soviet Union and the nations exchanged ambassadors, but relations were severed in October of 1947.

After the war the Soviet Union, while continuing to assert its leadership over the international movement, pretended to preserve the appearance of autonomy among the Latin American and other Communist parties. Soviet attempts to guide the parties were less direct than under the Comintern but nonetheless effective. A new network of front organizations was developed in order to coordinate labor, women, and youth. In September 1947 a new international party agency called the Communist Information Bureau (Cominform) was created, and a journal entitled *For a Lasting Peace, For a People's Democracy!* was made available to the parties in the local language. Through this journal were disseminated the orthodox Soviet interpretations of international developments. With the opening of the Cold War in 1947, anti-Communist policies were adopted by the Latin American governments, often to win support from the United States; and consequently all but three (Argentina, Mexico, and Uruguay) of the fifteen nations that had recognized the Soviet Union broke relations.

Despite the cooling in diplomatic relations, the PCB maintained close ties with Moscow. Then in the last years of the Stalin era the Soviet Union increased its direct contacts with the Latin American Communist parties, and after 1952 Brazilian and other Latin American delegations traveled to the Soviet Union frequently and in larger numbers than ever before, to attend the Soviet party congresses. Some twelve Latin American parties sent delegates to the Soviet party's Nineteenth Congress in 1952, and were counseled there to capture the leadership of national liberation movements and to denounce reactionary imperialist regimes. Representatives of eighteen Latin American parties, including the PCB, attended the Twentieth Congress in 1956, to be exposed to the anti-Stalinist attacks on the "cult of personality" and advised to follow the new doctrine of "peaceful coexistence." Along

Table 8.1
Policy Impact of International Communism on the PCB

Event	International Communist Policy	PCB Policy	Policies Compared
Second Congress, Comintern, 1920	21 conditions for membership	Acceptance at founding Congress, 1922	Comintern provisionally accepts PCB only as "sympathizing party," Fourth Congress, December 1922
Founding of PCB, 1922	South American Secretariat influenced by Argentine party	Party statutes based on Argentine Communist party	Same
Fifth Congress, Comintern, 1924	Reorganization of parties on cell basis	Second Congress adopts policy, 1925	Same
Fifteenth Congress of Soviet party	Trotskyist oppositionists expelled; Trotsky exiled, 1929	PCB Trotskyists withdraw before and after party's Third Congress, 1928–29	Same
Sixth Congress, Comintern	"Third Period" hostility to democratic and reformist elements	Expulsion of Oposição Sindicalista, at party Third Congress, 1928–29	Same
Montevideo meeting of South American Secretariat, 1930	"Third Period" hostility	Denounced 1930 Revolution	Same

Event	International Communist Policy	PCB Policy	Policies Compared
Seventh Congress, Comintern, 1935	Popular Front	First National Conference, 1934, adoption of popular front. Party forms ANL, 1935	Same, although PCB policy predates that of Comintern
November 1935 revolts	Comintern agents assist in planning revolts	Prestes and party leaders participate in planning revolts	Same, although rising was probably touched off by police, not PCB
1937 Electoral Campaign	Nationalist front and support of Américo candidacy	Américo faction vs. Prestes faction	Prestes faction victorious
Second National Conference of the PCB, 1943	National unity and anti-fascism	National unity and anti-fascism Same "Independent line" but support for USSR	Same
Cominform established, 1947. PCB outlawed	Aggressively anti-imperialist, anti-Western	Increasingly anti-imperialist; unconditional adherence to USSR	Same
Korean War 1950–53	Favor Stockholm peace appeal, anti-germ warfare campaign, and other peace measures	"New line" favoring national front, nationalism, and party legality, but adherence to international campaigns, August 1950 and thereafter	Same, with attention to both national and international issues

Event	International Communist Policy	PCB Policy	Policies Compared
Nineteenth Congress of Soviet party, 1952	Seek leadership of national liberation movements; anti-imperialism	Seek democratic government of national liberation; fight "U.S. imperialism." Adopted at Fourth Congress of PCB, 1954	Same
Twentieth Congress of Soviet Party, 1956	Anti-Stalinist campaign against "cult of personality" and for "peaceful coexistence"	Open debate, October 1956 to April 1957; coexistence adopted in March, 1958	Same
Twenty-First Congress of Soviet Party, 1959	Peaceful coexistence reaffirmed	Stalinists defeated at PCB Fifth Congress, 1960: statutes and program modified to seek legal status, 1961	Same
Twenty-Second Congress of Soviet party, 1962, and Twenty-Third Congress, 1966	Peaceful coexistence reaffirmed	Promotes nationalist and democratic government	Same
Sino-Soviet conflict; Cuban Revolution; and establishment of Tricontinental	Armed struggle advocated	Condemns OLAS and China in defense of USSR at Sixth Congress, 1967	Same, but opposed to revolutionary tendencies

with other Latin American parties, the PCB sent a delegation to the ceremonies commemorating the fortieth anniversary of the Russian Revolution, and on this occasion they were directed to emphasize nationalism and to encourage non-Communists to lead the national liberation movement. Latin American delegates at the Twenty-First Congress in 1959 were instructed to convoke their own party congresses more frequently. In August 1960 the PCB sent a delegation to the Eighth Congress of the Cuban party, and in November joined with delegations from all other Latin American republics at a Moscow meeting of parties. The PCB sent delegates also to the Twenty-Second Congress in 1962, a year after the Brazilian government had re-established diplomatic relations (which remained in effect throughout the sixties) with the Soviet Union; and a delegation headed by Prestes attended the Twenty-third Congress in 1966.

While, as related earlier in the book, Stalin's death had serious repercussions on the Brazilian party during the fifties, a dissident Chinese position on many international issues led to factionalization, expulsion, and withdrawal during the sixties as well. Although weakened by these controversies, the party leadership under Prestes persisted in its allegiance to Moscow. During 1966 and 1967 the PCB's reluctance to support a policy of armed struggle engendered profound differences with the Cuban regime and the Havana-based Organización Latino-Americana de Solidariedad (OLAS), which considered the party backward and intransigent. As the Soviet hegemony over the international Communist movement was considerably strained by the independent stance of the Chinese, Albanian, Rumanian and other parties in the late sixties, the PCB again rallied behind the Sovet call to convene a world Communist conference. A resolution in support of the conference was approved at the PCB's Sixth Congress in December 1967; and at a consultation of parties in Budapest from February 26 to March 5, 1968, Prestes, representing the PCB, reaffirmed his party's position.[9] And the PCB attended the Moscow conference during June 1969.

Impact of the Ruling Parties on the PCB

Our assessment of the influence on the PCB of the ruling Communist parties—principally that of the Soviet Union—is based upon considerations of policy formation, choice of leadership, and ideological tendencies.

Policy
The impact of the international Communist movement on PCB policies is set forth schematically in Table 8.1, and differences between the

international movement and the Brazilian party during four periods are summarized. Thus, as we read above, the Comintern provisionally acknowledged the PCB only as a "sympathizing" party at the Fourth Congress in late 1922, since the anarchism of its founders appeared entrenched in the new party's idealism. Much later the Comintern favored the majority PCB faction in its support of José Américo de Almeida during the presidential campaign of 1937; but this Soviet-favored wing was challenged by a strong Prestista minority, and this minority won a quick victory—assuring Prestes dominance over the party for a generation thereafter. In a third contretemps, electoral successes during 1945 and 1947 and a commitment to function within the parliamentary order made for the party's noticeable moderation and reluctance to manifest a hard-line Cold War position in the USSR's favor during that period. Despite such differences, the party maintained and even intensified its allegiance to the Soviet position throughout the fifties, nor, as we saw earlier, did the debates on Stalin and the cult of personality deter the party from following the Soviet line in concentrating on national developments and emphasizing nationalist appeals in its propaganda. Compromised by its commitment to mainstream Brazilian politics and to the peaceful-coexistence policy of the Soviet Union, the PCB position was incompatible with the radical approach of the Cuban Revolution and even with the armed-struggle stance of many Marxist but non-Communist national liberation movements during the late sixties, not only in Brazil but elsewhere in Latin America, in Africa, and in Asia.

Not unexpected but vividly revealed in the table is the direct influence exerted by international Communist policy on the Brazilian party throughout more than four decades of existence. The pattern was obviously established by Lenin's twenty-one conditions for membership in the Comintern. The intent then had been to split the socialist parties in Europe, Latin America, and elsewhere, and to bring their left-wing elements under firm international discipline. Accordingly, each party was required to commit itself, in the Lenin document's terms, to "a complete and absolute break with reformism," strict discipline in the "systematic and persistent communistic" struggle for the revolution, and acceptance of the decisions of the International.[10] Although it was not explicitly stated in the conditions, there was in fact considerable flexibility to set positions on national issues, as was attested not only by the Brazilian experience but also by that of Communist parties elsewhere.

The PCB not only approved the twenty-one conditions—thus qualifying for eventual membership in the International—but also adopted, at its founding congress, party statutes modeled on those of the Argentine Communist party. Comintern directives mandated the PCB's reorganization in 1925, its anti-Trotskyist and isolationist postures in 1928 and 1929; and its adoption of popular frontism as a tactic while planning the abortive revolts of November 1935. A response to Soviet pressure was also evident in the party's call for national unity and opposition to facism as early as 1938 and again in 1943, at a national conference in its increasingly anti-"U.S. imperialist" stance after the formation of the Cominform in 1947, and in its support of a national front and opposition to the Korean War after August 1950. Party developments during the fifties likewise resonated with policies promulgated at the Soviet party congresses. Thus, resolutions at the PCB Fourth Congress in 1954 reflected decisions at the Soviet party's Nineteenth Congress in 1952, and, the open debates of 1956 and 1957 followed the anti-Stalinist campaign at the Soviet's Twentieth Congress in 1956. The Soviet policy of peaceful coexistence led to renewed efforts by the PCB leadership to seek legal status, even to the extent of a name change, as well as measures to demonstrate that the party was indeed national rooted.

Leadership

Although it is difficult to document the influence of ruling Communist parties upon the choice of leadership within the PCB, two patterns may be discerned. One is that of direct overtures on the part of Comintern agents to intervene in the selection of leaders. To illustrate, there was the late 1921 meeting between the English agent Ramison and Astrojildo Pereira, who in consequence provided the leadership during the formative years of the PCB, serving as its secretary general until the end of the decade.[11] Second, there was the consultation between Pereira and Prestes in Bolivia during December of 1927. After this initial contact Prestes sought exile in Buenos Aires, where he associated with Argentine Communists such as Rodolfo Ghioldi. From there he went to the USSR and was eventually appointed, as we know, to the Executive Committee of the Comintern.

In April 1935, probably at the Comintern's urging, he returned to Brazil (in the company of four Comintern agents) as a member of the PCB's Political Bureau and Central Committee.[12] Before his departure for Brazil, Prestes may well have been the one who persuaded the Comintern bosses to adopt the popular-front policy at its Seventh Congress. Back in Brazil, Prestes was named honorary president of the ANL alliance. It is not clear (although it is a possibility) that he was responsible for encouraging the Comintern to become involved in the November 1935 revolt; we do know that he participated in preparations for the risings, as did several foreign agents, among them the American Victor Allan Baron, the German Harry Berger, the Argentinian Rodolfo Ghioldi, and the Belgian Léon Jules Vallée.

The second pattern reflects the impact of Soviet and international Communist policies upon leadership allegiance, defection, and expulsion within the PCB. In theory the principles of democratic centralism and collective leadership should facilitate communication between the rank and file and the party officers, as well as ensuring open and free debate at all levels of the party, and the formulation of policy based on the beliefs of the majority of elected officers. In practice, however, under both Stalin and Prestes these principles were inoperative. Decisions were made at the top, and the PCB hierarchy, subdued by international Communist policy-makers, was shaken by dissidence. Thus, the party's own structure in combination with Soviet pressure could dictate both directly and indirectly the choice of top PCB leadership.

Moreover, the dominance of Prestes ensured the allegiance of an inner core of leaders from 1945 until 1956. This allegiance plus bureaucratic discipline were in essence maintained within the party even after the 1956–57 debates. These debates, however, encouraged the defection of individual members and groups opposed to the old PCB order, since that order ultimately refused to alter its intransigent control over decisions and policy. Whence the disruptive tendencies indicated in Table 5.5, which records seven major divisions within the party: in 1924, 1929, 1947, 1952, 1957, 1962, and 1967. In every incident the disagreements flowed either from intransigence in the party leadership or from arbitrary directives from Moscow.

Ideology

In Table 8.2 are enumerated the theses of each of the six congresses of the PCB from the first in the year 1922, as we have them in the documents of the congresses. In the political sphere, as the table shows, four of the congresses emphasized the party statutes, and three were dedicated to the party program. Democratic centralism and adherence to the

Table 8.2

Ideological Formation
Comparison of Theses of Six PCB Congresses

Principles Emphasized	I (1922)	II (1925)	III (1928 -29)	IV (1954)	V (1960)[1]	VI (1967)
Political						
Modify statutes	x	x		x	x	x
Modify program		x		x	x	
Democratic centralism	x	x	x	x	x	x
Anti-reformism	x	x	x			
Anti-fascism			x	x		
Popular frontism				x	x	x
Electoral participation				x	x	x
Support national bourgeoisie				x	x	x
Peace, anti-war, anti-violence			x	x	x	x
Adherence to USSR	x	x	x	x	x	x
Economic						
Dual-society contradiction		x	x	x	x	x
Anti-monopoly capitalism	x	x	x	x	x	x
Anti-imperialism	x	x	x	x	x	x
Nationalist development				x	x	x
Agrarian reform				x	x	x
Social-Cultural						
Urban labor base	x	x	x	x	x	x
Rural labor base			x	x	x	x
Youth base		x	x	x	x	x
Woman base		x	x	x	x	x
Party press and propaganda		x	x	x	x	x

x = supported by particular congress

Sources: First Congress: "Sociedades civis," p. 6970 in *Diário Oficial,* April 7, 1922, and *Movimento Comunista,* 7 (June 1922), cited in Bandeira *et al., O ano vermelho,* pp. 294–99. Second Congress: Pereira, *Formação do PCB,* pp. 65–71. Third Congress: *Ibid.,* pp. 114–35; Fourth Congress: "IV Congresso do Partido Comunista do Brasil," *Problemas,* 64 (December 1954–February 1955), 1–414, especially pp. 22–46 and 149–70. Fifth Congress: Statutes and program in *Novos Rumos,* Special Supplement, April 15–21, 1960, and reprinted in Inquérito Policial Militar No. 709, *O comunismo no Brasil,* Vol. II, pp. 104–11. Sixth Congress: "Teses," *Vos Operária* 19 (July 20, 1966), 1–16.

1. Program and statutes were modified in 1961.

Soviet Union were stressed at each congress. Opposition to reformism within the party was a concern of the first three meetings, and anti-fascism, at the third and fourth meetings. Peace and opposition to war were objectives of the last four meetings, popular frontism, electoral participation, and support for the national bourgeoisie, of the last three meetings.

In the economic sphere, anti-monopoly capitalism and anti-imperialism were concerns of all the congresses. Beginning with the Second Congress and in all congresses thereafter, the PCB analyzed Brazilian society in terms of a basic dualism between semi-feudal agrarian capitalism and modern industrial capitalism. Nationalistic developments were not of particular concern until the fifties, and proposals for agrarian reform were not elaborated until the Fourth Congress.

In social-cultural matters, in all six congresses importance was attached to urban labor in the party organization, and youth and women were recognized also as important at the party's Second Congress, and rural labor, at the Third Congress. The role of the party press and propaganda were specific concerns of the last five meetings.

What is the significance of these ideological principles? For one thing, all were emphasized in Soviet documentation, on which a good part of PCB doctrine was patterned. They also signified a certain dependence on explicit theory, and sometimes a rigidity and inflexibility. Further, while the theses reflected changes in world Communism and new policy directions for the PCB, they were not necessarily implemented in party action. While, for example, democratic centralism was advocated, rarely was it fully realized, for internal debate was not generally encouraged. The party's position on semi-feudal agrarian conditions and a semi-colonial economy, adapted from a European model of feudalism and applied to Brazil, was not really seriously challenged until the early sixties. Then too, its hopes for a progressive national bourgeoisie seems to have been unduly stressed, and its aspiration to be a revolutionary party within the context of Brazilian parliamentarianism proved unrealistic.

The party's failure to convene a congress during the intervening years 1929–54 distorts our analysis somewhat. During a large part of 1935 and the period 1945–47, the party ideology betrayed little relevancy to actual PCB policy and action. During those years the doctrinaire aims of Communism were played down, and the party concentrated instead on the immediate issues affecting Brazilian workers and the lower middle class. The revolutionary stance of the party's early years was undermined by appeals to the population to join in a program of national union. At the same time the party actively cooperated with the government to ensure that Communist activities would be tolerated. The party became reformist rather than revolutionary as it exploited Prestes' image as a national hero and directed its efforts to increasing party membership as rapidly as possible.

Impact of the PCB on the Ruling Parties

What is the perceived position of the PCB in the world Communist system? Today its position is confused by the tensions between the Soviet Union and China (aggravated by the foreign policy of the Nixon Administration), divisions in Eastern Europe, and the revolutionary stance of Cuba within the Third World. The PCB's recent decline in prestige within both Brazil and the whole Communist world was partially a consequence of the party's illegal status and its consequent loss in membership. Ideological divisions also impaired the party image, and adherence to the Soviet position within the Communist world cast the party in a reformist role, generally opposed to radical and revolutionary action.

It might be argued that the PCB never enjoyed a prominent place in the international Communist movement. One proponent of this position suggests that if during Stalin's reign, and particularly after the failure of the 1935 revolt, little attention was paid the Brazilian and other Latin American parties by the Soviet policy-makers, it was chiefly because they were convinced that the United States would never tolerate a Communist government in the hemisphere. Although Latin America was assigned a low priority—lower than any other part of the world except Africa—the Soviets nevertheless considered it useful to have a Brazilian branch and to assist it financially and in other ways. Such a party could generate popular support for Soviet foreign policy objectives.[13]

At times, however, the PCB was clearly important to the Communist world. There were periods, especially during 1935 and 1945 to 1948, when the Soviet Union viewed the PCB as the most important Communist party in Latin America, and Prestes as the most renowned of Communist leaders.[14] There were several reasons for such recognition.

Principally, there was the cult of Prestes, the hero of the 1920's who returned to Brazil to lead the ANL alliance in 1935. The adherence of hundreds of thousands of supporters to the popular-front movement was evidence of his appeal and charisma among the Brazilian masses. When Vargas eliminated the possibility that the alliance might come to power by peaceful means, the four Comintern agents who had accompanied Prestes to Brazil were able to enact an alternate (and probably main) strategy planned before the July demise of the ANL, specifying simultaneous barracks revolts in scattered parts of the country. The belief was that such uprisings would neutralize the Brazilian armed forces and set off a popular uprising. Only in one other Latin American country—El Salvador—had there been an attempt to seize the government by violent means; and although the participants probably miscalculated their potential strength, it is clear that Prestes through his counsel, action, and prestige had been influential in drawing international Communist attention to Brazil.[15]

Besides its allocation of funds to aid the PCB effort, the Soviet nation itself became a haven for large numbers of Brazilian exiles during the late thirties. One of the exiles, Octávio Brandão, broadcast regularly in Portuguese to Brazil from about the year 1938 until the end of World War II.[16] Then too, Soviet interest in Brazil was enhanced by increased trade after 1953. Until about 1959, trade fluctuated considerably from year to year but reached $30,900,000 in 1960, and that figure more than doubled (to $77,100,000) by 1963. Under President Quadros new commercial arrangements were negotiated with the Soviet Union to facilitate the exchange of coffee, cacao, iron ore, and vegetable oils for petroleum and wheat.[17]

PCB's Relations with Other Parties

Although the Soviet Union has maintained considerable respect for the PCB and in general considers Brazil as important to Soviet influence in Latin America, ruling parties in other Communist nations, and other non-ruling parties—in particular those in Latin America—have exhibited different attitudes and perspectives toward the PCB, as we realize when we recall the repercussions of the Sino-Soviet dispute, the Cuban Revolution, and the fast-moving developments in the Third World.

The Sino-Soviet Dispute

The divergent views of the Chinese and Soviet parties were exposed during the November 1960 conference of Communist parties, held in

Moscow, after an earlier attempt to achieve unanimity (at Bucharest in June 1960) had apparently failed; the chief points of dispute were revealed in an exchange of diplomatic letters during 1963. On the question of war, the Chinese charged the Soviet leaders with encouraging the illusion that war could be abolished while imperialism existed; in reply the Soviet Union charged that Chinese Communists premised the future on the ruins of a thermonuclear war. On revolution, the Chinese accused the Soviet leaders of seeking to weaken the world revolutionary movement by excessive emphasis upon legal and parliamentary means of overthrowing capitalism, while the Soviets condemned the Chinese for prematurely encouraging armed revolutions in the Third World.

The Chinese called the Soviet Union "adventurous" in placing missiles in Cuba and "capitulating" in withdrawing the missiles under the threat of a U.S. ultimatum; the Soviets claimed that the missiles were set up in Cuba to prevent armed aggression on the part of the United States and were withdrawn to prevent the outbreak of thermonuclear war. While the Chinese insisted that Soviet withdrawal of economic assistance to China signified the abandonment of international solidarity, the Soviets claimed that the Chinese were responsible for the drop in Soviet-Chinese trade and that they had unilaterally cut their trade with other smaller socialist countries. The Soviets also refuted the Chinese belief that they had encouraged illusions among the Soviet peoples that full Communism and complete abundance could be achieved in the USSR within a generation.

When the Chinese charged that the Soviet leaders had made unwise and exaggerated attacks on Stalin, the Soviets responded that the Chinese had betrayed Leninism by supporting the personality cult of Stalin. When the Chinese condemned the Soviets for forcing all Communist parties to accept Moscow's unilateral decisions as binding doctrine, the Soviets charged the Chinese with deliberately attempting to split world Communism by encouraging the formation of Chinese-oriented groups in many parts of the world.[18]

Apparently when this high-level hassle entered the public domain, well before 1960, the differences had affected the Communist movement in Brazil, for as we have seen, Chinese efforts to undermine the Soviet hegemony over the PCB had begun as early as 1956. At that time Diógenes Arruda Câmara had been invited to visit China after attending the Twentieth Congress of the Soviet party, and returned with glowing reports, according to Osvaldo Peralva, who met with him in Moscow during July 1956.[19] Peralva also recalled Sino-Soviet differences dating to 1949, when the Chinese refused to join the Cominform in order to avoid ideological clashes with the Soviets and also to maintain their own ideological position and win over other Communist parties in the Third World.[20]

As differences sharpened within the PCB during the debates of 1956 and 1957, the conservative clique around Prestes became isolated by the anti-Stalinism prevailing in leadership circles. Subsequently, when Arruda along with João Amazonas, Pedro Pomar, and Maurício Grabois lost their leadership offices, yet their influence remained strong among the party cadres. Although their expulsion was a setback for the Chinese, ultimately the PCB split when the dissidents (Arruda excepted) formed their own pro-Chinese PC do B in early 1962.[21]

In the early sixties when the Chinese managed to influence leftist developments in certain Latin American countries including Brazil, the PCB's adherence to the Soviet orientation remained intact despite the presence of the small PC do B.[22] The Chinese adapted their tactics accordingly, beaming broadcasts in Portuguese to Brazil for eight hours every day, sending representatives of the arts to Brazil, and participating in political meetings such as the Conference of Students from the Underdeveloped World, held in Bahia during July 1963.[23]

The split in the PCB occurred at a time when the Chinese were reluctant to support divisions in the Communist parties on an international scale. Thus, the founding of the PC do B was not reported in the Chinese press, and in March 1963 a two-man delegation of the splinter party that visited Peking and was received by Mao Tse-Tung was still described in *Peking Review* as a delegation from the PCB. Not until September was there any indication that the PC do B had been officially recognized by Peking.[24] Apparently the PC do B received funds from the Chinese—and, according to one observer, also from the Cubans—for operating their party, publishing house, and fortnightly newspaper, *A Classe Operária*. When Prestes, during a visit to Havana in March 1963, succeeded in persuading the Cubans not to subsidize the rival party, the dissident party became totally dependent on Chinese support. Most likely the Cubans were unwilling to split the international movement at just that time; perhaps, too, they believed with one writer that it was "the most sterile, rigid, and ineffective elements in the Brazilian Communist movement who were won over to the Chinese cause." [25]

Cuba and the Third World

After 1961 the ongoing Cuban Revolution became dependent on Soviet economic and technical assistance. The U.S. blockade and the Bay of Pigs invasion had pushed Castro farther into the Soviet camp; and in the uncertain aftermath of the overthrow of Khrushchev in late 1964, Castro consented to agreements with the Latin American Communist parties which compromised his previous independent position in the world Communist movement. His November 1964 agreement with the Latin American Communist parties endorsed armed struggle in six Latin American countries, but also allowed each party to determine its own tactics.[26] From Moscow's perspective the agreement undermined Chinese influence in the area.

Although the Cuban ruling party was given the orthodox name Partido Comunista, it was reorganized to deprive the old-line Communists of any meaningful power. The publication and widespread distribution of Ché Guevara's manual on guerrilla warfare signified a measure of rapport with China, for there were similarities in the two parties' positions on guerrilla warfare and national liberation movements.[27] Cuba also was the only Latin American nation with diplomatic relations with Communist China; it refused to sign the Soviet-supported nuclear test-ban treaty; and it published the full documentation of the Sino-Soviet dispute.

The Tricontinental Conference of January 1966, which marked Castro's independence within the international Communist movement, was followed up by Cuban attacks on Yugoslavia, by criticism of the Soviet Union, and finally by the organization of a united faction consisting of Cuba, North Korea, and North Vietnam—an axis that could be distinguished from the Chinese sphere of influence and yet act as a pressure group to mobilize European Communist governments into greater revolutionary effort in the Third World. In addition, the Tricontinental Conference provided Castro with the opportunity to take his place alongside other Third World leaders. He unexpectedly attacked the Chinese for limiting their rice shipments to Cuba. Then taking his position against Soviet attempts to urge moderation, Castro stated, at the close of the conference that: "If . . . it is understood once and for all that sooner or later all or almost all peoples will have to take up arms to liberate themselves, then the hour of liberation for this continent will be advanced . . . we believe that on this continent . . . the battle will take on the most violent forms." [28]

Following the conference the Organización Latino-Americana de Solidaridad (OLAS) was created. When it convened in late July 1967, however, internal ideological divisions were immediately apparent in the debates between Communist delegates and less orthodox radical Marxist delegates. The Cuban position prevailed in the documents of the commissions: thus, revolutionary violence offered the most concrete and manifest possibility for defeating imperialism; armed struggle constituted the fundamental line; and solidarity would characterize the struggle in the form of guerrilla war and liberation armies throughout the continent.[29]

Neither the PCB nor the PC do B sent delegations to the OLAS conference, although Carlos Marighella, the former PCB leader, was there, as was José Anselmo dos Santos, who had led the March 1964 naval strike and now represented the Movimento Nacionalista Revolucionário (MNR). Anselmo dos Santos was quoted as stating that the OLAS would "end the myth that a party is necessary in order to make a revolution." [30] Apparently he was alluding to the PCB, and the attack became official policy with the publication of an article in *Teoria y Prática* (an organ of the Partido Comunista de Cuba) denouncing the traditional line of the Communist parties in Brazil and Argentina.[31] The PCB seems not to have defended its position but to have reaffirmed its allegiance to the Soviet Union. Thus, in supporting the International Conference of Communist and Workers' Parties held in Moscow June 5–17, 1969, Prestes expressed "full agreement" with the meeting's conclusions and reiterated that all Latin American countries were going through "the same stage of the revolution, which is a national-democratic revolution." [32]

Other Latin American Communist Parties

Among the Latin American Communist parties, the Argentine party has probably exerted the greatest influence on the PCB. In 1922, as noted above, the PCB based its statutes on the Argentine model; during 1928 to 1931, while in Buenos Aires, Prestes associated with Communists; and in 1930, PCB policies were subjected to self-criticism with the South American Bureau of the Comintern, which was strongly influenced by the Argentine party. Further, in 1935 the Argentine Communist Rodolfo Ghioldi worked with Prestes in Brazil and was later imprisoned there for his part in the November uprisings. Although differences grew up between the two parties over Argentine dictator Juan Perón after the Second World War,[33] unity continued during the late fifties and the sixties. Under attack from both the Cuban regime and the

OLAS, the Brazilian and the Argentine parties reasserted their position in a joint statement in late 1968. Urging unity of action on the part of all forces against tyrannical regimes, the parties condemned U.S. imperialism and called for solidarity among the Latin American Communist movements "on the basis of proletarian internationalism and the general principles of the Moscow Statement of 1960 and the Havana Conference of 1964." Further, they supported "the victory achieved in Czechoslovakia by the participation of the Soviet Union and other Warsaw Treaty countries" during August 1968.[34]

Conclusion

By way of conclusion we are now ready to reformulate the PCB's relations with the Communist world, drawing heavily on the interpretations of leftist Brazilian intellectuals.

In its early, formative years, the PCB concentrated on elaborating an ideological line, a political program, and perspectives on the Brazilian revolution. With its roots in the working class, however, the party lacked the participation of militant intellectuals; and, not being involved in any mass struggle, its impact on the nation was slight. This early handicap may have contributed to the party's difficulty in affiliating with the Third International.

The first PCB schism happened over the role of the front organization, the BOC, which was eventually dissolved in consequence of the party's indecisive leadership in the face of the international Communist line, on the one hand, and failure to comprehend internal political conditions, on the other. According to one observer, the indecisiveness of the PCB leadership "revealed the lack of preparation of the jealous labor leaders in the confrontation with the bourgeois revolution." [35]

It is believed also that Prestes, the national hero who became a prominent figure in international Communist circles, jeopardized PCB development beginning in the early thirties. The impact of Prestes' failure to participate in the 1930 revolution has been described by "Antônio Palmares" as "disastrous—it weakened the most radical wing of the petty bourgeoisie." [36] According to Fernando Lacerda, Prestismo brought a "lack of confidence to the proletarian and peasant masses, motivating forces against feudalism and imperialism, and a lack of faith in the capacity of the proletariat to lead the revolution." [37] Eventually, "under the inspiration of the leftist line of the Third International the sectarianism of the PCB and of Prestes aligned against the progress of the country." [38] Prestes' entry into the PCB destroyed the remaining proletarian element and ensured the domination in the party of a radical petty bourgeoisie.

The politics of the International worked other damage on the PCB, according to its critics. The 1935 uprising, for example, was written off as "a petty bourgeois adventure" demonstrating the dominance of bourgeois, radical revolutionaries within the party, who under the guise of Stalinism, transformed the revolution into a compromise among the bourgeoisie, latifundistas, and imperialists.[39] In the aftermath, the near-demise of the party rallied all the classes (the peasantry excepted) under the Estado Novo, and the labor and welfare legislation of the regime was to diminish the PCB's relations with organized labor. In 1943 the PCB advocated the formation of a "national union," and two years later supported Vargas in an opportunistic yet successful move to obtain legal status. Years later Prestes came around to a critical assessment of party policy and a denunciation of the national-union line; yet one Brazilian leftist interpreted this 1949 criticism as "a mere reflection of the changes in the world Communist movement." The PCB, he claimed, had not yet become a Marxist-Leninist party; "it remained in the periphery of Marxism." [40]

While the Prestes manifesto of August 1950 was an effort to break with the old reformist and opportunist line of national union, it was also a response to the Cold War and the success of the Chinese revolution. As one critic claims, however, the insurrectionary line conflicted with a phase of rapidly expanding Brazilian capitalism and that "sectarianism replaced opportunism, widening the gap between the PCB and the masses." [41]

Again, the world Communist movement, disrupted by the termination of the Korean War, the death of Stalin, the stabilization of European economies, the Hungarian and Polish revolts, and the consolidation of Soviet politics under Khrushchev, brought changes to the PCB. After the death of Vargas in 1954, the party supported an alliance with the national bourgeoisie and aligned itself with nationalist forces and goals. Many of the new ideas were incorporated into the agenda of the party's Fourth Congress.[42]

Clearly the changes in the Communist world throughout the fifties and sixties allowed the PCB to attempt to transform itself. Eagerness to be integrated into national society became virtually an obsession, along with the felt need for legal existence. To those ends the party took pains to demonstrate that it was not dependent on the Soviet Union or the world Communist movement. It also tried to change its image from that of a proletarian party to one more closely identified with the Brazilian middle classes.[43] It was precisely these moves that provided at least part of the pretext for the military takeover in 1964—though of course the party's strength and effectiveness at the time were greatly exaggerated by the anti-Communist military leaders. At any rate, forced underground, the PCB found its activities suppressed and its unity and strength weakend by subsequent internal divisions brought about by the party's continued dependence on Soviet Communism and by ideological differences within the world movement.

9 • Principal Determinants of Party Performance

This chapter sets forth some propositions in an attempt to provide a framework for evaluating the performance of the PCB through historical periods since its formation and within its national and cross-national environments. As we have been at pains to demonstrate in previous chapters, the history of the PCB corresponds in its varying patterns to developments in the international Communist world and within Brazil itself. The Russian Revolution provided the exemplar of revolutionary effectiveness; Marx, Lenin, and others gave radicals an ideological frame of reference; and the Communist International supplied the guidelines for national party organization. Yet the party's performance was conditioned even more by political and cultural considerations in Brazil.

Party behavior was a reflection of the challenges to the national system—among them the desire for self-determination, for improvement of social conditions, and for representative government—that confronted the hierarchy of political, economic, and social structures dominating Brazilian history well into the present century. In addition, these challenges were accompanied by protest and conflict, manifested in the form of continuous racial, rural, and urban discontent. The past traces of indigenous protest and resistance to the ruling order in Brazil are constantly recalled by the political left. Frequently this discontent led to the formation of radical movements. As a radical movement the PCB has related to such discontent, at least symbolically, although it has also based itself solidly on an international framework.

Then too, much of the discontent during the present century was brought about by changes in the areas of industrialization and urbanization. Accompanying these changes was the evolution of organized labor, and this in turn was informed by the ideologies of socialism and especially of anarchism. Socialism captured the imagination of progressive intellectuals, and anarchism appealed to the expanding working class. While both radical currents contributed to the Communist movement in Brazil, when they failed to mobilize the masses of workers in the struggle to restructure national society they were displaced by the PCB as the major contemporary Marxist movement. With the assistance of some radical intellectuals, a labor-oriented segment of the lower classes had originated the PCB, but, as we have noted often in previous chapters, this segment quickly succumbed to middle-class bureaucratic elements that were to guide the party after the 1930 revolution. The PCB evolved from this combination of circumstances.

We have already identified several patterns in our early chapters tracing the evolution of the party through eight historical periods. First, we recall, a correlation is clearly discernible between the party's actions and policies within Brazil and the decisions of the international Communist movement. The party moreover tended to support popular forces—labor leaders, intellectuals, middle-class elements, and disenchanted military—to manifest dissatisfaction with oligarchic government and to oppose conservative forces, including the military and police, industrialists and businessmen, landowners, and foreign interests.

The above patterns produced two conflicting orientations. One, based on disciplined organization and action, was particularly susceptible to pressures from international Communism. The other, based on personalism and pragmatism, reflected Brazilian politics in general. The proximity to or deviation from one style or the other determined the party's degree of dependence on or independence from the world-wide Communist movement, as well as its effectiveness in the national milieu. In addition, two major themes provided the party's perspective of national and world politics: nationalism and anti-imperialism. The party's concern with nationalism was partially a vague expression of Prestes' personal ambition to dominate the Brazilian revolution, but more important, it was linked closely with the party's anxieties over foreign capitalist penetration of Brazilian economic life.

Lastly, the PCB was torn by division and conflict, the result of ideological differences, dissension over national and international pressures and policy, and eventually the isolation of an inner core of career-oriented bureaucratic leaders from other echelons of party life.

These patterns affected party performance in a kind of chain-reaction. Thus:

- Dependence on the Soviet model of party structure and the highly centralized and hierarchical rule of a clique-styled minority over the mass membership resulted in lack of mass participation and a decline in membership.
- The hierarchical centralization and the non-involvement by the mass membership facilitated rigid leadership control at all levels of party organization.
- The dominant leadership and the lack of mass participation contributed substantially to the party's vulnerability to government repression at times when it advocated a militant course of action.
- On the other hand, a policy of collaboration with popular elements or in support of the government tended to undermine the rigid control by leadership, especially when that policy coincided with efforts to expand the size of the rank and file membership—an expansion that inevitably relaxed party discipline and encouraged divisiveness.
- The persistent dominance of a single charismatic leader over the administrative inner core and the mass membership both benefited and weakened the party. The personal appeals aroused mass aspirations for social, economic, and political change, and at the same time enhanced public toleration for Communist participation in Brazilian society. Yet the determination to remain in the mainstream of politics undermined the party's vanguard role in clarifying the vital issues of Brazilian society.
- The mainstream position of the party often blinded the PCB leadership not only to the vital issues but also to recognition of the rank and file's demands. The resultant breakdown in communication between leaders and followers encouraged defections and disunity.
- Despite these disruptive tendencies, the party probably offered the chance of social mobility and status for some of its working-class supporters; and, as suggested earlier, its leaders in the labor movement quite possibly got the feeling of bourgeois dignity in their association with the predominantly middle-class party leadership. Although empirical data is not yet available to support these assumptions, we may hypothesize tentatively that improved status sometimes contributed to conservatism and to defense of the status quo by way of preserving the new prestige.

That the growth and performance of the PCB were shaped by its interaction with the national and cross-national environments, we brought out in Chapter 8. In large measure, however, the party's effectiveness was determined by a set of conditions in the national environment. While we have adverted to all of them earlier, here they are brought together as follows:

• Party theory vis-à-vis national development conflicted sharply with actual Brazilian practice. In the absence of effective centralized planning, the government promoted import-substituting industrialization, which favored the developed regions of the country and the high-income segments in the population and brought disparities in regional development, especially in the traditionally backward Northeast. The PCB opposed such governmental policy.

• Despite the generally conservative, elitist control over Brazilian society, the PCB's effort for reforms to improve conditions for wage earners in the new industrial society was undermined by the complex labor legislation and unionization measures sponsored by the government. It would appear that the resultant artificially high industrial wages and the general welfare benefits served to co-opt important segments of the labor movement in urban areas where PCB strength was highest. With government protection, collective bargaining was controlled by the Ministry of Labor, and hence the PCB found it expedient to ingratiate itself with the Ministry as well as the labor movement itself.

• As a result of labor legislation and replacement of labor leaders the Brazilian government helped decisively to alienate the older, more aggressive labor leadership (including Communists) from the new masses of industrial workers. With the end of the Estado Novo, the PCB could operate in the labor movement through coalitions either with the governmental cadres or with prestigious independent leaders. But labor reform was contingent less upon revolutionary Marxist policy than upon dedicated militants and activists many of whom belonged to the PCB. Having accepted the operational limits of activity imposed by the government, however, the PCB was unable to distinguish itself among its collaborators, so that when the party was outlawed, its working-class followers simply transferred their allegiance to another party.

• The general nationalist sentiment shared by the intellectuals and political parties reinforced Communist allegiance to a model premised on the need for a bourgeois-democratic revolution that would eliminate the obstacles to development such as were to be found in a feudal agrarian economy and the imperialistic control of natural resources. Clearly after 1958 the party emphasized the nationalist aspects of the bourgeois revolution, insisting at the same time that it could come to power peacefully through the constituted electoral process. That objective was based primarily on its possibility of forming a united front of progressive forces, comprising the national industrial bourgeoisie and the urban middle class, an alliance of workers and peasants, and all others who opposed imperialism and favored land reform. In effect, the PCB became a pressure group, committed to the task of radicalizing the bourgeoisie to oppose U.S. imperialism. The party's traditional commitment to class conflict was replaced by a commitment to nationalism.

• The PCB tendency toward moderation in national politics conditioned in part by its experience as a legal party and by its electoral and organizational successes of the 1945–47 period. Believing that it could operate within the existing political framework, it concentrated until 1964 on regaining its legal status.

• By way of enhancing its image in the labor movement, the PCB sought to establish itself as the legitimate broker between labor and the government, and thus to capture mass support in the urban areas. Likewise, it moved in among rural wage earners and sought influence in the government-sponsored rural unions and the peasant leagues, especially in the Northeast.

• When the Goulart regime allowed the PCB control of a few strategic segments of the government apparatus, the party found its role as broker between labor and government threatened and undermined by this opportunity to institutionalize itself as a party within the government. Having accepted its new role and perceiving the possibility of losing control altogether (to the military and reactionary forces that eventually seized power), the PCB radicalized itself in the last days of the Goulart regime and demanded a new government coalition.

• It would appear that during the period after 1945, in a regime of welfarism and state intervention, the PCB found itself characterized by two conflicting images from which it struggled to extricate itself: that of a rightist and opportunistic party dependent on the state for its existence or that of a leftist and conspiratorial party sworn to the overthrow of the state. The party had slim hope of becoming a revolutionary mass movement.

It is clear from this formulation that the PCB had over the years—but more markedly between 1945 and 1964—transformed itself from a party of particular and individual representation to a party of integration with national society. Two strategies were utilized by the PCB in the process. One involved open revolution, general strikes, and prolonged terrorism and sabotage. At the outset of the party's existence this strategy was utilized in its maneuvers toward the working class (from which, as we know, the early leadership and membership were principally drawn). The second strategy—more familiar to Brazilian politics—was that of peaceful association with organizations and segments of the population outside the party. Thus, since its inception the PCB was concerned to organize or penetrate labor unions, student societies, and women's groups, creating popular-front organizations, and to operate within institutions that influence public opinion. Party effectiveness in interaction with national society obviously depended largely on the interlocking front groups and Communist-led mass organizations through which it could infiltrate professional societies, cultural associations, ethnic groups, and other special-interest groupings. Despite success in these activities, the party was never permitted a decision-making role in Brazilian society.

In its effort to involve itself in Brazilian society, the party frequently encountered intense competition among its Marxist and non-Marxist revolutionary rivals. As the party moved toward mainstream politics, it found itself sometimes supporting the status quo of a bourgeois-dominated government that offered few alternatives to pressing needs. But party ideology itself offered few solutions to the problems of the existing order; and then too, the party strategy frequently was influenced by the directives of international Communism. And, of course, party ideals succumbed to the personalist and pragmatic leadership of Prestes. Hence it is not surprising that the PCB in the sixties found itself outflanked by a more radical student vanguard and progressive Catholic and Marxist movements.

As for the PCB's international environment, we need recall only that since its founding, the PCB has remained subservient to world Communist policies dictated by the Soviet Union, which has been able to control the direction of PCB policy, its choice of leadership, and its ideological formation; and that, secondarily, the PCB has occasionally been regarded as important to the Communist world, despite the fact that within Latin America the party's earlier prestigious position (largely attributable to the charisma of Prestes) declined by reason of loss of its legal status with consequent drop in membership, internal ideological divisions, a reformist stance, and opposition to radical and revolutionary action—a situation in turn affected by the party's ambiguous relations with Cuba and China as well as disagreements over policy and action with revolutionary movements in other Third World countries.

In general, while the PCB's formation, strategy, and policy were indeed modified by its cross-national environment, that environment did not enhance the party's position in the world Communist system nor did it benefit the party on the home front. From its inception the party represented a challenge to the established Brazilian order; and of course the established order reacted to militant and revolutionary activities by suppressing and several times nearly bringing Communism to an end in Brazil. But as the party sought to improve its national image and to solicit additional support, it practiced accommodation and found collaboration. Brief periods of success in 1935 and 1945 to 1947 persuaded the party that its continued existence depended upon a moderate course whenever possible within mainstream Brazilian politics.

It may be that our generalizations are applicable to the experience of other Communist parties in Latin America. In any case these generalizations do support the assumptions in the introduction to our book; and subsequent pages have borne out that the PCB, despite its occasional bold and revolutionary stance, evolved into an organization controlled by a few leaders whose power was highly centralized and anti-democratic and whose policies became internally conservative.

Moreover, we have shown that the party's commitment to principles and to a radical perspective of Brazilian society tended to deteriorate at times when a broad mass base was deemed essential. Such a mass base required support from either voters or sympathizers; and a decline in such support meant also a decline in membership and prestige. Thus our assumption is verified that the conservative character of the party is found in the relation between party and state: the party ends by acquiring a vigorous organization of its own and is based on the same principles of authority and discipline that characterize the organization of the state. Instead of gaining revolutionary fervor as strength and unity increase, a policy of caution and timidity guides party action. The revolutionary party of the proletariat becomes a rival of the bourgeois parties, a competitor and collaborator, no longer seeking to struggle against the very system that provoked its emergence, but becoming instead merely a force of limited pressure and moderation within the established order.

Appendix

Elected Political Representatives of the PCB: 1925-1972

Elections of 1925: Municipal Councilmen
SANTOS
Unsuccessful first attempt to run PCB candidates for office.

Elections of February 24, 1927: Federal Deputies
João Batista de Azevedo Lima (elected under Bloco Operário)

Elections of October 1928: Municipal Councilmen[1]
RIO DE JANIERO
Octávio Brandão
Minervino de Oliveira (elected under BOC)

Elections of May 3, 1933: Constituent Assembly and Federal Deputies
SANTA CATARINA:
Alvaro Ventura [2]

Elections of October 14, 1934: State Deputies [3]
PCB sympathizers in Congress arrested March 1936:[4]
   Federal Deputies
   Abguar Bastos[5]
   João Mangabeira [6]
   Octávio da Silveira[7]
   Domingos Velasco[8]

---

1. Leônico Basbaum, *História sincera da república,* Vol. II, p. 315, and Robert Alexander, *Communism in Latin America,* p. 97.

2. Jorge Amado, *O cavaliero da esperança,* note 133, p. 239. Alvaro Ventura, a stevedore, was elected an alternate federal deputy from Federal District on December 2, 1945.

3. Under the União Operária e Camponesa, the PCB presented Agostinho Dias de Oliveira. Although he did not win a seat in 1934, he was elected a federal deputy from Pernambuco in 1945 under PCB.

4. Charges against these men were included in Eurico Bellens Porto, *A insurreição de 27 de novembro,* pp. 241–55. All were associated with the ANL and opposed repression of the ANL and PCB after November 1935.

5. Bastos was author of *Prestes e a revolução social,* a sympathetic biography of Prestes. He was a founder of ANL, a radical deputy from Goiás, and a supporter of Prestes.

6. Mangabeira later was PSB presidential candidate in the 1950 elections in which he received less than 10,000 votes.

7. Silveira, a deputy from Curitiba, was active in ANL and founded the Paraná section of ANL. After the 1935 revolt he read a message from Prestes to the Chamber of Deputies.

8. Velasco probably is a socialist sympathizer of PCB.

Senators
Abel Chermont[9]

Elections of December 2, 1945: Federal Deputies and Senators[10]

PERNAMBUCO

	Vote (more than 500)
Federal Deputies	
Gregório Lourenço Bezerra	14,341
Luiz Carlos Prestes (replaced by Morais Coutinho)	9,270
Agostino Dias de Oliveira	5,160
Alternates	
Dr. Alcedo de Morais Coutinho	2,917
Ilvo Furtado Soares de Meireles	1,516
Sindulfo Correia Josué	1,016
Adalgisa Rodrigues Cavalcanti	849
Dr. Rui de Costa Antunes	706
Carlos Augusto de Rêgo Cavalcanti	651
Alfredo Richmond	554
Antônio Marques da Silva	
Manuel Casimiro de Lima	
Joaquim Cavalcanti Filho	
José Francisco Monteiro	
Vicente Barbosa da Silva	
Dr. Frederico Freire	
Brivaldo Leão de Almeida	
José Francisco Lins	
João Rodrigues Sobral	

BAHIA

Federal Deputies	
Carlos Marighella	5,188
Alternates	
Juvenal Luiz do Souto Jr.	2,824
Diógenes Arruda Câmara	2,735
Luiz Carlos Prestes	1,368
Nelson da Silva Schaun	932
Edgard Paulo da Mata	925
João da Costa Falcão	870
Joaquim S. do Vale Cabral	713
Valdir de Oliveira e Sousa	624
Eusíno Gaston Levigne	
Vicente Paulo de Jesus	
Demócrito Gomes de Carvalho	
Manuel Batista de Sousa	
Giocondo Gerbasi Alves Dias	

9. Chermont later was elected PCB suplente to Senator Luiz Carlos Prestes in Federal District, January 19, 1947.

10. All data for 1945 and 1947 elections in Tribunal Superior Eleitoral, *Dados estatísticos. Eleições, federal, estadual e municipal realizadas no Brasil a partir de 1945*, Vol. I, Rio de Janeiro: Departamento de Imprensa Nacional, 1950.

	Vote *(more than 500)*
Armênio Guedes	
Mecenas da Silveira Mascarenhas	
Alfredo Moreira de Freitas	
João do Carmo	
Aurélio Justiniano da Rocha	
Aristeu Nogueira Campos	
Ariston Andrade	
Estanislau José de Santana	
Jacinta Passos Amado	

RIO DE JANEIRO

Federal Deputies

| Claudino José da Silva | 11,291 |
| Alcides Rodrigues Sabença | 6,403 |

Alternates

Henrique Cordeiro Oest	5,379
José Barreto Gomes	4,508
Celso Cabral de Melo	2,694
Luiz Carlos Prestes	2,668
Maria Geni Gerreira da Silva	1,028

DISTRITO FEDERAL

Federal Senator

| Luiz Carlos Prestes | 157,397 |

Federal Deputies

Luiz Carlos Prestes (replaced by Batista Neto)	27,664
João Amazonas de Souza Pedroso	18,379
Maurício Gabrois	15,243

Alternates

Joaquim Batista Neto	14,177
Francisco Gomes	13,683
Agildo da Gama Barata Ribeiro	1,549
Iquatemi Ramos da Silva	1,453
Manuel Venâncio Campos da Paz	1,274
Pedro Paulo Sampaio da Lacerda	836
Manuel Alves da Rocha	563
Eugênia Alvaro Moreira	
Abel Abreu Chermont	
Pedro de Carvalho Braga	
Antônio Soares de Oliveira	
Hilton Machado de Vasconcelos	
Alvina Correia do Rêgo	
Alvaro Soares Ventura	

SÃO PAULO

Federal Deputies

José Maria Crispim	36,657
Osvaldo Pacheco da Silva	18,420
Jorge Amado	15,315

	Vote (more than 500)
Mário Scott	13,570
Alternates	
Milton Caires do Brito	10,595
Luiz Carlos Prestes	10,476
Caio Prado Júnior	9,315
Euclides Savieto	7,297
Gervásio Gomes de Azevedo	5,662
Antônio Patrocínio Oliveira	4,790
Roque Trevisan	4,353
Ernesto Alves	4,005
Luiza Pessanha Camargo Branco	3,783
Francisco Siedler	3,301
Lázaro Maria da Silva	3,206
João Mendoça Falcão	3,013
Samuel Barnsley Pessoa	3,003
Antônio Tavares de Almeida	2,992
Maria Carlota Vizotto	2,544
Antônio Campos	2,542
Juvenal Alves de Oliveira	2,431
João Sabino Primo	2,286
Catulo Branco	2,217
Abelcio Bitencourt Dias	1,984
Jair Rocha Batalha	1,924
Reginaldo Xavier de Carvalho	1,752
Eurico Paranhos	1,591
Cândido Portinari	1,585
Rafael Corrêa Sampaio Filho	1,453
Luiz Franceschini	1,097
Lutgardes Bastos	1,092
José Maria do Nascimento	1,065
Benedito Dias Batista	899
Antônio Alves dos Santos	615
Enrico Magalhães da Silveira	596

RIO GRANDE DO SUL

Federal Deputies

Luiz Carlos Prestes (replaced by Abílio Fernandes)	11,849
Alternates	
Abílio Fernandes	5,947
André Trifino Correia	3,508
Oto Alcides Ohlweiler	3,079
Dyonelio Tubino Machado	2,320
Lucas Fortes dos Santos	1,481
Deburgo de Deus Vieira	1,432
Manoel Jover Telles	1,206
Júlio de Sousa Teixeira	814
Gashypo Chagas Pereira	809
Arlindo Ferreira de Sousa	807
Santos Soares	798

	Vote (*more than 500*)
Peroy de Abreu Lima	742
Antônio Teixeira e Silva	586
Deborah Sousa Ribeiro	
Albino Portela Fagundes	
César Augusto da Costa Avila	
Sérgio Olmos	
Carlos Lima Aveline	
Alvaro Moreyra	
Richard Ellwanger	
Nicácio Fernandes da Costa	

Elections of January 19, 1947: Alternates to Senators, Federal Deputies, State Deputies, Municipal Councilmen.[10]

Federal Senator: Alternate
Abel Chermont (alternate for Senator Luiz Carlos Prestes)   96,547

SÃO PAULO

Federal Deputies
Pedro Ventura A. Pomar (elected under PSP)
Diógenes de Arruda Câmara (elected under PSP)

PARÁ

State Deputies
Henrique Felipe Santiago   699

Alternates
Guilherme de La-Rocque   520
Ritacínio Ramos Pereira   514
Diego Narciso Coêlho da Costa
João Gomes Pereira
Saturnino Arlindo Ribeiro

CEARÁ

State Deputies
José Pontes Neto   4,295
José Marinho de Vasconcelos   876

Alternates
Aldi Mentor Couto Melo   664
Euclides Maia   661
Antônio dos Santos Teixeira   478
Pedro Teixeira de Oliveira   544
Humberto Lucena Lopes

PARAÍBA

State Deputies
João Santa Cruz de Oliveira   1,654

Alternates
Felix de Sousa Araújo   1,516
Alegicio dos Santas Lima   607

Vote
(*more than 500*)

Geraldo Moura Baracul
José Feodripe
José Vandregiselo de Araújo Dias

PERNAMBUCO

State Deputies

David Capistrano da Costa	3,117
Rui da Costa Antunes	2,839
Valdo Cardoso de Aguiar	2,676
Amaro Francisco de Oliveira	2,658
Adalgisa Rodrigues Cavalcanti	2,305
José Leite Filho	1,817
Francisco Antônio Leivas Otero	1,760
Eliazar Machado	1,757
Etelvino de Oliveira Pinto	1,737

Alternates

Demócrito Ramos da Silveira	1,525
Alfredo Richmond	1,476
Luiz Braz de Luna	1,037
Valdemar Luiz Alves	980
Otávio Ramos do Nascimento	959

ALAGÔAS

State Deputies

André Papini Góis	895
José Maria Cavalcanti	506
Moacir Rodrigues de Andrade	

Alternates

José Almeida
Jaime Barbosa da Silva
José Francisco de Oliveira
José Lira Sobrinho
Oscar Silva

SERGIPE

State Deputies

Armando Domingues da Silva	657

Alternates

Carlos Garcia	509
João Batista de Lima e Silva	
Manuel Francisco de Oliveira	
Ofenísia Soares Freire	
Júlio Bispo dos Santos	

BAHIA

State Deputies

Giocondo Gerbasi Alves Dias	1,904
Jaime da Silva Maciel	1,174

	Vote (*more than 500*)
Alternates	
Mário Alves de Sousa Vieira	718
Eusínio Gaston Lavigne	621
José Ferreira de Sousa Filho	556
João Ribeiro dos Passos	536
Saul Coriolano Rosas	

ESPÍRITO SANTO

State Deputies

Benjamin de Carvalho Campos	999

Alternates

Luís Simões de Jesus	523
Pedro Correia Reis	
Antônio Ribeiro Granja	
Rodrigo de Sá Cavalcanti	
José Ribeiro Filho	

RIO DE JANEIRO

State Deputies

Pascoal Elídio Danielli	2,465
Lincoln Cordeiro Oest	2,379
Valquirio de Freitas	2,124
José Brigagão	1,965
Josias Ludolf Reis	1,859
Celso Paulo Fernandes Tôrres	1,831

Alternates

Horácio Valadares	1,436
Edgard Leite Ferreira	1,414
Caetano Regis Batista	1,364
Benigno Rodrigues Fernandes	1,223
Mário Paulo de Matos	1,183

SÃO PAULO

State Deputies

Milton Caires de Brito	17,692
Maurílio Muraro	10,041
Roque Trevisan	8,530
João Taibo Cadorniga	8,329
Lourival Costa Villar	8,288
Estocel de Moraes	7,356
Clóvis de Oliveira Neto	6,502
João Sanches Segura	6,267
Armando Mazzo	6,140
Catulo Branco	5,448
Caio Prado Júnior	5,257

Alternates

Lázaro Maria da Silva	5,054
Zuleika Alambert	4,654
Celestino dos Santos	4,637

	Vote *(more than 500)*
Mário Schenberg	3,092
Rio Branco Paranhos .	3,081

PARANÀ

State Deputies

| José Rodrigues Vieira Neto | 775 |

Alternates

Manuel L. da Costa Júnior	775
Antônio Carlos Raimundo	
Nelson Tôrres Galvão	
Mozart de Oliveira Valim	
Miguel Pan	

RIO GRANDE DO SUL

State Deputies

Oto Alcides Ohweiller	2,327
Antônio Ribas Pinheiro Machado Neto	2,231
Dionélio Machado	1,876

Alternates

Júlio de Sousa Teixeira	1,679
Antônio Lustenes Peres Barros	1,413
José César de Mesquita	1,134
Manoel Jover Telles	1,108
Antônio Ferreira Martins	1,068

MINAS GERAIS

State Deputies

| Armando Ziller | 2,845 |

Alternates

Lindolfo Hill	1,600
Jacinto Augusto de Carvalho	1,201
Sebastião Francisco de Azevedo	1,150
Roberto Margonari	1,122
Orlando Bonfim Júnior	944

GOIÁS

State Deputies

| Abraão Isaac Neto | 635 |
| Afrânio Francisco de Azevedo | 583 |

Alternates

| Paulo Alves da Costa | 557 |
| Epifânio Bezerra | 543 |

MATO GROSSO

State Deputies

| José Gomes Pedroso | 510 |
| Rádio Maia | |

Alternates

| Benedito Domingues da Silva | |

Vote
(*more than 500*)

Vicente Bezerra Neto
Alberto Neder
Cid Apolinário de Morais
João Avila de Mesquita

DISTRITO FEDERAL

Municipal Councilmen

Pedro de Carvalho Braga	10,520
Agildo Barata	9,689
Otávio Brandão Rêgo	5,257
Manuel Lopes Coêlho Filho	4,075
Bacelar Couto	3,872
Manuel Venâncio Campos de Paz	3,755
Arcelina Mochel	3,704
Aparício Torelly	3,699
Arlindo Pinho	3,189
João Massena	3,187
Ari Rodrigues	2,907
Aloísio Neiva	2,742
Antônio Soares de Oliveira	2,641
Amarílio Vasconcelos	2,604
Hermes de Caires	2,374
Iguatemí Ramos	2,189
Odila Schmidt	2,129
Joaquim José Reio	2,121

Alternates

Joaquim Barroso	2,078
Elvira Prestes	1,807
Carlos Fernandes	1,801
Lía Correia Dutra	1,784
Sebastião Luiz dos Santos	1,767

Elections of October 3, 1950: Federal Deputies, State Deputies, and Municipal Councilmen [11]

PERNAMBUCO

State Deputies

Paulo de Figueiredo Cavalcanti (elected under PSP)	3,996

FEDERAL DISTRICT

Federal Deputies

Roberto Morena (elected under PRT)	7,654

Municipal Councilmen [12]

Aristides Saldanha (elected under PRT)	4,477

---

11. Data for elections in Tribunal Superior Eleitoral, *Dados estatísticos. Eleições federal, e estaduais realizadas no Brasil em 1950*, Vol. II. Rio de Janeiro: Departamento de Imprensa Nacional, 1952.

12. Alexander, *Communism in Latin America*, p. 128, states that four Communists were elected councilmen under the PRT ticket, yet only the three councilmen below are identified in Tribunal Superior Eleitoral, *Dados estatístcos*, 1952, p. 107.

	Vote (*more than 500*)
Milton José Lobato (elected under PRT)	4,388
Elizeu Alves de Oliveira (elected under PRT)	2,492

SÃO PAULO [13]

Elections of October 3, 1954: Federal Deputies and Municipal Councilmen [14]

FEDERAL DISTRICT

Federal Deputies

Antônio Bruzzi de Mendonça (elected under PRT)	45,137

Municipal Councilmen [15]

Waldemar Viana de Carvalho (elected under PRT)	1,684[16]
Francisco Durso (elected under PRT)	1,223

Elections of October 3, 1958: Federal Deputies and State Deputies [17]

PERNAMBUCO

Alternate State Deputies

Miguel Batista (elected under PTB)	2,615
Clodomir Santos de Morais (elected under PTB)	2,353

BAHIA

Federal Deputies

Fernando de Santana (elected under PTB)	9,154

GUANABARA

Federal Deputies

Lício Silva Hauer (elected under PTB)	15,664

---

13. According to Alexander, *Communism in Latin America,* four PCB members were elected councilmen in São Paulo, two under PST and two under the PTN. These four were replaced by other representatives of the two parties after the electoral court declared the election of the Communists null and void. See Alexander, p. 128 and note 101, based on his interview with Plínio Mello, June 16, 1953.

14. Data for 1954 elections from Tribunal Superior Eleitoral, *Dados estatísticos . . . 1954 e 1955,* Vol. III, Part II, Rio de Janeiro: Departamento de Imprensa Nacional, n.d., esp. p p. 164, 171–72. Unconfirmed sources state that two PCB members and four supporters were elected on non-Communist tickets. One of these, Bruzzi de Mendoça (below), defected from the PCB in May 1957 but retained his seat in Congress. According to Osvaldo Peralva, *O retrato,* pp. 202, 205–76, Bruzzi de Mendonça was the only PCB deputy as of 1956. In 1958 he ran last as an alternate deputy on the PRT ticket.

15. In a communication to the author on July 24, 1970, Rollie Poppino states that the city of Rio de Janeiro's section of the PRT was taken over by the PCB in 1950 and 1954. This would confirm Alexander's information (note 13). Councilmen elected under the PRT, however, may not have been Communists.

16. Carvalho was re-elected in 1958.

17. Electoral data for 1958 from Tribunal Superior Eleitoral, *Dados estatísticos . . . 1958,* Vol. IV, 1961, especially pp. 145–46, 163, 178, 192, 210, 229, 262. Santana, Hauer, Melo, Cerqueira, Domingos Velasco, and Abguar Bastos are identified as members of the PCB in Inquérito Political Militar No. 709, *O Communismo no Brasil,* Vol. II, pp. 274, 390–91. One should be cautious with this often unreliable source, however.

	Vote (more than 500)
Alternates	
Benedito Cerqueira (elected under PTB)	11,087 [18]
Olímpio Fernandes Melo (elected under PTB)	10,707

RIO DE JANEIRO

Alternate Federal Deputies
Domingos Velasco (elected under Aliança Popular
    Nacionalista)   12,644 [19]

SÃO PAULO

Alternate Federal Deputies
Rafael Martineli (elected under PTB)   9,112
Abguar Bastos (elected under PTB)   7,448
Aldo Lins e Silva (elected under PTB)   3,422
Lindolfo Silva (elected under PTB)   43

State Deputies
Francisco Luciano Lepera (elected under PTB)   8,865

*Elections of October 3, 1962: Federal Deputies, State Deputies,
and Municipal Councilmen* [20]

CEARÁ

Alternate State Deputies
Aníbal Fernandes Bonavides (elected under Partido Socialista
    Trabalhista)   3,564

RIO GRANDE DO NORTE

Federal Deputies
Djalma Aranha Marinho (elected under UDN-PST)   49,352 [21]

Alternate State Deputies
Luiz Maranhão Filho (elected under UDN-PST alliance)   1,587

BAHIA

Federal Deputies
Fernando de Santana (elected under Aliança Democrática
    Trabalhista Cristã)   3,564

MINAS GERAIS

State Deputies
Clodsmidt Riani (elected under PTB)   14,328 [22]

---

18. Cerqueira probably was a socialist and sympathizer of PCB.
19. See note 8.
20. Electoral results for 1962 drawn from Tribunal Superior Eleitoral, *Dados estatísticos . . . 1962*, Vol. VI, 1964, esp. pp. 137, 154, 166–67, 169, 171, 201–2, 252, 258, 260, 298.
21. In a communication to the author on July 27, 1970, John W. F. Dulles notes that he was informed during a visit to Natal that Marinho had been censured by PCB about 1942 but had made a self-criticism and rejoined the party.
22. Riani was a sympathizer, apparently not member, of the PCB.

Vote
(more than 500)

GUANABARA

Federal Deputies
Benedicto Cerqueira (elected under PTB-PSB) 3,564 [23]
Marco Antônio Tavares Coêlho (elected under PSD-PST) 21,300
Alternates
Lício Silva Hauer (elected under PTB-PSB) 192
State Deputies
Hércules Corrêa dos Reis (elected under PTB) 13,273
João Massena Mello (elected under PST) 8,149

RIO DE JANEIRO

State Deputies
Francisco Alves da Costa (elected under PSB) 4,359 [24]

SÃO PAULO

State Deputies
Osvaldo Lourenço (elected from Santos but declared null
  and void)
Alternates
Lazaro Paulino Maia (elected under PTB) 201

Municipal Councilmen

SÃO PAULO
Matilde de Carvalho
Moacir Longo
Odon Pereira da Silva

RIBEIRÃO PRETO
Pedro Augusto de Azevedo Marques

SANTOS
Luiz Rodrigues Corvo

Elections of November 15, 1966: Federal Deputies
GUANABARA
Federal Deputies
Hermano Alves (elected under MDB) [25]

23. See note 18.
24. Costa was supported by PCB; see *Novos Rumos,* 188 (September 20, 1962), 8.
25. Alves, who was purged from Congress in December 1968 and sentenced to 27 years in prison for subversive activities, was identified as a member of the PCB Central Committee in a March 1969 report in *Este y Oeste* of Caracas, trans. as "Problems of Subversion in Brazil Reviewed," *Joint Publications Research Service,* 47, 950; Translations on Latin America No. 170, VII (1969), 46.

Appendix B

Leadership of the PCB: Composition of the Executive Commission and Central Committee: 1946–1967

	December[1] 1946 26 (plus 19 alternates)	August[2] 1960 38	June[3] 1964 26	January[4] 1967 22
Alambert, Zuleika		X	X	
Almeida, Neri Reis de			X	
Alves, Hermano				X
Alves, Plínio				X
Alves de Souza Vieira, Mário		X*	X*	
Amazonas, João	X*			
Arruda Câmara, Diógenes	X*			
Bahia, Sabino				X
Barata, Agildo	X			
Batista, Miguel		X	X	
Benaim, Lourdes		X		
Bento, Augusto				X
Bonavides, Aníbal			X	
Bonfim Júnior, Orlando		X*	X[5]	
Braga, Pedro Carvalho	X			
Brasil, Ely				X
Cabral, Celso	X			
Caires de Brito, Milton	X*			
Capistrano da Costa, David	X	X		
Carvalho, Apolônio Pinto de		X	X	
Carvalho, Benedito de	√	X		
Chamorro, Antônio		X		
Chermont, Abel				X
Coêlho, Marco Antônio Tauares		X*	X	
Corrêa, Gentil				X
Costa, Elson		X*		
Costa, Sérgio		X*		
Crispim, José Maria	X			
Dias, Giocondo Alves	X	X*	X*	X*
Dias de Oliveira, Agostinho	X*	X	X	
Ferreira, Joaquim Câmara		X		
Francisco, José			X	
Gomes, Francisco	X*		X	

X—Member of Central Committee
*—Member of Executive Commission
√—Alternate to Central Committee (1946 only).

	December[1] 1946 26 (plus 19 alternates)	August[2] 1960 38	June[3] 1964 26	January[4] 1967 22
Gorender, Jacob		X	X*	
Grabois, Maurício	X*			
Granja, Antônio Ribeiro		X		
Guedes, Amênio	√	X		
Hill, Lindolfo	X			
Holmos (or Olmos), Sérgio	X*		X	
Humberto, Francisco			X	
Kondor, Valério				X
Lima, Firmino de				X
Luchesi, Ramiro		X*	X	
Maranhão Filho, Luís			X	
Maranhão, Olga				X
Marighella, Carlos	X	X*	X*	X
Martins, José	X			
Massena Melo, João	X			
Menesse, Luís				X
Miranda, Jaime Amorim de			X[5]	
Morias, Estócelde	X			
Morena, Roberto		X	X	
Muraro, Mautílio	X			
Oliveira, José Francisco	X			
Oliveira Mota, Renato		X		
Otero, Francisco Antônio Leivas	√	X		
Pacheco da Silva, Osvaldo	√	X		
Pereira, Astrojildo	√	X	X	
Pomar, Pedro	X*			
Praz, Marcel				X
Prestes, Luiz Carlos	X*	X*	X*	X*
Reis, Marco Dinarco	√	X	?[5]	
Ribeiro, Iracena				X
Ribeiro, Ivan Ramos		X*	X	
Rodrigues, Felipe				X
Rodrigues, Orestes Timbaúba	√	X		
Rodrigues dos Santos, Geraldo		X*	X[5]	
Santos, Oto				X
Schenoval, Isaac			X	
Segovia, Maria				X
Segura, João Sanches	X			
Telles, Manoel Jover	√	X*	X	X
Tenório de Lima, Luís		X		X
Timoteo, Adalberto		X		
Vasconcelos, Amarílio	X			
Vieira de Azevedo, Agilberto	X	X	X	
Vila, Jorge				X
Vilar, Lourival da Costa	X	X		

	December[1] 1946 26 (plus 19 alternates)	August[2] 1960 38	June[3] 1964 26	January[4] 1967 22
Vinhas, Moises			X	
Ziller, Armando		X		
Total	26	37	28	22

1. From Partido Comunista do Brazil, Comitê Nacional, "A direção nacional de Partido Comunista do Brasil," *Fôlha do Povo*, 226 (December 17, 1946), 1. A total of 19 alternates is given, including Fernando Lacerda and Octávio Brandão. The eight checked were in leadership positions 15 years later.

2. A list of the leadership is in John W. F. Dulles, "Brazilian Communism and the Military Movement of 1964," Austin, October 20, 1969, unpublished MS, note 6.

3. "Problems of Subversion in Brazil Reviewed," *Joint Publications Research Service*, 47, 950; Translations on Latin America No. 170, VII (1969), 37. Trans. from *Oeste y Este* (March 1969), 1-27. This list is the same as that published in *O Estado de São Paulo,* July 1, 1964, based on information given to police by Neri Reis de Almeida, and is probably accurate.

4. *Ibid.,* pp. 45–46. A very tentative, perhaps incomplete, and not reliable list. By the end of 1967, Gorender, Marighella, and Telles had been expelled from the party. Other than Prestes and Giocondo Alves Dias, no Central Committee member is identified as part of the Executive Commission. Marighella resigned from the Commission in December 1966.

5. According to Dulles, "Brazilian Communism and the Military Movement of 1964," p. 27, Bonfim, Dinarco Reis, Rodrigues dos Santos, and Miranda were named to the Executive Commission at a Central Committee meeting in São Paulo in May 1965 along with Prestes, Marighella, and Giocondo Alves Dias.

Bibliography

Books, Monographs, Pamphlets

This section of the Bibliography consists of secondary works as well as primary documentation on the PCB and on the Marxist and other radical groups with which the Communists compete, party texts, and writings of party leaders. Certain general works on Brazil are included, but their annotations pertain only to Communism. A number of the references in the chapter notes do not directly concern the PCB and so have been excluded from the Bibliography. Titles entered in the Bibliography are preceded by an asterisk on their first appearance (if any) in the chapter notes. In addition, a number of anti-Communist works are included; and while most of these are not particularly useful, those by former party members are especially important.

To assist the researcher, materials in the Municipal Library of Recife are coded *MLR;* those in the Municipal Library of São Paulo, *MLSP;* those in the National Library of Brazil (Biblioteca Nacional do Brazil), *NLB.* Generally only secondary materials are found in these libraries. Some of these materials may be located also in some U.S. libraries, to mention only the Library of Congress, the New York Public Library, and the libraries at universities with strong collections on Latin America, such as Columbia, Florida, Stanford, and Texas. The primary materials, often ephemeral, are in private archives of PCB intellectuals as well as in police archives in Rio, Recife, and São Paulo.

Abreu Ramos, Plínio de. *Como agem os grupos de pressão.* Rio de Janeiro: Cadernos do Povo Brasileiro (20), Editôra Civilização Brasileira, 1963. Pp. 86.

Ação Popular. "Estrategia revolucionária." N. p. 1966. Pp. 12, mimeo. Call for violent revolution in the overthrow of capitalism and "imperialism."

———. "Resolução sôbre o debate teorético e ideológico." N.p., April 1967. Pp. 56, mimeo. Resolution in preparation for AP Second National Congress urging its members to read Marx, Lenin, and Mao.

———. "Textos para militantes." Rio de Janeiro? 1966. Pp. 56, mimeo. Call for complete restructuring of Brazil's social and political order to establish a pure socialism. Through guerrilla warfare the ultimate violent overthrow of capitalism and "imperialism" would be achieved.

———. National Committee. "Asuntos gerais." N.p., May 1967. Pp. 5, mimeo. Plans for the Second National Congress. Analyzes impact on politics that pressure groups (particularly leftist) may exert in order to effect structural changes. Representative of nationalist and revolutionary thought of the early sixties.

Aguiar, Hernani d'. *A guerra revolucionária comunista* . . . Recife: Imprensa Universitária, 1964. Pp. 61. Anti-Communist polemic.

Aguilar, Luis E. (ed.). *Marxism in Latin America.* New York: Alfred A. Knopf, 1968. Pp. 271. Includes a long introd. and a selection by Luiz Carlos Prestes, "Brazilian Communists in the Fight," pp. 139–44, and "Self-Criticism," pp. 250–56, a 1965 document of PCB.

Alexander, Robert J. *Communism in Latin America.* New Brunswick, New Jersey: Rutgers University Press, 1957. Pp. 449. Includes detailed history of PCB, based on documents and personal interviews. "Luiz Carlos Prestes and the Partido Comunista do Brasil," chap. 7, pp. 93–134.

———. *Labor Relations in Argentina, Brazil, and Chile.* New York: McGraw-Hill, 1962. Pp. 387. A useful historical analysis and description of the Brazilian labor movement, its organization and activities, and ties with the left, including PCB. Part I, pp. 25–136, focus on Brazil.

Allen, Robert Loring. *Soviet Influence in Latin America: The Role of Economic Relations.* Washington, D.C.: Public Affairs Press, 1959. Pp. 108. Brief study of Soviet economic influence in Latin America.

Alves, Márcio Moreira. *El despertar de la revolución brasileña.* Havana: Casa de las Américas, 1972. Pp. 284. Critical assessment of recent development in Brazil by a former Catholic-leftist deputy, now in exile for his outspoken views of the military. This work, chosen as the best memoir of the year by the Cuban staté publishing house, exposes the weaknesses of the Brazilian bourgeoisie (of which the author is a member) and of the failings, both of PCB and the revolutionary splinter groups that broke from PCB in the late 1960's. Trans. to English as *A Grain of Mustard Seed. The Awakening of the Brazilian Revolution.* Garden City, N.Y.: Doubleday/Anchor, 1973. Pp. 194.

Alves, Mário, and Paul Singer. *Análise do plano trienal.* Rio de Janeiro: Editôra Universitária da União Nacional de Estudantes, 1963. Pp. 90. A critique of the economic plan presented by the Goulart government. At the time Alves was a prominent PCB officer, and Singer, a PSB member, was associated with the University of São Paulo.

Amado, Jorge. *O cavaleiro da esperança: vida de Luiz Carlos Prestes.* 10th ed. Rio de Janeiro: Coleção Novos Horizontes No. 1, Editorial Vitória, 1956. Pp. 356. Also consulted: 6th ed., São Paulo: Livraria Martins Editôra, 1945. Romantic biography (to 1956) of Brazilian Communist leader by national literary figure and member of PCB. *NLB*

————. *Le chevalier de l'esperance (vie de Luís Carlos Prestes).* Trans. by Julia and Georges Soria. Paris: Editeurs Français Réunis, 1949. Pp. 377. French edition of the author's biography of Prestes.

————. *Homens e coisas do Partido Comunista.* Rio de Janeiro: Edições Horizonte, 1946. Pp. 63. Impressions of PCB, apparently inspired by electoral success during party's legal stage initiated in 1945. *NLB*

————. *Luís Karlos Prestes: zhizn' i revoluitsionnaia bor'ba* (Luiz Carlos Prestes; his life and revolutionary struggle). Moscow: Izdatel'stvo Inostrannoi Literatury, 1951. Pp. 308. Russian edition of the author's biography of Prestes.

————. *O mundo da paz: União Soviética e democracias populares.* Rio de Janeiro: Editorial Vitória, 1951. Pp. 402. Favorable perspectives of the Soviet Union and the Communist world, based on author's visit to socialist-bloc nations in 1949 and 1950. *NLB*

————. *Der Ritter der Hoffnung: Das Leben v. Luis Carlos Prestes.* Translated by Karl Heinrich. Berlin: Verlag Volk und Welt, 1952. Pp. 515. German edition of biography of Prestes.

————. *Seara Vermelha.* 12th ed. São Paulo: Obras de Jorge Amado (12), Livraria Martins Editôra, 1965. Pp. 340. Novel based in part on 1935 Natal revolt. *NLB*

————. *Os subterrâneos da liberdade.* I. *Os ásperos tempos.* II. *Agonia da noite.* III. *A luz no túnel.* 10th ed. São Paulo: Livraria Martins Editôra, 1964. 3 vols. Trilogy on the clandestine period of the PCB during the thirties and early forties, when Communists were persecuted by Vargas dictatorship.

————. *Vida de Luiz Carlos Prestes: o cavaleiro de esperança.* 6th ed. São Paulo: Livraria Martins Editôra, 1945. Pp. 366. Biography of the leader of the Brazilian Communist movement in the original language.

Amaral, Antônio Carlos Cintra da. *O socialismo.* Recife: Imprensa Oficial, 1955.

Pp. 12. Theoretical essay, reprinted from *Revista Pernambucana de Sociologia,* II, 2 (1955). *NLB*

Amazonas, João. *Contra a cassação dos mandatos e pela defesa da economia nacional.* Rio de Janeiro: Editorial Vitória, 1947. Speech in Congress by a Communist deputy.

――――. *Pelo fortalecimento e unidade sindical.* Rio de Janeiro: Edições Horizonte, 1946(?). Pp. 54. Communist role in strengthening the labor movement analyzed by PCB leader.

Amazonas, João, Carlos Marighella and Maurício Grabois. *Em defesa dos mandatos do povo e pela renúncia do ditador.* Rio de Janeiro: Editorial Vitória, 1947. Pp. 20. The authors, deputies in the national Congress, defend the PCB against the ban on its activities. *NLB*

Arruda Câmara, Alfredo. *Contra o comunismo.* Rio de Janeiro: Imprensa Nacional, 1946. Pp. 28. Anti-Communist polemic. *NLB*

Arruda Câmara, Diógenes de. *Forjemos un poderoso partido comunista.* Rio de Janeiro: Edições Horizonte, 1946(?). Pp. 54. Prospects for the PCB analyzed by a leader of party.

――――. *Nosso partido, nossa tatica, nossas tarefas atuais . . . . Informe político da Comissão Executiva ao Plano do Comitê Nacional do PCB, em Fevereiro de 1951.* Rio de Janeiro?, 1951?, Pp. 38. Report on PCB tactics and the objectives, presented to the party's National Committee. *NLB*

――――. *O programa do Partido Comunista do Brasil—bandeira da luta e da vitória: informe apresentado em nome do Comitê Central ao IV Congresso do Partido Comunista do Brasil. . . .* Rio de Janeiro: November 1954. Pp. 50. Report submitted to the PCB Fourth Congress during November 1954. Summarizes internal party debate over Draft Program issued in January of that year and contrasts moderate 1954 statement with the more radical August 1950 manifesto.

Autuori, Luiz. *O sentido comunista da democracia . . . .* Rio de Janeiro: Livraria Editôra, Z. Valverde, 1956. Pp. 250. Not consulted. *NLB*

Avila, Fernando Bastos de. *Neo-capitalismo, socialismo, solidarismo.* Rio de Janeiro: Agir, 1963. Pp. 177. General perspectives and theoretical analysis.

Azevedo, Agilberto Vieira de. *Minha vida de revolucionário,* N.p., 1967. Pp. 64. Memoirs of a Communist who participated in the 1935 revolts and served many years in prison.

Azevedo do Amaral, Ignácio M. *Ensaio sôbre a revolução brasileira. Contribuição para o estudo dos problemas da brasilidade.* Rio de Janeiro: Imprensa Naval, 1963. Pp. 331. An interpretive and descriptive synthesis of revolutionary movements in Brazil since 17th C. Superficial analysis, but useful for identification of protest that has interested many Communist writers.

Backheuser, Everardo. *A sedução do comunismo.* Rio de Janeiro: Edition Centro d. Vital, Série Jackson de Figueiredo (9), Gráficas O Livro Vermelho do Telefone, 1933. Pp. 77. Anti-Communist view. *NLB*

Báez-Camargo, Gonzalo (Pedro Gringoire, pseud.). *A verdade e os erros do marxismo, versão de Júlio Camargo Nogueira.* Rio de Janeiro: Centro Brasileiro de Publicidade, 1936. Pp. 101. Polemical critique of Marxism. *NLB*

Bailby, Edouard. *Que é o imperialismo?* Rio de Janeiro: Cadernos do Povo Brasileiro (17), Editôra Civilização Brasileira, 1963. Pp. 141. A polemical analysis of concept of "imperialism" and its impact on an underdeveloped nation.

A bancada comunista na constituinte de 1946. Rio de Janeiro: Edições Horizonte, 1947. Pp. 43. Communist document describing role of Communist members of the Constituent Assembly.

Bandeira, Moniz, Clóvis Melo, and A. T. Andrade. *O ano vermelho: a revolução russa e seus reflexos no Brasil*. Rio de Janeiro: Retratos do Brasil (64), Civilização Brasileira, 1967. Pp. 418. A resynthesis of the years following the Russian Revolution and formation of the PCB. Important documents are included. The best analysis of radical leftist activities during the period.

Barata, Agildo. *Vida de um revolucionária: memórias*. Rio de Janeiro: Editóra Melso, n.d. Pp. 415. Interesting autobiography in which author relates his experience in the 1924 São Paulo revolt, his association with PCB and the Rio uprising of November 1935, his activity as a PCB councilman and his defection from party.

Barbêdo, Alceu. *O fechamento do Partido Comunista do Brasil (os paraceres Barbêdo) 1. Parecer de 8/2/47. 2. Parecer de 12/4/47. 2. Parecer de 22/8/47*. Rio de Janeiro: Imprensa Nacional, 1947. Pp. 114. Brief summary of events dealing with the ban on PCB. *NLB*

Barros, Adirson de. *Ascenção e queda de Miguel Arraes*. Rio de Janeiro: Editóra Equador, 1965. Pp. 174. Analysis of political career of former governor Pernambuco.

————, Almiro Bica Buys de. *Os movimentos sociais e o socialismo*. 3rd ed. Rio de Janeiro: J. Konfino, 1956. Pp. 278. Historical summary of socialism. *NLB*

————, João Alberto Lins de. *Memórias de um revolucionário*. Rio de Janeiro: Editóra Civilização Brasileira, 1954. Pp. 258. Memoirs by a participant in the 1924 revolt of São Paulo and the Prestes March, a *tenente* and interventor in the state of São Paulo.

Barroso, Gustavo. *Comunismo, cristianismo e corporativismo*. Rio de Janeiro: Edições ABC, 1938. Pp. 164. Attack on Communism by well-known writer and Integralista leader. *NLB*

Basbaum, Leôncio. See also Machado, Augusto (pseud.).

————. *Caminhos brasileiros do desenvolvimento; análise e perspectivas da situação brasileira*. São Paulo: Editóra Fulgor, 1960. Developmental perspectives for Brazil by Marxist nationalist and former Communist. *NLB*

————. *História e consciência social. Das conexões entre a psicologia, a sociologia e a história*. São Paulo: Editóra Fulgor, 1967. Pp. 236. According to the author, his study examines formation of "the social superstructure" or "the manifestations of human activity . . . art, philosophy, religions and institutions, revolutions and wars."

————. *História sincera da república*. 2nd ed. São Paulo: Coleção Temas Brasileiros, Editôra Edaglit, 1962. Vol. I: *Das origens até 1889*. Vol. II: *1889–1930*. Vol. III: *1930–60*. Memoirs and autobiographical notes on author's Brazilian experience, esp. useful for candid and incisive analysis of PCB, of which he once was a member.

————. *História sincera de república*. Vol. IV: *De Jânio Quadros a Costa e Silva (1961–1967)*. São Paulo: Editôra Fulgor, 1968. Pp. 216.

————. *O processo evolutivo da história. Apontamentos críticos à filosofia da história e à sociología*. São Paulo: Biblioteca de História e Sociologia (1), Editôra Edaglit, 1963. Pp. 301. Studies "the material conditions of social existence . . . the infrastructure of societies and history."

————. *Sociología del materialismo*. Buenos Aires: Americalee, 1964. Pp. 398. Theoretical essay.

Bastos, Abguar. *Prestes e a revolução social. Factos políticos, condições socais e causas econômicas de uma fase revolucionária do Brasil*. Rio de Janeiro: Editorial Calvino, 1946. Pp. 366. Sympathetic biography of PCB leader by a Brazilian Communist, and particularly useful for inclusion of significant documents by Prestes and PCB. *NLB*

————. José Lessa. *A doutrina comunista*. Rio de Janeiro: Imprensa Nacional, 1946. Pp. 128. Emphasis on Marxist theory. *NLB*

Bezerra, Gregório. *Eu, Gregório Bezerra, acuso!* N.p. 1967. Pp. 30. Personal account, written in prison, of author's experiences as a Communist in Pernambuco. He recalls his activity as a PCB federal deputy and organizer of peasant leagues, and his years of imprisonment for subversive activity.

Bôa-Vista, Jaime. *Sôbre nulidade de registro e diplomação de candidatos, comunistas por outras legendas partidárias. Fraude, délo e simulação. Associação ilegal. Petição ao juiz eleitoral. Recurso ao Tribunal Regional Eleitoral. Recurso ao Superior Tribunal Eleitoral. Voto vencido Juiz Moreno Loureiro Lima, Parecer do dr. Gonçalo Rollemberg Leite . . . . Memorial do Supremo Tribunal Eleitoral.* 1948. Pp. 26. Documents and the case against PCB legalization. *NLB*

O bolchevismo e a religião. São Paulo: Edições ABC, 1949. Pp. 20. Anti-Communist polemic. *NLB*

Brandão, Octávio. See also Fritz Mayer (pseud.).

————. *Os intelectuais progressistas.* Rio de Janeiro: Organização Simões Editor, 1956. Exalts the work of Tobias Barreto, who recognized Marx as "the most courageous thinker of the 19th century in the area of economic sciences," Euclides da Cunha, who "wrote a brilliant page on Marx in *Contrastes e confrontos,*" and Lima Barreto, who supported the Russian Revolution.

Brazil. Agência Nacional. *Defendemos o futuro. A participação de elementos extrangeiros no levante comunista de novembro de 1935.* Rio de Janeiro: Imprensa Nacional, 1936. Pp. 17. The role of foreign Communist agents in the uprisings of November 1935. *NLB*

————. Escola Superior de Guerra. *O comunismo e os movimentos da juventude.* Rio de Janeiro, 1965. Pp. 50. Army report on Communism and youth movements in Brazil.

————. Ministério de Guerra. Secretaria Geral. *As vitimas das atentados comunistas de 1935.* Rio de Janeiro: Imprensa Nacional, 1941. Pp. 48. Army report on the 1935 uprisings.

————. Polícia Militar do Distrito Federal. *Guía de combate ao comunismo, para uso dos quadros e da tropa da polícia militar do distrito federal.* Rio de Janeiro: Tipografia da Polícia Militar, 1938. Pp. 106. Police guide for combating Communism. *NLB*

"Brazil'skaia Kommunisticheskaiia Partiia," in *Sovetskaia Istoricheskaia Entschklopediia,* Vol. II, Moscow, 1962, pp. 689–92. Brief summary of PCB history.

Bueno, Francisco da Silveira. *Visões da Russia e do mundo comunista.* São Paulo: Editôra Saraiva, 1961. Pp. 253. Perspectives on USSR and the Communist world. *NLB*

Cabral, C. Castilho. *Batalhões patrióticos na revolução de 1924.* São Paulo: Livraria Liberdade, 1927. Pp. 237. On 1924 revolt in São Paulo.

Callado, Antônio. *Tempo de Arraes: padres e comunistas na revolução sem violência.* 3rd ed. Rio de Janeiro: José Alvaro, 1964. Pp. 158. Sympathetic description of activities of Francisco Julião and others who organized the Northeast peasantry before 1964.

Calmon, João. *Duas invasões.* Vol. I. *Invasão vermelha.* Rio de Janeiro: Editôra O Cruzeiro, 1966. Noted for debate he maintained with ex-Deputy Leonel Brizola and for denouncing control of parts of the Brazilian press by North American interests, the author analyzes the "Red Invasion" preceding the 1964 political movement; a second volume, "White Invasion," deals with economic interests seeking control of the Brazilian press.

Cannabrava Filho, Paulo. *Militarismo e imperialismo en el Brasil.* Buenos Aires: Colección Mundo Actual, Editorial Tiempo Contemporáneo, 1970. Pp. 214. Examines the dominant class and the military supporters of imperialism in Brazil. Chap. 6 focused on the left with attention to the rise of PCB and its difficulties after the coup of 1964.

Capistrano de Costa, David *et al.,* "Tese para discussão." Recife? May 1964. Pp. 5, mimeo. Attack on nationalist party leadership for Communist setback after the 1964 coup.

Carmo, José Arimateia Pinto do. *Diretrizes partidárias, VON-PRD-PSD-PTB-PRP-PL-PR-PSP-PDC-PGT-PST-PTN-PCB.* Rio de Janeiro: Editôra Pongetti, 1948. Pp. 329. Useful information on the PCB and other legal parties for the period 1945–47.

Carneiro, Glauco. *História das revoluções brasileiras.* Vol. I: *Da revolução da república a Coluna Prestes (1889–1927).* Rio de Janeiro: Edições O Cruzeiro, 1965. Pp. 354. Useful case-by-case analysis, including documentation, photographs, and critical commentary by Osvaldo Tôrres Galvão.

————. *História das revoluções brasileiras.* Vol. II: *Da revolução liberal a revolução de 31 de Marco (1930–1964). Ibid.* Pp. 715. Esp. helpful on PCB's role in the 1930 revolution, the November 1935 uprising, and the March 31, 1964, military coup.

Carone, Edgard. *Revoluções do Brasil contemporâneo 1922/1938.* São Paulo: Coleção Buriti (11), São Paulo Editôra, 1965. Pp. 174. Excellent brief synthesis of revolutionary developments during the period, including PCB role.

Carpenter, Luiz Frederico Saverbronn. *Sociedade nova e república nova. Brasil: República socialista do trabalho e da cultura.* Rio de Janeiro: Gráficas Alba, 1930. Pp. 127. Not consulted. *NLB*

"Carta + Denuncia, a tôdas as organizações e a todos os membros do PCB." Guanabara, 1967? Pp. 3, mimeo. Attack on PCB theses for Sixth Congress, signed by "Um velho militante comunista da GB."

Carvalho, Apolônio de. *Os problemas da juventude brasileira.* Rio de Janeiro: Edições Horizonte, 1947. Pp. 16. Communist report on Brazilian youth.

Carvalho, Ferdinando de (ed.) *IPM sôbre actividades comunistas, Paraná e Santa Catarina.* Curitiba: Fifth R.M. and Fifth D.I., 1967. Pp. 128. Regional army report of Communism.

Carvalho, J. Nunes de. *A revolução no Brasil, 1924–1925; Apontamentos para a história.* 3rd ed., Rio de Janeiro: Typografia de Terra de Sol, 1931. Pp. 294. Account by a participant, including useful documentation.

Carvalho, Rafael de. *Carta de Alforria do camponês . . . . do deputado Francisco Julião.* Recife? Editôra Jotapê, 1961 (?). Pp. 63. Peasant Poetry on Peasant Leagues, unions, cooperatives, laws, and a demand that the illiterate be entitled to vote.

Carvalho e Souza, O. *Evolução do comunismo no Brasil.* Rio de Janeiro: Departamento Nacional de Propaganda, 1938. Pp. 88. Anti-Communist account, including some documentation of PCB attempts to establish a popular front in Brazil, the 1935 revolts, and the aftermath.

Castro, Orlando Ribeiro de. *E as ordens vieram de Moscou.* Rio de Janeiro: Editôra A. Noite, 1949. Pp. 196. Supports thesis that Communist activity in Brazil is directed from the Soviet Union. *NLB*

Cavalcanti, Paulo. *Eça de Queiroz, agitador no Brasil.* São Paulo: Brasiliana (311), Companhia Editôra Nacional, 1959. Pp. 367. Important critical study of famous 19th-C. Portuguese novelist by a journalist and PCB leader in Pernambuco. *MLR, NLB*

———. *Os equivocos de Caio Prado Júnior.* São Paulo: Argumentos, 1967? Pp. 44. Critical reply to Caio Prado Júnior's *A revolução no Brasil,* with especial attention to Marxist interpretations of feudalism is Brazil.

César, Osório. *Que é o estado proletario? Reflexões sôbre a Russia soviética.* 2nd ed. São Paulo: Editorial Udar, 1933. Pp. 190. Critical view of the USSR.

Chacon, Vamireh. *História das idéias socialistas no Brasil.* Rio de Janeiro: Editôra Civilização Brasileira, 1965. Pp. 415. Undertakes to examine the roots and evolution of socialism in Brazil. Hastily written and disorganized, but a generally useful secondary account. *MLR*

———. *Reflexões sôbre a humanismo maxista; tese apresentada a IV Semana de Estudos Jurídicos de Curitiba em outubro de 1954.* Recife, 1955. Pp. 58. Theoretical essay by a Pernambuco Marxist.

Chaves Neto, Elías. *A revolta de 1924.* São Paulo: Almeida Filho, 1925. Pp. 103, Brief analysis of the 1924 revolt in São Paulo by a Communist who later edited *Revista Brasiliense. MLSP*

Chevalier, Carlos. *Os 18 do Forte. Collectanea organisada pelo Capitão Carlos Chevalier sôbre Siqueira Campos, Commandante dos 18 do Forte de Copacabana, 1922–1930.* n.p., n.d. Pp. 96. Poetry, newspaper articles, and interesting photographs.

Communist Party of Brazil. "Self-criticism," pp. 250–56 in Aguilar, *Marxism in Latin America* (q.v.). Trans. from La situación en Brasil," *Principios,* 108 (August 1965), 142–62.

Congresso Continental de Solidariedade a Cuba. *Anais.* Nitoròi, March 28–30, 1963. Pp. 116. Contains list of Brazilian delegates, and texts of speeches by Francisco Julião, Max da Costa Santos of the PSB, Alvaro Ventura of the Sindicato dos Operários Navais, Roberto Morena, and others.

Costa, Bolívar. *Quem pode fazer a revolução no Brasil?* Rio de Janeiro: Cadernos do Povo Brasileiro (7), Editôra Civilização Brasileira, 1962. Pp. 91. Analysis of right, center, and left political forces in Brazil. Author attempts to determine who will bring about Brazil's revolution. The right is a counter-revolutionary force; the center is apt to form an alliance with the right to achieve reforms.

Costa, Dante. *O socialismo; conceito, raízes históricas, posição atual no Brasil.* Rio de Janeiro: Coleção Rex. Problemas Atuais (1), Organização Simões, 1954. Pp. 128. Socialism in theory and practice in Brazil. *NLB*

Costa Lima, Alvaro Gonçalves *et al. Aspectos da atividade do comunismo em Pernambuco.* Recife: Secretaria da Segurança Pública, Delegacia Auxiliar, 1958. Pp. 218. Police report on PCB in Pernambuco, espec. important for biographical documentation on party leadership; based on files confiscated in a raid on local PCB headquarters. *University of Pernambuco, Law Library.*

Cruzada Brasileira Anticomunista. *Como se desenvolve a ofensiva comunista.* Petropólis. Editôra Vozes, 1961. Pp. 125. Anti-Communist polemic. *NLB.*

Cruzada Brasileira Anticomunista. *Manifesto à nação.* Rio de Janeiro; Jornal do Brasil, 1952. Pp. 23. Anti-Communist polemic. *NLB*

Cunha, Tristão Ferreira da. *Sistemas socialistas: doutrinas e experiências.* São Paulo: Editorial Atlas, 1945? Survey of socialism. *NLB*

Decter, Moshe. *Cartilha de comunismo: teoria e prática.* Trans. by Donaldson M. Garschagen. Rio de Janeiro: Edições GRD, 1964. Pp. 161. Anti-Communist guidelines.

Delamore, Alcibiades. *A bandeira do sangue (combate ao comunismo).* Rio de

Janeiro: Tipografia Jornal do Commercio, 1932. Pp. 108. Anti-Communist polemic. *NLB*

Detrez, Conrad (ed.). *Carlos Marighella pour la libération du Brésil.* Paris: Editions du Seuil, 1970. Pp. 138. Collection of Marighella's writings, incl. a letter to PCB Executive Committee explaining his resignation; a letter to Fidel Castro, August 18, 1967; an interview with Conrad Detrez; and his manual of urban guerrilla warfare published by ALN June 1969. Also an introd. by the editor.

Dias, Everardo. *História das lutas sociais no Brasil.* São Paulo: Temas Brasileiros No. 8, Editôra Edaglit, 1962. Pp. 330. Autobiographical impressions and insights on labor movement in Brazil, by a printer and writer long involved in Socialist currents. Most chapters originated in *Revista Brasiliense,* but there are important documents as well as a chronology of labor strikes and activities, 1798–1934.

Dillon, Dorothy. *International Communism and Latin America: Perspectives and Prospects.* Gainesville: Latin American Monograph No. 19, School of Inter-American Studies, University of Florida Press, 1962. A brief survey.

Diniz, Almachio. *Preparação socialista do Brasil.* Rio de Janeiro: Calvinho Filho, 1934. Pp. 228. Guidelines for socialism in Brazil. *NLB*

Os dois mundos, antiteses enganosas. São Paulo: ADC, 1950. Pp. 12. Anti-Communist polemic. *NLB*

Doria, Antônio de Sampaio. *O comunismo caminha no Brasil.* São Paulo: Editorial Vitória (?), 1933. Pp. 38. Optimistic Communist report. *NLB*

Dubois, Florent Auguste. *Piadas (entre vermelhos).* Belém: Editôra São José, 1954. Pp. 110. Anti-Communist in orientation. *NLB*

Dulles, John W. F. "Brazilian Communism and the Military Movement of 1964." Unpublished MS, Austin?, October 20, 1969. Pp. 53 plus notes. Description of activities and analysis of PCB and its Marxist competitors during the period 1964–1969.

————. "Brazilian Communism: Efforts at Recovery, 1964–1969," Unpublished MS, Austin? April 4, 1971. Pp. 70 plus 15 pages of notes. Review of PCB activities during late 1960s.

————. *Unrest in Brazil. Political-Military Crises, 1955–1964.* Austin and London: University of Texas Press, 1970. Pp. 449. Useful chronological account, including information on PCB and labor movement.

————. *Vargas of Brazil: A Political Biography.* Austin: University of Texas Press, 1967. Pp. 395. Solid biography with occasional references to PCB impact on his policies and actions.

Edmundo, Claudio. *Um engenheiro brasileiro no Russia.* Rio de Janeiro: Calvinho Filho, 1933. Pp. 203. Sympathetic impressions of 5-year visit.

Efimov, A. V., and others. *Brazilija: ekonomika, politika, kul'tura.* Moscow: Izdatel'stvo Akademii Nauk SSR, 1963. Pp. 525. Joint effort by Soviet and Brazilian scholars.

Em guarda (contra o comunismo). Rio de Janeiro: Imprensa do Estado-Maior do Exército, 1937. Pp. 242. Army warning on Communism in Brazil. *NLB*

"Escola de delatores." Rio de Janeiro? 3rd ed., July 1967. Pp. 13, mimeo. Dissident POLOP view attacking organization's leadership. Reflects views of Luís Alberto Moniz Bandeira.

Facó, Rui. *Brasil siglo XX.* Buenos Aires: Editorial Platina, 1963. Pp. 269. Polemic by a Brazilian nationalist, journalist, and PCB member.

————. *Braziliia XX stoletiia* (Brazil in the 20th Century). Moscow: Izdatel'stvo Inostrannoi Literatury, 1962. Pp. 303. Russian trans. of *Brasil século XX.*

————. *Cangaceiros e fanáticos: gênese e lutas.* Rio de Janeiro: Editôra Civilização Brasileira, 1965. Pp. 226. Marxist analysis and provocative interpretation of social banditry, Canudos and O Conselheiro, and Juàzeiro and Padre Cícero. Contains brief chronology and bibliography.

————. "*A Classe Operária*" *20 anos de luta*. Rio de Janeiro: Edições Horizonte, n.d. Pp. 31. Brief history of the PCB organ, *Classe Operária*. *NLB*

Fairbanks, João Carlos. *Refutação científico ao comunismo*. São Paulo: Companhia Editôra Panorama, n.d. Pp. 207. Anti-Communist polemic. *NLB*

Faleão, Waldemar. *Contra o comunismo anti-christão*. Rio de Janeiro: Irmãos Pongetti, 1938. Pp. 180. Anti-Communist polemic. *NLB*

Faria, Octávio de. *Destino do socialismo*. Rio de Janeiro: Ariel, 1933. Pp. 375. *NLB*.

Feitosa, Antônio. *O comunismo e a maçonaria*. 2nd ed. São Salvador: Editora Mensageiro da Fe, 1955. Pp. 123. The misgivings of a Catholic priest. *NLB*

Ferreira, Oliveiros S. *As Fôrças Armadas e o desafio da revolução*. Rio de Janeiro: Edição GRD, 1964. Pp. 152. Though written in 1963, this analysis of armed forces participation in the politics of "Sergeants Revolt" of 1963 and its suggestion of an alliance between civil and military authorities in order to "liberate the unions, organize society and to give predominance to industry" provides background for study of 1964 movement.

Ferreira, S. Dias. *A marcha da coluna Prestes*. With the collaboration of Sady Valle Machado. Pelotas: Livraria do Globo, 1928. Pp. 297. Memoirs of the Prestes march of the 1920's.

Figueiredo, W., and others. *Os idos de março e a queda em abril*. 2nd ed. Rio de Janeiro: José Alvaro Editor, 1964. Pp. 403. Consists of articles by various journalists on the 1964 movement and provides good documentation and excellent background for reconstructing last days of Goulart government.

Fonesca, Gondin da. *Bolchevismo*. Rio de Janeiro: J. R. de Oliveira, 1935. Pp. 411. Russian history (1919–39) and Communism. *NLB*

Franco, Cid. *Anotações de um cassado*. São Paulo: Livraria Martins Editôra, 1965. Pp. 128. Author was deputy of the Brazilian socialist party in São Paulo.

Frank, Andrew Gunder. *Capitalism and Underdevelopment in Latin America. Historical Studies of Chile and Brazil*. New York: Monthly Review Press, 1967. Pp. 298. Sections III and IV focus on capitalist development of underdevelopment, and capitalism and the myth of feudalism in Brazilian agriculture, and constitute a reassessment of Marxist economic thought and a critique of prevailing PCB views.

Freire, Paulo. *O desafio comunista*. Rio de Janeiro: Imprensa Nacional, 1958. Pp. 12. This Catholic reformer became involved in the popular literacy campaign of the sixties in Recife and Pernambuco; the military coup of 1964 forced him into exile in Chile.

Frente Obrero Revolucionário Democrático Cubano. *Derrota comunista en el Brasil. El fracaso de la CUTAL*. Miami: Ediciones FORDC (2), 1964. Pp. 35. Cuban exile polemic on CUTAL activities in Brazil.

Gallejones, Eustaquio. *AP socialismo brasileiro*. Rio de Janeiro: Centro de Informação Universitária, 1965. Pp. 47. Not consulted.

Garôfalo, Rafael. *A superstição socialista*. São Salvador: Livraria Progresso, 1955. Pp. 179. Not consulted *NLB*

Gerson, Brasil. *Tiradentes: herói popular*. Rio de Janeiro: Edições Horizonte, 1946. Pp. 64. Brief, superficial examination of an 18th-century independence movement, an example of interest of PCB writers in historical movements of protest.

Gil, Federico G. "Communism in Latin America," pp. 184–209 in Dan N. Jacobs (ed.), *The New Communisms*, New York: Harper and Row, 1969. Brief synthesis identifying conditions characterizing Latin American Communism, the periods of evolution of the parties, and the impact of the Cuban Revolution.

Glinkin, A. N. *Noveishaya Istoriya Brazilii (1939–1959)*. Moscow, 1961. Cited by John Paul Van Huning as a major work on radical Brazilian politics; "draws extensively on PCB sources for the entire period covered, and is useful even to the reader unacquainted with Russian for its detailed bibliography."

Godhino, Antônio de Oliveira. *Catolicismo, comunismo e outros asuntos (conversa com dois comunistas)*. Rio de Janeiro: Livraria Agir, 1947. Pp. 96. Not consulted.

Gonçalves, Carlos Torres, and Geonisio Curvello de Mendonça. *Positivismo e comunismo; a propósito do surto comunista*. Rio de Janeiro: Jornal do Commercio, 1947. Pp. 28. Not consulted; anti-Communist in orientation. *NLB*

Gordon, Lincoln. "Unclassified Statement on Communism in Brazil," in *Hearings on Castro Communist Subversion in the Western Hemisphere*, Washington, D.C., House Subcommittee on Inter-American Affairs, March 1963. Pp. 245–48.

Gringoire, Pedro, pseud. See Báez-Camargo, Gonzalo.

Guanabarino, Juvenal. *O que vi em Roma, Berlim e Moscou*. Rio de Janeiro: Calvinho Filho, Editor, 1934. Pp. 192. Favorable impressions.

Guilherme, Wanderley. *Quem dará o golpe no Brasil?* Rio de Janeiro: Cadernos do Povo Brasileiro (5), Editôra Civilização Brasileira, 1962. Pp. 98. Author analyzes political situation since August 1961 and speculates on a military coup or a "popular" coup. He prefers the second and outlines conditions for such a takeover.

Halperin, Ernst. "Peking and the Latin American Communists." Cambridge: International Communism Project (C/66-5), Center for International Studies, Massachusetts Institute of Technology, November 1966. Pp. 69, mimeo. Essay on Chinese policy, principally in relation to Cuba.

————. "Proletarian Class Parties in Europe and Latin America. A Comparison." Cambridge: International Communism Project (C/67-7), *ibid.*, August 1967. Pp. 60, mimeo. Comparative analysis with considerable attention to the PCB in an effort to demonstrate that Communists and other Marxist groups have failed to implant revolutionary doctrines and class-consciousness in the Latin American industrial working class.

Harding, Timothy F. "A Political History of the Brazilian Labor Movement." Calif., 1968. Unpublished MS, 9 chaps. Also as Ph.D. dissertation, Stanford University, 1973. Based on library research and personal interviews with Communist and non-Communist labor leaders. Interpretive history of labor movement and the radical left, including the PCB.

Hervé, Egydio. *Democracia liberal e socialismo entre os extremos: integralismo e comunismo*. Pôrto Alegre: Livraria do Globo, 1935. Pp. 206. Interpretive essay on moderating and polarizing currents of the mid-thirties. *NLB*

História universal do proletariado: vinte séculos de oppressão capitalista (a éra da escravidão). Rio de Janeiro, 1927. Pp. 48. Preface by Celso Corrêa. Appeals to workers to unite and correct injustices against them. The text focuses on the discipline, moral fiber, and courage of the ancient Spartans as an example to the Brazilian worker.

Holanda, Nestor de. *Como seria o Brasil socialista?* Rio de Janeiro: Cadernos do Povo Brasileiro (8), Editôra Civilização Brasileira, 1963. Pp. 97. Describes Brazil under socialism.

Horowitz, Irving Louis. *Revolution in Brazil: Politics and Society in a Developing Nation*. New York: E. P. Dutton & Company, 1964. Pp. 430. Besides the author's useful commentary, includes trans. of valuable documents by Brazilian nationalists, including Prestes and Gorender.

Infiltração comunista no Brasil. São Paulo: I PES, Cadernos Nacionalistas (1), 1964. Pp. 43. Auti-Communist attack by right-wing-financed business group.

Inquérito Policial Militar No. 709. *O Comunismo no Brasil.* Vol. I: *Introdução.* Rio de Janeiro: Coleção General Benicio (47–252) Biblioteca do Exército Editôra, 1966. Pp. 298. Superficial overview of PCB "subversion" with attention to the ideological bases, international aspects, historical synthesis of the party, general characteristics of PCB behavior, policy line, and PCB in national politics.

———. Vol. II: *A construção. A infiltração.* Coleção General Benedicio (50–255), *ibid.* Pp. 414. Further results of a military investigation of PCB activities. Here attention is to party organization and to organizational peripheries (e.g., labor, youth, women, intelligentsia).

———. Vol. III: *A agitação e a propaganda. A movimentação de massas.* Coleção General Benedicio (52–257). Biblioteca do Exército Editôra, 1967. Pp. 611. Esp. useful for information on the PCB press and the themes of its propaganda.

———. Vol. IV: *A ação violenta.* Coleção General Benicio (53-258), *ibid.* Pp. 415. Attempts to identify a consistent policy of violence and revolution.

Jackson, D. Bruce. *Castro, The Kremlin, and Communism in Latin America.* Baltimore: Studies in International Affairs (9), The Washington Center of Foreign Policy Research, Johns Hopkins Press, 1969. Pp. 163. Concerns general divisions within the Communist world and their impact on Latin America in the 1960's, with little attention to Brazil.

Jacobs, Dan N. (ed.) *The New Communisms.* New York: Harper & Row, 1969. Pp. 326. See esp. Federico G. Gil, "Communism in Latin America," Chap. 7, pp. 184–209.

Julião, Francisco. *Até quarta, Isabela.* Rio de Janeiro: Editôra Civilização Brasileira, 1965. Pp. 97. Ex-deputy of Brazilian Socialist Party and ex-director of Peasant Leagues narrates his experiences in prison in the form of a letter to his daughter.

———. *Escucha campesino.* Montevideo: Ediciones Presente, 1962. Pp. 76. Actually written by an Uruguayan journalist of the weekly *El Sol* who in an introductory essay traces Julião's and Liga's development. Includes: "Cartillo del Campesino" presented by Julião in October 1960, and "Cartas a los Campesinos."

———. *Que são as ligas companesas?* Rio de Janeiro: Cadernos do Povo Brasileiro (1), Editôra Civilização Brasileira, 1962. Pp. 94. History and program of Ligas.

Jurema, Abelardo. *Entre os Andes e a revolução.* Rio de Janeiro: Editôra Leitura, 1965. Pp. 200. Author, Minister of Justice in the Goulart government, records primarily the events of 1964 as lived by members of the deposed government.

———. *Sexta-Feira, 13: os últimos dias do govêrno Goulart.* Rio de Janeiro: Editôra O Cruzeiro, 1964. Pp. 241. Journalistic account of period prior to the military coup of March 1964.

Kröning, H. *Kontinent Brasilien.* Leipzig, 1963. Pp. 268.

Lacerda, Carlos. See Marcos (pseud.).

Lacerda, Fernando, Luiz Carlos Prestes, and Sinani. *A luta contra o prestismo e a revolução agrária e anti-imperialista /por/ Fernando Lacerda, Luiz Carlos Prestes e Sinani.* Rio de Janeiro (?), 1934. Pp. 152. Attempts to demonstrate that PCB need not be dominated by the personalism of Prestes. *NLB*

Lafayette, Pedro. *Os crimes do Partido Comunista.* Rio de Janeiro: Editôra Moderno, 1946. Pp. 101. Polemic against PCB. *MLSP*

Landucci, Italo. *Cenas e episódios da revolução de 1924 e da Coluna Prestes.* São Paulo: Editôra Brasiliense, 1947. Pp. 212. 2nd ed., rev., 1952; pp. 212. Memoirs by a participant. *NLB*

Leão, Koscioszko Barbosa. *A visão da miseria através da polícia (socialismo-cooperativismo)*. Rio de Janeiro: Andersen, 1936? Pp. 326. Not consulted. *NLB*

Leite, Eurico de Souza, and João Neves de Fontoura. *Defesa do Senador Abel Chermont*. Rio: 1937. Defense of radical Senator accused of subversive activity in November 1935 uprisings.

Leuenroth, Edgard. *Anarquismo—roteiro da libertação social: antologia de doutrina crítica, história, informações*. Preface by Agustin Souchy. Rio de Janeiro: Editôra Mundo Livre, 1963. Pp. 235. Selection of writings by Brazilian anarchists.

———— and Hélio Negro. See entry under Negro below.

Levine, Robert M. "Revolution in Brazil: November 1935." Riverside and Los Angeles: Latin American Research Program, Latin American Center, and African Studies Center, University of California, February 1968. Pp. 29, mimeo. Paper presented to Brazil-Portuguese Africa colloquium, on the revolts in Natal, Recife, and Rio November 23–27, 1935.

————. "The Vargas Regime and the Politics of Extremism in Brazil, 1934–1938." Princeton, New Jersey: Ph.D. dissertation, 1967. Pp. 305. Published as *The Vargas Regime: The Critical Years, 1934–1938*. New York: Columbia University Press, 1970. Based on research in civil police archives in Rio, Recife, and Natal, in the Superior Military Tribunal, and personal archives of Vargas, Caio Prado Júnior and others, this study includes chapters on the left and ANL and the uprisings of 1935.

Liga Socialista Independente. *Projeto de programa e estatutos da Liga Socialista Independente*. São Paulo, 1956. Pp. 31. Party statutes and program as presented to its National Conference.

Lima, Lourenço Moreira. *A Coluna Prestes: marchas e combates*. Prefaces by Caio Prado Júnior, Jorge Amado, and Col. Felipe Moreira Lima. São Paulo: Editôra Brasiliense Limitada, 1945. Pp. 631. Memoirs and important documents by secretary to Prestes Column.

Linhares, Hermínio. *Contribuição à história das lutas operárias no Brasil*. Rio de Janeiro: Baptista de Souza, 1955. Pp. 130. Chronological account of attempts to organize labor in Brazil, with identification of strikes and movements since about 1823. Author, a participant in some of the events he describes, also traces influence of anarchism, socialism, and communism on labor movement.

Livro branco sôbre a guerra revolucionária no Brasil. Pôrto Alegre. 1964. Analysis of "Communist infiltration" in Goulart government; a justification for April 1964 coup.

Lobato, José Bento Monteiro. *Zé Brasil*. Rio de Janeiro: Editôra Vitória, 1948. Pp. 28. Popular poetry by Communist sympathizer and important literary figure. *NLB*

Luís, Pedro. *Para onde irá o comunismo?* São Paulo: Nova Jurisprudencia, n.d. Pp. 225. Anti-CP. *MLSP*

Lyra, Roberto. *O socialismo para o Brasil; cristianismo, nacionalismo, democracia. Vida e pensamento do autor por Evaristo Costa*. Rio de Janeiro: Editôra Civilização Brasileira, 1962. Pp. 107. Sympathetic to socialism and nationalism in Brazil.

Machado, Augusto (pseud. of Leôncio Basbaum). *O caminho da revolução operária e camponeza*. Rio de Janeiro: Calvino Filho Editor, 1934. Pp. 196. Communist appraisal of Brazil under Vargas, especially critical of Prestes' role in 1930 revolution and of PCB as well. Provides detailed program to "realize an agrarian anti-imperialist revolution." *NLB*

Machado, Raul Campelo. *A insídia comunista nas letras e nas artes do Brasil*. Rio de Janeiro: Imprensa Militar, 1941. Pp. 20. Voices concern over Communist penetration into Brazilian arts and letters, by a judge in the court trial of Prestes, Berger, and other Communists. *NLB*

Magalhães, Sérgio. *Prática de emancipação nacional.* Rio de Janeiro: Editôra Tempo Brasileiro, 1964. Pp. 221. Ex-deputy and leader of now extinct Frente Parlamentar Nacionalista analyzes political activity of nationalist movement and reproduces Frente charter.

Mangabeira, Francisco. *Imperialismo, petróleo, Petrobrás.* Rio de Janeiro: Zahar Editores, 1964. Pp. 210. On significance of state-controlled oil monopoly for "imperialism" and Brazilian petroleum reserves.

Mangabeira, João. *Análise do momento político (discurso . . . a 17–6–48).* Ed. by Comissão do Distrito Federal (do Partido Socialista Brasileiro). Rio de Janeiro: Imprensa Nacional, 1948. Pp. 17. Perspectives on current political situation by leading Socialist. *NLB*

Manifesto da Comissão Executiva do P.C.B. (conferência). Rio de Janeiro: Edições Horizonte, 1946. Pp. 32. Official PCB document.

Manifesto liberal-socialista dos estudantes da Faculdade de Direito do Recife al povo do Brasil. Recife: Publicação do Diretório Acadêmico da Faculdade de Direito da Universidade do Recife, 1953. Pp. 16. Liberal-socialist manifesto of law students of Federal University of Pernambuco.

Marcos (pseud. of Carlos Lacerda). *O quilombo de Manoel Congo.* Rio de Janeiro: R. A. Editôra, 1935. Pp. 50. At the time this now-conservative nationalist was pro-Communist.

Mariani, Clemente. *Democracia e comunismo: discurso proferido na Assembleia Nacional Constitutinte.* Rio de Janeiro: Imprensa Nacional, 1947. Pp. 42. Not consulted. *NLB*

Marighella, Carlos. *Escritos de Marighella la guerrilla en Brasil.* Chile: Ediciones Pensa Latinoamericana, 1971. Pp. 304. Documents by the author, 1964–69.

———. *Por que resisti á prisão.* Rio de Janeiro: Edições Contemporâneas, 1965. Pp. 139. Memoirs of author's imprisonment after military coup of March 1964 and after his defection from PCB.

———. *Uma prova em versos (e outros versos).* Rio de Janeiro: Edições Contemporâneas, 1959. Pp. 42. Poems on Prestes and PCB.

Marques, Aguinaldo N. *De que morre o nosso povo?* Rio de Janeiro: Cadernos do Povo Brasileiro (16), Editôra Civilização Brasileira, 1963. Pp. 155. Polemic advocating eradication of problems of disease and health in Brazil; alleges that such problems are caused by oligarchic and "imperialist" forces.

———. *Fundamentos do nacionalismo.* Preface by Oswaldo Costa. São Paulo: Editôra Fulgor, 1960. Pp. 236. A leftist attempts to describe Brazilian nationalism.

Martins, Ivan Pedro. *La liberación nacional de Tiradentes a Prestes.* Montevideo, 1940. Pp. 32. Brief essay linking protest in Brazil from Tiradentes to Prestes and his march.

Matos, Almir. *Em agôsto Getúlio ficou só.* Rio de Janeiro: Editôra Problemas Contemporâneos, 1963. Pp. 86. Polemic by a PCB journalist concerned with U.S. influence in Brazil and party secretarianism during the early fifties.

Maul, Carlos. *Nacionalismo e comunismo.* Rio de Janeiro: Baptista de Souza, 1936. Pp. 270. Not consulted. *NLB*

Mayer, Fritz (pseud.). See also Octávio Brandão.

———. *Agrarismo e industrialização.* Rio de Janeiro (?), 1926 (?) Examines 1924 Paulista revolt and attempts to relate it to "imperialism" and agrarianism in Brazil.

Medeiros, João. *Meu depoimento: sôbre a revolução communista e outros as-*

sumptos. Natal: Imprensa official, 1937. Pp. 144. Documentation in an attempt to exonerate Medeiros, Natal police chief held by rebels in uprising of November 1937.

Madeiros, Maurício de. *Outras revoluções virão.* . . . 9th ed. Rio de Janeiro: Editôra Calvino Filho, Freitas Bastos, 1932. Pp. 270. Contains preface on Communism and chapter on São Paulo revolt.

Mello, B. *Luiz Carlos Prestes. El caballero de la esperanza y la revolución brasileña.* Buenos Aires. n.p., n.d. Favorable impressions of Prestes.

Mello, José Barbosa. See entry under Pedro Motta Lima.

Mello, Olbiano de. *Comunismo ou fascimo?* Preface by Plácido M. Modesto de Mello. Rio de Janeiro: Terra do Sol, 1931. Pp. 193. 2nd ed., Rio de Janeiro: Irmãos Pongetti Editores, 1937. Pp. 143. Favors a fascist path in struggle to reform Brazil. *NLB*

Mello, Robespierre de. *As democracias e a ditaudra soviética.* São Paulo: Irmãos Dupont, 1949. Pp. 116. Critical of Soviet dictatorship.

Melo, Clóvis. *Colonialismo, problema internacional.* Recife: Edição Revista Encontro, 1954. Pp. 144. Survey of colonialism by Pernambuco intellectual, writer, and leader of local PCB.

Mendes, Raymundo Teixeira. *A ordem social e o comunismo.* Rio de Janeiro, 194? Pp. 16. Anti-Communist polemic. *NLB*

Menezes, Florentino. *A ilúsão comunista e a realidade soviética.* Rio de Janeiro: Editôra Moderna, 1934. Pp. 1411. Anti-Communist polemic.

Mergulhão, Benedicto. *O bagageiro de Stalin.* Preface by Oscar Fontenelle. 2nd ed. Rio de Janeiro: Editôra Moderna, 1946. Pp. 172. Anti-Communist polemic. *NLB*

Monteiro, Sylvio. *Como atua o imperialismo ianque?* Rio de Janeiro: Cadernos do Povo Brasileiro (13), Editôra Civilização Brasileira, 1963. Pp. 134. Nationalist discusses tactics for strike action in labor movement.

Miranda, Francisco Cavalcante Pontes de. *Anarchismo, comunismo, socialismo.* Rio de Janeiro: Adersen, 1933. Pp. 142. Not consulted. *NLB*

Moniz, Heitor. *Comunismo.* Rio de Janeiro, n.d. Pp. 122. Not consulted.

Monteiro, Sylvio. *Como atua o imperialismo ianque?* Rio de Janeiro: Cadernos do Povo Brasileiro (12), Editôra Civilização Brasileira, 1963. Pp. 199. Polemic against U.S. "imperialism."

Monteiro, Sylvio. *A ideologia do imperialismo.* São Paulo: Universidad do Povo (20), Editôra Fulgor, 1964. Pp. 87. A nationalist polemic on "imperialism."

Motta Lima, Pedro, and José Barbosa Mello. *El nazismo en el Brasil: proceso del estado corporativo.* Buenos Aires: Editorial Claridad, 1938. Pp. 215. Communist indictment of the Estado Nôvo.

Movimento subversivo de julho (polícia de São Paulo). 2nd ed. São Paulo: Casa Garraux, 1925. Pp. 263. Police report alleging subversion in São Paulo revolt of 1924.

Muricy, (Gen.) Antônio Carlos da Silva. *A guerra revolucionária no Brasil e o episódio de novembro de 1935.* Natal: 1966. Roughly accurate but not carefully documented account of the Natal Revolt.

Negro, Hélio, and Edgard Leuenroth. *O que é o maximismo ao bolchevismo: programa comunista.* São Paulo, 1919. Pp. 128. Anarchist perspectives on Marxism and the Russian Revolution. Analysis of the pamphlet, including excerpts from the original, is in Bandeira et al, *O ano vermelho;* pp. 169–76.

Neruda, Pablo, Pedro Pomar, and Jorge Amado. *O Partido Comunista e a liber-*

dade de criação. Rio de Janeiro: Edições Horizonte, 1946. Pp. 36. Speeches by Neruda, Pomar and Amado. *NLB*

Niemeyer, Waldir. *Movimento syndicalista no Brasil.* Rio de Janeiro, 1933. Pp. 163. Essay on Brazilian labor movement. *NLB*

Nogueira, José Antônio, *et al., O Partido Comunista. Sua condenação pela justicia brasileira.* Rio de Janeiro: Imprensa Nacional, 1947. Pp. 45. Pro and con views of the judges who banned the PCB in May 1947. *NLB*

Oiticica, José. *Ação direta (meio século de pregação libertária).* Ed. with introd. by Roberto das Neves. Rio de Janeiro: Editôra Germinal, 1970. Collection of author's writings from 1901 to late 1950's, reflecting his anarchist perspectives.

————. *A doutrina anarquista ao alcance de todos.* Rio de Janeiro: Editôra Germinal, 1954. Pp. 124. Published originally in newspaper he edited, *Ação Direta,* this is an analysis of anarchist doctrine and ideology. *NLB*

Oliveira, Franklin de. *Que é a revolução brasileira?* Rio de Janeiro: Cadernos do Povo Brasileiro No. 9, Editôra Civilização Brasileira, 1963. Pp. 100. Two lectures given in May 1962 in Faculty of Law at the University of Brazil.

————. *Revolução e contra-revolução no Brasil.* Rio de Janeiro: Cadernos do Povo Brasileiro (Volume Extra), Editôra Civilização Brasileira, 1962. Pp. 131. Preface dedicated to Leonel Brizola. Author seeks revolution that need not be violent.

Oliveira, Nelson Tabajara. *1924. A revolução de Isidoro.* São Paulo: Companhia Editôra Nacional, 1956. Pp. 200. On the São Paulo revolt of 1924 and its aftermath.

Osório, Antônio J., *et al. Prestes, estudos e depoimentos.* N.p., 1947? Pp. 84. Collection of documents by Osório, José Rodrigues, Lourenço Moreira Lima, Jorge Amado, and Pedro Motta Lima.

Palha, Américo. *Jornada sangrenta; campanha contra o comunismo.* Rio de Janeiro, 1936. Pp. 113. Anti-PCB polemic. *NLB.*

Palmares, Antônio. "La izquierda brasileña, historia y perspectivas." Concepción, Chile, 1968. Pp. 79, typescript. Incisive critique by Brazilian Marxist, writing under pseudonym.

Palmeira, Sinval. *Liberdade de ser comunista: razões de recurso dirigidas ao Supremo Tribunal Federal pelo Partido Comunista do Brasil, no processo de cassação de seu registro eleitoral.* Rio de Janeiro: Editorial Vitória, 1947. Pp. 48. Communist rebuttal efforts to ban PCB and an appeal to Supreme Court.

Partido Comunista Brasileiro. Comitê Central. "Resolução política." Rio de Janeiro?, May 1965. Pp. 9, mimeo. Resolution based on report of PCB Executive Commission. Ten-point statement on 1964 coup, U.S. "imperialism" in Brazil, policies of the military dictatorship and measures to deal with it, and need to unite all forces to overthrow the government.

————. Comitê Central. "Teses, aprovadas na reunião do Comitê Central, primeira quinzena do mês de Junho de 1966." São Paulo?, 1966. Theses of PCB Sixth Congress.

————. Comitê Estadual de São Paulo. "Unidade e ação do Partido pela revolução brasileira: resolução do Comitê Estadual de São Paulo do Partido Comunista Brasileiro." São Paulo, September 1967. Pp. 7, typescript. Published in English as "CP State Committee Airs Differences with CC," Foreign Broadcast Information Service, November 21, 1967. Emphasizes "ideological divergences between the majority of the Party and the group dominating the Central Committee."

Partido Comunista Brasileiro. Convenção Municipal de Curitiba do PCB. "Resolução." Curitiba, 1967. Pp. 3, mimeo. Calls on PCB national leadership to modify its "petty-bourgeois" composition and become a genuine party of workers and peasants.

――――. *Estatuto do Partido Comunista Brasileiro*. São Paulo? December 1967. Pp. 35. Approved at party's Sixth Congress.

――――. VIII° Conferência Estadual do PCB do Rio Grande do Sul. "Resolução política do Conferência Estadual do Rio Grande do Sul." Pôrto Alegre? 1967? Pp. 8, mimeo. State resolution opposed to theses for PCB Sixth Congress, approved by Central Committee.

――――. VI° Congresso. *Estatutos do Partido Comunista Brasileiro*. São Paulo? December 1967. Pp. 8. Party statutes approved at Sixth Congress.

――――. VI° Congresso. *Resolução política*. São Paulo? December 1967. Pp. 19. Policy resolution approved at party's Sixth Congress.

――――. "Tópicos do Programa de Ação do Partido Comunista." Reprinted as Document No. 8 in Glauco Carneiro, *História das revoluções brasileiras,* Rio de Janeiro: Edições O Cruzeiro, 1965, Vol. II, pp. 608–11. Allegedly a Communist blueprint for revolutionary action, found in Minas Gerais after coup of 1964.

――――. "Trabalho especial." São Paulo? 1966. Pp. 4, typescript. Advocates that the party maintain a "permanent front" with "self-defense" groups to be organized to oppose repression against party activities.

Partido Comunista do Brasil. Comitê Central. *La guerra popular en el Brasil*. Montevideo: Bandera Roja (15), Nativa Libros, 1970. Pp. 57. Analysis of contemporary Brazil; adopts a Maoist position in favor of armed struggle and popular war.

Partido Comunista do Brasil. Commissão Central Executiva. *Estatutos approvados no Congresso Comunista reunido no Rio de Janeiro a 25, 26 e 27 de março de 1922*. Rio de Janeiro: Edição da Commissão Central Executiva, 1922. Statutes approved at PCB's First Congress.

――――. Comitê National. *Estatutos. Projeto de reforma*. 2nd ed. Rio de Janeiro: Edições Horizonte, 1946. Pp. 27. Another edition of PCB statutes.

――――. Comitê Nacional. *Luta pela constituinte*. Rio de Janeiro: Edições Horizonte, 1946. Pp. 39. PCB position on Brazilian constitution.

――――. Conferência Nacional Extraordinário. "Em defesa do Partido." São Paulo, February 1962. Reprinted in Inquérito Policial Militar No. 709, *O comunismo no Brasil . . . ,* Vol. III, pp. 435–39. Justification of dissident policies of PC do B and condemnation of old PCB.

――――. *Estatutos do Partido Comunista do Brasil. Projecto de reforma*. Rio de Janeiro: Comitê Nacional do Partido Comunista, 1946. Pp. 32. PCB statutes.

――――. *Manifesto de convocação. (Teses). Resoluções. III Conferência Nacional do PCB*. Dio de Janeiro: Edições Horizonte, 1946. Pp. 32. Theses of PCB's Third National Conference.

――――. *Programa do Partido Comunista do Brasil*. Rio de Janeiro: Imprensa Popular, 1954. Pp. 21. PCB Program adopted at party's Fourth Congress.

――――. Sixth Conference. "Resolução da Sexta Conferência do Partido Comunista do Brasil (junho de 1966): União dos Brasileiros para livrar o país da crise, da ditadura e da ameaça neocolonialista." Guanabara? June 1966. Pp. 48, mimeo. Conference of dissident PC do B paralleling PCB Sixth Congress. Approved new statutes and a policy resolution in favor of violence and in assent that peaceful coexistence with United States was a mistaken policy.

――――. *Um ano de legalidade . . .* Preface by Pedro Pomar. Rio de Janeiro: Editorial Horizonte, 1946(?) Pp. 27. Review by Communist leader of PCB accomplishments during legal existence 1945–46. *NLB*

Partido Comunista Brasileiro Revolucionário. "Reencontro histórico ou simples mistificação?" Rio de Janeiro? 1968? 11 pp., typescript. Accusation by Manoel Jover Telles of fellow PCBR leaders for taking an "intermediate position" between revisionism and Marxism-Leninism..

————. "Resolução da Comissão Executiva Nacional do Partido Comunista Brasileiro Revolucionário (PCBR) sôbre atividades divisionistas no Comitê Estadual do Guanabara." Rio de Janeiro? June 1968. Pp. 5, typescript. Attacks PC do B.

Partido Operário Revolucionário. *Por um 1° de maio anti-capitalista: Pelo triunfo da revolução socialista mundial.* Rio de Janeiro: Direção Nacional de Partido Operário Revolucionário, 1956. Pp. 4. Trotskyist document. *NLB.*

Partido Socialista Brasileiro. *Estatutos.* Rio de Janeiro: Comissão Executiva do Estado da Guanabara, 1960. Pp. 19. PSB statutes.

————. *Estatutos. Comissão Executiva Nacional.* Rio de Janeiro: Comissão Executiva do D.F. Rio de Janeiro, Departamento de Imp. Nacional, 1951. Pp. 11. PSB statutes. *NLB*

————. *Programa do Partido Socialista Brasileiro.* Rio de Janeiro: n.p., n.d. Pp. 2. PSB program.

Pedreira, Fernando. *Março 31: civis e militares no processo da crise brasileira.* Rio de Janeiro: José Alvaro Editor, 1964. Pp. 208. One of the most interesting works on causes of 1964 political movement; analyzes Goulart government, role of the "moderating power" of the armed forces, "Nasserism" in Brasilian political life, the Brazilian "Left," alternatives of development, and the first six months of Castello Branco regime.

Peralva, Osvaldo. *Pequena história do mundo comunista.* Rio de Janeiro: Edition of the Author, 1964. Pp. 197. Brief historical survey of international Communism by former Communist journalist who left PCB in 1957 and later joined PC do B. *NLB*

————. *O retrato.* Belo Horizonte: Editôra Itatiaia, 1960. Pp. 400. Best-selling, anti-Communist analysis by journalist formerly an editor of the Communist daily, *Tribuna Popular.*

————. *O retrato: impressionate depoimento sôbre o comunismo no Brasil.* Rio de Janeiro: Editôra Globo, 1962. Pp. 275.

Perdigão, José Maria Reis. *O manifesto do Partido Socialista Brasileiro, e um documento do escandalosa mistificação.* São Paulo: São Luiz, 1933. Pp. 73, Not consulted. *NLB*

Pereira, Astrojildo. *Crítica impura (autores e problemas).* Rio de Janeiro: Coleção Vera Cruz (Literatura Brasileira IX), Editôra Civilização Brasileira, 1963. Pp. 347. This respected literary critic and a PCB founder presents essays on diverse Brazilian topics, including Monteiro Lobato and the trade union movement; on the "new China;" and on "culture and society."

————. *Formação do PCB, 1922–1928.* Rio de Janeiro: Editorial Vitória, 1962. Pp. 143. Memoirs and historical analysis of first phase of PCB by one of its founders, and secretary general during period 1922–28. Important and useful.

————. *Interpretações.* Rio de Janeiro: Edições CEB, Livraria-Editôra da Casa do Estudante do Brasil, 1944. Pp. 301. Critical essays on persons and topics, including Machado de Assis, Lima Barreto, and Rui Barbosa.

————. *Machado de Assis. Ensaios e apontamentos avulsos.* Rio de Janeiro: Editôra São José, 1959. Interpretative critical essays.

————. *USSR-Itália-Brasil.* Rio de Janeiro: Editôra Alba, 1935. Impressionistic essays.

Pereira da Silva, Gustão. *A mulher no regime proletário. A verdadeira situação da mulher no Russia.* Rio de Janeiro: Calvinho Filho, Editor, 1934. Pp. 210. 2nd ed. Rio de Janeiro: Editôra Panamericana, n.d. Pp. 206. Sympathetic view of working woman.

Peri, Marcos. *Perspectiva da revolução brasileira.* Rio de Janeiro?: Edições Autores Reunidos, 1962. Pp. 163. First two-thirds of this critical assessment focus on international aspects of Communism, with data on PCB. The last third concerns PCB's integration with national Brazilian poiitics, and concludes with recommendations for modification of PCB and its policies aimed at working class and peasants.

O periódo comunista: esclarecendo o povo brasileiro. Preparativos bolchevistas para a implantação da república popular brasileira. Recife: I. Nery da Fonseca, 1958. Pp. 171. Anti-communist polemic plus documentation on PCB.

Peterson, Phyllis J. "Brazilian Political Parties, Formation, Organization and Leadership, 1945–1959." Unpublished Ph.D. dissertation, University of Michigan, 1962. Pp. 370. Political analysis, including leftist parties.

Pimentel, A. Figueiredo. *A inspiradora de Luiz Carlos Prestes.* 3rd ed. Preface by Azevedo Amaral. Rio de Janeiro: Calvinho Filho, Editor, 1933. Pp. 202. Romance based on march of the Prestes column.

Pinto, Alvaro Franco. "Sob a signo do cruzeiro ou o operário brasileiro e o comunismo." São Paulo: Ramos Franco Ed., 1947. Pp. 37, mimeo.

Pinto, Olympio. *Socialização do Brasil.* Rio de Janeiro: Tipografia Luzitania, 1933. Pp. 150. Not consulted. *NLB*

Pires, Jurandir. *A extinção dos mandatos e a tática comunista; debates parlamentares.* Rio de Janeiro: Imprensa Nacional, 1948. Pp. 45. On PCB tactics in Congress and banning of the party. *NLB*

Política Operária. "Declaração política do 4° Congresso do OBMPO." N.p., September 1967. Pp. 5, mimeographed. Declaration of POLOP's Fourth National Congress; advocates a strictly proletarian uprising, guerrilla warfare, and formation of a truly Marxist-Leninist party in Brazil.

————. "Por que anular o voto nas eleições estaduais da Guanabara?" Rio de Janeiro? 1965? Pp. 2, mimeographed. Concern over new legislation by Castelo Branco government to thwart the opposition in future elections.

Pomar, Pedro. *O PCB no trabalho de massa; informe de trabalho de massa da Comissão Executiva ao Comitê Nacional do Partido Comunista do Brasil, apresentado . . . em janeiro de 1946.* Rio de Janeiro: Edições Horizonte, 1946. Pp. 36. Report on Communist efforts to mobilize labor, presented to PCB leadership.

Poppino, Rollie. *International Communism in Latin America: A History of the Movement, 1917–1963.* New York: The Free Press of Glencoe, 1964. Pp. 247. General survey of Communism in Latin America, with detailed sections on the movement in Brazil.

Porto, Eurico Bellens. *A insurreição de 27 de novembro.* Rio de Janeiro: Polícia Civil no Districto Federal, Imprensa Nacional, 1936. Pp. 265. Indictment of PCB for its role in 1935 uprisings. Invaluable documentation, including biographical sketches and personal accounts by Communist leaders and rank and file.

Pôrto Sobrinho, Antônio. *A guerra psicológica no Brasil.* Rio de Janeiro: Editôra Fundo de Cultura, 1965. Pp. 143. Analysis of "psychological war" as one of the instruments employed for "Communist subversion in Brasil."

Prado Júnior, Caio. *The Colonial Background of Modern Brazil.* Trans. by Suzette Macedo. Berkeley and Los Angeles: University of California Press, 1967. Pp. 530. Classic study by Brazilian Marxist, former PCB deputy from São Paulo. Its three parts focus on "population and settlement," "material life," and "social and political life."

————. *Dialética do conhecimento*. São Paulo: Editôra Brasiliense, 1952. 2 vols. *NLB*

————. *Esbôço dos fundamentos da teoria econômica*. São Paulo: Editôra Brasiliense, 1957. Pp. 227. *NLB*

————. *Evolução política do Brasil e outros estudos*. 2nd ed. São Paulo: Editôra Brasiliense, 1957. Pp. 264. 3rd ed., 1961; 4th ed., 1963.

————. *Evolução política do Brasil; ensaio de interpretação dialética de historia brasileira*. 2nd ed. São Paulo: Editôra Brasiliense, 1947. Pp. 203.

————. *Formação do Brasil contemporâneo. Colônia*. São Paula: Livraria Martins, 1942. Pp. 388.

————. *Formação do Brasil contemporâneo. Colônia*. 7th ed. São Paulo: Editôra Brasiliense, 1963. Pp. 390.

————. *História econômica do Brasil*. São Paulo: Coleção Grandes Estudos Brasilienses (2), Editôra Brasiliense, 1945. Pp. 318. 8th ed., 1963; pp. 354. Interpretative economic history, 1500 to 1960, from Marxist perspective presented according to consecutive chronological periods.

————. *O mundo do socialismo*. São Paulo: Editôra Brasiliense, 1962. Pp. 183. Based on author's travels to Soviet Union and Communist China in 1960.

————. *A revolução brasileira*. São Paulo: Editôra Brasiliense, 1966. Pp. 332. Marxist reinterpretation of prevailing Marxist conceptions in Brazil. An important statement.

————. *U.R.S.S., um novo mundo*. São Paulo: Coleção Viagens (3), Editôra Nacional, 1934. Pp. 241. *NLB*

Praxédi, Zé. *O sertão é assim* . . . . Rio de Janeiro: Editorial Vitória, 1960. Pp. 99. Popular peasant poetry, published by PCB.

Prestes, Luiz Carlos. "Brazilian Communists in the Fight for Democracy," pp. 139–44 in Aguilar, *Marxism in Latin America*. Trans. from *Os comunistas na luta pela democracia*, pp. 6–12.

————. *Cinco cartas da prisão*. Rio de Janeiro: Edições Horizonte, 1938? Pp. 14. Letters from imprisoned PCB leader on ANL and the future of PCB, written in 1938 to Tenente Severo Fournier. *NLB*

————. *Os comunistas e a Conferência de Petrópolis*, n.p., n.d. Pp. 7. Interview.

————. *Os comunistas e a religião*. Rio de Janeiro: Sabatinas de Luiz Carlos Prestes, Edições Horizonte, 1945. Pp. 14. Excerpts from two speeches on religion.

————. *Os comunistas e o monopólio da terra*. Rio de Janeiro: Sabatinas de Luiz Carlos Prestes (2), Edições Horizonte, 1945. Pp. 15. Excerpts from writings and speeches.

————. *Os comunistas lutam pela ordem e pela consolidação da democracia*. Rio de Janeiro: Edições Horizonte, 1947. Pp. 14. Speech to the Senate, November 26, 1946.

————. *Os comunistas na luta pela democracia; informe político da Comissão Executiva ao Comitê Nacional do Partido Comunista do Brasil, apresentado na solenidade de instalação do C.N., realizada em 7 de agosto de 1945, no Instituto Nacional de Música*. Rio de Janeiro: Edições Horizonte, 1945. Pp. 45. Reviews of international situation and PCB evolution to 1945. Pp. 6–12 trans. as "Brazilian Communists in the Fight for Democracy," pp. 139–44 in Aguilar, *Marxism in Latin America* (*q.v.*).

————. *Contra a guerra e o imperialismo*. Rio de Janeiro: Editorial Vitória, 194(?). Speech in Constituent Assembly on American "imperialism," March 26, 1946.

————. *Depoimento perante a comissão de inquérito sôbre atos, delituosos da ditadura.* Rio de Janeiro: Editorial Vitória, 1948. Pp. 32. Review of tortured "democrats" held in prison. *NLB*

———. *Documentos de Luís Carlos Prestes.* Buenos Aires: Ediciones Tiempos Nuevos, 1947. Pp. 177. Collection of public speeches and reports trans. to Spanish. Overlaps his *Problemas atuais da democracia (q.v.).*

———. *Dolores Ibarruri, La Pasionaria.* Rio de Janeiro: Edições Horizonte, 1946. Pp. 28. Speech of December 9, 1945, on leader of Partido Comunista de España. NLB

———. *Em marcha para um partido comunista de massas.* Rio de Janeiro: Editorial Vitória, 1944. Pp. 44. Presented at plenary session of National Committee of PCB, December 6, 1946. *NLB*

———. *Frente nacional para salvação da pátria; discurso pronunciado no senado federal, na sessão de 5 de agosto de 1947.* Rio de Janeiro: Editorial Vitória, 1947. Pp. 35. Advocates formation of Frente Nacional of leftist parties. *NLB*

———. *Organizar o povo para a democracia; discurso, pronunciado a 15 de julho no estádio de Pacaembú.* Rio de Janeiro: Edições Horizonte, 1945. Pp. 32. Attack on national problems and outlines organization of União Nacional, the Comitês Democráticos Populares, CGTB, and youth movement. *NLB*

———. *A palavra de Prestes na constituinte—discurso pronunciado pelo Senador Luiz Carles Prestes, na Assembléia Constituinte, na sessão de 5 de fevereiro de 1946.* Rio de Janeiro: Edições Horizonte, 1946. Pp. 15. Speech of February 5, 1946, to Constituent Assembly.

———. *O PCB na luta pela paz e pela democracia—informe político da Comissão Executiva ao Comitê Nacional do Partido Comunista do Brasil, apresentado por Luiz Carlos Prestes, no solenidade de instalações do Pleno Ampliado do C.N. em 4 de janeiro de 1945 no Instituto Nacional de Música.* Rio de Janeiro: Edições Horizonte, 1945. Pp. 75. Political report of Comissão Executiva to plenary session of PCB Comitê Nacional, January 1946.

———. *Paz indivisível. Comemoração da vitória e contra a política de blocos; discurso pronunciado na Assembléia Constituinte em 8-15-1946.* Rio de Janeiro: Edições Horizonte, 1946. Pp. 30. Report of meeting of PCB Comissão Executiva, May 6, 1946. *Hoover Institution Library.*

———. *Por que os comunistas apoiam Lott e Jango.* Rio de Janeiro: Coleção Documentos Políticos (3), Editorial Vitória, 1960. Pp. 46. Two documents, dated September 1959 and March ·1960, in support of Presidential candidate Lott and Vice Presidential candidate Goulart.

———. *O problema de terra e a constituição de 1946.* Rio de Janeiro: Imprensa Nacional, 1946. Pp. 30. Same as following reference.

———. *O problema da terra e a constituição de 1946—discurso pronunciado na Assembléa Nacional Constituinte pelo . . . ."* Rio de Janeiro: Edições Horizonte, 1946. Pp. 64. Speech to Constituent Assembly on the land problem.

———. *Problemas atuais da democracia.* Preface by Pedro Pomar. Rio de Janeiro: Editorial Vitória, 1948. Pp. 519. Collection of speeches and documents 1935–1946. Important for PCB policy. *NLB*

———. *Relatório e accordão do process em que são accusados Luiz Carlos Prestes, Harry Berger, Dr. Pedro Ernesto e outros . . . .* Rio de Janeiro: Imprensa Nacional, 1937. Pp. 171. *NLB*

———. *Resistência. Unidade. Organização.* São Paulo: Pequena Biblioteca Popular, 1947. Pp. 12. Speech of November 5, 1947.

———. *A situação no Brasil e no mundo.* Rio de Janeiro, 1945. Pp. 16. Speech on general conditions in Brazil and the world, reprinted from *O Globo* of March 15, 1945.

BOOKS, MONOGRAPHS, PAMPHLETS 263

————. *A situação política e a luta por um governo nacionalista e democrático.* Rio de Janeiro: Coleção Documentos Políticos (1), Editorial Vitória, 1959. Pp. 74. In favor of nationalist government. *NLB*

————. *Solução imediata para os problemas do povo.* Rio de Janeiro: Edições Horizonte, October 1946. Pp. 51. Political report to Third National Conference of PCB.

————. *The Trial of Luiz Carlos Prestes.* Introd. by Prof. Roger Picard. Paris: Association Juridique Internationale, 1936? Pp. 24.

————. *União Nacional para a democracia e o progresso.* Rio de Janeiro: Edições Horizonte, 1945. Pp. 29. Speech of May 23, 1945.

————. "The United States, the Soviet Union, and Communism in Brazil," in Irving Louis Horowitz, *Revolution in Brazil,* New York: Dutton, 1964, pp. 341–45. Advocates breaking U.S. monopoly of Brazilian foreign trade and a reorientation of foreign policy toward Soviet Union.

———— and K. E. Vorochilov. See entry under Vorochilov.

Quartim, João. *Dictatorship and Armed Struggle in Brazil.* Trans. by David Fernbach. New York: New Left Books, Monthly Review Press, 1971. Pp. 250. Best available analysis of the armed struggle of revolutionary groups to the left of the PCB, covering period 1964–70.

O que é o trotskismo. Rio de Janeiro: Editôra Verdade, 1933. Pp. 77. Brief sketch of Trotskyism in Brazil. *NLB*

Queiroz, Nelson Araújo. *Até eu sería comunista.* Belo Horizonte: Edições Loyola, n.d. Pp. 62. Catholic "exposé" of Communism.

Quintiliano, Aylton. *A grande muralha (romance).* 2nd ed. Rio de Janeiro: Bruno Buccini Editor, 1960. Pp. 287. Autobiography by defector from PCB and former journalist of *Imprensa Popular;* focuses on grassroots Communist activities and attacks Prestes.

Relatório e accordão do processo em que são accusados Luiz Carlos Prestes, Harry Berger, dr. Pedro Ernesto e outros. Juiz relator Dr. Raul Machado. Preparadores dr. Raul Machado, al. Costa Netto e Dr. Pereira Broya. Rio de Janeiro: Imprensa Nacional, 1937. Pp. 171. The trial of Prestes and other Communists and non-Communists for their role in November 1935 uprisings. *NLB*

Rezende, Leonidas. *Pequena história da revolução bolchevique.* Rio de Janeiro: Editorial Calvino Limitada, 1945. Pp. 274. Brief history of Russian Revolution by former editor of *A Nação.*

Ribeiro, Luiz de Prado ¿*Qué é communismo? O credo russo em face da atualidade brasileira.* Rio de Janeiro: Norte Editôra 1937. Pp. 74. Anti-Communist pamphlet. *NLB*

Rodrigues, Edgar. *Socialism e sindicalismo no Brasil, 1675–1913,* Rio de Janeiro: Gráfica Editôra Laemmert, 1969. Pp. 342. Best study to date of anarcho-syndicalist movement in Brazil.

Rodrigues, Felix Contreiras. *O socialismo e a liberdade do comércio.* Pôrto Alegre: Tipográfica do Centro, 1948. Pp. 31. Concerned with impact of socialism on free enterprise. *NLB*

Rodrigues, Leôncio Martins. *Conflito industrial a sindicalismo no Brasil.* São Paulo: Difusão Européia do Livro, 1966. Pp. 222. One of the best surveys of labor movement, with emphasis on state domination of labor in post–1938 period.

Rossi, Agnelo. *A filosofia do comunismo.* Petrópolis: Editôra Vozes, 1947. Pp. 127. Anti-Communist polemic. *NLB.*

Rui, Affonso. *A primeira revolução social brasileira.* São Paulo: Brasiliana, Biblioteca Pedagógica Brasileira, Companhia Editôra Nacional, 1942. Polemical and pro-communist.

Ruy, Affonso. *A primeira revolução social brasileira.* 2nd ed. Preface by Helio Viana. Salvador: Tipografia Beneditina, 1951. Pp. 192.

Salgado, Plínio. *Doutrina e tática comunistas (noções elementares).* Rio de Janeiro: Livraria Clássica Brasileira, 1956. Pp. 151. Polemic by leader of Integralist movement in Brazil. *NLB*

Sampaio, Doria. *O comunismo caminha no Brasil.* São Paulo, 1933. Pp. 38. Anti-PCB.

Santa Rosa, Virginia. *Que foi o tenentismo?* Rio de Janeiro: Cadernos do Povo Brasileiro (22), Editôra Civilização Brasileira, 1963. Pp. 135. Classic study of tenentismo, originally published in 1933 as *O sentido do tenentismo.*

Santos, Brenno dos. *Contra o comunismo russo e contra a democracia plutocrática, programa político.* Rio de Janeiro: n.p., 1955. Pp. 6. Anti-Communist political platform. *NLB*

Santos, Mário Ferreira dos. *Análise dialéctica do marxismo.* São Paulo: Logos, 1953. Pp. 223. *NLB*

Santos de Oliveira, Antenor. *Você conhece o comunismo? Mas conhece mesmo?* São Paulo: Editôra Antenor Santos de Oliveira, 196? Pp. 155. Anti-Communist polemic.

São Paulo. Secretaria da Segurança Pública, Departamento de Ordem, Política e Social. *Actividades comunistas junto a campanha do petróleo.* São Paulo: 1949. Pp. 14. Police document alleging Communist participation in nationalist campaign in defense of Brazilian petroleum reserves. *NLB*

————. *Relatório: inquérito instaurado contra Luiz Carlos Prestes e outros por ocasião da revolução de Março de 1964.* São Paulo, 1964. Pp. 76. Published findings of the São Paulo investigation of Prestes and others.

Sasso, R. *In Hungry Northeast Fidel and Nasser Are Gods, As Is Julião the Prophet.* Washington, D.C.: Government Printing Office, 1961. Pp. 7.

Schooyans. Michel. *O comunismo e a futuro da igreja no Brasil.* São Paulo: Editôra Herder, 1963. Pp. 96. Catholic attack on Communism.

Severo, Alfredo. *As falsas bases do comunismo russo.* Rio de Janeiro: Imprensa Naval, 1931–59. 2 vols. Attack on Communism. *NLB*

Silva, Hélio. *O ciclo de Vargas.* Vol. 1: 1922 . . . ; Vol. II: 1926 . . . ; Vol. III: 1930 . . . ; Vol. IV: 1931 . . . ; Vol. V: 1932 . . . ; Vol. VI: 1933 . . . ; Vol. VII: 1934 . . . ; Vol. VIII: 1935 . . . ; Vol. IX: 1937 . . . ; Vol. X: 1938 . . . ; Vol. XI: 1939 . . . ; Vol. XII: 1942 . . . . Rio de Janeiro: Coleção Documentos da História Contemporânea, Editôra Civilização Brasileira, 1965–72.

Simão, Azis. *Sindicato e estado: suas relações na formação do proletariado do São Paulo.* São Paulo: Dominus, 1966. Pp. 245. Sociological and historical analysis of labor, with emphasis on São Paulo during period 1920–40.

Simonsen, Roberto Cochrane. *As classes produtoras do Brasil e o Partido Comunista; discurso proferido . . . no sessão do dia 2 de junho de 1947, no Senado Federal.* Rio de Janeiro: Imprensa Nacional, 1947. Pp. 12. Anti-Communist speech by distinguished economist and conservative.

Skidmore, Thomas E. *Politics in Brazil, 1930–1964. An Experiment in Democracy.* New York: Oxford University Press, 1967. Pp. 446. One of the most useful political histories of contemporary Brazil, esp. for information on emergence of nationalism during the period and Communist influences on nationalist activity. Occasional references to PCB activities.

"Sôbre a 'Tese para discussão'." São Paulo?, 1964? Pp. 11, mimeo. Rebuttal to Pernambuco denunciation of PCB national leadership for mistakes of 1964.

Sodré, Nelson Werneck. *As classes socias no Brasil.* Rio de Janeiro: Textos de

História do Brasil (1), Instituto Superior de Estudos Brasileiros, 1957. Pp. 51. Analysis of social classes in Brazil by Marxist historian, participant in ISEB.

———. *Formação da sociedad brasileira*. Rio de Janeiro: Coleção Documentos Brasileiros (47), J. Olympio, 1944. Pp. 338.

———. *Formação histórica do Brasil*. Rio de Janeiro: Coleção Documentos Brasileiros (47), Liv. José Olympio, 1944. Pp. 338. Interpretative history from Marxist perspective.

———. *Formação histórica do Brasil*. 3rd ed. São Paulo: Editôra Brasiliense, 1964. Pp. 338.

———. *História da burguesia brasileira*. Rio de Janeiro: Retratos do Brasil (22), Editôra Civilização Brasileira, 1964. Pp. 418. Historical analysis in attempt to evaluate role of national bourgeoisie in the Brazilian revolution.

———. *História militar do Brasil*. Rio de Janeiro: Retratos do Brasil (40), Editôra Civilização Brasileira, 1965. Pp. 439. Systematic and documented study of Brazil's armed forces.

———. *Introdução à revolução brasileira*. Rio de Janeiro: Coleção Documentos Brasileiros (98), José Olympio, 1958. Pp. 257. Guidelines on the future Brazilian revolution.

———. *O que se deve ler para conhecer o Brasil*. Rio de Janeiro: Centro Brasileiro de Pesquisas Educacionais, INEP, Ministério da Educação e Cultura, 1960. Pp. 388. Useful bibliography on Brazil in general.

———. *Quem é o povo no Brasil?* Rio de Janeiro: Cadernos do Povo Brasileiro (2), Editôra Civilização Brasileira, 1962. Pp. 60. Attempt to define classes in Brazil; author foresees "Brazilian Revolution."

———. *Raízes históricas do nacionalismo brasileiro*. Rio de Janeiro: Textos de Formação Histórica do Brasil (3), Ministério da Educação e Cultura, Instituto Superior de Estudos Brasileiros, 1959. Pp. 40. Important statement on nationalism.

Solomin. *A emancipação da mulher na URSS*. São Paulo: Edições Nosso Livro, 1934. Pp. 114. The "liberation" of women in Soviet Union.

Stoiano, Constantino *et al. Operários paulistas na União Soviética*. São Paulo: Edições Fundamentos, 1951? Pp. 71. Impressions of São Paulo workers visiting Soviet Union.

Telles, Manoel Jover. *O movimento sindical no Brasil*. Rio de Janeiro: Editorial Vitória, 1962. Pp. 301. Historical treatment with emphasis upon recent years, by a PCB labor leader.

Un ano de Legalidade: Documentário fotográfico de legalidade do P.C.B. Rio de Janeiro: Edições Horizonte, 1946 ?. Pp. 32. Photographs portraying PCB's legal existence during 1945–46.

União de Resistência Nacional. *O comunismo contra o Brasil; história e atualidade de assalto stalinista; a verdad sôbre o mito Prestes*. São Paulo: S.C.P., 1945. Pp. 48. Attack on Communism, PCB, and Prestes. *NLB*

U.S. Joint Publications Research Service. "Communist Political Activities in Brazil." Washington, D.C., 1963. Pp. 34. Mimeo. Articles from *Novos Rumos,* Rio de Janeiro, 200 (December 14–20, 1962), 4, 6, 8. "A Political Resolution of the Brazilian Communists," pp. 1–23; "Peasant Congress in Rio Grande du Sul," pp. 24–27; "Popular Reaction to Brazilian Court Decisions Repealing the Election of Sergeants and Deputies," pp. 28–34.

Van Hyning, John Paul. "From 'Sectarianism' to Reformism: The Communist Party of Brazil, 1950–1954." Madison: M.A. thesis, University of Wisconsin, 1969. Pp. 137. Useful analysis of PCB's evolution during period leading to its Fourth Congress.

Veiga, Gláucio. *Revolução keyneseana e marxismo.* Recife: Imprensa Official 1954. Pp. 186. Marxist comparison of economic systems.

Velloso, Manoel Joaquim Pimenta. *Comunidade ou comunismo? Carta aos brasileiros.* Rio de Janeiro: Livraria Agir, 1946. Pp. 151. Anxiety about Communism in Brazil, in letter form. *NLB*

Vieira, Clóvis Botelho. *Pela libertade do Luiz Carlos Prestes.* São Paulo, 1957 Pp. 7. In defense of Prestes. *NLB*

Vieira Pinto, Alvaro. *Consciência e realidade nacional.* Rio de Janeiro: Institute Superior de Estudos Brasileiros, 1960. Pp. 639. Very useful work on Brazilian nationalism by well-known intellectual of the political left.

————. *Ideologia e desenvolvimento nacional.* Rio de Janeiro: Instituto Superior de Estudos Brasileiros, 1956. Pp. 45. Brief statement on developmental nationalism before author became director of ISEB.

————. *Por que os ricos não fazem greve?* Rio de Janeiro: Cadernos do Povo Brasileiro (4), Editôra Civilização Brasileira, 1962. Pp. 118. Analysis of the extremely rich and the extremely poor classes in Brazil.

Vilela, Orlando O. *Atitude cristã em face da política; comunismo, capitalismo, integralismo, outros temas.* Belo Horizonte: Ed. Menezes, 1951. Pp. 209. Anti-Communist view, by a priest. *NLB*

Vinhas, Moisés. *Estudos sôbre o proletariado brasileiro.* Rio de Janeiro: Coleção Retratos do Brasil (75), Editôra Civilização Brasileira, 1970. Pp. 279. Theoretical and empirical examination of Brazilian proletariat.

————. *Operários e camponeses na revolução brasileira.* Preface by Mário Schenberg. São Paulo: Editôra Fulgor, 1963. Pp. 131. Role of workers and peasants in the Brazilian revolution discussed by PCB member, with special attention to São Paulo.

Vorochilov, K. E., and Luiz Carlos Prestes. *O exército vermelho.* Trans. by Júlio Vargas. São Paulo: Editôra São Paulo, 1930?. Pp. 128. Includes essay by Prestes, "O exército vermelho e suas grandes realizações," pp. 31–43.

Voz Operária, Editorial Board. *O orgão central e a democratização do partido.* Rio de Janeiro, 1957. Criticism by Renovadora faction of PCB leadership for its silence and for reducing funds promised for publication of documents of Soviet Twentieth Congress.

Wilson, Edith Dulles. "The Political Evolution of the Partido Comunista Brasileiro: 1922–1970." Austin: M.A. thesis, University of Texas, August 1970. Pp. 146. General survey of the party, including its history, the Soviet Union and PCB, the impact of Vargas, the image of PCB, and internal party politics.

Young, Jordan M. *The Brazilian Revolution of 1930 and the Aftermath.* New Brunswick, New Jersey: Rutgers University Press, 1967. Pp. 156. General account, useful chiefly on the 1930 Revolution, with only occasional reference to PCB.

Bibliography B

Communist and Radical-Left Periodicals

Most of the following publications are rarely found in Brazilian libraries and only occasionally are they found in private archives. Those sources consulted in preparation of the present work are marked with an asterisk (*). The author has profited immensely from the use of complete runs of *Fôlha do Povo* (1935, 1945–62); *Problemas*, Nos. 1–71 (August 1947–November/December 1955); *Novos Rumos* (1959–March 1964), *A Hora* (1961–March 1964). Also *Ação Socialista* (1959–60); *Classe Operária* (1948 to 1951, 1962–64, sporadic issues thereafter); *Divulgação Marxista* (1946–47); *Fundamentos* (1950–51); *Novos Tempos* (1957–58); *Problemas da Paz e do Socialismo* (1959–62); *O Popular* (1948); *Vanguarda Socialista* (1946–47); and *Voz Operária* (1950–59, 1964–   ).

Where information may be questionable, various sources are cited in parentheses in the annotations below. These sources are Hermínio Linares, "O comunismo no Brasil—III," *Revista Brasiliense,* 28 (March–April 1960), 139–41 or his *Contribuição à história* (cited hereafter as "Linares"); Bela C. Maday *et al., U.S. Army Handbook for Brazil,* Washington, D.C., 1964, pp. 278 (cited as "Handbook"); Nelson Werneck Sodré, *História da imprensa no Brasil,* Rio de Janeiro: Editôra Civilização Brasileira, 1966 ("Sodré"); and Chapter 4, "A imprensa comunista," pp. 89–138 in Inquérito Policial Militar No. 709, *O Comunismo no Brasil,* Vol. III, 1967 (cited as "Inquérito"). Some titles below were drawn from the Biblioteca Nacional in Rio. Omitted in the following list are PCB-controlled or PCB-influenced periodicals published in 1927 and 1928, referred to in Linhares' writings including *O Internacional, O Trabalhador Gráfico, A Vida, O Sapateiro, A Voz do Gráfico, A Abelha, Voz Cosmopólita, Boletim da ATIMO, Boletim da ISV (Internacional Sindical Vermelha)*. The titles below are for the period 1922–72 and exclude those of anarchist and socialist orientation mentioned in our chapter 2. Sources available in the National Library of Brazil are identified as NLB, those in the Municipal Library of Recife, as MLR.

Ação Direta (Rio de Janeiro). Anarchist organ ed. by José Oiticica and published in Rio 1928–29, and from 1946 until 1959, when it ceased.

Ação Popular (Belo Horizonte). Leftist Catholic biweekly first issued on January 6, 1962, and ceased publication in early 1963. Ed. by L. N. Pereira, Marco António Rodriques Dias *et al.*

Ação Socialista (São Paulo). Organ of Liga Socialista Independente, issued from December 1958 to No. 9 late 1960. This self-styled Trotskyist publication included articles by A. Barreto, Carlos Roth, António I. Martínez, and Alvaro Santiago.

Alerta (Rio de Janeiro). Ideological organ of "a group of radical Marxist students"; first issued in 1963 in mimeographed form.

O Alfaiate (São Paulo). Communist-edited organ of tailors' union of São Paulo; first issued in 1920's.

Aurora (Rio de Janeiro). Organ of the PCB Comitê Regional Marítimo; published after 1964.

Auto-Crítica (Rio de Janeiro). Started by PCB in a period of self-criticism before Third Congress of the party. 8 numbers issued, 6 in 1928 before the congress and 2 in 1929 after the congress. Each number had 16 pages. Issues discussed included Communist activity in the unions; political line and tactical policies of PCB in the BOC; the peasant problem; relations between the Juventude Comunista and PCB; character of the Brazilian revolution; the fight against anarcho-syndicalism; documents of the Comintern.

Avante! (Rio de Janeiro). National socialist daily published by H. de Almeida Filho (Linhares).

Avante (Rio de Janeiro). Official organ of Comitê Secundarista da Guanabara, published clandestinely after 1964 coup.

Bancário (Rio de Janeiro). Communist periodical (Inquérito) ed. by Antônio Pereira da Silva Filho. Published 123 numbers, 1933–63.

Boletim Sindical (Rio de Janeiro). Official organ of Comissão Sindical do Comitê Estadual da Guanabara, published clandestinely after 1964 coup.

Brasil, Urgente (São Paulo). Leftist Catholic newspaper, published by Ação Popular, first issued on March 17, 1963. Ed. by Carlos Josaphat, Josimar Moreira et al. until No. 50, February 23–28, 1964.

Clarté, Revista de Sciencias Sociaes (Rio de Janeiro). Organ of the Grupo da Clarté, first published September 1, 1921. No. 1 (September 1921) through No. 7 (January 1922).

A Classe Operária (Rio de Janeiro). First issued on May 1, 1925, as official organ of the Partido Comunista do Brasil. Suppressed on its 12th number of July 18, 1925, it reappeared in May 1928 until mid-1929, when it was again stopped by police. Originally its motto was "Jornal dos Trabalhadores, feito por trabalhadores, para trabalhadores." A new publishing phase was initiated after the PCB was legalized in 1945; first issued in January 1946 and edited by Maurício Grabois. Published weekly until at least 1949; in 1951–52 issued monthly. After the split and change of name of the pro-Soviet party to Partido Comunista Brasileiro the dissident pro-Peking PCB continued to publish *A Classe Operária* during March 1962 (issue 418) to March 1964 (issue 463 dated March 16–31, 1964). *NLB: February 1948—June 1952*

O Combate (São Paulo). Official organ of Comitê Estadual de São Paulo (PCB), published clandestinely after 1964.

Combater (Recife). Publication of Pernambuco State Committee of PCB, begun after 1964 coup.

Comício (Rio de Janeiro). Independent weekly ed. by Joel Silveira, Rafael Corrêa, and Rubem Braga from May to October 1952.

Communist International (Leningrad). Published 1919–40 as a journal reflecting developments in international Communist world. Only a few scattered references to Brazil.

O Combate (Rio de Janeiro). A quarterly Marxist journal founded 1921 and ed. by Astrojildo Pereira (Sodré).

O Comunista (Rio de Janeiro). Launched 1954 (Linhares).

Democracia Popular (Rio de Janeiro). Published in 1950 and ed. by J. Sá de Carvalho (Linhares).

Democrata (Fortaleza). Communist newspaper first issued in 1945 and known to be published in 1948 (Linhares). Ed. by Anníbal Bonavides, Odalves Lima, Luiz Batista, and Fernando Ferreira (Inquérito).

O Democrata (Mato Grosso). Communist journal published in 1948 and ed. by Amorésio de Oliveira (Inquérito).

Diário do Povo (Rio de Janeiro). Founded in 1948 (Linhares).

Diretrizes (Rio de Janeiro). Literary pro-Communist journal initiated in 1938 and ed. by Azevedo Amaral and Samuel Waener. *NLB: 1942 scattered issues.*

Divulgação Marxista (Rio de Janeiro). Biweekly ed. by Calvino Filho and S. O. Hersen. First issued as biweekly July 1, 1946. Most articles are of foreign origin.

Emancipação (Rio de Janeiro). Founded in 1948 and ed. by Gen. Felicíssimo Cardoso, Col. Hildebrando Pelágio Rodrigues Pereira. An economic journal of PCB (Linhares).

Espírito Novo (Rio de Janeiro). Socialist literary journal ed. by João Calazans and A. M. Lage with collaboration of Arthur Ramos, Carlos Lacerda, Jorge Amado, and others. First published January 1934.

Esquerda (Rio de Janeiro). Leftist, pro-Communist, "tenentista" newspaper first published on July 5, 1927. Ed. by José Augusto Lima and Pedro Motta Lima (Linhares).

Estado de Goiás (Goiânia). Communist newspaper founded in 1932 in Pires do Rio. Moved to Uberlândia, Minas Gerais, and in 1946 to Goiânia, where it became a PCB organ ed. by A. Isaac Neto and A. Xavier de Almeida (Linhares).

*Estudos Sociais (Rio de Janeiro). Bimonthly theoretic organ of the official PCB, first issued in May–June 1958 and ed. by Astrojildo Pereira until late 1963. *NLB*.

Ex-Combatente (Rio de Janeiro). Published in 1946 under the motto "Liberdade e Democracia" (Linhares).

Fôlha Capixaba (Vitória). Weekly organ of Espírito Santo Regional PCB (Handbook).

*Fôlha do Povo (Recife). Communist-owned daily published in July 9—November 21, 1935. Ed. by Osório Lima until August and by José Cavalcanti thereafter. Reappeared November 19, 1945 until May 19, 1948, when suspended until November 28, 1948. Thereafter published until October 18, 1960. Succeeded by *A Hora*. *MLR*: 1935, 1945–60.

Fôlha Popular (Aracajú). First published in 1954 and ed. by Roberto Garcia, Agnaldo Pacheco da Silva, Walter de Oliveira Ribeiro, and Gervásio dos Santos (Inquérito).

Fôlha Popular (Natal). PCB paper ed. by Luís Maranhão (Linhares).

*Fôlha Socialista (São Paulo). Organ of Comissão Estadual de São Paulo do Partido Socialista Brasileiro, first issued November 27, 1947, and published until 1964. Original editors were Antônio Cândido and Arnaldo Pedroso d'Horta.

For a Lasting Peace, for a People's Democracy! (Belgrade and Bucharest). Published 1947–1956 as official weekly of the Communist Information Bureau (Cominform). Coverage of PCB is sparse through 1950, but expanded thereafter as the international movement took interest in Brazilian developments. Tends to emphasize international rather than domestic aspects of PCB affairs.

*Frente Operária (São Paulo). Trotskyist monthly first issued in 1951. Ed. by Sidney Marquês dos Santos at Av. Queiroz Filho, 459, Vila Humaitá, Caixa Postal, 4562.

Frente Popular (Goiás). Populist weekly first published on December 27, 1950, and ed. by Alóisio Crispim (Linhares).

*Frente Universitária (Rio de Janeiro?). Youth organ of Partido Operária Revolucionário (POR), Trotskyist movement affiliated with the Fourth International. First issue (not dated) probably appeared in early 1964. Address unavailable.

*Fundamentos (São Paulo). Founded by Monteiro Lobato in 1948; editorial committee included Afonso Schmidt, Arthur Neves, Caio Prado Júnior, J. E. Fernandes, and Ruy Barbosa Cardoso.

Gazeta Sindical (Rio de Janeiro and/or São Paulo?). Founded in 1948 as Communist monthly focused on labor issues (Linhares, Handbook). Ed. by Jocelyn Santos, Roberto Morena, and Francisco Trajano.

O Guerrillheiro (clandestine). Newspaper of Brazilian revolutionary groups referred to in Marighella's "Minimanual of the Urban Guerrilla."

*O Guia (Rio de Janeiro). Mimeographed "Orgão dos comunistas da orla marítima" first published in 1965 with the banner "O marxismo é um guia para a ação."

Hoje (São Paulo). First published October 5, 1945, as a PCB-oriented periodical, ed. by Milton Caires de Brito (Linhares).

*A Hora (Recife). Weekly of Pernambuco regional PCB and successor of *Fôlha*

do Povo, published August 5, 1961, through no. 141, March 21–27, 1964. Ed. by Claudio Tavares and David Capistrano. *MLR*

Horizonte (Pôrto Alegre). Ed. by Fernando Guedes, Demétrio Ribeiro Lila Ripoll, Carlos Scliar, and Nelson Souza; from 1951 (Linhares).

Horizontes do Mundo (São Paulo). "Mensário de cultura e divulgação. Arte-Paz Cultura." Ed. by Affonso Schmidt beginning in 1955 (Linhares).

*Imprensa Popular (Rio de Janeiro). PCB daily founded in 1948, and published until August 3, 1958. Ed. by Pedro Motta Lima. *NLB:* 1951–58.

*Information Bulletin (Supplement to *World Marxist Review;* Toronto). Interna tionally-oriented Communist organ, occasionally including important texts and statements by PCB and its leaders; published since 1963.

Informe Nacional. Clandestine bulletin of Partido Operaria Comunista, known to be published in the late 1960's.

O Isqueiro (Rio de Janeiro). "The Spark," official publication of PCB commit tee for the Central Zone of Guanabara after the 1964 coup. In September 1967 censured by PCB Central Committee for its "Fractionalist" tendencies.

*Insurreição (Rio de Janeiro). Mimeographed "Orgão dos comunistas universi tários' first published August 1966.

International Press Correspondence (London), Official publication of the Com intern, 1921–38, succeeded by *World News and Views.* Articles on Brazil and PCE appear sporadically from 1923 through 1937.

Jornada (Rio de Janeiro). University publication, begun in 1952 and ed. by Murilo Vaz (Linhares).

Jornal da Semana (Rio de Janeiro). Allegedly Communist weekly published in 1961, with editors Sebastião Nery, Rui Simões, Macário Teixeira, and Antônio Ney (Inquérito).

Jornal do Povo (Curitiba). Communist newspaper known published during 1948 Suspended in early December.

Jornal do Povo (João Pessõa). Communist paper of João Pessõa owned by João Santa Cruz; suspended in May 1947. A paper with the same title known to be published by the PCB also, in Aracajú.

Jornal do Povo (Minas Gerais). First published in 1948 and ed. by Orlandc Bomfim (Inquérito).

Jornal do Povo (Rio de Janeiro). Published during 1934–35 and ed. by Aparície Torelly (Linhares).

O Jovem Proletário. (Rio de Janeiro?) Mimeo. publication of Juventude Com unista produced "regularly" probably from January 1927 until it stopped (for financial reasons) April 1928; it had reached a circulation of 1000. Reappeared in 1934, and in 1935 was the short-lived title of the ANL student movement and was run principally by students in law and medical schools in Rio and in law school in São Paulo (Linhares).

*Leitura. Crítica e Informação Bibliográfica. (Rio de Janeiro). Marxist, pro Communist literary magazine ed. by Dioclécio D. Duarte and Raul de Góes. Nos 1–41 (1943–46).

A Liberdade (Natal). Single issue published on November 27, 1935, as the "Orgãc oficial do Gôvẹrno Popular Revolucionário."

Liberdade (São Paulo). Organ of political prisoners of the Prisão Maria Zélia issued during 1937 (Linhares).

*Liberdade (São Paulo). Leftist socialist journal irregularly issued after Apri 1964. Its motto: "Unir tódas as fôrças do povo brasileiro para reconquistar as liber dades democráticas."

Liberdade Sindical (São Paulo). First published 1951 (Linhares).

O Libertador (Rio de Janeiro?). Distributed sporadically by the Prestes Column in the 1920's; in 1935 became official organ of the ANL.

O Libertador (Rio de Janeiro). Small newspaper ed. by Agildo Barata and his leftist "Coletivo" group during their imprisonment 1935–37.

O Libertário (Rio de Janeiro). Anarchist sheet first published during 1959.

*A Liga (Rio de Janeiro). Organ of Ligas Componesas of Northeast Brazil and ed. by Francisco Julião. Issued as a weekly from October 1962 until March 1964.

Literatura (Rio de Janeiro). Communist literary journal ed. by Astrojildo Pereira (Sodré).

Luta (Manaus). Communist newspaper published in 1946 under the motto "Democracia e Paz" and ed. by Francisco Alves dos Santos.

*A Luta (Recife). PCB daily ed. by Rui Antunes, José Leite Filho, and Clóvis Melo, and first issued on January 19, 1948. Replaced the banned *Fôlha do Povo* and continued until No. 103, August 25, 1948, when suppressed and replaced by *O Popular*. MLR

A Luta (Rio de Janeiro). Official organ of Comitê Estadual da Guanabara. (PCB), published clandestinely after 1964.

Luta de Classes (Rio de Janeiro). Illegal journal of Trotskyist Partido Socialista Revolucionário distributed alternately in printed and mimeographed forms in late 1930's.

A Manhã (Rio de Janeiro). Daily PCB paper, ed. by Pedro Motta Lima. Prestes' letter acknowledging his adherence to ANL published in No. 16 on May 14, 1935 (Linhares).

Marcha (Rio de Janeiro). Ed. by Francisco Mangabeira with assistance of Rubem Braga, Newton Freitas, and Carlos Lacerda in 1935 for ANL Municipal Executive Committee of Federal District (Linhares).

Missão Operária (São Paulo). Radical Catholic, Marxist-oriented publication ed. by Father Antônio Ritter, with collaboration by Fathers Afonso Ritter, Tranquido Moterle, and José M. Gonzalez Ruiz. Sixth number, issued November 1968, called for creation of a Partido Operário Brasileiro under leadership of workers and peasants.

*O Momento (Salvador). Communist organ begun in 1945; suspended briefly in May 1947 but reappeared thereafter. Ed. by Almir Matos, J. Quintino de Carvalho, Ariovaldo Matos, and Aristeu Negueira (Inquérito).

Movimento (Rio de Janeiro). Journal of ANL's Modern Culture Club of Rio, whose editorial board included writers Jorge Amado and José Luis do Rêgo; published in 1935.

*Movimento (Rio de Janeiro). Organ of União Nacional dos Estudantes (UNE) first issued on August 23, 1963, and known to have continued to No. 4, September 13, 1963. Ed. by Humberto Kinjo and Luciola Silva Lima.

*Movimento Comunista (Rio de Janeiro). Communist theoretical organ. Suspended by police on June 10, 1923, after 24 numbers. Published 3 numbers in 1922 and 11 in 1923.

Movimento Feminino (Rio de Janeiro). Monthly Communist woman's magazine (Handbook).

O Movimento Sindical Mundial (Rio de Janeiro). Monthly magazine ed. by Moacir Ramos Silva. Begun in 1954 (Linhares).

*Movimento Socialista (Rio de Janeiro). Independent Marxist journal first issued July 1, 1959. Apparently an earlier journal with same name ed. by Astrojildo Pereira (Sodré).

A Nação (Rio de Janeiro). Begun in 1922; after a period of suppression, reap-

peared from January 3, 1927, to August 11, 1927. Generally leftist, but Com
munist-oriented during the period of PCB's legality, and ed. by Leonidas de Resende
(Linhares, Pereira). During its early phase, ed. by Resende and Maurício de Lacerdz
(Sodré). *NLB: 1924*

O Nacional (Rio de Janeiro). Weekly published by dissident Renovadora factior
after its break from PCB in May 1957; ceased in 1958. Ed. by Aydano do Coute
Ferraz.

Nossa Imprensa (Rio de Janeiro). First published in 1953 as "orgão de defesa dz
classe jornalística" (Linhares).

Nossos Tempos (São Paulo). Official organ of União Estadual dos Estudante:
de São Paulo, first issued on July 22, 1963. Ed. by Marco Antônio.

Notícias de Hoje (São Paulo). Successor to *Hoje* and published first in 1949 undei
banner "A verdade ao serviço do povo" (Linhares).

Novos Rumos (Rio de Janeiro). Published in 1954 under editorship of Emmc
Duarte. *NLB*

Novos Rumos (Rio de Janeiro). Weekly organ of pro-Soviet Partido Comunistz
Brasileiro, issued March 6, 1959—March 1964. Ed. by Mário Alves along witr
Fragmon Carlos Borges, Luiz Gazzaneo, and Guttenberg Cavalcante. A Belo Hori
zonte edition was under direction of Edson Costa Ney Velloso (Inquérito). *NLB*

Novos Tempos (Rio de Janeiro). Alternately monthly and bimonthly magazine
of the Renovadora faction, published from September 1957 to May 1958 aftei
breaking from the PCB. Ed. by Osvaldo Peralva and a board composed of Armandc
Lopes da Cunha, Benito Papi, Calvino Filho, Ernesto Luiz Maia, Eros Martins
Teixeira, Horácio Macêdo, Leôncio Basbaum, Roberto Morena, and Wilson Lopes
de Souza. *NLB: 1957–58*

Orientação (Recife). Pernambuco Communist magazine first issued in Septembei
1951; published by Clóvis Melo, ed. by Paulo Cavalcanti.

Orientação Socialista (Rio de Janeiro?). Semi-legal newspaper of Troskyis:
Partido Socialista Revolucionário; published in 1934.

Orientação Socialista (São Paulo). Biweekly "Organ of Marxist thought" ed. by
José Stacchini.

Orla Marítima (Rio de Janeiro). Communist newspaper of maritime worker:
published monthly after 1944 and focused on labor issues (Handbook). Ed. by
Emílio Bonfanto Demária and Waldir Gomes dos Santos.

Panfleto (Rio de Janeiro). Leftist nationalist weekly issued from January tc
March 1964. Its editorial board included Leonel Brizola, Almino Afonso, anc
Alvaro Vieira Pinto.

Panfleto (Rio de Janeiro). Leftist magazine embracing collaboration of Com
munist writers; first issue dated June 1958. Ed. by Lourival Coutinho.

Para Todos (Rio de Janeiro). Communist-oriented peace journal founded ir
1951 by Alvaro Moreyra (Linhares).

Partidários da Paz (Rio de Janeiro). First published in 1951. Ed. by Gracilianc
Ramos, with staff including Fernando Guedes, Demócrito Ribeiro, Lila Ripoll,
Carlos Scliar, and Nelson de Sousa (Linhares).

Peking Review (Peking). Scattered articles with infrequent reference to Braziliar
Communist developments from 1958. After 1962 carries articles dealing with position and activities of Peking-oriented PC do B.

A Platéia (São Paulo). ANL daily published in 1935.

A Plebe (São Paulo or Rio de Janeiro?). Pro-Soviet anarchist newspaper knowr
published in 1919 and in 1920's; reappeared briefly in 1933 (Linhares). It later was
critical of the Russian Revolution.

PN (*Política e Negócios*). Published 1951—March 1964, identified as pro-Communist (Inquérito).

Política Operária (São Paulo). Small leftist publication, 1962–64 (also issued in Rio de Janeiro). Edited by Luiz Alberto Dias Lima (Inquérito). By 1968 it had become the organ of POC.

O Popular ("Um Jornal para a Defesa do Recife"). PCB daily replacing *A Luta*, first issued August 28, 1948; ed. by Clóvis Melo. Ceased with No. 78 (November 27, 1948), when *Fôlha do Povo* was allowed to resume.

O Popular (Rio de Janeiro). First published in 1951 (Linhares).

Problemas (Rio de Janeiro). Communist monthly and sometimes bimonthly theoretical organ first issued in August 1947. Ed. by Carlos Marighella until No. 15 and by Diógenes Arruda Câmara thereafter until No. 71 (November–December 1955). Contains important party documents and speeches by PCB leaders. *NLB*

Problemas da Paz e do Socialismo (Rio de Janeiro). Monthly Communist theoretical and international news journal ed. by Rui Facó. First issued in 1959, and featuring foreign articles.

Reforma Agrária (Pôrto Alegre). Weekly organ of Rio Grande do Sul regional PCB focused on rural issues (Handbook).

Renovação (Rio de Janeiro). Socialist organ first published on March 18, 1933; ed. by Jocelyn Santos, Martins Carlos and Juvenil Silva (Linhares).

Resenha Socialista (Rio de Janeiro). Monthly Socialist organ first issued in 1956; ed. by Nestor Peixoto de Oliveira, with collaborators Hermes Lima, João Mangabeira, and Mário Pedrosa.

Resistência (Pôrto Alegre). Weekly with general PCB line (Handbook).

Revista do Povo (Rio de Janeiro). Cultural and popular magazine founded 1945, and ed. by Alvaro Moreira, Fróes da Mota, and Emmo Duarte (Linhares).

Revista Módulo (Rio de Janeiro). Monthly, pro-Communist journal oriented to technical architectural matters (Handbook).

Revista Brasiliense (São Paulo). Founded by Caio Prado Júnior and ed. by Elias Chaves Neto as an independent Marxist and nationalist journal in 1956; terminated in early 1964. An important social-science journal for the period.

Seiva (Salvador). Communist-oriented literary monthly first issued in 1947.

O Semanário (Rio de Janeiro). Leftist nationalist weekly published April 1956–March 1964; ed. by Osvaldo Costa with Edmar Morel, José Frejat, *et al.*

O Sol (Rio de Janeiro). Ed. in 1951 by Abelardo Rojas (Linhares).

O Sol (Rio de Janeiro). Official organ of Comitê da Zona Central do Brasil na Guanabara, published clandestinely after 1964.

O Soldado Vermelho (Rio de Janeiro?). Military-oriented PCB newspaper known to have been published during mid-1930's.

Solidaridade (Recife). An irregular publication of Pernambuco workers organized by ANL in 1935.

Tempo Brasileiro (Rio de Janeiro). First published in 1962 as leftist nationalist journal.

Terra Livre (Rio de Janeiro and/or São Paulo). Communist weekly first published in 1948 (Linhares) or 1949 (Inquérito) for rural workers. Ed. by Oswaldo R. Gomes, H. Sosthenes Jambo, Derdieux Crispim, and Rodorico N. Guimarães (Inquérito, Handbook).

Trabalho (Rio de Janeiro). Published in 1934 under motto "Jornal proletário, feito por proletários, para proletários"; ed. by Jocelyn Santos (Linhares).

Tribuna Capixaba (Vitória). Communist newspaper known to be publishing in 1948.

Tribuna do Pará (Belem). Communist newspaper definitely published in 1948 and in 1960's by the Pará regional PCB (Handbook).

Tribuna do Povo (Curitiba). Weekly of Paraná regional PCB (Handbook). Published in 1949 and ed. by Hermógenes Lazier (Inquérito).

Tribuna do Povo (São Luiz). PCB paper suspended in May 1947.

Tribuna do Povo (Uberlândia). Weekly of Minas Gerais regional PCB (Handbook).

Tribuna do Sul (Ilhéus). Communist organ ed. by Nelson Schaun and Umberto Vita (Inquérito).

Tribuna Gaúcha (Pôrto Alegre). Newspaper of PCB, first published in 1945 and known to be active in 1948 (Linhares) and in 1960's, by the Rio Grande do Sul regional PCB.

Tribuna Popular (Rio de Janeiro). Communist official daily first appearing on May 23, 1945. Published by Pedro Motta Lima and ed. by Aydano do Couto Ferraz. *NLB:* July–December 1945; January 1946–December 1947.

*Ultima Hora (Recife). Leftist daily issued from July 18, 1962, until April 17, 1964. Reflects news of left groups, including Communists, and is particularly useful for its incisive, objective analysis of Pernambuco politics. *MLR*

*Ultima Hora (Rio de Janeiro, São Paulo, Belo Horizonte, and Pôrto Alegre). Most important of the left dailies during early 1960's, but limited by its leftist nationalist bias. *NLB*

Unidade (São Paulo). Journal published by a small dissident Communist group led by José Maria Crispim after they had been expelled in 1952 from the PCB. Ed. by Darwin Silveira Pereira (Inquérito).

*Vanguarda Socialista (Rio de Janeiro). Begun in August 1945 as a weekly and became a biweekly with No. 110, October 3, 1947. Ed. by Mário Pedrosa and Trotskyists who had in 1945 broken with the Fourth International. By October 1947 Hermes Lima had become editor, signifying its new socialist orientation, although earlier it had published writings of Trotsky and his followers. *NLB: August 30, 1946–August 29, 1947*

Voz Cosmopólita (Rio de Janeiro). Communist-edited periodical of Hotel and Restaurant Employees Union of Rio, first published in the 1920's.

A Voz Livre (Recife). Organ of Setor Estudantil de Pernambuco, published clandestinely after 1964.

Voz do Povo (Maceió). PCB daily owned by André Papini. Suspended in May 1947 and later reappeared as a weekly, assuming a pro-Castro and regional PCB line (Handbook).

Voz do Povo (Rio de Janeiro). Anarchist periodical appearing in the early 1920's.

Voz do Trabalhador (Rio Grande do Sul). Published during 1945 (Linhares).

*Voz Operária (Rio de Janeiro). Weekly first published in 1949, replacing *A Classe Operária* as the central organ of the (illegal) PCB. Ceased on February 20, 1959; new phase initiated clandestinely in 1964. NLB: 1951–59

*World Marxist Review (Toronto). Internationally-oriented Communist publication with scattered references to PCB and documents of party and its leaders 1958–63. See also *Information Bulletin* above.

World News and Views (London). Successor of *International Press Correspondence,* official publication of Comintern. Published articles on Brazil and PCB 1938–46.

Notes

Notes to Chapter 1
Titles preceded by asterisk on first appearance have complete entries in Bibliography.

1. Joseph LaPalombara and Myron Weiner (eds.), *Political Parties and Political Development*, Princeton: Studies in Political Development (6), Princeton University Press, 1966. Chap. 1, "The Origin and Development of Political Parties," p. 6, quotation on p. 29.
2. *Ibid.*, pp. 7–20.
3. The literature can be identified in two excellent collections of essays, each of which contains an extensive bibliography. The earlier collection, ed. by Sigmund Neumann, is entitled *Modern Political Parties; Approaches to Comparative Politics*, Chicago: University of Chicago Press, 1956, see esp. pp. 425–46. The other study, by LaPalombara and Weiner, *op. cit.*, includes a bibliography selected and classified by Naomi E. Kies, pp. 439–64.
4. See Robert (Roberto) Michels, *Political Parties: A Sociological Study of the Oligarchial Tendencies of Modern Democracy*, trans. Eden and Cedar Paul, introd. by Seymour M. Lipset, Glencoe, Ill.: Free Press, 1949, and New York: Collier Books, 1962; and Maurice Duverger, *Political Parties, Their Organization and Activity in the Modern State*, trans. Barbara and Robert North, with foreword by D. W. Brogan, New York: Science Editions, 1963.
5. For a critique of Duverger, see Aaron B. Wildavsky, "A Methodological Critique of Duverger's *Political Parties*," *Journal of Politics*, XXI (1959), 303–18.
6. Roberto Michels, "Some Reflections on the Sociological Character of Political Parties," *The American Political Science Review*, XXI (November 1927), 762–63, 765.
7. Although other of Michels' observations could be useful in our examination of the PCB, it should be emphasized that many of his provocative assumptions contradict Marxist-Leninist theory. For example, he argues that organization is oligarchical in nature and leads to power, but that because power is always conservative, internal party policy will be absolutely conservative. Again, organization based on bureaucratic principles results in the suppression of the struggle for great principles. Further, the profoundly conservative nature of the party emanates from the relation between the party and the state. Although the working-class party struggles for the overthrow of the state, the party itself quickly acquires a centralization of its own, based on the same principles of authority and discipline that characterize the organization of the state. Marxists would argue, however, that power was radical and revolutionary, not always conservative, in the Russian, Chinese, and Cuban experiences. In the case of Cuba there is a constant struggle to thwart bureaucratic sectarianism and to provide for the material needs such as food, clothing, health, education. Also, if the state (which in Marxist terms is the rulers and their apparatus of oppression) is overthrown and a classless society is established, the rules of the game would be modified and the party would be subject to a very different set of forces. Michels' generalizations are extracted from *Political Parties*, pp. 333–39.
8. Fals Borda, a Colombian sociologist, places positive emphasis upon the con-

cept "subversion," whose elements, he posits, are "dialectically articulated" when "the social order is refracted with a Utopian impact." These elements are counter-values, counter-norms, disorgans (innovating groups or institutions that challenge the established order), and technological innovations. They seem to be inherent in the philosophy, theory, and practice of the PCB and likely would be manifested in that conflict, described by Fals Borda, as "implicit in all strategic endeavors for collective self-improvement." As he observes, "The model that emerges from the analysis of national historical processes is that of social disequilibrium." See Orlando Fals Borda, *Subversion and Social Changes in Colombia*, New York: Columbia University Press, 1969, pp. x, 189–96.

9. From V. I. Lenin's "What Is To Be Done?" reprinted in *Lenin, Collected Works*, Vol. I, Moscow: Foreign Language Publishing House, 1947, pp. 207–8.

10. Gabriel A. Almond, *The Appeals of Communism*, Princeton: Princeton University Press, 1954.

11. Almond, *op. cit.*, esp. the analysis in chaps. 6 and 11.

12. Hadley Cantril, *The Politics of Despair*, New York: Basic Books, 1958.

13. Cantril, *op. cit.*, chap. 4, "The Ingredients Required for Faith," for explication of the model.

14. Lucian W. Pye, *Guerrilla Communism in Malaya: Its Social and Political Meaning*, Princeton: Princeton University Press, 1956.

15. Pye, *op. cit.*, pp. 7–8.

16. *Ibid.*, p. 5. This emphasis on differences is also stressed by Thomas H. Green, "The Communist Parties of Italy and France: A Study in Comparative Communism," *World Politics*, XXI (October 1968), 1–38; and by H. Gordon Skilling, who reviews some of the criticism of the totalitarian model as used in the study of Communism in his "Interest Groups and Communist Politics," *World Politics*, XVIII (April 1966), 435–51.

17. Among monographs on non-Communist political parties in Latin America are: Robert J. Alexander, *The Venezuelan Democratic Revolution*, New Brunswick, Rutgers University Press, 1964, on Acción Democrática; Robert Anderson, *Party Politics in Puerto Rico*, Stanford: Stanford University Press, 1965; Federico G. Gil, *Genesis and Modernization of Political Parties in Chile*, Gainesville: University of Florida Press, 1962; Harry Kantor, *The Ideology and Program of the Peruvian Aprista Movement*, Berkeley: University of California Press, 1953; John D. Martz, *The Acción Democrática: Evolution of a Modern Political Party in Venezuela*, Princeton: Princeton University Press, 1966; Edward Williams, *Latin American Christian Democratic Parties*, Knoxville: University of Tennessee, 1967; and Ronald Snow, *Argentine Radicalism: The History and Doctrine of the Radical Civil Union*, Iowa City: University of Iowa Press, 1965.

18. We have no published monograph in English on the PRI of Mexico, although Robert Scott has written a book exploring the party's activities in Mexican life: *Mexican Government in Transition*, Urbana: University of Illinois, 1959 and 1964. Karl M. Schmitt has published a study of the Partido Comunista de México, *Communism in Mexico: A Study in Political Frustration*, Austin: University of Texas Press, 1965.

19. We know of no published study in English focusing specifically on the Chilean Communist party, although two works are useful for information and interpretation of that party: Ernst Halperin, *Nationalism and Communism in Chile*, Cambridge, Mass.: M.I.T. Press, 1965; and Eudocio Ravines, *The Yenan Way*, New York: Scribner, 1951. The latter book is by a former Peruvian Communist and describes his role in the formation of the Chilean popular front of the late

thirties. The reader may wish to consult the unpublished Ph.D. dissertation by Cole Blasier, "The Cuban and Chilean Communist Parties: Instruments of Soviet Policy, 1935–48," Columbia University, 1954. In September 1970 Salvador Allende, coalition candidate of the Chilean Communist and Socialist parties, won a plurality of votes in the Presidential elections.

20. See Robert J. Alexander, *The Communist Party of Venezuela*, Stanford: Hoover Institution Press, 1969.

21. The major works are Robert J. Alexander, * *Communism in Latin America*, and Rollie Poppino, * *International Communism in Latin America: A History of the Movement, 1917–1963*. Other, less successful, works discussing international Communist influences are Robert Loring Allen, * *Soviet Influence in Latin America: The Role of Economic Relations;* Dorothy Dillon, * *International Communism and Latin America: Perspectives and Prospects;* and D. Bruce Jackson, * *Castro, the Kremlin and Communism in Latin America*.

22. Federico G. Gil, "Communism in Latin America," pp. 184–87 in Dan N. Jacobs, ed., * *The New Communisms*.

23. Alexander, *Communism in Latin America*, chap. 2, "The History of Communism in Latin America," p.. 18–31.

24. Ernst Halperin, * "Proletarian Class Parties in Europe and Latin America. A Comparison," pp. 23–30.

25. The writer, Fernando Pedreira, and his ideas are cited in Halperin, "Proletarian Class Parties . . . ," pp. 49–50.

26. This anti-intellectualism is evident in Jorge Amado, * *Os subterrâneos da liberdade*. See Halperin, *op. cit.*, pp. 54–57, for reference and analysis of Amado's trilogy.

27. The renowned historian, Caio Prado Júnior, is an example of Marxist intellectual whose adherence to the party has not deterred him from criticism of party policy.

28. Alexander, *Communism in Latin America*, p. 93.

29. These hypotheses, stated almost verbatim, were advanced by Jan F. Triska in his "Comparative Studies of the Non-ruling Communist Parties," n.d., pp. 2–3.

Notes to Chapter 2

Titles preceded by asterisk on first appearance have complete entries in Bibliography.

1. Caio Prado Júnior is author of * *Evolução política do Brasil*, * *História económica do Brasil*, and * *Formação do Brasil contemporânea. Colônia*, trans. and published in 1967 as *The Colonial Background of Modern Brazil*.

2. On Palmares, the 17th-century center of black Africa resistance to the established colonial system, see Edison Carneiro, *O quilombo dos Palmares, 1630–1695*, São Paulo, Editôra Brasiliense, 1947. On Bahian movements led by black Muslims 1807–35, see Clóvis Moura, *Rebeliões de senzala: quilombos, insurreições, guerrilhas*, São Paulo: Edições Zumbi, 1959; and Aderbal Jurema, *Insurreições negras no Brasil*, Recife: Edições da Casa Mozart, 1935.

3. See Rui Facó, * *Cangaceiros e fanáticos, gênese e lutas*. The *Cangaceiros* or bandits of the Brazilian backlands were motivated not only by desire for revenge or self-defense. They were "social" in orientation inasmuch as they provided the rural areas of achievement. Rather than basing recruitment on ascription that characterized patriarchal communities, the bands were open to dynamic elements from the lower strata whose chief attribute was prowess. For a definitive essay on the subject see Amary de Souza, "The Cangaço and the Politics of Violence," pp. 109–31 in Ronald H. Chilcote (ed.), *Protest and Resistance in Angola and Brazil: Com-*

parative Studies, Berkeley and Los Angeles: University of California Press, 1972.

4. Events leading up to Canudos as well as the war itself are vividly described by Euclides da Cunha in *Rebellion in the Backlands* (*Os Sertões*), trans. by Samuel Putnam, University of Chicago Press, 1944.

5. See Brasil Gerson, *Pequena história dos fanáticos do Contestado*, Rio de Janeiro: Imprensa Nacional, 1955; and Maurício Vinhas de Queiroz, *Messianismo e conflito social: a guerra sertaneja do Contestado, 1912/1916*, Rio de Janeiro: Editôra Civilização Brasileira, 1966. Contestado is the topic of Maria Isaura Pereira de Queiroz' *O messianismo no Brasil e no mundo*, São Paulo: Editôra da Universidade de São Paulo, 1965, pp. 246–60, and her *La guerre sainte au Brésil: le movement messianique du Cantestado*, São Paulo: Facultade de Filosofia, Ciência e Letras da Universidad de São Paulo, 1957.

6. See Facó, *Cangaceiros e fanáticos*, pp. 125–210. There are more than a score of books on Padre Cícero, including Edmar Morel, *Padre Cícero, o santo de Joàzeiro*, Rio de Janeiro: Empresso Gráfica O Cruzeiro, 1964; Xavier de Oliveira. *Beatos e cangaceiros*, Rio de Janeiro, 1920; Lourenço Filho, *Joàzeiro de Padre Cícero: scenas e quadros do fanatismo no Nordeste*, São Paulo: Melhoramentos, n.d.; and an excellent political history of the case by Ralph Della Cava, *Miracle at Joàzeiro*, New York, Institute of Latin-American Studies, Columbia University Press, 1970.

7. For description of these heroes, see Facó, pp. 38–46; Gustavo Barroso, *Heróes e bandidos*, Rio de Janeiro: Livraria Francisco Alves, n.d.; Carlos D. Fernandes, *Os cangaceiros*, 3rd ed., São Paulo; Monteiro Libato, 1922.

8. On the Prestes march (which had urban origins), see Italo Landucci, * *Cenas e episódios da Coluna Prestes*, and Lourenço Moreira Lima, * *A coluna Prestes: marchas e combates.*

9. Apparently the first Communist peasant league in Northeast Brazil was reported in the Communist daily *Fôlha do Povo*, 114 (April 6, 1946), 4, and there are scattered references to rural activity thereafter. One Communist active in rural organization was Gregório Bezerra, whose autobiographical account is in * *Eu, Gregório Bezerra, acuso!* (1967), a pamphlet written in prison and clandestinely published by the PCB. Although the PCB manifested support for the peasant leagues of Julião, there were serious differences between the two groups, differences which were occasionally aired in public.

10. A Marxist-Leninist perspective of the rural worker is Moisés Vinhas, * *Operários e camponeses na revolução brasileira*. On Julião, see his * *Escucha campesino*

11. Brasil Gerson, * *Tiradentes: herói popular.*

12. Amaro Quintas, *Atualidade de Inconfidência*, Recife: Editôra Nordeste, 1952; also his *A gênese do espírito republicano em Pernambuco e a revolução de 1817*, Recife, 1939; and *O sentido social da revolução Praieira*, Rio de Janeiro; Editôra Civilização Brasileira, 1967. For another Marxist perspective, see Edison Carneiro, *A insurreição Praieira*, Rio de Janeiro: Coleção Temas Brasileiros (3), Conquista, 1960.

13. Manuel Correira de Andrade, *A guerra dos Cabanos*, Rio de Janeiro: Coleção Temas Brasileiras (7), Conquista, 1965.

14. Paulo Cavalcanti, * *Eça de Queiroz, agitador no Brasil.*

15. These developments "agitated all social classes except the rural workers, who passed from almost complete slavery to a period of freedom without any particular feeling of group consciousness." Quoted in J. V. Freitas Marcondes, *First Brazilian Legislation Relating to Rural Labor Unions: A Sociological Study*, Gaines-

NOTES   281

ville: University of Florida Press, 1962, p. 51, a monograph on the first labor legislation and specifically the law of January 3, 1903, on rural labor.

16. The 1912 congress, sponsored by the government, was officially called the "fourth" Congresso Operário Brasileiro, an interpretation generally accepted by Socialists who claim that the first three congresses occurred in 1892, 1902, and 1906. Anarchists claim that the first congress was in 1906 and the second in 1913. Brazil's second major congress, sponsored by COB, is generally accepted as having taken place in September 1913, convoked by its secretary-general Astrojildo Pereira. Two years later the COB sponsored an international peace conference, and a third labor congress took place in April 1920. See Everardo Dias, * História das lutas sociais no Brasil, p. 283. Proceedings, resolutions, and names of participating organizations are in three important documents of the congresses of 1906, 1912, and 1913; see "Resoluções do Primeiro Congresso Operário Brasileiro," Estudos Sociais, IV (March 1963), 387–98; "Congresso Operário de 1912," in Estudos Sociais, V (June 1963), 69–87; and Un relatório datado de 1913," Estudos Sociais, V (November 1963), 194–206.

17. Mancur, Olson, Jr., "Rapid Economic Growth as a Destabilizing Force," Journal of Economic History, XXIII (December 1963), 529–52.

18. These and other ideological positions of Lenin contributed to the splits brought about in the socialist parties almost everywhere by the First World War and the Russian Revolution. The gathering together of left-wing elements under Russian leadership led to the founding of the Third or Communist International (Comintern) in Moscow in March 1919.

19. Hermínio Linhares, * Contribução, à história das lutas operárias no Brasil, p. 55.

20. The very early roots of socialism in Brazil, of course, date before the formation of political parties. A periodical, O Socialista, was published in Rio de Janeiro as early as 1939. During 1842–43 Benoît-Jules Mure attempted to found a socialist community near São Francisco do Sul in Santa Catarina. On August 1, 1845, Manuel Gaspar de Siqueira Rêgo initiated publication in Niterói of O Socialista da Província do Rio de Janeiro, which circulated three times a week until August 1847. The details are in Moniz Bandeira, Clóvis Melo, and A. T. Andrade, * O ano vermelho: a revolução russa e seus reflexes no Brasil, pp. 6–7. Amaro Quintas in his extensive writings on the Praieira Revolution of 1848 suggests that the revolution, Antônio Pedro de Figueiredo ("one of the first Brazilian socialists"), and the magazine O Progresso all contributed to "popular agitation" corresponding to "the existence of an intellectual elite prone to the comprehension of socialist principles"; see Amaro Quintas, * O sentido social da Revolução Praieira, pp. 8–9.

While socialism of this early period was influenced by the utopians and later by Marx and Engels and other philosophers, attempts to establish a socialist or workers' party in Brazil paralleled developments elsewhere, especially in Germany and Russia. By 1894, at age 24, Lenin had become a Marxist. Four years later a Russian Social Democratic Workers' party was formed, even though Marxism had been winning adherents among the revolutionary intelligentsia for more than a decade. In 1902 Lenin advocated the formation of a tightly organized and disciplined party (see his What Is To Be Done?). A year later his views prevailed in the majority faction at the Second Congress of the party; the majority faction thereafter became known as Bolshevik, the minority faction as Menshevik. Lenin's views were challenged by Rosa Luxemburg, a founder of the Spartacus League, later the nucleus for the German Communist party in 1919. Although her basic Marxist stand differed little from that of Lenin, she attacked his concept of the centralized party (see esp. her *Leninism or Marxism,* Glasgow, 1935). Like Rosa Luxemburg, Leon Trotsky represented ultra-radical sentiment that could not be reconciled to Lenin's stress on party organization (see Trotsky's *Our Political Tasks,* Geneva, 1905); in 1917 however, he joined Lenin.

21. Astrojildo Pereira in "Silvério Fontes, pioneiro do marxismo no Brasil," in *Estudos Sociais,* III (April 1962), 405, dates Brazilian socialism to 1889, to the movement in Santos initiated by Silvério Fontes, Sóter de Araújo, and Carlos de Escobar. According to Pereira, this group published a "Manifesto Socialista ao Povo Brasileiro" on December 12, 1889. Pereira believes that Silvério Fontes elaborated upon socialist principles in the first issue (September 15, 1895) of *A Questão Social,* published by the Centro Socialista de Santos, and quotes a lengthy passage from that document (Pereira, "Silvério Fontes . . . ," p. 407). Silvério Fontes joined the PCB in 1922 and, according to Pereira, thereby carried on the struggle that since the first days of the Republic had been influenced by "the banner of socialism." Pereira quotes in its entirety a document published in *O Estado de São Paulo* on August 28, 1902, possibly being the original manifesto attributed to Silvério Fontes in 1889 (see Partido Socialista Brasileiro, "O Conselho Geral do Partido aos habitantes de Brasil, especialmente aos proletarios, Manifesto," quoted in Pereira, pp. 411–19). Octávio Brandão, like Pereira a founder of the PCB, minimized the role of Silvério Fontes, alleging that Pereira's interpretation was based on *ex post facto* examination of information in 1928; see Brandão, "Combates de classe operária," *Revista Brasiliense,* 46 (March-April 1963), 74–75.

22. According to Bandeira *et al., O ano vermelho,* p. 15, the São Paulo congress founded the PSB, which had "an ephemeral existence" and was influenced by the French Socialist party. Reference to this congress and party is omitted in the above cited writings of Dias, Linhares, and Pereira.

23. Pereira, "Silvério Fontes . . . ," p. 406, suggests that the number of 400 delegates was exaggerated by Linhares, *Contribuição . . . ,* p. 39, who gives details on the party's founding; Linhares also identifies two short-lived socialist publications with the title *O 1° de Maio,* published in São Paulo, one in 1892 and the other in 1895. Leôncio Basbaum, * *História sincera da república,* Vol. II, p. 312, refers to a Centro Socialista in Santos which published *O Socialista;* Pereira, *op. cit.,* p. 407, documents the existence of a União Operária, a Partido Operário, and a Centro Socialista—all in Santos during 1895. Manoel Jover Telles, * *O movimento sindical no Brasil,* p. 21, refers to a Partido Operário Progressista, also established in 1895 (and possibly the same as Partido Socialista Operário). Among other publications thereafter were the daily *O Povo* (São Paulo) in 1899; the daily, *La Parola dei Socialista* (São Paulo), in 1900; and the sporadic *Pelestra Social* (São Paulo), in 1900. Jover Telles also cites a Clube Democrático Socialista, founded in São Paulo.

24. The congress was organized by Italian and Brazilian socialists (including Silvério Fontes) residing in São Paulo who in 1900 had founded the periodical *Avante!* The party disappeared two years later, according to Pereira, "Silvério Fontes . . . ," p. 406; details of the party's program are in Linhares' *Contribuição . . . ,* pp. 48–49, and Dias, *História das lutas . . . ,* p. 244.

25. See Dias, *op. cit.,* pp. 245–46; Linhares, *Contribuição . . . ,* pp. 35, 54; and Basbaum, *História sincera . . . ,* Vol. II, p. 312. Dias identifies a Círculo Karl Marx in São Paulo in 1906 and names 17 Ligas Socialistas as existing at that time.

26. These socialist organizations are identified in Bandeira *et al., O ano vermelho,* pp. 141–42, 154–56, 158. The PSB leadership included Nestor Peixoto de Oliveira

as secretary general and Evarista de Moraes, an unsuccessful PSB candidate for federal deputy in 1918.

27. See "Clarté" in *Clarté*, I (September 1, 1921), 1–5. Although difficult to document, Linhares in "O comunismo no Brasil—I," *Revista Brasiliense*, 25 (September-October 1959), p. 152, refers to a socialist party as existing in 1911 and 1919.

28. Political events, including a state of siege, prevented this party from effective activity. Details, including excerpts from *Clarté*, are in Dias, *op. cit.*, pp. 104–11. The party statutes are in "Estatutos da Sociedade Civil Clarté," *Clarté*, I (September 1, 1921), 16–18.

29. From Woodcock's *Anarchism* . . . , p. 13. His excellent synthesis of the ideas of Proudhon, Bakunin, Kropotkin, and other thinkers is in chaps. 2 to 8, pp. 37–238. Irving Louis Horowitz suggests an interesting typology of anarchist strategies and beliefs, including utilitarian anarchism ("an expression by the déclassé wealthy on behalf of the underprivileged of society"); peasant anarchism ("within a narrow and parochial circle entailing negative attitudes toward the processes of industrialization and urbanization"); anarcho-syndicalism ("the anarchism practiced and preached by radical trade unionism"); collectivist anarchism ("freeing anarchism from a class base and placing it upon a mass base"); conspirational anarchism ("a process of systematic assassination of the rulers and stimulating widespread insurrection"); communist anarchism ("violence should be intrinsic and organic to the goal sought"); individualist anarchism ("sought to preserve the principle of rights over law . . . to make anarchism a respectable doctrine"); pacifist anarchism ("pacifism in the state of political victory involved itself in the betrayal of its anarchist premises"). See Horowitz (ed.), *The Anarchists,* New York: Dell Publishing, 1964, pp. 28–55. The contrast in various anarchist positions is evident in the following major works: Michael Bakunin, *God and State,* Boston, 1893, and *Marxism, Freedom, and the State,* London, 1950; Peter Kropotkin, *The Conquest of Bread,* London, 1906; G. V. Plekhanov, *Anarchism and Socialism,* Chicago, 1908; Pierre-Joseph Proudhon, *The General Idea of Revolution in the Nineteenth Century,* London, 1923.

30. The Spanish Confederación Nacional del Trabajo was undoubtedly influential in the growth of anarchism in Latin America. The largest, most militant of the organizations was the Federación Obrera Regional Argentina (FORA), founded in 1901. In Mexico, Ricardo Flores Magón and his anarcho-syndicalist newspaper, *Regeneración,* played an important role in arousing urban working-class sentiment against the Porfirio Díaz dictatorship; Magón is remembered as a father of the Mexican Revolution of 1910. For additional details see George Woodcock, *Anarchism: A History of Libertarian Ideas and Movements,* Cleveland and New York: World Publishing Co., 1962, esp. pp. 425–28.

31. An excellent analysis of Spanish anarchism and anarcho-syndicalism is in Gerald Brenan, *The Spanish Labyrinth,* London, 1943.

32. The ideological conflict between anarchists and Marxists has centered on the question of the transitional period between existing and future social orders. Whereas Marxists generally respect the anarchist notion of the withering away of the state, they contend that in the transition period the state must be controlled by the dictatorship of the proletariat. These contrasting positions are reflected in the thought of Bakunin and Marx, according to Woodcock: "Marx was an authoritarian, Bakunin a libertarian; Marx was a centralist, Bakunin a federalist; Marx advocated political action for the workers and planned to conquer the state; Bakunin opposed political action and sought to destroy the state; Marx stood for what we now call

nationalization of the means of production; Bakunin stood for workers' control." From *Anarchism* . . . , p. 171.

33. The periodicals (probably only part of the whole output) are described in the writings of two participants: Everardo Dias, *História das lutas sociais* . . . , pp. 243–308; and Hermínio Linhares, *Contribuição* . . . , pp. 38–81. Among other works consulted, see Leôncio Basbaum, *História sincera* . . . , Vamireh Chacon, * *História das idéias socialistas no Brasil;* and Nelson Werneck Sodré, *História da imprensa no Brasil,* Rio de Janeiro: Editôra Civilização Brasileira, 1966. The 30 periodicals published between 1894 and 1920 were: *L'Avenire* (São Paulo), first issued in 1894 in Portuguese and Italian; *O Despertador* (Rio de Janeiro), first issued in 1898 (ed. by J. Sarmento); *O Protesto* (Rio de Janeiro), an anarcho-communist periodical, 1899; *Il Diritto* (Curitiba) and *La Canaglia* (Ribeiro Preto, São Paulo), both 1899 and in Italian, *Avanti* (São Paulo, a socialist organ that until 1909 maintained its primitive libertarian program), *L'Azione Anarchica* (São Paulo), and *La Bataglia* (São Paulo), all 1900; *1º de Maio* (São Paulo), one issue 1901; *XX Settembre* (São Paulo), also one issue in 1901; *Germinal* (São Paulo), 1902–3; *O Amigo do Povo* (São Paulo), ed. by Neno Vasco in 1902; *O Libertário* (Rio de Janeiro), 1902; *La Nuova Gente* (São Paulo), a bimonthly ed. by Luigi Magrassi in 1903; *O Trabalhador* (Rio de Janeiro), a biweekly, 1903; *Kultur* (Rio de Janeiro), 1904; *O Libertário* (Rio de Janeiro), 1904; *Aurora* (São Paulo), a monthly, 1904; *A Terra Livre* (São Paulo), ed. by Edgar Leuenroth in 1905; *La Battaglia* (São Paulo), 1905; *Fôlha do Povo* (São Paulo), 1908–9; *A Luta* (Pôrto Alegre), 1909–10; *Le Barricata* (São Paulo), 1911; *A Guerra Social* (São Paulo), 1911; *A Luta* (Pôrto Alegre), 1911; *La Propaganda Libertária* (São Paulo); *Germinal* (São Paulo), 1913; *Spartacus* (Rio de Janeiro), weekly, 1919; and *A Plebe* (São Paulo) and *A Vanguarda* (São Paulo), both 1919.

34. By 1911 there existed a Grupo Anarquista Guerra Social and a Centro Libertário de Estudos Sociais Aurora e Libertade in Rio; a Centro Libertário, a Grupo Libertário Aurora-Libertás, a Círculo de Estudo Sociais Francisco Ferrer, a Círculo de Estudos Sociais Conquista do Porvir, and a Grupo Guerra Social in São Paulo; a Grupo Anarquista Sementeira in Pôrto Alegre, and a Grupo de Operários de Estudos Sociais Germinal in Nitorói.

35. Historians generally emphasize anarchism as the basis for evolution of Communist movements and the PCB. See Poppino, *International Communism in Latin America,* pp. 70–72; and Alexander, *Communism in Latin America,* pp. 93-96. The best study of anarchism to date is Edgar Rodrigues, * *Socialismo e sindicalismo, no Brasil, 1675–1913.*

36. In some cases anarchists mistakenly believed that the Russian Revolution was libertarian-inspired. According to Linhares, in early 1918 anarchists published a pamphlet, *A revolução russa e a imprensa,* which was followed on May 1 by a demonstration in Rio to manifest "sympathy for the Russian people . . . against capitalism." Quoted in Linhares, *Contribuição* . . . , pp. 77–78.

37. Leuenroth was secretary-general of the anarchist-controlled COB, an editor of *A Terra Livre* and *Fôlha do Povo,* as well as founder of *A Plebe* and *A Vanguarda,* and editor of a collection of essays, * *Anarquismo—roteiro da libertação social: antologia de doutrina crítica, história, informações.* José Oiticica was the author of * *A doutrina anarquista ao alcance de todos,* a collection of articles originally published by the anarchist newspaper, *Ação Direta,* ed. by Oiticica 1946–57. Leuenroth, Oiticica, and other names cited above are in Dias, *História das lutas* . . . , p. 103; Alexander, *Communism* . . . , 94, includes also Rudolpho

Felippe António Domingues, and Ricardo Cipolla as leaders of anti-Bolshevist anarchists. See note 42 for further details.

38. The alternative was affiliation with the Red International of Labor Unions, The conflicting positions and international groupings are discussed in Alexander, *Communism* . . . , p. 94.

39. These and other examples of Brazilian information on the Russian Revolution are cited by Astrojildo Pereira, "Lutas operárias . . . ," in *Problemas, 39* (April-May 1952), 75–87, and his * *Formação do PCB*, pp. 26–30; Basbaum, *História sincera* . . . , Vol. II, p. 313; and Alexander, *Communism* . . . , p. 93. Pereira was an editor of *Spartacus*.

40. The best synthesis of these developments is in Bandeira *et al., O ano vermelho,* pp. 283–300.

41. Pereira, *Formação do PCB,* p. 51; and Poppino, *International Communism* . . . , p. 71, identify the movement as "União"; Linhares *Contribuição* . . . , p. 77, calls it a "Centro." Brandão in "Combates da class operária," pp. 75–76, minimizes the importance of the União Maximalista, which later joined the PCB after its leader, Abílio de Nequete (a barber), was expelled from the PCB as "a traitor." The Brazilian ideological roots of the Maximalistas appear to be found in a famous article, "No ajuste de contas," today known as the "Manifesto Maximalista," published in 1918 by Lima Barreto as a political manifesto and revolutionary program inspired by "the Russian Revolution." He called for elimination of the national debt; confiscation of religious property; abolition of rights to inherit property; and legalization of divorce. It is reprinted in Bandeira *et al., O ano vermelho,* pp. 363–67, where it is entitled "Manifesto da União Maximalista aos operários" and dated November 1, 1918, Pôrto Alegre. On pp. 355–62 of the same work appears Lima Barreto's "Sôbre a Maximalismo", in which he states that his manifesto was published on May 11, 1918, in the magazine *ABC.* Pereira's claim that Lima Barreto favored the PCB (*Formação do PCB,* p. 54) is challenged by Brandão ("Combates . . . ," p. 74) who, although acknowledging Barreto as a defender of the worker and the Russian Revolution, cannot accept him as a Marxist. "His ideological roots were Comte and Spencer, Réclus and Kropotkin, Balzac and Dostoevski"—and adds, "an alcoholic, he died in 1922." Additional details are in Linhares, "O comunismo no Brasil—I," pp. 149–52.

42. On June 21, 1919, the PCB conference was inaugurated in Rio de Janeiro, according to a news report, "Primeira Conferência Communista do Brasil," in *A Plebe* of São Paulo, III (June 21, 1919), reproduced in Bandeira *et al., O ano vermelho,* photo opposite p. 212. *A Plebe* published the resolutions of the conference on June 28, 1919 (reprinted in *O ano vermelho,* pp. 162–63). Pereira, *Formação do PCB,* pp. 42–43, stated that under the leadership of José Oiticica, the party sponsored a congress in late June in Niterói after police prohibited the meeting in Rio. The congress approved Oiticica's program, "Princípios e fins do comunismo," which Pereira labels as "communism in name only." Pereira judged this movement as premature, since Oiticica and others proved to be "pure" or "intransigent" anarchists and critics of Russian Communism. The program of the anarchist PCB was prepared by Hélio Negro and Edgard Leuenroth, * *O que é o maximismo ao bolchevismo: programa comunista.*

43. The founding of the Grupo Comunista occurred almost simultaneously with that of the earlier mentioned socialist-backed Grupo da Clarté and an apparently anarchist-oriented Coligação Social, comprised of intellectual and labor elements who proposed "a Congresso da Vanguarda Social do Brasil in order to found a

party of intense action, rigid principles and a well-defined program." See Dias, *História das lutas . . .* , pp. 105.

44. Besides Pereira, the other founders are Manuel Abril, João Argolo, Antônio Branco, Antônio de Carvalho, Antônio Cruz Júnior, José Alves Diniz, Aurélio Durães, Francisco Fereira, Sebastião Figueiredo, Olgier Lacerda, and Luiz Pérez.

45. Modified to a biweekly in January 1923, *Movimento Comunista* published 24 numbers until it ceased in June 1923 when police seized its press.

46. This socio-economic data is extracted from Linhares, *Contribuição . . .* , p. 84; Dias, *História das lutas . . .* , p. 54, and Pereira, *Formação do PCB,* p. 46. Pereira notes that only nine delegates attended the founding congress of the Russian (1898) and Chinese (1921) Communist parties.

47. An appeal from the South American Bureau of the Comintern was read before the First Congress. Acceptance of the 21 conditions assured the PCB of its place at the Fourth Congress of the Comintern (Moscow, November 1922). The appeal is quoted in Dias, *História das lutas . . .* , pp. 112–13.

48. These names are identified, perhaps erroneously, in Inquérito Policial Militar No. 709, *O comunismo no Brasil,* Vol. I, Rio de Janeiro: Biblioteca do Exército-Editôra, 1966, p. 126; substitute delegates (*suplentes*) were Cristiano Cordeiro, Rodolfo Coutinho, Antônio de Carvalho, Joaquim Barbosa, and Manuel Cendón. Antônio Canellas represented the PCB at the Fourth Congress of the Comintern, but his report was not accepted by the Central Committee of the PCB, which expelled him. His report, "Relatório Canellas," was reprinted in *Novos Tempos,* 4 (January 1958), 40–44.

49. Our emphasis has been upon ideologies of alien and international origin. Obviously they influenced national developments. Socialism, positivism, and nationalism, e.g., all had an impact on Brazilian revolutionary thought. Perhaps the best source for interpretative synthesis of Brazilian thought is João Cruz Costa, *A History of Ideas in Brazil. The Development of Philosophy in Brazil and the Evolution of National History,* Berkeley and Los Angeles: University of California Press, 1964.

Notes to Chapter 3

Titles preceded by asterisk on first appearance have complete entries in Bibliography.

1. A useful history of these events is John W. F. Dulles, **Vargas of Brazil: A Political Biography;* also see the multi-volume work, * *O ciclo de Vargas,* by Hélio Silva; and Glauco Carneiro, *História das revoluções brasileiras,* Rio de Janeiro: Edições O Cruzeiro, 1965 (2 vols.). Jordon M. Young in * *The Brazilian Revolution of 1930 and the Aftermath,* sketches a similar historical period but with less detail and interpretation.

2. Many army officers and esp. the Military Club in Rio de Janeiro had opposed the dominant political machine in 1921–22. The opposition led to later rebellions, the Prestes march, and the rise of *tenentismo.* For a popular account of these events, see Glauco Carneiro, *O revolucionário Siqueira Campos. A epopêia dos 18 do Forte e da Coluna Prestes . . .* , Rio de Janeiro: Gráfica Record Editôra, 1966 (2 vols). Also interesting are photographs in *Os 18 do Forte: Collectânea organisada pelo Capitão Carlos Chevalier sôbre Siqueira Campos . . .* , n.d.

3. The classic study of tenentismo is Virginia Santa Rose, * *O sentido do tenentismo,* 1933, (in a 2nd ed., *Que foi a tenentismo?*), 1963. Among important articles on the tenente movement, see Robert J. Alexander "Brazilian 'Tenentismo,' " *Hispanic American Historical Review,* XXXVI (May 1956), 229–42; Ann Quiggins Tiller, "The Igniting Spark—Brazil, 1930," *Hispanic American Historical*

Review, XLV (August 1965), 384–92; John D. Wirth, "Tenentismo in the Brazilian Revolution of 1930," *Hispanic American Historical Review,* XLIV (May 1964), 161–79; and Jordan Young, "Military Aspects of the 1930 Brazilian Revolution," *Hispanic American Historical Review,* XLIV (May 1964), 180–96.

4. For a description of the 1924 events and aftermath, see Nelson Tabajara de Oliveira, *1924: a revolução de Isidoro,* São Paulo: Companhia Editôra Nacional, 1956. Also see J. Nunes de Carvalho, * *A revolução no Brasil, 1924–1925: Apontamentos para a história.*

5. See the memoirs of Cabanas in *A columna da morte sob o comando do Tenente Cabanas,* 6th ed., Rio de Janeiro: Livraria Editôra Almeida e Torres, 1928.

6. Barros' memoirs are in * *Memórias de um revolucionário.*

7. See Távora's *A guisa de depoimento sôbre a revolução brasileira de 1924,* Vol. 1: *O combate,* São Paulo, 1927. A descriptive but poorly organized study of this revolutionary is Abelardo F. Montenegro, *Juarez Távora e a renovação nacional,* Fortaleza, 1957, esp. pp. 41–58.

8. Other interesting personal accounts of the march are those of a former Italian artillery captain, Italo Landucci, * *Cenas e episódios da Coluna Prestes;* and the secretary to the column, Lourenço Moreira Lima, * *A Coluna Prestes: marchas e combates,* including letters and documents. Two accounts of particular events, respectively in Rio Grande do Norte and in Paraíba, are Raimundo Nonato, *Os revoltosos em São Miguel, 1926,* Rio de Janeiro: Editôra Pongetti, 1966; Manuel Otaviano, *Os martires de Piancó,* João Pessoa: Editôra Teone, 1955; also on Paraíba, Apolônio Nobrega, *História republicana da Paráiba,* João Pessoa, 1950, pp. 168–69.

9. Prestes consistently displayed outstanding leadership, became Miguel Costa's chief of staff, and because of prestige among the common soldiers, was promoted to the rank of revolutionary general; he thus stood above such widely acclaimed leaders (all revolutionary commanders), as Barros, Siqueira Campos, Djalma Dutra, and Oswaldo Cordeiro de Farias (the latter climaxed his career as a cabinet minister in the Castelo Branco regime). Jorge Amado characterized Prestes as the "cavalier of hope" in the biography of that title, * *O cavaleiro de esperança: vida de Luiz Carlos Prestes.* The other important biography (also sympathetic) is by Abguar Bastos, * *Prestes e a revolução social.* A Communist explanation for the failure of the Prestes march and antecedent events was based on: first, "the failure to deliver the city of São Paulo to a council of workers and soldiers . . . ," this being attributable to the PCB's inability to assume leadership, its lack of a policy on "the petty bourgeoisie," and its failure to provide political direction to the masses; and, second, the "total lack of . . . military strategy." See Armando Guerra, "The Political Situation of Brazil," *Political Affairs,* IX (November-December 1930), 1034–35.

10. In 1923 the PCB reached an agreement with or infiltrated the Confederação Sindicalista Cooperativa Brasileiro in Rio and consequently for more than a year was able to publish its news on one full page of the pro-Bernardes daily newspaper, *O Paiz.* This information was provided by Rollie Poppino in a private communication of November 21, 1969, citing Carlos Lacerda's "A exposição anti-comunista," in *O Observador* (January 1939), 129.

11. Documentation of the Second Congress is in Pereira, *Formação do PCB,* pp. 66–71. The party's emphasis on semifeudal agrarian capitalism suggests a transition period in which capitalism has began to penetrate and dominate the feudal structure upon which agrarian society presumably is based in Brazil. This interpretation of feudalism, essentially maintained by the party today, was chal-

lenged by some Marxist scholars, including Caio Prado Júnior in his * A revolução brasileira, esp. chap. 2, pp. 33–114.

12. Pereira, op. cit., pp. 72–84, includes separate chapters on A Classe Operária and A Nação.

13. Resende later became a Trotskyist, according to Guerra's "The Political Situation of Brazil," p. 1036.

14. See Partido Comunista do Brasil, Comissão Central Executiva, "Carta aberta à Maurício de Lacerda, à Azevedo Lima, ao Partido Socialista, ao Centro Político dos Operários do Distrito Federal, ao Centro Político dos Choferes, ao Partido Unionista dos Empregados no Comércio, ao Centro Político Proletário da Gávea, ao Centro Político Proletário de Niterói," in A Nação, 2 (January 5, 1927), 1, and reprinted in Pereira, op. cit., pp. 87–100. According to Pereira, many of the proposals in this document were later incorporated into the Vargas government's labor legislation.

15. The PCB first ran candidates, without success, for public office in the municipal election of 1925 in the port city of Santos. The name change from the BO to BOC (thereby including peasants as well as workers in the name) was the result of the Lei Celerada of August 1927, which gave the PCB semi-legal status. With the name change the PCB technically ceased to function and the Bloco became its front organization, with sections established in the Federal District, Niterói, Petrópolis, São Paulo, Santos, Juiz de Fora, Recife, and Ribeirão Prêto. PCB disassociation with the BOC occurred with the party's Third Congress (see below).

16. Pereira, Formação do PCB, pp. 110–13, mentions Barbosa's pamphlet, Uma carta aberta aos membros do PCB, which touched off the debate; and elaborates on the content of the six numbers of Auto-crítica published before the Third Congress and the two numbers issued thereafter.

17. Octávio Brandão, "Combates da classe operária," p. 73, labels this faction "liquidacionista" because its 48 members desired to eliminate existing labor organizations, the PCB itself, and to impede the founding of a Brazilian labor federation. Earlier Barbosa and apparently Costa Pimenta as well had cast the only two dissenting votes against a resolution of the Executive Central Committee to send secretary general Pereira to Bolivia to meet with Prestes (see Pereira, op. cit., p. 106). Linhares in "O comunismo no Brasil—I," p. 161, interprets this decision as a response to the rapidly growing prestige of Prestes and to the expectation that the "third explosion" (following those of 1923 and 1924) would be led by the working class in alliance with the petty bourgeoisie and its leader Prestes.

18. Barbosa returned to the PCB in 1943; Costa Pimenta became a Trotskyist and about 1946 joined the newly established Brazilian socialist party. See Alexander, Communism in Latin America, p. 97, information based on his interview with Hilcar Leite in Rio de Janeiro, June 11, 1953.

19. Alexander, Communism . . . , p. 98, states that these Trotskyists had more popular support and labor influence than their PCB rivals. Alexander identifies also Pedrosa and Coutinho, both of whom travelled to Europe in 1929, as the principal leaders in the dissident faction. There was apparent Trotskyist strength among printers and metallurgical unions in Rio and São Paulo. Based on his interview with Hilcar Leite on June 11, 1953, Alexander believes that in the years immediately following the 1930 revolution the Trotskyists "had more popular support and trade union influence than their Stalinist rivals."

20. Prado Júnior, op. cit., pp. 47–48, attributes the party's emphasis on feudalism to "the European model" adopted at the Sixth Congress of the Comintern on September 1928 in Moscow.

21. Pereira's detailed summary, analysis, and assessment are in *Formação do PCB*, pp. 115–35.

22. See Pereira's reservations, note 56; Basbaum, *História sincera* . . . , Vol. II, pp. 400–1; and Brandão, "Combates da classe operária," p. 65. Brandão condemns the PCB for moving in late 1929 toward a political line "more and more leftist," culminating in 1930–34 under the command of the Soviet Union and resulting in the decimation of the party, which, he says, suffered "a real catastrophe." Commenting a few years later at the Seventh Congress of the Comintern, Comrade Marques, a Brazilian delegate, blamed the party's failing on Pereira: "The party emerged from the whole period during which it led an energetic struggle against the rotten Menshevik line of its former secretary general, Astrojildo Pereira, and then against serious sectarian mistakes." See Marques, "The Seventh World Congress of the Communist International," *International Press Correspondence*, XV, 41 (August 25, 1934), 1068–69. Writing under the pseudonym "Augusto Machado" in * *O caminho da revolução operária e camponeza*, pp. 139–40, Basbaum analyzed the prospects for an agrarian, anti-imperialist revolution as dependent on four conditions: a profound and abrupt crisis in Brazil; a deep alienation of the masses; a solid consciousness of class; and the existence of a Communist party "ideologically strong, Marxist-Leninist, capable of guiding the masses, of unmasking social fascists." He argued that only the first two conditions existed in Brazil.

23. These developments are described by Prado Júnior in *História econômica do Brasil*, 8th ed. (1963), pp. 263–74.

24. The FSRR held its first congress April 27–30, 1927, and anarchists and Communists were represented, although Communist influence apparently was dominant, according to Alexander, *Communism* . . . , p. 96. The congress discussed the organization of regional workers federations in all Brazilian states as well as the founding of a Confederação Geral dos Trabalhadores do Brasil (CGTB); see Dias, *História das lutas* . . . pp. 312–13; Pereira, *Formação do PCB*, pp. 77–78. The CGTB was formally established in Rio at the second congress of the FSRR, under the domination of the PCB (Alexander, *idem.*, information based on his interview with Roberto Morena, August 28, 1946). The CGTB held its first congress in April 1929 and sent representatives to the founding Communist congress of the Sindical Latino Americano in Montevideo a month later (Alexander, *idem.*); the CGTB later was replaced by the government-controlled Confederação Nacional do Trabalho (Basbaum, *História sincera* . . . Vol. III, p. 34; Dias, *idem.*, p. 155).

25. See note 16. Pereira's interview was published in the *tenentista* daily, *A Esquerda*, ed. by Pedro Motta Lima, January 3 to 5 or 6 (See Pereira, *Formação do PCB*, pp. 108–9). Jorge Amado, *O cavaleiro da esperança* ,p. 133, notes that *A Esquerda* was confiscated from the Biblioteca Nacional in Rio and burned by the Estado Novo regime of Vargas, but that the interview was published also in *Diário da Manhã* of Recife. Amado also cites an article by the Paraguayan Communist leader, Oscar Creydt, "Tres etapas de una vida heróica," in *El Siglo* (Santiago de Chile), January 10, 1941, in which Creydt recalls meeting Prestes in Santa Fe, Argentina, in 1928.

26. Leôncio, Basbaum, *História sincera* . . . , Vol. II, 402–03.

27. *Ibid.*, pp. 404–05.

28. Getúlio Vargas, *A nova política do Brasil*, Vol. I: *Da Aliança Liberal* . . . . Rio de Janeiro: Livraria José Olympio Editôra, 1930, pp. 26–29. The Aliança also called for amnesty for all the 1922–26 revolutionaries, autonomy for the states, a new election law, reorganization of justice, and education; it promised economic

development, especially in poor areas of the Northeast and the Amazon, and protection for the coffee and cattle-raising industries.

29. See, e.g., the views by Antônio Augusto Borges de Medeiros of Rio Grande do Sul and others in Affonso Henriques, *Ascenção e queda de Getúlio Vargas*. Vol. I: *Vargas, o maquiavélico*, Rio de Janeiro: Distribuidora Record, 1966, pp. 92–98.

30. In Paraíba, for example, João Pessôa drew up a congressional slate of new Liberals opposed to José Pereira, the wealthy oligarch of the interior Princesa sector. Pereira, aligned with Júlio Prestes, organized his followers into, groups of *cangaceiros* or professional outlaws. On May 3 the Paraíba slate favored by Pereira was seated. In Minas authorities refused to accept the credentials of 14 Aliança deputies. See Dulles, *Vargas of Brazil* . . . , pp. 57–58. On the Princesa rebellion, see José Gastão Cardoso, *A heróica resistência de Princesa*, Recife, 1954; João Lelis, *A campanha de Princesa*, 1930, João Pessôa: A União Editôra, 1944; and Adhemar Vidal, *1930, História da revolução na Parahyba*, São Paulo: Companhia Editôra Nacional, 1933.

31. Dulles, *op. cit.*, p. 58.

32. Prestes believed that his followers would have to wait two years before rebelling and one year if the Aliança attempt failed. See Dulles, *op. cit.*, p. 60, information based on interview with Emídio Miranda, July 19, 1963.

33. Prestes' "Manifesto de Maio" was published in *Diário da Noite* (São Paulo), 2nd ed., May 29, 1930, and reprinted in full in Bastos, *Prestes e a revolução social*, pp. 225–29; and in Hélio Silva, * *O ciclo de Vargas*. Vol. III: *1930, a revolução traída*, pp. 417–21; two short excerpts are translated in Alexander, *Communism* . . . , pp. 104–5. About a month before the May Manifesto, Prestes offered a program focused on political liberties (six points), political action (five points), and the rural problem (two points); see Alexander, pp. 103–4, for English text of this moderate program, and Bastos, pp. 249–51, and *A Noite*, June 4, 1930, for the Portuguese version.

34. Dulles, *op. cit.*, p. 61.

35. For information of Juarez Távora's statement and for full text of Isidoro's letter (published in *Estado de São Paulo*, July 15, 1930), see Bastos, *Prestes e a revolução social*, pp. 230–36.

36. Virgílio A. de Mello Franco, *Outubro, 1930*, Rio de Janeiro: Schmidt, 1931, p. 218.

37. The full text of the PCB reply is in Basbaum, *História sincera* . . . , Vol. II, pp. 444–47; and a comment is in Guerra, "The Political Situation of Brazil," pp. 1031–43. The original PCB declaration was published in *Voz Operária*, 96 (August 1930).

38. Basbaum, *op. cit.*, Vol. II, pp. 408–10, suggests that both Prestes and the PCB erred in refusing to join the Aliança. Evidence of dissension with the PCB over Prestes had been apparent since the party's 1927 decision to establish contact with him in Bolivia (see note 16); and apparently in 1930 some leaders such as Brandão and Pereira were jealous because Prestes had been received by the party. Brandão published lengthy replies to Prestes' various announcements (in *O Journal* of Rio), and Fernando Lacerda attacked Prestismo as an ideology based on a belief in "elites, heroes, and cavaliers of hope" which tended to retard the development of revolutionary consciousness (see Alexander, *Communism* . . . , pp. 107–8). The impending revolution was certainly weakened by the loss of support from the labor movement (which was influenced by the PCB), although there was apparent labor sympathy with tenente rebels. Everardo Dias, at the request of Maurício de Lacerda, wrote a program for a Frente Unida das Esquerdas which called for

government control over foreign and domestic trade, legislation to prevent factory shutdowns, the guarantee of full employment, protection of small property owners through rent controls and other measures, and a revision of the discriminating tax system; his 32-point action program included dissolution of national, state, and municipal legislatures, and the implementation of laws to protect urban and rural workers. Such a program would be initiated after labor and rebel soldiers had launched their revolution; it was, however, unacceptable to the tenentes. See Dias, *História das lutas . . .* , pp. 161–67.

39. Linhares, "O comunismo . . . . —I," p. 163.

40. Thomas E. Skidmore, * *Politics in Brasil, 1930–1964: An Experiment in Democracy,* pp. 9–10, distinguishes between two major positions in the Vargas government: the liberal constitutionalists who favored free elections, constitutional government, and full civil liberties, and whose position was strongest in São Paulo state and in the small middle class of a few large cities; and the semi-authoritarian nationalists, including the tenentes, who desired changes in the government, social services, and an increase in the level of national consciousness. Their view was represented by the Clube 3 de Outubro (the day on which the 1930 revolt began), founded in 1931. The tenentes began to lose influence in 1932, and they wielded little influence in the Vargas government after 1934. For details of this decline, see Hélio Silva, *O ciclo de Vargas,* esp. Vol. IV: *Os tenentes no poder,* and Vol. VI: *A crise do tenentismo;* in the latter volume see the document, "Princípios básicos do tenentismo," pp. 284–87.

41. This authorization is quoted in full in Bastos, *Prestes e a revolução social,* p. 248, and in Alexander, *Communism . . .* , pp. 99–100. Communist labor groups in São Paulo also attempted to build the labor movement through a Comitê Provisório de Reorganização Sindical (Dias, *op. cit.,* p. 176).

42. Linhares, "O comunismo . . . —II (*Revista Brasiliense,* 26 November–December 1959), 187; Alexander, p. 100; Basbaum, *História sincera . . . ,* Vol. III, pp. 87–89. João Alberto came under attack once it was known his brother was a Communist. His first cabinet resigned before the end of 1930 and by July 1931 he too had resigned; see Dulles, *Vargas of Brazil . . . ,* p. 93.

43. The full text of Prestes' March 12 letter is in *Diário da Noite,* March 24, 1931, and reprinted in Bastos, *Prestes e a revolução social,* pp. 252–66. In denouncing the Trotskyists Prestes singled out Aristides Lobo, who had visited him in Buenos Aires, apparently convinced him to give up the LAR, and drafted several statements which Prestes issued under his own signature (see Alexander, *op. cit.,* p. 102).

44. The letter is reprinted in Bastos, *op. cit.,* pp. 269–72; a partial translation is in Alexander, p. 107. In Moscow he directed the construction of workers' housing projects and counselled the Comintern on South American affairs, eventually (at the Seventh Congress of the Comintern) assuming a position with the Executive Committee (see Bastos, p. 317). He did not affiliate with the PCB, however, until August 1, 1934 (*A Classe Operária,* 17 [1934], cited in Linhares, "O Comunismo . . . —II," p. 186, and confirmed by Alexander in his interview with Prestes on August 27, 1947—see pp. 109, 412).

45. Bastos, *op. cit.,* pp. 272–73.

46. Alexander, *op. cit.,* p. 99.

47. Basbaum, *História sincera . . . ,* Vol. III, pp. 85–88, refers also to the November 1932 meeting as a National Conference. The party's Second National Conference was held in 1943, and thus Basbaum is either incorrect or the 1932 meeting was not recognized as the First National Conference. There were probably two conferences, but we shall refer to the 1934 meeting as the First National Confer-

ence. Among the old militants removed from the Central Committee in 1934 were Heitor F. Lima, Mário Grazini, and Leôncio Basbaum himself.

48. Jorge Amado, *Cavaleiro de esperança*, 1945 ed., note 133, p. 239, notes that there was one PCB member in the 1934 Constituent Assembly: Alvaro Ventura, a stevedore from Santa Catarina elected an alternate federal deputy from the Federal District under the PCB in 1945.

49. Linhares, "O comunismo . . . —II," p. 188, citing *Jornal do Povo*, October 17, 1934. See Salgado's *O integralismo perante a nação*, 3rd ed., Rio de Janeiro: Livraria Clássica Brasileira, 1955, and *O que é o integralismo*, Rio de Janeiro, Schmidt, 1933.

50. The 1934 constitution, based on the German Weimar model, and in large measure upon the Brazilian constitution of 1891, symbolized a return to electoral democracy. A unique feature provided for representation of classes as well as parties. For details see Karl Loewenstein, *Brazil under Vargas*, New York: MacMillan, 1944, especially pp. 20–29.

51. The "popular front" policy adopted at the seventh and last congress of the Communist International in August 1935 called for cooperation with liberal and socialist groups wherever alliances could be arranged, and popular-front governments came to power in Chile, France, and Spain. The Comintern policy was formulated after a revision in 1934 of Soviet foreign policy, resulting in the Soviet government's pressing for "collective security" against Germany and Japan, joining the League of Nations, and forming a military alliance with France. According to Marques, *op cit.*, p. 1068, the PCB accepted the popular front line at an October 1934 conference of Latin American Communist parties.

52. Alexander, *op. cit.*, p. 109. Officially the conference was under ANL sponsorship.

53. The repressive National Security Law, passed by Congress on March 30, 1935, gave the government special power to repress subversive political activities and in effect, to move against the ANL.

54. Significantly the ANL headquarters were in the offices of the defunct Clube 3 de Outubro, the "jacobin" military-civilian club that had coalesced tenente supporters of the 1930 revolution. The club was disbanded in 1932 "after a dispute between conservative and radical members, and thereafter conservatives like War Minister Pedro Góis Monteiro moved toward the rightwing authoritarianism of *integralismo* and the Estado Novo, and other members, like Cascardo, moved left toward the ANL"; see Dulles, *op. cit.*, pp. 105, 146.

55. Allegedly Lacerda, under PCB orders, acted without the knowledge of ANL officials, although he denied this. See Robert Levine, "The Vargas Regime and the Politics of Extremism in Brazil, 1934–38," Princeton: Princeton University, unpublished Ph.D. dissertation, 1967, p. 94; chap. 4 focuses on the ANL. Another useful source is Thomas E. Skidmore, "Failure in Brazil; From Popular Revolt to Armed Revolt," *Journal of Contemporary History*, V, No. 3 (1970), 37–57. Lacerda later became a fervent anti-Communist nationalist and publisher of a Rio daily, *Tribuna da Imprensa*, which launched severe attacks on Presidents Vargas, Quadros, and Goulart.

56. The text of the ANL platform is in Bastos, *Prestes e a revolução social*, pp. 280–81; and in Linhares, *Contribuição* . . . , pp. 93–94 and *"O comunismo* . . . ," pp. 188–99; Levine, "The Vargas Regime . . . ," p. 100, states that the program was issued in March 1935, although it was analyzed in *Terceira República*, I, 1 (July 5, 1935), a date cited by Alexander, *Communism* . . . , p. 110.

57. Levine, "The Vargas Regime . . . ," p. 96, estimates membership in the Federal District as divided among businessmen, professionals, and commissioned officers

(37 per cent); workers and soldiers (52 per cent); and unclassified (11 per cent, including 2 per cent "agricultural").

58. The entire text of Prestes' speech appears in *Fôlho do Povo*, 1 (July 9, 1935), 1, 2, 4; and in Bastos, *op. cit.*, pp. 304–15.

59. In the Soviet Union Prestes had convinced the Comintern of the necessity of a military coup and establishment of a popular-front government under his leadership. The Vargas government was aware of the plans, however, because one of its agents, Antônio Maciel Bomfim, had become secretary general of the PCB after the imprisonment of the top leadership in 1932 and had even traveled to Moscow to support Prestes' coup plans. Bomfim (also known as Miranda, as Adalberto de Andrade Fernandes, and as Américo de Carvalho) had been a leader of the Liga de Ação Revolucionária and was elected secretary general at the PCB's First National Conference in 1934. The PCB National Secretariat in 1935 comprised Bomfim, Honório de Freitas Guimarães, Lauro Reginaldo da Rocha, and Adelino Deycola dos Santos. Details of these developments are in Basbaum, *História sincera . . .* , Vol. III, 87–89. That Vargas was aware of the plans is evident in his letter to Benedito Valvadares of July 5, 1935, reprinted from the Arquivo Getúlio Vargas in Hélio Silva, *1935, a revolta vermelha*, Vol. VIII, Rio de Janeiro: Editôra Civilização Brasileira, 1969, pp. 180–81. Further evidence is cited in Silva, pp. 398–400, including a statement by Vargas' daughter, Alzira Vargas do Amaral Peixoto, and police chief, Filinto Miller. For a description of the 1935 revolts, see Carneiro, *História das revoluções brasileiras*, Vol. II, chap. 18, "A revolta comunista," pp. 415–35.

60. Medeiros relates details of the Natal revolt and his capture and includes police documents in * *Meu depoimento: sôbre a revolução comunista e outros assumptos*, pp. 45–144. A photograph on p. 1 of *A Liberdade*, a rebel newspaper that claimed revolutionary success in João Pessôa, Recife, and São Paulo appears after p. 48 (the first issue is dated Wednesday, November 27, 1935). Medeiros confirms knowledge of a Communist conspiracy that was to have occurred on December 5, information based on secret messages given to Rio police "by a certain Communist agent."

61. The five committee members were Quintino Clementino de Barros, a sergeant rebel leader who had become Minister of Defense; Lauro Cortez Lago, a former police official and ex-director of the state prison who served as the Comitê's Minister of Interior; José Macedo, a former head of the state's postal service who was named Minister of Finance; João Baptista Galvão, a journalist who was Minister of Public Works; and José (Zé) Praxedes de Andrade, the Provisions Minister, a shoemaker, and the only committee member from the working class, who disappeared after the collapse of the revolt (see Medeiros, *Meu depoimento . . .* , pp. 111–12. Levine, "The Vargas Regime . . . ," p. 163, cites Luiz Machado, "Revolution in Brazil," in *International Press Correspondence* (London), XVI (January 11, 1936), 36, as asserting that Praxedes escaped to the interior with 500 rebels to organize peasants. Levine identifies Praxedes as the shoemaker Luiz in Jorge Amado's * *Seara Vermelha*, although this novel is dedicated to "Zé" who might be Praxedes as well as another character in the novel, *Zé Trevoada;* in any case Amado focuses on the Natal revolt (see pp. 266–319). The PCB also published the poetry of Zé Praxédi, *O sertão 'é assim . . . ;* the name (probably a pseudonym) may have relevance to the Natal revolt.

62. Although the revolt was ostensibly led by the ANL, which claimed 2,000 members in Recife alone, in fact the PCB dominated the state organization. PCB leaders, like Bezerra, had influenced local railroad strikes in Jaboatão but in the name of the ANL. ANL news was carried in the regional PCB newspaper, *Fôlha do Povo*. PCB domination was particularly evident after Silo Meireles' arrival from

Rio in May up to his personal control of the ANL state organization; see Levine *op. cit.,* p. 175. Levine also cites documentary evidence that Harry Berger (Arthur Ernest Ewert), a German Comintern agent sent to Brazil to assist the PCB in the uprising, had personally visited the São Francisco region where the party planned work in impoverished districts.

63. Death casualty estimates in Recife ranged from 60 to 800 and apparently were considerably less in Natal; see Levine, "The Vargas Regime . . . ," pp. 180–201.

64. Documentary evidence cited by Levine, *op. cit.,* p. 183; see Prestes' message in Agildo Barata, * *Vida de um revolucionário,* p. 261.

65. Barata was imprisoned in 1932 for fighting with the São Paulo constitutionalists, exiled to Portugal, and returned to Rio in December 1933. An amnesty in 1934 allowed him to return to army service. He was transferred to Rio Grande do Sul, and according to his own statement, became a militant in the PCB in February 1935 and in the ANL a month later. Under unclear circumstances he returned to Rio in October and November 8 began serving a 20-day sentence at the Praia Vermelha garrison. His narrative of the November conspiracy and events is in *Vida . . . ,* pp. 253–300. The official police version of these events, including documents and useful details of the rebels is in Eurico Bellens Porto, * *A insurreição de 27 de novembro.*

66. Secretary general of the ANL, Roberto Sissón, was informed in mid-1935, but after the ANL was declared illegal, the PCB assumed control, and Sissón was told that the revolution was postponed indefinitely, according to Levine, *op. cit.,* p. 188. Basbaum, *História sincera . . . ,* Vol. III, pp. 90–96, presents a convincing argument that the police were also aware of the plans. In an interesting letter to Sissón, written in September 1935, Prestes attempts to distinguish the ANL from the PCB and calls upon the ANL to take up "partial armed struggles," i.e., organize small groups for self-defense against police suppression; these struggles would lead to guerrilla warfare and to mass struggle. See Prestes' letter in his * *Problemas atuais de democracia,* pp. 15–19. Also see note 59 for evidence of police awareness of the uprising.

67. Medeiros, *Meu depoimento . . . ,* pp. 47–48, suggests that through the message Rio police intended "to sacrifice one state . . . for the sake of the Nation." See also Edgard Carone, * *Revoluções do Brasil contemporâneo, 1922/1938,* p. 145.

68. Basbaum alleges police infiltration and manipulation over events; the police, he asserts, knew of Prestes' activities in Russia and his plans to return to Brazil and may have encouraged the formation of the ANL (the ANL was closed by military groups who were unaware of the government's plans) as well as the transfer of Barata from Rio Grande do Sul to Rio (see Basbaum, *op. cit.,* Vol. III, pp. 90–96).

69. Alexander, *Communism . . . ,* p. 111, places emphasis on labor strikes and unrest in the countryside. In a communication to this writer, dated December 1, 1969, Alexander noted that local political rivalries played a large part in the Natal uprising, and they may have set off the revolt prematurely. He also noted that in an interview Roberto Sissón informed him that the November revolts were carried on against the wishes of non-Communist ALN leaders. Timothy Harding in "A Political History of the Brazilian Labor Movement," chap. 3, p. 13, argues that the PCB failed to inform labor of the plans to take power; as evidence he cites refusal of Communist-led workers in São Paulo to strike.

70. The local PCB in Natal received word of the decision to revolt and only a few hours in advance, according to Levine, "The Vargas Regime . . . ," p. 154, 161, and "The Brazilian Revolts of 1935," 1968, mimeo. p. 11 of paper delivered at the Brazil—Portuguese Africa Colloquium, Riverside, Calif., February 13, 1968.

Loewenstein, *Brazil under Vargas,* p. 28, agrees "that the outbreak was a purely military revolt; labor and the masses at large had nothing to do with it and did not participate." He errs, however, in dismissing Communist participation altogether. In a general criticism of the party's role in the 1935 revolt, Lacerda in "The Fascist Coup d'Etat in Brazil," *Communist International* XV (January 1938), 46, identifies five errors: "a false political line was adopted"; there was "neglect" of mass organizations; "the forces of the enemy were underestimated"; "there was insufficient revolutionary vigilence"; and there was "an overestimation of the role of individual heroism."

71. Allegedly in a concentration camp, but this is denied by Levine, *op. cit.,* p. 190, who states that she died of tuberculosis in a Swiss Red Cross hospital a few months after her arrival and after the delivery of a daughter, who eventually returned to Brazil in 1945. In May 1946, however, the PCB published an unsigned letter from Berlin recording Maria Wiedmayer's impressions of Olga Prestes in a Nazi concentration camp just prior to the latter's death; see "Olga Benário Prestes, a prisoneira No. 435 . . . a última testemunha . . . ," *Fôlha do Povo,* 153, Second Section (May 26, 1946), 1, 2. Ruth Eberle, another witness, stated in an interview with *Manchete* (December 21, 1957) that Olga died on March 4, 1942, in the concentration camp of Ravensbruck, a victim along with five other women of fire from a Nazi machine gun; the interview is reprinted in Henriques, *Ascenção e queda . . . ,* Vol. I, p. 440.

72. Of the 238 persons implicated in the Rio revolt, 156 were held in prison for periods up to two and one-half years, even though nearly half were acquitted for lack of evidence. At a secret trial of 35 of the principal defendants, the Tribunal sentenced Prestes to 16 years and 8 months in prison; Berger, 14 years; Barata, 10 years; Ghioldi, 4 years; and Pedro Ernesto and João Mangabeira, each 3 years and 4 months. The accusations against the 238 persons are in Porto, *A insurreição . . .* and a full list of names is also in Bastos, *Prestes e a revolução social,* pp. 326–28; the prison terms above are listed in Alexander, *op. cit.,* p. 111, although Levine, *op. cit.,* pp. 207–8, gives slightly different figures, probably because some, like Prestes, received additional sentences for subversive activities before November 1935 (after nine years in prison, Prestes was pardoned in 1945 when Vargas was forced to call elections). Of the 371 implicated in the Natal revolt, 66 were given prison terms ranging from 2 to 13 years; see Bastos, p. 336, for a list of those condemned.

73. A primary source on this period is Lourival Coutinho, *O General Góes depõe . . . ,* Rio de Janeiro: Livraria Editôra Coêlho Branco, 1955.

74. See Loewenstein, *Brazil under Vargas,* for a detailed analysis of the constitution and other legalistic aspects. Francisco Campos, author of the constitution, propagated the regime's credo in *O Estado Nôvo: sua estrutura, seu conteudo ideológico,* Rio de Janeiro: Livraria José Olympio Editôra, 1940.

75. Details on the suppression of the integralistas are in Levine, *op. cit.,* chap. 9, "The Eclipse of Integralism," pp. 254–72, and Dulles, *op. cit.,* pp. 178–93.

76. A useful synthesis of developments is in Skidmore, *Politics in Brazil . . . ,* pp. 24–47. Vargas' Labor Ministry was able to place its men in positions of leadership in many unions, thereby isolating independent militants, including Communists who had exerted much influence before 1937.

77. Harding suggests that Vargas added labor to his coalition because "Brazil lacked a nationalist industrialist class with enough power and consciousness to lead development at the expense of traditional landowners" and that such coalitions are not uncommon in less developed countries. See Harding, "A Political History . . . ,"

chap. 6, pp. 3–4, typescript. An explanation of this government-labor relation is in Leôncio Martins Rodrigues, * Conflito industrial e sindicalismo no Brasil, pp. 39–40, 184.

78. Alexander, Communism . . . , pp. 113–14, based on his interview with former secretary general of the PSR, Hermínio Saccheta, in São Paulo, June 16, 1953.

79. Levine, "The Vargas Regime . . . ," p. 208, bases this information on police files. The group was called the Grupo Comunista Lenino in 1929 and Legião dos Comunistas about 1931 (see note 19).

80. Alexander, op. cit., p. 114.

81. Alexander, p. 113, quotes from the party's "new program of 1938 which also called for an amnesty for anti-fascist prisoners; establishment of heavy industry; solution of the economic crisis; and application of the minimum wage law. Another perspective on the PCB's tenuous position is in Marina Lopes, "The People's Struggle against fascism in Brazil," The Communist, XVII (June 1938), 513–25. Prestes' counsel to the party is contained in a series of five letters to tenente Severo Fournier, November and December 1938; he proposed a three-point program embracing democracy, nationalism, and the people's welfare. His emphasis on nationalism (advocating organization of a steel industry and national defense) is particularly interesting and generally parallels the nationalist tendencies of Vargas' Estado Novo (see Prestes, Problemas atuais . . . , pp. 23–37). The party line also is advocated by P. Monteiro, "For a Nationwide Democratic United Front," World News and Views, XVIII, 38 (August 6, 1938), 902.

82. Linhares, "O comunismo . . . —II," pp. 194–95, condemns the party leadership as "opportunist," "bourgeois," and "liquidationalist" for its abandonment of a "revolutionary" policy. It would appear that the party leadership (like the Comintern movement itself) was confused by the nonaggression treaty of August 1939 between the Soviet Union and Germany.

83. Dulles, Vargas of Brazil . . . , p. 213. Also see Pedro Lafayette, * Os crimes do Partido Comunista, pp. 41 ff. Henriques, Ascenção e queda . . . , Vol. I, pp. 349–55, states that Elza Fernandes (or Copelo Polônio) was the mistress of Bomfim (or Fernandes, see note 59), and that a police investigation after her murder affirmed that she had not betrayed the PCB, that Bomfim had indeed been the police informer. Repression of Communists during 1940 is reported in the New York Times (April 3, 1940), 3; (April 14, 1940), 31; (April 15, 1940), 5; (April 16, 1940), 2; (April 27, 1940), 4; (April 28, 1940), 32.

84. Basbaum, História sincera . . . , Vol. III, p. 147. Germany invaded the USSR in June 1941. The realignment of world powers led to the anti-revolutionary dissolution of the Comintern in May 1943 as the supreme goal of Communism became victory over Germany. Soviet dominance over Communist movements, however, in reality continued unabated.

85. Basbaum, op. cit., Vol. III, pp. 148–49; Linhares, "O Comunismo . . . —II," pp. 195–97. Linhares believed that the conference was of immense significance for the party, while Basbaum identified two "fundamental errors," including Prestes' election (the party thereafter was dominated by "Prestes' cult of personality"); and the unconditional support for Vargas ("based on the abstentionist policy of the liquidationists"). See also "A significação histórica de Conferência da Mantiqueira," Problemas, 49 (September 1953), 1–8.

86. See Prestes' 13-point document, "Comentários a um documento Aliancista aparecido nos últimos meses de 1943," in Problemas atuais . . . , pp. 45–49.

87. See Prestes, "Projecto de declarção da ANL e do PCB," in Problemas atuais . . . , pp. 51–59.

88. The constitution of 1937 had provided for a plebescite on November 10, 1943. On that date Vargas, in a speech to the nation, promised a "political modification"; this he reiterated six months later in April 1944.

89. On October 24, 1943, intellectuals and politicians in Minas Gerais had issued a manifesto calling for the redemocratization of Brazil. The statement is reprinted in Henriques, *op. cit.*, Vol. II: *O Estado Novo*, pp. 154–62.

90. Published in *O Globo*, March 15, 1945, and reprinted as "A situação no Brasil e no mundo," in Prestes, *Problemas atuais . . .*, pp. 71–74, a document dated May 23, 1944.

Notes to Chapter 4

Titles preceded by asterisk on first appearance have complete entries in Bibliography.

1. José Ribeiro de Lira (?), "Três etapas do comunismo brasileiro," *Cadernos do Nosso Tempo*, 2 (January-June 1954), p. 123.

2. Alexander, *Communism in Latin America*, p. 117, cites a report in the *Daily Worker* of New York, June 9, 1945, in affirming that PCB withdrawal from the UDN occurred in June.

3. Basbaum, *História sincere da república*, Vol. III, pp. 158–60, compares the UDN to the Partido Republicano of the *Velha República*, which consisted of democrats divided between a wing of bankers and industrialists, on the one hand, and the *ala moça* of "idealists and romanticists," on the other. The Esquerda Democrática was formally instituted on August 25, 1945, at which time it issued a manifesto signed by 63 members, including João Mangabeira, Hermes Lima, Hercolino Cascardo, José Lins do Rêgo, Rubem Braga, Sérgio Buarque de Holanda, and Juracy Magalhães. On August 25, 1946, at its First National Conference, the Esquerda approved its statutes and officially became a party. At its Second National Conference in April 1947 it changed its name to the Partido Socialista Brasileiro. See Linhares, *Contribuição à história das lutas . . .*, pp. 99–104.

4. Dulles, *Vargas of Brazil*, p. 262.

5. Earlier Vargas had attempted to organize workers into a mass political movement under the control of Labor Ministry officials. The idea was rejected by military leaders in 1937 and 1938, but Vargas' creation of a labor commission in 1943 was apparently part of a plan to insure that he continue in office through indirect elections by the corporativist unions of the Estado Novo. This plan was not carried out, but Viana became head of the PTB. (Harding, "A Political History . . . ," chapt. 6, p. 40, note 40.)

6. Barata, *Vida de um revolucionário*, pp. 320–21. The author refers to division among Communist prisoners on Ilha Grande, where Prestes also was held, between one group led by ex-tenente Carlos da Costa Leite ("a nihilist group . . . infiltrated and destroyed by the police") and the "grupo do Agildo" (which supported the CNOP and along with Prestes provided PCB leadership until 1957). In 1945 Prestes confirmed the importance of the CNOP, stating that it was "the positive factor in the reorganization and recovery of our party." See his *Problemas atuais da democracia*, p. 135.

7. Barata, *op. cit.*, p. 321. Dulles, *Vargas of Brazil*, p. 260, states that the liaison between Prestes and Vargas was Orlando Leite Ribeiro, a well-regarded high official in the Foreign office during the Estado Novo and a fellow conspirator with Prestes in the 1920's.

8. Prestes' speech was published as * *União Nacional para a democracia e o progresso. Discurso pronunciado do comício de 23 de maio no estádio Vasco da*

Gama, esp. pp. 23–25. The speech is reproduced in Prestes' *Problemas atuais . . . ,* pp. 77–94. In another statement Prestes viewed the tasks of the MUT as necessary and preliminary to the establishment of a Confederação Geral dos Trabalhadores do Brasil—"the maximum organization of the proletariat, defender of its rights, and the vertical column of national union." The MUT was the labor front of the União Nacional, which had been organized into peasant and youth groups (see Prestes, *Problemas atuais . . . ,* "Organizar a povo para a democracia," pp. 95–119, a speech in São Paulo). Thus Prestes apparently anticipated the possibility that Vargas, desiring to remain in power against the will of the military, would call upon the PCB and the labor movement for support; furthermore, that any delay in elections would allow Communists more time to counter Vargas' own attempt at co-optation of labor (through the PTB) and permit the PCB to build strength through domination of the labor movement. Alexander, *Communism . . . ,* p. 119, emphasizes that the PCB labor policy allowed the party to infiltrate the Estado Novo apparatus and through control of official unions to have available ample funds, since the Vargas system required a compulsory contribution to the unions of one day's wage per year by every worker.

9. See details in Dulles, *Vargas of Brazil,* pp. 271–74. Young states that the U.S. Embassy had learned details of a Vargas plot to stay in power and refers to pressure by Ambassador Adolph Berle. See Young, *The Brazilian Revolution of 1930 . . . ,* p. 94. See also details in Alexander, *Communism . . . ,* pp. 116–18, and Basbaum, *História sincera . . . ,* Vol. II, pp. 167–70.

10. See Prestes, "Discurso proferido no grande comício, a nordeste a Luiz Carlos Prestes, no Parque 13 de Maio, no Recife, em 26 de novembro de 1945," pp. 167–82 in *Problemas atuais . . . .*

11. Reported in *Tribuna Popular,* November 14, 1945, and *Fôlha do Povo,* 1 (November 19, 1945), 1 ff., and partially quoted in Alexander *Communism . . . ,* p. 120. A resumé of the 12-point program is in Prestes' *Problemas atuais . . . ,* pp. 221–23.

12. The PCB program is outlined in Prestes, "Os comunistas na luta pela democracia," *ibid.,* pp 121–63; also in *Fôlha do Povo,* 90 (March 9, 1946) to 128 (April 25, 1946).

13. For election returns, see Tribunal Superior Eleitoral, *Dados e estadísticos— eleições federal, estadual e municipal realizadas no Brasil a partir de 1945,* Rio de Janeiro: Imprensa Nacional, 1950, pp. 15, 20, 28–30, 33–35, 37–39, 41, 43, 47, 49–50.

14. Alexander, *Communism . . . ,* p. 121.

15. See Prestes, "Informe político da Comissão Executiva ao Comitê Nacional do Partido Comunista do Brasil, apresentado por Luiz Carlos Prestes, no solenidade de instalação do Pleno Ampliado do C.N. em 4 de janeiro de 1946, no Instituto Nacional do Música," in *Problemas atuais . . . ,* pp. 185–247.

16. Prestes' first major address before the Constituent Assembly is entitled "A bancada comunista na constituinte," speech of February 5, 1946, in *Problemas atuais . . . ,* pp. 251–59. His major objections to the Constitution are in a speech before the Constituent Assembly, "O problema da terra e a constituição de 1946," *ibid.,* pp. 363–414; this speech, dated June 16, 1946, appears also in *Divulgação Marxista,* I (July 15, 1946), 121–59, see also *Fôlha do Povo,* 52 (January 22, 1946), 4. The Constitution was promulgated on September 18, 1946.

17. See Prestes, "Contra a guerra e o imperialismo," speech of March 26, 1946, in the Constituent Assembly, reprinted in *Problemas atuais . . . ,* pp. 263–328;

quotation from p. 327; reprinted in *Fôlha do Povo,* 108 (March 30, 1946) to 138 (May 8, 1946). A PCB attack on "imperialism" and U.S. Ambassador Berle appears in "O Partido Comunista denuncia os planos de grupos imperialistas americanos," *Fôlha do Povo,* 107 (March 29, 1946), 1, 2, 4.

18. See Prestes, "Paz indivísivel," speech before the Constituent Assembly based on document by the Comissão Executiva do Partido Comunista do Brasil," Rio de Janeiro, May 6, 1946, reprinted in *Problemas atuais . . . ,* pp. 329–60.

19. See Prestes, "Informe político apresentado à III Conferência Nacional do PCB em Julho de 1946," *ibid.,* pp. 417–56. See the Resolutions of the Conference in *Fôlha do Povo,* 202 (July 24, 1946), 1–4; 203 (July 25, 1946), 2.

20. See the PCB's "Manifesto do Partido Comunista dos trabalhadores . . . ," *Fôlha do Povo,* 220 (August 14, 1946), 1, 3, 4.

21. The theses approved at the Congresso are reprinted as "Firmada a opinião do proletariado sôbre os vinte pontos do temário do Congresso Sindical . . . ," in *Divulgação Marxista,* I (October 1, 1946), 116–25; a closing statement contains details of the proceedings and names of the CTB provisional executive committee; see pp. 126–28. See also "Temário do Congresso Sindical dos Trabalhadores do Brasil," *Fôlha do Povo,* 235 (August 31, 1946), 4. According to Alexander, *Communism . . . ,* p. 123 (based on his interview with Coelho Filho), the CTB maintained a legal existence of about six months and claimed to control 200 unions. See also Jover Telles, *O movimento sindical no Brasil,* pp. 39–40, and a speech by Jover Telles, pp. 255–72, "A verdade sôbre a Congresso Sindical realizado no Rio de Janeiro em setembro de 1946," June 13, 1947. To counter the CTB, the Ministry of Labor attempted to establish the Confederação Nacional dos Trabalhadores (CNT).

22. Poppino, *International Communism in Latin America,* p. 77; *New York Times* (January 22, 1947), 2.

23. The party policy and tactics prior to the January 1947 elections are described by Prestes in "Em marcha para um grande Partido Comunista de massa, informe político da Comissão Executivo ao Pleno do Comitê Nacional de PCB em 6 de dezembro de 1946," reprinted in *Problemas atuais . . . ,* pp. 475–515 (esp. pp. 509–10). An example of the PCB's opportunism was its bargain with Adhemar de Barros, who won the São Paulo gubernatorial race thanks to Communist support and working-class votes. At the same time the PCB replaced the UDN as the third-ranking party in total vote.

24. PCB protests against the suppression were "Preso, ontem, a presidente do MUT (José Viana)," *Fôlha do Povo,* 135 (May 4, 1946), 4; 137 (May 7, 1946), 14. See also 138 (May 8, 1946), 1, 4; 139 (May 10, 1946), 1; 146 (May 18, 1946), 1. See also *New York Times* (May 21, 1946), 4.

25. *Fôlha do Povo,* 427 (April 16, 1947), 1. *New York Times* (April 16, 1947), 19.

26. The opinions of the three judges who favored the ban (the vote was 3 to 2) are in *O Partido Comunista, sua condenação pela justiça brasileira,* Rio de Janeiro: Imprensa Nacional, 1947. The bases for suppressing the PCB were, first, the discovery that the party statutes differed slightly from those originally submitted to the Supreme Electoral Court; and second, that the party name ("do Brasil" rather than "Brasileiro") signified that it was foreign. The purge applied only to those on the PCB ticket, allowing Pomar and Arruda Câmara to remain in the Chamber of Deputies. At this time Prestes went underground for ten years. After being banned, there were unsuccessful efforts to have the party legally re-established, first in June 1947 as the Partido Constitucionalista Brasileira, and later in June 1949

as the Partido Popular Progressista. See Phyllis Peterson, "Brazilian Political Parties, Formation, Organization, and Leadership, 1945–1959," Ann Arbor, Unpublished Ph.D. dissertation, University of Michigan, 1962, p. 106.

27. Skidmore, *Politics in Brazil* . . . , p. 67; *Fôlha do Povo*, 450 (May 14, 1947), 1, 4; Jover Telles, *O movimento sindical* . . . , p. 40, states that more than 400 unions were intervened. Prestes' response to government suppression is in "Os comunistas lutam pela ordem e pela consolidação da democracia, resposta à circular do Ministro da Justiça aos Interventores, enviada em novembro de 1946," reprinted in *Problemas atuais* . . . , pp. 459–72.

28. Prestes, *op. cit.*, p. 499; *Fôlha do Povo*, 222 (August 16, 1946), 1, 4; 223 (August 17, 1946), 1, 3; 310 (November 28, 1946), 1.

29. The aggressive Communist international line was a response to the Cold War maneuvers of the United States and Great Britain. A first indication of this line was the unseating in March 1946 of Earl Browder as secretary general of the Communist Party of the United States after Browder had been attacked by French Communist leader Jacques Duclos for "opportunistic politics." The Communist position was institutionalized into the Communist Information Bureau (Cominform), established in September 1947 to link the Communist parties of the Soviet Union and East Europe to the two powerful Western European parties in France and Italy.

30. These theses are summarized in Ribeiro de Lira (?), "Três etapes do comunismo brasileiro," pp. 126–27. A portion (40 points) of the theses is in Partido Comunista do Brasil, Comitê Nacional. "O Comitê Nacional do PCB apresenta as teses para discussão no IV Congresso," *Fôlha do Povo*, 409 (March 25, 1947), 4; 410 (March 26, 1947), 4; 411 (March 27, 1947), 4.

31. Basbaum, *História sincera* . . . , Vol. III, 218–19.

32. The PCB response—an attack on the Dutra government—is in *Fôlha do Povo*, 587 (October 22, 1947), 1, 8; 501 (October 26, 1947), 6.

33. Harding, "A Political History . . . , chap. 7, p. 50, based on information in *A Classe Operária*, March 15, 1947. The policy of worker-employer cooperation also was in accordance with the general Communist tendency throughout Latin America, notably in Mexico.

34. Among the economists were Rômulo Almeida, "Experiência brasileira de planejamento, orientação e contrôle da economia," *Estudos Econômicos*, I, 2, (June 1950), 6–115; and Evaldo Corrêa Lima, who along with other economists was responsible for criticizing the neo-liberal views of the U.S.-Brazilian delegation, which issued its findings in June 1949. See "Relatório Abbink," *Estudos Econômicos*, I, 1 (March 1950), 175–91. See also Skidmore, *Politics in Brazil* . . . . for excellent economic analysis of the 1946–1949 period.

35. The PCB's call in June 1947 for a party of the masses—the União Popular Constitucionalista—was in part influenced by the legacy of past policy, but also probably attributable to the government's return to central planning. See Pedro Pomar, "Um novo partido para as massas . . . ," *Fôlha do Povo*, 485 (June 24, 1947), 1, 2. In 1948 the PCB joined with Socialists to establish Centros de Estudos e Defesa do Petróleo; see *A Luta*, 23 (May 23, 1948), 1.

36. These arguments are summarized in Ribeiro de Lira (?), "Três etapes do comunismo brasileiro," pp. 127–28.

37. Linhares, "O comunismo no Brasil—III," *Revista Brasiliense*, 28 (March-April 1960), 123. The PCB's difficulties with Trotskyism are alluded to by Jorge Amado in *Homens e coisas do Partido Comunista*, pp. 21–24.

38. In January 1946 the PCB expelled one group of dissidents, including Cristiano Cordeiro, Silo Meireles, Mota Cabral, and José Medina; see detail in *Fôlha do*

Povo, 48 (January 17, 1946), 1. In July the party expelled Eduardo Marquês dos Santos; see *Fôlha do Povo,* 198 (July 19, 1946), 4; and in December, Amaro Ferreira de Miranda, *Fôlha do Povo,* 330 (December 21, 1946), 2.

39. In 1950 Roberto Morena (under the PRT) was elected to Congress, where he was recognized as PCB party spokesman. In Recife, Paulo Cavalcanti (elected under the PSP) was a vociferous member of the Pernambuco state assembly. Running on the PTB ticket, four Communists were elected to the Rio municipal council. The election of four Communists to the city council in São Paulo was voided. See Alexander, *Communism* . . . , p. 28.

40. The change in attitude toward the Dutra government is apparent in Prestes' "Manifesto," in Antônio J. Osório *et al,* * *Prestes, estudos e depoimentos,* pp. 78–84, a statement dated November 15, 1947, in São Paulo. The PCB antagonism toward the Dutra government, however, did not necessarily affect the party's traditional opportunism. In late 1947, e.g., Prestes agreed to support São Paulo Governor Adhemar de Barros in exchange for the release of Communists in prison, press freedom, and personal assurances to Prestes. This secret pact was made after an earlier bargain in 1946 in which the PCB supported Adhemar for the governorship. Despite this pact Prestes and Vargas joined forces to oppose Adhemar's candidate for Vice Governor in the election of November 9, 1947. Adhemar's candidate won with 46.5 per cent of the vote, and the Vargas-Prestes coalition received 33.8 per cent; see Henriques, *Ascenção e queda* . . . , Vol. II, pp. 413–14; 440–46.

41. Skidmore, *Politics in Brazil* . . . , p. 75.

42. Basbaum, *História sincera* . . . , Vol. III, p. 238.

43. See Prestes, "Forjar . . . ," *Problemas,* 19 (June-July, 1949), 59–63.

44. Basbaum, *op. cit.,* Vol. III, pp. 228–29.

45. "Nossa política: Prestes aponte aos brasileiros o caminho da libertade," *Problemas,* 29 (August-September 1950), 3–17; also the interesting analysis by Maurício Grabois, "O programa da Frente Democrática de Libertação Nacional, um poderoso instrumento de luta," *Problemas,* same issue, pp. 24–39. The English version is in "Programme of Democratic Front of National Liberation," *For a Lasting Peace,* III (September 1, 1950), 4.

46. Partido Comunista do Brasil, Comitê Nacional, "As tarefas atuais dos comunistas na luta pela paz e pela independência nacional," *Problemas,* 33 (March-April 1951), 3–12.

47. See *The New York Times,* (August 22, 1950), 6; (September 15, 1950), 17; and (October 1, 1950), 56.

48. *Correia da Manhâ,* I (November 7, 1953), 12.

49. The PCB campaigns for peace coincided with Communist activities around the world. See Linhares, "O comunismo . . . —III," pp. 125–27.

50. *Imprensa Popular,* (January 23, 1953), 1, 8, and (February 7, 1953), 2.

51. The PCB peace position is clarified in a series of party documents, esp. "Nossa política: mais um passo para a guerra," *Problemas,* 39 (March-April 1952), 3–6; Prestes, "A luta pela paz, nossa tarefa central e decisiva," *Problemas,* 39 (March-April 1952), 7–48, based on a February 1952 report to PCB National Committee; "Em defesa da paz, contra o tratado de guerra e colonização," *Problemas,* 42 (September-October 1952), 3–9; "Nossa política: o povo unido pôde derrotar o acôrdo militar: resolução do Comitê Nacional do Partido Comunista do Brasil sôbre o 'Acôrdo' . . . ," *Problemas,* 43 (November-December 1952), 1–9.

52. John Paul Van Hyning, * "From Sectarianism to Reformism: The Communist Party of Brazil," 1950–1954," p. 46.

53. *Imprensa Popular,* (April 2, 1954), 1, 5, and (April 6, 1954), 1, 5. The latter reference contains text of the LEN charter.

54. *Imprensa Popular,* (March 27, 1953), 1, 5, and (April 3, 1953), 1, 3.

55. *Correia da Manhã,* I (May 6, 1954), 7, and I (May 15, 1954), 2.

56. *Imprensa Popular,* (January 22, 1953), 6.

57. *Imprensa Popular,* (June 7, 1953), 3, 6.

58. On the April strike see "Nossa política: manifesto de 1° de maio do PCB," *Problemas,* 46 (May-June 1953), 1–4; and "Apoio e solidaridade aos grevistas de São Paula," *Problemas,* 46 (May-June 1953), 5–7. Alexander, "Brazil's CP . . . ," p. 23, analyzes the failure of the PCB to exploit these strikes. In a communication to this writer dated December 1, 1969, Alexander noted that strikes during this period were counter-productive, since workers grew wary of walkouts which frequently were politically motivated.

59. See Prestes, "Por um 1° de maio de luta e de unidade," *Problemas,* 57 (May 1954), 3–21; and PCB Central Committee statement in *Problemas,* 58 (June 1954), 1–2.

60. This followed the victory of Jânio Quadros in the São Paulo mayoralty elections of 1953 in which the PCB candidate polled only twenty thousand votes. See Alexander, *Communism* . . . , pp. 128–30; also "Nossa política: manifesto eleitoral do Partido Comunista do Brasil," *Problemas,* 61 (September 1954), 1–7; and "Comunistas e trabalhistas na luta contra o enemigo común," *Problemas,* 62 (October 1954), 7–12.

61. *Imprensa Popular,* (January 1, 1954), 1–2.

62. See "Programa do Partido Comunista do Brazil," in *Problemas,* 64 (December 1954-February 1955), 21–46. The proceedings of the Fourth Congress are reported in this issue of *Problemas.* In his book, *A revolução brasileira,* pp. 75 ff., Prado Júnior singled out the 1954 program for "its theoretical promises of an imaginary anti-feudal revolution."

63. These "new" positions are identified by Linhares, "O comunismo no Brasil . . . —III, pp. 128–29.

64. Prestes, "Informe de balanço do Comitê Central do PCB ao IV Congresso . . . ," *Problemas,* 64 (December 1954-February 1955), 47–104.

65. Van Hyning, "From Sectarianism to Reformism . . . ," pp. 96–106, emphasizes these differences. Prado Júnior, *op. cit.,* pp. 75–79, attacks the reformist nature of the 1954 program.

66. The PCB attack on Crispim, who was accused of right-wing, bourgeois, and sectarian tendencies, is in Diógenes Arruda, "Reforçar, a vigilância revolucionária, tarefa vital do partido," *Problemas,* 39 (March-April 1952), 49–72; on Lacerda see Prestes, "A situação de Fernando Lacerda . . . ," *Problemas,* 61 (September 1954), 8–20, and "Resolução de Comitê Central do PCB," *Problemas,* 61 (September 1954), 21. Alexander, *Communism* . . . , p. 132, doubts that Crispim's split represented a break with Stalinism. In fact, it appears that the expulsion occurred without discussion of the Crispim faction's disagreements over the August 1950 manifesto. See *New York Times* (March 26, 1952), 13, "Brazilian Titoists Form New Party," by Sam Pope Brewer.

67. Basbaum, *História sincera* . . . , Vol. III, pp. 272–73; also Linhares, "O comunismo no Brasil . . . —III," pp. 135–37, quotes criticism of A. Dias de Oliveira and cites *Voz Operária,* May 18, 1957. Peralva, * *O retrato,* pp. 44–47, describes PCB's subservience to the Soviet line, attributing a major role to "a functionary of the Foreign Section of the Central Committee of the CPSU—Andrei Mikhailovich Sivolobov."

68. Van Hyning, *op. cit.*, p. 106. In 1958, after emerging from clandestinity, Prestes acknowledged that the PCB's principal error had been "its incomprehension of world problems and especially of the Brazilian reality." He attributed this to the party's classification of Brazil as a "colony" at a time when the nation had "gained its sovereignty" under Vargas, who came to power in the fifties despite "imperialist" pressure. See Lourival Coutinho, "Conversa com o Sr. Prestes," *Panfleto*, 1 (June 1958), 48–58.

69. The PCB position on the elections was set forth by Prestes in "As eleições presidenciais de 1955 e as tarefas de nosso partido . . . ," *Problemas*, 66 (April 1955), 14–41; "Nossa política . . . ," *Problemas*, 67 (May-June 1955), 1–4; and "Manifesto eleitoral . . . ," *Problemas*, 69 (August 1955), 7–10. Also see Election Manifesto of the Brazilian Communist Party, *"For a Lasting Peace, for a People's Democracy,"* 355 (August 26, 1955), 4.

70. Pedro Pomar met with Kubitschek, who agreed only to defend Petrobrás in the national interest, according to John W. F. Dulles' interview with Mário Schenberg in São Paulo on November 14, 1966; see Dulles' * *Unrest in Brazil, Political-Military Crises, 1955-1964*, p. 19.

71. See the PCB position in *Problemas*, 71 (November-December 1955), pp. 3–7.

72. Peralva, *O retrato*, pp. 204–5, bases his conclusion on an interview with a member of PCB's Central Committee; apparently Communist leaders went into hiding.

73. Alexander, *Communism . . .* , pp. 130, 134.

74. For analysis of the target plan and economic growth rates during the Kubitschek regime, see Helio Jaguaribe, *The Brazilian Structural Crisis*, Riverside: Seminar Series Report No. 1, Latin American Research Program, December 1966, p. 8–10.

75. Among social scientists and technocrats who helped to shape the ISEB thinking were Hélio Jaguaribe, Alberto Guerreiro Ramos, Evaldo Corrêa Lima, and Cândido Mendes de Almeida. Some of the group's early ideas are in *Introdução aos problemas do Brasil*, Rio de Janeiro: ISEB, 1956. An excellent review of the ISEB experience is Frank Bonilla, "A National Ideology for Development: Brazil," Chapter 7, pp. 232–64 in K. H. Silvert, *Expectant Peoples: Nationalism and Development*, New York: Random House, 1963. See also Ronald H. Chilcote, "Development and Nationalism in Brazil and Portuguese Africa," in *Comparative Political Studies*, II (January 1969), 501–25.

76. Partido Comunista do Brasil, Comitê Central, "Manifesto do PCB, aprovado no Pleno Ampliado de janeiro de 1956," *Fôlha do Povo*, 62 (January 4, 1956), 1; this statement reiterated in "Plataforma do PCB," *Fôlha do Povo*, 103 (March 25, 1956), 1.

77. See Peralva, *O retrato*, p. 255, who refers to an article published in *Voz Operária* in late March 1956. The first news on the Twentieth Congress in *Fôlha do Povo* was Miguel Alves, "As grandes ensinamentos do XX Congresso," 111 (April 5, 1956), 3.

78. See articles in *Fôlha do Povo:* 114 (April 8, 1956), 3; 119 (April 14, 1956), 3; and 133 (May 3, 1956), 2, 3, by Prestes.

79. Partido Comunista do Brasil, Comitê Central, "Projeto de Resolução do Comitê Central . . . ," *Fôlha do Povo*, 179 (October 26, 1956), 3, 4.

80. Peralva, *op. cit.*, pp. 253–54.

81. *Ibid.*, pp. 254–55; "A crise no seio do PCB," *Novos Tempos*, 1 (September 1957), 56–59.

82. Peralva, *op. cit.*, pp. 254–55.

83. *Ibid.*, p. 338; the name Pántano is used by Peralva.

84. This shuffle followed a similar development in the Soviet Union in June 1957, when Molotov, Malenkov, and others were demoted from leadership of the Communist party. The Soviet power shift apparently convinced the pragmatic Prestes to support revisionism. See "Reply to Khrushchev. Resolution of the Central Committee of the Communist Party of Brazil," *Peking Review*, VI (September 13, 1963), 39.

85. See Maia's "O direito inalienável do povo húngaro," *Fôlha do Povo*, 185 (November 3, 1956), 3; 186 (November 4, 1956), 3.

86. *Imprensa Popular*, November 4, 1956, cited by Peralva, *O retrato*, p. 308.

87. See Pereira's statement in *Fôlha do Povo*, 189 (November 8, 1956), 3; and Cavalcanti in 191 (November 10, 1956), 3.

88. See Prestes, "Importante carta de Luiz Carlos Prestes ao C.C. do PCB sôbre o debate político," *Fôlha do Povo*, 201 (November 23, 1956), 1, 3.

89. Partido Comunista do Brasil, Comitê Central, "Resolução," *Fôlha do Povo*, 327 (April 27, 1956), 3. Between the November pronouncement and the April resolution many of the debates were published in *Fôlha do Povo*: see Ferraz in 192 (November 11, 1956), 3; Peralva in 193 (November 13, 1956), 3; Carvalho and Samico in 194 (November 14, 1956), 2–3; Lacerda in 199 (November 21, 1956), 3, and 200 (November 27, 1956), 3; Flavier in 202 (November 24, 1956), 3, 2; Kondor in 204 (November 27, 1956), 3; Carvalho in 206 (November 29, 1956), 3; 217 (December 13, 1956), 3; 219 (December 15, 1956), 3; Tavares in 220 (December 16, 1956), 3; Maia in 224 (December 21, 1956), 3; José Gorender in 227 (December 25, 1956), 3; Souto Maior in 231 (January 1, 1957), 3; Barata in 236 (January 8, 1957), 3, and 237 (January 9, 1957), 3, 2; Marighella in 238 (January 10, 1957), 3 and 239 (January 11, 1957), 3; Amazonas in 243 to 246 (January 16 to January 19, 1957), 3; Amazonas in 255 (January 30, 1957), 3, and 256 (January 31, 1956), 3; Pereira in 280 (February 28, 1957), 3, 2, and 326 (April 26, 1957), 3, 2.

90. Agildo Barata, "Pela renovação e o fortalecimento do Partido," *Novos Tempos*, 1 (September, 1957), 42–47.

91. A useful discussion of the internal PCB struggle is in Peralva, *O retrato*, pp. 307–8; its Appendix I, pp. 377–90, contains excerpts from the debates.

92. *Ibid.*, pp. 329–33.

93. Barata's letter to the Central Committee is included in his *Vida de um revolucionário*, p. 352; he outlines his criticisms of the party on pp. 354–69. The PCB's denunciation is in "Declaração do Presidium do Comitê Central do PCB em face das declaraçãoes feitas por Agildo Barata a um semanário burguês contra o partido e a movimento operário," *Fôlha do Povo*, 354 (May 30, 1957), 3. Also see "A que se reduz o "caso" defecção de Agildo Barata," *Fôlha do Povo*, 360 (June 6, 1957), 3, and Jacob Gorender, "A extrema direita do nacionalismo," *Fôlha do Povo*, 372 (June 20, 1957), 3; 376 (June 27, 1957), 3; 383 (July 6, 1957), 3; Maurício Grabois, "Uma plataforma tipicamente burguêsa," *Fôlha do Povo*, 385 (July 9, 1968), 3, 2.

94. Peralva's letter of resignation (emphasizing four points) to the Central Cobmittee is included in his *O retrato*, pp. 390–91. Mendonça's resignation was reported in the *New York Times* (June 23, 1957), 10.

95. Peralva, *O retrato*, p. 351.

96. Evaldo Martins and Pedro Salustio, "Que é a Corrente Renovadora?," *Novos Tempos*, 1 (September 1957), 14–18, 22.

97. Eros Martins Teixeira, "Nossa revolução," *Novos Tempos*, 1 (September 1957), 23–29, and 2 (October-November 1957), 20–27. A defense of this leftist

opposition is Luiz Alberto, "O carater socialista da revolução no Brasil, *Novos Tempos,* 2 (October-November 1957), 28–30.

98. Carleto Ferrer Favalli *et al,* "Manifesto de Convocação da Convenção de Fundação do Movimento Socialisto Renovador," *Novos Tempos,* 2 (October-November 1957), 66–67.

99. Criticism of the MSR Congress program was expressed by Raimundo Schaun and Hélio Oliveira, "Caminhos da Renovação Socialista no Brasil," *Novos Tempos,* 3 (December 1957), 36–39. They urged adoption of a "Carta de princípios" favoring the path toward national and social liberation" rather than a struggle by a "Dominant Party."

100. This emphasis on nationalism is evident in Peralva's statements, O caráter popular no nacionalismo brasileiro," *Novos Tempos,* 3 (December 1957), 42–47, the article by ISEB director, Roland Corbisier, "A propósito de 'Sortilégio,'" in *Novos Tempos,* 5 (March 1958), 6–8, and reviews of books published by ISEB; see *Novos Tempos,* 3 (December 1957), 49–50.

101. Partido Comunista do Brasil, Comitê Central, "O C.C. do PCB traça a nova política dos comunistas," *Fôlha do Povo,* 99 (March 20, 1958), 2, 3; excerpts reprinted in Inquérito Policial Militar No. 709, *O comunismo no Brasil,* Vol. I, pp. 192–97.

102. The PCB position on the election is clarified in a collection of documents by Prestes, * *Por que os comunistas apoíam Lott e Jango.*

103. The theses were published four months before the Fifth Congress in the party weekly, *Novos Rumos,* Special Supplement (April 15–21, 1960). Reprinted in Inquérito Policial Militar No. 709, *O comunismo no Brasil,* Vol. II, pp. 104–11.

104. Prado Júnior, in *A revolução brasileira,* p. 79, identifies the 1954 program as the first party statement after World War II in which a theory of the Brazilian revolution·was discussed and approved The resolution was published as "Revolução política," *Novos Rumos,* 81 (September 16–22), Supplement, pp. 3–5.

105. Prado Júnior, *op. cit.,* pp. 80–81.

106. Editorial entitled "Em defesa do undade do movimento Comunista," *Novos Rumos,* 152 (January 5–11, 1962), 1–2; in *A Hora,* 28 (January 20–27, 1962) 3, 5; and reprinted in Inquérito Policial No. 709, *O comunismo no Brasil,* Vol. III, pp. 401–10. Although this editorial explicitly states that Pomar, Arroio, and Danielli "were retained in the national leadership," the list of party leadership published by Dulles excludes their names. See his * "Brazilian Communism and the Military Movement of 1964," note 6.

107. Jacob Gorender's position is in "O V Congresso dos comunistas brasileiros," *Estudos Sociais,* III (October 1960), 3–11.

108. See program and statutes in *Novos Rumos,* Supplement 127 (August 11–17, 1961), 1–7.

109. Published later as "Em defesa do partido," *A Classe Operária,* 419 (April 1962), 6–7, and reprinted in Inquérito Policial Militar No. 709, *O comunismo no Brasil,* Vol. III, pp. 412–21. The document claims that Prestes' attempt to obtain legal status for the PCB violated "party principles and the decisions of the Fifth Congress."

110. João Amazonas, Maurício Grabois, Pedro Pomar, Calil Chade, Angelo Arroio, and Lincoln Oest, "Manifesto-Programa . . . ," *A Classe Operário,* 418 (March 1962), 5, 6. Reprinted as Supplement to *A Classe Operária,* 445 (June 15–30, 1963), 2–4; and in Inquérito Policial Militar No. 709, *O comunismo no Brasil,* Vol. III, pp. 422–32. The document itself is dated February 18, 1962.

111. Partido Comunista do Brasil. Conferência Nacional Extraordinária. "Em

defesa do Partido," São Paulo, February 1962; reprinted in Inquérito Policial Militar No. 709, *O comunismo no Brasil*, Vol. III, pp. 435–39.

112. An excellent brief synthesis of differences among various Communist parties and groups is Peralva, "Mais um PC," *Observador Econômico e Financeiro*, XXVI (December 1961), 14–15. Peralva notes that after it captured control of the PCB in August 1957, the Pántano (Grupo Baiano) permitted the old-guard conservatives to wield power over regional committees in the states of Rio de Janeiro, Rio Grande do Sul, and São Paulo, where they won support for their dissident position and formation of a new party.

113. For statistics and details on growth, consumption, and rural and urban wages, see Brazil, Presidência da República, *Plano Trienal de desenvolvimento econômico e social, 1963–1965: síntese*, December 1962, pp. 23–30.

114. An excellent analysis of these developments and those after 1960 until 1964 is Timothy F. Harding, "Revolution Tomorrow: The Failure of the Left in Brazil," *Studies on the Left*, IV (Fall 1964), 30–54. Also useful is Skidmore, *Politics in Brazil . . .*, pp. 163–302. Basbaum, *História sincera . . .*, Vol. III, pp. 280–82, suggests that Lott's defeat was attributable to Kubitschek's failure to endorse the candidate and his interest in a UDN victory. Additionally there was the high cost of living, diminishing real wages, PSD's "secret" support for the UDN, propaganda based on abstract nationalist slogans that alienated the masses, and the absence of a party of mass interests.

115. Dulles, *Unrest in Brazil*, pp. 109–11.

116. Prado Júnior, "As eleições de 3 de Outubro," *Revista Brasiliense*, 32 (November-December 1960), 1–18.

117. There was widespread sympathy throughout Brazil for the Cuban Revolution in its early stages. Castro's declared adherence to Marxism-Leninism on December 2, 1961, however, alienated a large segment of this support and also aggravated dissension in the PCB; whereas for Prestes, Castro's loss of prestige tended to justify his own moderate policies in Brazil, the PC do B emphasized Castro's success and revolutionary course as the example for Brazil.

118. Elaborated in Jaguaribe, *The Brazilian Structural Crisis*.

119. These and other developments, including formation of a Movimento Unitário do Povo Brasileiro in October and the failure of a general strike demanding a Christmas holiday or "thirteenth month" bonus, are assessed by Basbaum, *História sincera . . .*, Vol. III, pp. 283–87.

120. *Novos Rumos*, 133 (September 1961), 1. While the PCB emphasized causes popular with the left, there was speculation that a radical alternative might be a possibility. According to Prestes' notes found in his home during April 1964, Soviet leaders Nikita Khrushchev and Mikhail Suslov counselled Prestes in Moscow during November 1961 "to increase the demands of the great peasant masses . . . leading them thus to insurrection." As it was explained, "You speak of agrarian reform. This is right when the situation is not revolutionary. In a revolutionary situation we must know how to fight for the agrarian revolution." Quoted from São Paulo State, Secretaria da Segurança Pública, Departamento de Ordem Político Social, * *Relatório: inquérito instaurado contra Luiz Carlos Prestes e outros por ocasião da revolução de março do 1964*, p. 23, and reprinted in Dulles *Unrest in Brazil*, p. 168. Nearly a year later, however, Prestes delivered over 53,000 signatures on petitions demanding legalization of the PCB.

121. Quotes from "Communists Review the Situation in Brazil," *World Marxist Review*, V (November 1961), 40–43, and similar to the PCB document in *Novos Rumos*, 143 (November 3–9, 1961), 3, and reprinted in Inquérito Policial Militar

No. 709, *O comunismo no Brasil,* Vol. III, pp. 246–59. This PCB position was supported by the detailed analysis of Jacob Gorender, "Brazil in the Grip of Contradictions," *World Marxist Review,* VI (February 1963), 27–33, and reprinted in Irving Louis Horowitz, * *Revolution in Brazil,* pp. 328–41.

122. Harding, "Revolution Tomorrow . . . ," p. 40.

123. Background in labor developments during 1962 and 1963 is in Neuma Aguiar Walker, "The Organization and Ideology of Brazilian Labor," in Horowitz, *op. cit.,* pp. 242–56. A Communist perspective and description of state and national labor conferences, strikes, and other labor matters is in Jover Telles, *O movimento sindical . . . ,* pp. 87–186. These pages contain important documentation on the labor movement.

124. In the Pernambuco and Brazilian press Julião was criticized for vagueness on agrarian reforms and for excessive "mysticism." This criticism is reflected in the Recife daily, *Ultima Hora* in an exchange of views with Sêrgio Magalhães, 195 (January 4, 1963), 3; see also 250 (March 2, 1963), 1.

125. Lêda Barreto, *Julião, nordeste revolução,* Rio de Janeiro: Editôra Civilização Brasileira, 1963, pp. 83–84.

126. Political Resolution of August 1962, reprinted in Inquérito Policial Militar No. 709, *O comunismo no Brasil,* Vol. IV, pp. 276–88. Also see Partido Comunista Brasileiros, "Os comunistas brasileiros definem sua posição ante a grave situação do pais," *Novos Rumos,* 185 (August 31–September 6, 1932), 4.

127. Dulles, *Unrest in Brazil,* p. 184.

128. *Novos Rumos,* 196 (November 16–22, 1962), 1, cited and reprinted in a three-point Political Resolution in Inquérito Policial Militar No. 709, *O comunismo no Brasil,* Vol. IV, pp. 290-93.

129. *Novos Rumos,* 200 (December 13–20, 1962), 4, reprinted in Inquérito Policial Militar No. 709, *O comuniso no Brasil,* Vol. IV, pp. 293–309.

130. *Novos Rumos,* 207 (February 1963), 3.

131. Harding, "Revolution Tomorrow . . . ," p. 41.

132. Documents and proceedings at the congress are in Congresso Continental de Solidaridade a Cuba, *Anais,* Niterói, March 28–30, 1963. A full list of Brazilian delegates, including labor leaders, student leaders, artists, intellectuals, university professors, diplomats, clergy, deputies and others is on p. 17–28; their speeches are on pp. 83–95, 98–101, 105–106, 108–110. Five resolutions are on pp. 110–15.

133. The PCB's Political Resolution is in *Novos Rumos,* 229 (July 12–18, 1963, 3, and cited and reprinted in Inquérito Policial Militar No. 709, *O comunismo no Brasil,* Vol. IV, pp. 313–20.

134. Dulles, *Unrest in Brazil,* pp. 230–33. Dulles also states that Chinese Communists assisted in organizing the uprising, citing Chinese documentation published in *O Estado de São Paulo,* May 10, 1964. Other sources, however, tend to stress past evidence of revolutionary potential among the enlisted men—e.g., their support for Goulart's assumption of the Presidency in 1961. See Nelson Werneck Sodré, * *História militar do Brasil,* pp. 372–89; and Carneiro, *História das revoluções brasileiras,* Vol. II, pp. 533–50, for analysis of the revolt. Alfred Stepan, "Patterns of Civil-Military Relations: the Brazilian Political System," Santa Monica: Rand Corporation, 1970, pp. 247–60, emphasizes the technical training, professionalization, and rise in educational status of these military men, who were dissatisfied at not having also the legal status of officers. This study was published as *The Military in Politics: Changing Patterns in Brazil,* Princeton: Princeton University Press, 1971.

135. *Novos Rumos,* 242 (October 5, 1963), 1. Goulart's request on October 4 for a state of siege was withdrawn three days later, and this move was favorably

appraised by the PCB in *Novos Rumos*, 242 (October 11–17, 1963), 1, cited and reprinted in Inquérito Policial Militar No. 709, *O comunismo no Brasil*, Vol. IV, pp. 325–29.

136. The March 13 speeches of Goulart, Brizola, and Miguel Arraes are in Inquérito Policial Militar No. 709, *O comunismo no Brasil*, Vol. IV, pp. 326–57. An interesting letter from Humberto de Alencar to his uncle, Arraes, on pp. 330–35 reports dialogue between Goulart and the PCB, and Jango's desire to lead a Frente Unica; also in Carneiro, *História das revoluções brasileiras*, Vol. II, pp. 616–19.

137. The PCB supported amnesty for the sergeants; see *Novos Rumos*, 251 (December 13–19, 1963), 2, 8. A statement of the party's position on conditions in late 1963 is in Giocondo Dias, "Some Problems of the Class Struggle in Brazil," *World Marxist Review*, VII (January 1964), 21–25.

138. Prestes, "A situação política e o papel da imprensa do povo," *Novos Rumos*, 264 (March 20–26, 1964), 3.

139. Basbaum, *História sincera* . . . , Vol. IV, p. 89, quotes Prestes to illustrate his "self-deception."

140. Details of the naval mutiny are in Mário Victor, *Cincos anos que abalaram o Brasil, de Jânio Quadros ao Marechal Castelo Branco*, Rio de Janeiro: Editôra Civilização Brasileira, 1965, chap. 29, "A sublevação na marinha," pp. 493–514.

141. Partido Comunista Brasileiro, "Os comunistas e a situação política: intensificar as ações de massas para garantir a vitória do povo," *Novos Rumos*, Extra Edition (March 27, 1964), 3.

142. The theses for the 1964 Sixth Congress were published in "Teses para discussão," *Novos Romos*, Special Supplement to 265 (March 27–April 2, 1964), 1–15, and reprinted in Inquérito Policial Militar No. 709, *O comunismo no Brasil*, Vol. II, pp. 111–25.

143. Prado Júnior, e.g., who attacked the theses as "being inspired faithfully in the same conceptions which 36 years earlier had served . . . what had been arbitrarily generalized for Latin America and Brazil." Quoted in his *A revolução brasileira*, p. 100. Later, even Prestes acknowledged that the theses "exaggerated the strength of the mass movement, its militancy and organization . . . at the very time when many of the urban middle class were going over to the side of the reaction we were claiming that they were joining the anti-imperialist struggle." Quoted in Prestes, "Political Line and Tactics of Brazilian Communists in the New Conditions," *World Marxist Review*, XI (June 1968), 34.

144. Quoted in Harding, "Revolution Tomorrow . . . ," p. 43, where he describes Goulart as "a wealthy landowner playing the role of a leftist-nationalist, trading favors with the Communists, and negotiating foreign loans which were used to buy political support."

145. Twenty-six documents on the coup are in Carneiro, *História das revoluções brasileiras*, Vol. II, pp. 600–49, including a declaration by José Anselmo, a "Programa de Ação do Partido Comunista," and manifestos by UNE, the Comando Terrorista Nacional and the Grupos de Onze.

146. This military school, founded in 1949, received assistance from the U.S. Army under the U.S.-Brazilian military agreements of the fifties. Intellectuals associated with the ISEB attempted also to influence with their ideology of "developmental nationalism" the officers in the school through lectures and even in writings in military journals. See, e.g., Jaguaribe, "Situação atual do Brasil," *Revista do Clube Militar*, CXXXV (January-February 1955), 5–12, and "Sucinta análise do nacionalismo brasileiro," in CXLVII (1957), 11–14.

147. The Ato Institucional is reprinted in Carneiro, *op. cit.,* pp. 647–49.

148. Useful analyses in English of the coup and its immediate aftermath are Andrew Gunder Frank, "The Goulart Ouster: Brazil in Perspective . . . ," *The Nation,* 190 (April 27, 1964), 408–11; Eduardo Galeano, "Brazil: The Defeat and After," *Studies on the Left,* IV (Fall 1964), 55–76; Horowitz, "Revolution in Brazil: The Counter-revolutionary Phase," *New Politics,* III (Spring 1964), 71–80; and Chilcote, "Brazil: Suppressing the Future," *The Nation,* 190 (November 23, 1964), 368–70. A more detailed analysis is James W. Rowe, "Revolution and Counterrevolution in Brazil," *American Universities Field Staff Reports Service,* XI, 4 (January 4, 1964), 649–65, and XI, 5 (June 1964), 667–81. The most useful synthesis of these military events is in Stepan's *The Military in Politics,* and Ronald M. Schneider, *The Political System of Brazil: Emergence of a "Modernizing" Authoritarian Regime, 1964–1970,* New York: Columbia University Press, 1971.

149. Still another Institutional Act was declared by President Costa e Silva in mid-December 1968 after MDB and ARENA Congressmen joined in opposing a government move to purge MDB deputy Mário Moreira Alves, accused of insulting the Armed Forces. The Act closed Congress.

150. For a dispassionate analysis see Skidmore, *Politics in Brazil,* Appendix, "The United States Role in João Goulart's Fall," pp. 322–30.

151. See Prestes, "Defeat of Putschists will Pave Way for the Brazilian Revolution . . . ," *Information Bulletin* (Supplement to *World Marxist Review*), 15 (August 4, 1964), 67–69, and his "Policy of the Military Dictatorship in Brazil," in *World Marxist Review,* VIII (April 1965), 34–35, and "Interview" in *Information Bulletin* (Supplement to *World Marxist Review*) 55 (October 6, 1965), 39–42.

152. This reassessment and summary of the policy position adopted by the PCB Executive Commission is in Lucas Romão, "Democratic and National Struggle in Brazil and its Perspectives," *World Marxist Review,* VIII (February 1965), 41–45; the above quote is by Romão.

153. Quotes from The Communist Party of Brazil, "Self-Criticism," pp. 250–56 in Luis E. Aguilar, ed., *Marxism in Latin America,* trans. from *Principios,* 108 (August 1965), 142–62.

154. Reported in *New York Times,* October 16, 1964. Another source stated that a triumverate was established of elements from the Bahia group (probably among Giocondo Dias, Mário Alves de Souza Vieira, Carlos Marighella, and Jacob Gorender). This triumverate provided the leadership, removing Prestes from leadership function, but allowing him to remain as titular head of the party in order to avoid embarrassment as well as dissension provoked from the left, especially to PC do B which subsequently unleashed a campaign against Prestes. See "Problems of Subversion in Brazil Reviewed," *Joint Publications Research Service,* 47, 950, Translation on Latin America No. 170 (1969), 38; trans. from *Este y Oeste* (March 1969), 1–27.

155. Basbaum, *História sincera . . . ,* Vol. IV, pp. 88–89.

156. One of the 20 notebooks was inadvertently lost, yet from the 3,426 handwritten pages the police produced a 2,087-page study in 10 volumes. A summary of the findings is in São Paulo State, Secretaria de Segurança Pública, Departamento de Ordem Política e Social, *Relatório: Inquérito instaurado contra Luiz Carlos Prestes. . . .* Most of the defendants received prison sentences, although only one, Luís Tenório de Lima, a São Paulo labor leader already serving a term for another conviction, was present at the court sentencing in July 1966 (he was eventually released for good behavior). In general the military seemed not to desire to keep

Communists in jail—with the notable exception of Gregório Bezerra, and he finally was released along with 14 other political prisoners in September 1969 in exchange for kidnapped U.S. Ambassador C. Burke Elbrick.

157. Inquérito Policial Militar No. 709, * O Comunismo no Brasil, op. cit. The Castelo Branco government prevented Carvalho from injecting his findings into the October 1965 elections, and he was later transferred to Curitiba, Paraná, where in late 1967 he issued a report on the Communist activities in Paraná and Santa Catarina. See IPM sôbre atividades comunistas, Paraná e Santa Catarina, Curitiba: Fifth RM and Fifth DI, 1967. This information and the above report are cited by Dulles, "Communism and the Military Movement of 1964," pp. 23–24.

158. Details of the May meeting are in Dulles, op. cit., pp. 26–27, where he records names of the new Executive Commission: Prestes, Carlos Marighella, Giocondo Alves Dias, Dinarco Reis, Orlando Bonfim Júnior, Geraldo Rodrigues dos Santos, and Jaime Amorim de Miranda.

159. Partido Comunista Brasileiro, Comitê Central, * "Resolução política," São Paulo, May 1964; quotation on p. 4 and also p. 44 in Brazilian Communist Party, Central Committee, "Resolutions of the CC, Brazilian Communist Party," Information Bulletin (supplement to World Marxist Review, 52 [August 26, 1965], 39–52).

160. David Capistrano de Costa, * "Tese para discussão." An 11-page mimeographed reply, "Sôbre a tese para discussão," stressed that the thesis was a violation of Marxist-Leninist theory. Both documents are cited in Dulles, "Communism and the Military Movement of 1964," pp. 25–26. The Pernambuco thesis eventually was generally accepted by the national leadership.

161. The Guanabara dissent appeared in * O Isqueiro, 30 (April 1967) and 33 (July 1967). That of Rio Grande do Sul was published in VIII° Conferência Estadual do PCB do Rio Grande do Sul, "Resolução política do Conferência Estadual do Rio Grande do Sul." That of Paraná appeared as Convenção Municipal de Curitiba do PCB, * "Resolução." All documents are analyzed by Dulles, op. cit., p. 31.

162. The theses were published well in advance of the Sixth Congress, as "Teses," Voz Operária, Special Supplement, 19 (July 20, 1966), 1–16. The theses were debated in subsequent issues of Voz Operária, official organ of the PCB.

163. Intercontinental Press, VII (January 13, 1969), 14, an article trans. and reprinted from La Gauche, December 21, 1968. The June resolution was the focus of J. B. Tavares de Sá, "Against the Dictatorship in Brazil," World Marxist Review, IX (September 1966), 69–70.

164. See Brazilian Communist Party, "Political Resolution on the Sixth Congress of the Brazilian Communist Party," Information Bulletin (Supplement to World Marxist Review) 115 (March 1968), 5–30.

165. Carlos Marighella, "Carta de Carlos Marighella al ejecutivo del Partido Comunista Brasileño solicitando su renumcia," Pensamiento Crítico, 7 (August 1967), 209–18; trans. as "Letter of Resignation from Carlos Marighella to the Executive Commission of the Brazilian Communist Party," Joint Publications Research Service, 43450, Translations on Latin America, No. 3 (1967), 12–22. The sequence of events leading to Marighella's ouster is documented by Dulles, "Communism and the Military Movement of 1964," pp. 31–32, citing, * Unidade e ação do Partido pela revolução brasileira—resolução do Comitê Estadual de São Paulo do Partido Comunista Brasileiro," São Paulo (September 1967), an example of the persistent attack by São Paulo dissidents on the national party leadership, this in defiance of the Central Committee's order in March 1967 to end the debate on the theses and internal differences. See also Partido Comunista Brasileiro, Con-

ferência Estadual, *Documentos e resoluções: São Paulo,* São Paulo, April 1967, 31 p. Marighella's memoirs of imprisonment after April 1964 and some of his criticisms of the PCB prior to the coup are in his * *Por que resistí à prisão.*

166. The expulsions were announced in the party's "Political Resolution on the Sixth Congress of the Brazilian Communist Party," p. 30. Dulles, *op. cit.,* p. 33, adds that two others, one of them journalist Neri Reis de Almeida, were expelled for informing police on the party.

167. Dulles, *ibid,* citing *Voz Operária,* 32 (October 1967), 3.

168. Quoted in *World Outlook (New York),* VI (January 19, 1968), 41. This source also reported an earlier PCB attack on OLAS. The party denied sending Marighella as its representative to a 1967 OLAS Conference; see *World Outlook,* V (October 20, 1967), 830.

169. In defiance of the Central Committee's order of March 1967 to end the debate over the Sixth Congress theses and to heal internal differences, three São Paulo dissidents published their statement in September as Partido Comunista Brasileiro, Comitê Estadual de São Paulo, "Unidade e ação do partido pela revolução brasileira—resolução do Comitê Estadual de São Paulo do Partido Comunista Brasileiro," (see note 165 above).

170. São Paulo State Committee *et al.,* Statement published as "State CP's Denounce CC Stand on Insurrection," in *Foreign Broadcast Information Service,* November 17, 1967, 4 p. In August 1968 the Comitê Central de Guanabara formally joined the PC do B. See "PCs do Brasil continuam se dividindo," *Jornal do Brasil,* (September 1, 1968), 35.

171. Prestes, "Political Line and Tactics of Brazilian Communists in the New Conditions," pp. 31–38.

172. See Prestes' interview with Paulo Patarra, "Este é a camarada Prestes," *Realidade* 33 (December 1968), 38–58. Prestes attended the mid-1969 International Meeting of Communists and Workers' Parties in Moscow, and as head of PCB delegation gave his full support to the Soviet position in international Communist affairs. See his comments in *World Marxist Review,* XII (August 1969), 19–21.

173. Brazilian Communist Party, Central Committee, "Promote the Struggle Against the Dictatorship—Resolution of the CC, Brazilian Communist Party, September 1968," *Information Bulletin* (supplement to *World Marxist Review*), 133–34 (December 12, 1968), 53–63.

174. Brazilian Communist Party, Central Committee, "Resolution of the CC, CP of Brazil, February 1969," *Information Bulletin* (supplement to *World Marxist Review*), 143–44 (May 22, 1969), 16–20.

175. Márcio Moureira Alves, *Torturas e torturados,* Rio de Janeiro: Idade Nova, 1966. For a later and more in-depth analysis of development in Brazil see his * *El despertar de la revolución brasileña.*

176. Since April 1969 other professors have been purged. For details see Philippe C. Schmitter, "The Persecution of Political and Social Scientists in Brazil," *P.S.,* III (Spring 1970), 123–28, and Fagundes Bandira, "Brazil: Subverting the Universities," *The New Republic,* CLXI (November 8, 1969), 17–19.

177. President Arthur da Costa e Silva had planned to restore a measure of civilian government, but he suffered a stroke in late August 1969, and this prompted a takeover by a military junta and the imposition two months later of a new President, General Emílio Garrastazú Médici.

178. The activities of these organizations, esp. the CCC, are described in depth by Pedro Medeiros in an article in *O Cruzeiro,* (November 9, 1968), 19–23, trans. as "Terrorist Organization Seeks out Communist," *Joint Publications Research*

Service, 46, 968, Translations on Latin America No. 116, VII (1968), 9–18; and an article in *Jornal do Brasil* (November 3, 1968), 23, trans. as "Communist Pursuit Command Terrorizes the Country," *Joint Publications Research Service,* 47, 017, Translations on Latin America No. 118, VII (1968), 3–9. Torture and terror of the rightwing groups and the government is documented by the American Committee for Information on Brazil, *Terror in Brazil, a Dossier,* New York, April 1970, 18 p. A series of letters from Brazilian political prisoners appeared as "Torture in Brazil," *The New York Review of Books,* XIV (February 26, 1970), 44–45.

179. The message was probably read by Marighella. See "Texto del mensaje transmitido en la voz de Marighella por la Radio Nacional de São Paulo, cuando este emisora fue tomada por un grupo revolucionaria de Acción Libertadora Nacional," *Pensamiento Crítico,* 37 (February 1970), 20–24.

180. Most of those exchanged went to Mexico and then to Cuba. Descriptions of them and interviews were reported in Havana English ed. of *Granma,* IV (October 12, 1969), 17. As a result of the kidnapping, U.S. security agents become conspicuous in Brazil. A year earlier a U.S. military officer, Charles R. Chandler, had been assassinated by revolutionaries for his "criminal" role in Vietnam and for counterinsurgency work in Brazil.

181. For details of bank robberies and bombings after the 1964 coup, see article in *Correio da Manhã* (April 6, 1969), 5, trans. as "Terrorist Crimes Frequent in 1964–1969, List Shows," *Joint Publications Research Service,* 47, 970, Translation on Latin America, No. 171, VII (1969), 21–34. Details reported by Gerry Foley, "The Kidnapping of Ambassador C. Burke Elbrick, *Intercontinental Press,* VII (September 22, 1969), 834–37. See manifesto published by the ALN and MR-8 in *COLAS,* I (October 1969), 1, 3, and in *Intercontinental Press,* VII (September 22, 1969) 838. A similar statement by Marighella, "Secuestro de un embajador," *Pensamiento Crítico,* 37 (February 1970), 80–85, was originally issued in Brasília during October 1969.

182. Partido Operária Comunista, "The Debate over the Elbrick Kidnapping," *Intercontinental Press,* VII (October 13, 1969), 911–12.

183. For an interesting interview with the VPR revolutionary, Ladislas Dowbor, who organized the kidnapping of the Japanese Consul General, see Sanche de Gramont, "How One Pleasant, Scholarly Young Man from Brazil Became a Kidnapping, Gun-Toting, Bombing Revolutionary," *The New York Times Magazine,* (November 5, 1970), Section 6, 43–46ff.

184. See "Guerrillas Win Release of 44 Political Prisoners," *Intercontinental Press,* VIII (June 29, 1970), 634.

185. Leonard Greenwood, "Brazil Toughens Stand on Kidnapers' Demands," *Los Angeles Times* (December 14, 1970), 20.

186. See Márcio Moreira Alves, "Brazil: What Terror is Like," *The Nation,* CCXII (March 15, 1971), 337–41, for an analysis of the impact of repression upon the revolutionary left.

187. For a portrait of Marighella by his successor, see Joaquim Câmara Ferreira, "Marighella: Creative Life and Action," *Tricontinental Bulletin,* 21–22 (November 1970–February 1971), 119–23.

188. João Carvalho, "Joaquím Câmara Ferreira," *Granma,* V (November 8, 1970, 10; and Joaquim Câmara Ferreira, "Last Interview Held with Joaquim Câmara Ferreira, Revolutionary Leader Murdered by the Brazilian Regime," *Granma,* V (November 8, 1970), 10–11.

189. "Vila pregressa de Lamarca," *Jornal do Brasil* (September 22, 1971) and "A cena final de um terrorista," *Veja,* 159 (September 22, 1971), 23–26. Lamarca's

diary of June 29 to August 16, 1971, was published in *O Globo* (September 20, 1971), 6. Other details are in Gerry Foley, "Carlos Lamarca Reported Killed," *Intercontinental Press*, IX (October 4, 1971), 837–38; and Lucía Sepúlveda, "El Capitán Lamarca: un héroe del pueblo brasileño," *Punto Final*, VI (September 28, 1971), 26–27.

190. Revolutionary movements tending to outflank the PCB in the late 1960's are described in more detail in chap. 6.

191. Brazilian Communist Party, Central Committee, "Unite and Organize the Working Class to Isolate and Defeat the Dictatorship," *Information Bulletin* (Supplement to *World Marxist Review*), 220 (August 25, 1972), 32–37.

192. Brazilian Communist Party, "Political Statement by Brazilian Communist Party," *op. cit.*, 193 (June 4, 1971), 29–32.

193. Brazilian Communist Party, "Sixth Plenum of CC Brazilian CP," *op. cit.*, 207–208 (December 30, 1971), 54–56.

194. Alves, Márcio Moreira, * *El despertar de la revolución brasileña*, reviewed in detail by Gerry Foley, "The Awakening of the Brazilian Revolution," *Intercontinental Press*, X (September 25, 1972), 1024–29.

195. Marvine Howe, "Assembly of Bishops Urges Defense of Human Rights in Brazil," *New York Times* (March 18, 1973).

196. Luís Carlos Prestes, "Lenin's Heritage and Fight Against Opportunism in the Brazilian Communist Party," *World Marxist Review* XIII (November 1970), 10–17.

197. Luís Carlos Prestes, "Battle of Brazil's Communists," *World Marxist Review*, XV (February 1972), 16–23.

198. These periods of international and Latin American Communist activity are discussed in Gil, "Communism in Latin America," pp. 187–202, which draws heavily on Alexander, *Communism . . .* , esp. chap. 2, pp. 18–31.

Notes to Chapter 5

Titles preceded by asterisk on first appearance have complete entries in Bibliography.

1. Roberto Michels, *Political Parties*, esp. pp. 342–56.

2. Some U.S. political scientists use the concept "stratarchy" to characterize party hierarchy in the United States. Originally employed by Harold Lasswell and Abraham Kaplan in *Power and Society*, New Haven: Yale University Press, 1950, pp. 219–20, stratarchy is characterized as "the proliferation of the ruling group and the diffusion of power prerogatives and power exercise." Quoted in Samuel J. Eldersveld, *Political Parties: A Behavioral Analysis*, Chicago: Rand McNally, 1964, p. 9; he explores the concept in chap. 5, pp. 98–119.

3. The following discussion draws heavily on party statutes of 1954 and 1961. See Partido Comunista do Brasil, "Estatutos do Partido Comunista do Brasil," *Problemas*, 64 (December 1954–February 1955), 151–70, and "Os estatutos do PCB e do PCUS," in Inquérito Policial Militar No. 709, *O comunismo no Brasil*, Vol. II, pp. 26–33; the latter attempts to demonstrate similarities between statutes of the Brazilian and the Soviet parties. The 1961 statutes differ from the 1954 in several respects: in the 1961, all references to Marx, Engels, Lenin, and Stalin are eliminated; references to "the international spirit" and "international solidarity of workers of all countries" are suppressed; and the international nomenclature of party organization is revised to substitute Comissão Executiva for Presidium, Convenção Nacional for Congresso Diretório Nacional, Comitê Nacional for Comitê Central, as well as Partido Comunista Brasileiro for Partido Comunista do Brasil. Confronted with

a military dictatorship since 1964, the party reverted to former designations such as Comitê Central and Congresso.

4. The present description of the structure and functions of the Brazilian party is similar to the model of Communist parties in Latin America sketched in Rollie Poppino, *International Communism in Latin America*, chap. 6, pp. 117–27.

5. Articles 23–27 of the 1954 statutes and articles 31 and 32 of the 1961 statutes refer to the structure and functions of party congresses.

6. Based on article 33 of the 1954 statutes and articles 34 and 35 of the 1961 statutes.

7. Articles 28, 31, and 32 of the 1954 statutes.

8. Article 29 of the 1954 statutes and article 37 of the 1961 statutes.

9. Article 29 of the 1954 statutes and article 38 of the 1961 statutes. Elaboration of functions of Executive Commission and Secretariat is in Partido Comunista Brasileiro, "Resoluções da reunião do CC de março 1961," reprinted in Inquérito Policial Militar No. 709, *O comunismo no Brasil*, Vol. II, pp. 120–25.

10. During the interim period (1934–37), Antônio Macial Bomfim, apparently a police agent, was secretary general, although the party clearly was dominated by the popular Prestes after his declaration of Communist allegiance in March 1931 and esp. after his return to Brazil from Russia in April 1935. After 1964 there were reports, apparently erroneous, that Prestes had been named party president, an honorary post devoid of real authority and created to accommodate an important Communist personality whose image may still be useful to the party but who no longer is acceptable as top executive officer. It would appear that by the late sixties the position of secretary general, still held by Prestes, had indeed become honorary, although his influence and that of top leadership adhering to his line remained predominant in the face of severe party factionalization, defections, and expulsions.

11. Partido Comunista Brasileiro, "Resoluções da reunião do CC de Março de 1961," *op. cit.,* pp. 124–25.

12. Articles 36–39 of 1954 statutes and articles 10 and 26–28 of the 1961 statutes.

13. Articles 40–44 of the 1954 statutes and articles 18–20 of the 1961 statutes.

14. Articles 45 and 46 of the 1954 statutes.

15. Pereira, *Formação do PCB*, p. 70.

16. These auxiliary organizations will be discussed in chap. 5. A brief discussion of their relationship to the party is in Prestes, *Problemas atuais da democracia*, pp. 157–63.

17. The principle of democratic centralism was incorporated in the Soviet party statutes of October 1952. A discussion of the relevance of this principle and the Soviet statutes to the Soviet party is in Frederick C. Barghoorn, "The USSR: Monolithic Controls at Home and Abroad," pp. 219–83 in *Modern Political Parties. Approaches to Comparative Politics,* Chicago: The University of Chicago Press, 1956, ed. by Sigmund Neumann.

18. The principles of democratic centralism and collective leadership are elaborated in articles 14–22 of the 1954 statutes and articles 9 and 10 of the 1961 statutes.

19. Michels, *Political Parties*, p. 341.

20. Eldersveld, *Political Parties . . . ,* p. 5.

21. For Communist behavior in England, France, Italy, and the United States, see Almond, *The Appeals of Communism* and for behavior in a less-developed area, see Pye, *Guerrilla Communism in Malaya . . . .*

22. The assumptions are reviewed by Jan Triska in "Comparative Studies of the

Non-Ruling Communist Parties," Stanford: Institute of Political Studies, n.d., pp. 18–19.

23. *Idem.*

24. Institute for the Comparative Study of Political Systems, *Brazil, Election Factbook*, No. 2, Washington, D.C., September 1965, p. 48, suggests as many as 10 seats, while Prestes claimed 17 seats, were held by PCB members, according to Dulles in *Unrest in Brazil*, p. 184.

25. A very brief analysis of the presidential elections is in the above-cited *Brazil, Election Factbook*, esp. pp. 53–55.

26. Such was the case of the Communist party in post-World War II France, according to Hugh Seton-Watson, *From Lenin to Khrushchev*, New York: Frederick Praeger, 1961, p. 294.

27. Triska, *op. cit.*

28. *Ibid.*, p. 19.

29. Basbaum holds that the PCB lacked theoretical formation with a Marxist perspective; see his *História sincera* . . . , Vol. II, pp. 316–17, in which he assesses party influence during its first phase, 1922–29.

30. Basbaum, *História sincera* . . . , Vol. III, p. 83, however, makes clear that Communist influence prior to 1935 was "weak," in consequence of party division over Prestes and the 1930 revolution.

31. Quoted from "Manifesto of the Communist Party," Vol. I, p. 46, in Karl Marx and Frederick Engels, *Selected Works in Two Volumes*, Moscow: Foreign Languages Publishing House, 1958.

32. Gabriel A. Almond in *The Appeals of Communism* identifies a model of the Communist party based on "(1) its explicitness, (2) its exclusiveness, and (3) its special approach to the problem of values and means." Quoted on p. 14 of the 1965 paperback edition.

33. V. I. Lenin, *Lenin, Selected Works,* Moscow: Foreign Language Publishing House, 1947, Vol. I. p. 340, from his "One Step Forward, Two Steps Back." For other relevant statements by Lenin on the role of the party, see pp. 183, 207–8, and 237.

34. Duverger suggests that Communist parties should perhaps be conceived as "devotee parties, more open than cadre parties, but more closed than mass parties." See his *Political Parties*, p. 70.

35. Articles 2–11 of the 1964 statutes and 1–8 of the 1961 statutes concern membership.

36. Michels, *Political Parties, passim,* and Duverger, *Political Parties,* esp. pp. 133 ff. Duverger emphasizes that leadership of political parties is "democratic in appearance and oligarchic in reality," and that "Democratic legitimacy is beginning to find itself opposed by a class legitimacy quite clearly admitted by the Communist parties. . . . "

37. See Pereira's *Formação do PCB*. Other works by Pereira are * *URSS-Itália-Brasil,* * *Interpretações,* and * *Machado de Assis: ensaios e apontamentos avulsos.* He was also editor (1958–63) of *Estudos Sociais,* a bimonthly journal.

38. See Augusto Machado (pseud. of Leôncio Basbaum), * *O caminho da revolução operária e camponeza,* esp. chap. 3, pp. 48–59, and Octávio Brandão e Luiz Carlos Prestes," Appendix III in Basbaum, *Histórica sincera da república,* Vol. II, pp. 448–50.

39. See chap. 3, notes 46 and 47.

40. Michels, *Political Parties,* p. 100.

41. Biographical sketches of Prestes are in Jacob Gorender, "Figuras do movimento operário—Prestes," *Problemas* 24 (January-February 1950), 118–28, and Jorge Amado, *O cavaleiro de esperança*, esp. chap. 27, pp. 220–31. A critical characterization is in Peralva, *O retrato*, pp. 262–77. Other accounts are *Communist International*, XIII (March-April 1936), 562–66; and John Nasht, "The Prestes Saga," *Inter-American*, IV (December 1945), 14–15, 43–45.

42. These characterizations imply a charismatic image for Prestes, charisma being "a certain quality of an individual personality by virtue of which he is set apart from ordinary men and treated as endowed with supernational, superhuman, or at least specifically exceptional powers or qualities." (Quoted from Max Weber *The Theory of Social and Economic Organization*, trans. by A. M. Henderson and Talcott Parsons, Glencoe: Free Press, 1947, p. 358. Richard R. Fagen has drawn five propositions from Weber's conceptualization of charisma by way of showing how the concept might be used in empirical inquiry; his analysis may be applicable to a study of Prestes. See Fagen's "Charismatic Authority and the Leadership of Fidel Castro," *Western Political Quarterly*, XVIII (June 1965), 275–84. Also see Carl J. Friedrich, "Political Leadership and the Problem of Charismatic Power," *Journal of Politics*, XXIII (1961), 3–24.

43. Peralva in his *O retrato*, pp. 278–89, includes penetrating and obviously biased sketches of Arruda, Amazonas, Grabois, and Pomar. Peralva was close to these leaders until his defection, and his analysis may help explain why these leaders left the party in 1962—and Marighella in 1967. On pp. 278–81, he describes Arruda as "rude, abrupt, and arrogant," "semi-literate" but intelligent, with a strange personality, and explains how Arruda dominated over the inner circle and manipulated party activities. Arruda is portrayed as a hero in his memoir of imprisonment and torture (c. 1971); he states that he left the PCB in mid-1960. See his "De pie," *Tricontinental, 32* (1972), 98–115.

44. Peralva, pp. 282–83, considers Amazonas a good orator who served as federal deputy "without distinction," but was "humble and servile" and incapable of being "overly ambitious."

45. A biography of Amazonas is in *Fôlha do Povo*, 71 (February 13, 1946), 1.

46. Peralva, pp. 283–87, is especially critical of Grabois, whom he describes as an "inarticulate orator and writer," "cynical and an opportunist," an activist who abruptly dismissed theories and had read little of Marx, Engels, Lenin, and Stalin.

47. A biography of Grabois appears in *Fôlha do Povo, 72* (February 14, 1946), 1.

48. Peralva, pp. 181–82, is sympathetic to Pomar and calls him "one of the intellectuals" in the top leadership, the one chosen to write the preface to Prestes' *Problemas da democracia*.

49. Peralva, p. 287.

50. See chap. 4 for other details of Marighella's activities, esp. notes 165 and 179.

51. Biographical sketches below are drawn from information in Prestes' notebooks confiscated by police in 1964 and used as the documentation in São Paulo State. Secretaria da Segurança Pública . . . , *Relatório: inquérito instaurado contra Luiz Carlos Prestes*. . . .

52. These categories are suggested by Robert A. Scalapino in the introductory chapter to *The Communist Revolution in Asia. Tactics,, Goals, and Achievements*, Englewood Cliffs, New Jersey: Prentice-Hall, 1965, pp. 22–25.

53. Frederick C. Barghoorn noted in the early fifties that such power groups had developed in the Soviet Communist Party. See his "The USSR: Monolithic Controls

at Home and Abroad," p. 227 in Sigmund Neumann (ed.), *Modern Political Parties, Approaches to Comparative Politics.*

54. See Gastão Pereira da Silva, *Constituintes de 46: dados biográficos*, Rio de Janeiro: Editôra Spinoza, 1947. Based on biographies of Prestes, Milton Caires de Brito, Osvaldo Pacheo da Silva, Maurício Grabois, João Amazonas de Souza Pedroso, Joaquim Batista Neto, Claudino José da Silva, Jorge Amado, José Maria Crispim, Carlos Marighella, Alcides Rodrigues Sabença, Agostinho Dias de Oliveira, Gregório Lourenço Bezerra, Abílio Fernandes, Pedro Ventura Pomar, and Diógenes de Arruda Câmara.

55. Based on biographies in São Paulo State, Secretaria de Segurança Pública . . . , *Relatório: inquérito instaurado contra Luiz Carlos Prestes . . . .* The 74 persons identified in this investigation—those most frequently mentioned in Prestes' notebooks 1961–64—are representative of the top party leadership. The fact that 54 per cent resided in São Paulo and 23 per cent in Guanabara is indicative of relative party strength in those states.

56. Michels, *Political Parties*, pp. 241–42, suggests that such ideals often become associated with "aesthetic sensibilities—those endowed with political aptitudes and with the fervent knowledge and imagination can more readily grasp the extent and depth of human suffering." This, he believe, explains why we find so many radicals among poets and writers—e.g., Jack London, George Bernard Shaw, William Morris, and many others. A Brazilian list would include Jorge Amado, Monteiro Lobato, Graciliano Ramos, Lins do Rêgo, and more.

57. Michels, *op. cit.*, p. 239, explains this worker's behavior as "the spontaneous outcome of his class egoism."

58. This leadership is identified in chap. 2. See also Pereira, *Formação do PCB*, p. 46.

59. The 1934–36 leadership consisted of the following: Antônio Maciel Bomfim, Honório de Freitas Guimarães, Lauro Reginaldo da Rocha, and Adelino Deycola dos Santos (members of the National Secretariat); José Medina Filho, Carlos da Costa Leite, and Silo Soares Furtado de Meireles; and Agildo Barata and other military leaders of the Rio uprising. The leadership of the Natal revolt included an army sergeant, a former police official, a former head of the state postal service, a journalist, and a shoemaker (see chap. 2), although it is doubtful that all these were Communists. The Recife revolt leaders included Gregório Bezerra, a known Communist and soldier of peasant background. Of the above, only Rocha would classify as an intellectual; Barata and Leite were military men, and Medina was of the working class. This information is in Porto, *A insurreição de 27 de Novembro . . .* , esp. pp. 52–69.

60. The names of the 1946 leadership were published in *Fôlha do Povo*, 326 (December 1, 1946), 1. The Executive Commission included Prestes, Arruda, Pomar, Francisco Gomes, Amazonas, Grabois, Milton Caires de Brito, Agostinho Dias de Oliveira, and Sérgio Holmos with Marighella, David Capistrano, and Mautílio Muraro as alternates. Besides these, the Central Committee included Crispim, Barata, and Giacondo Alves Dias, with Fernando Lacerda, Jover Telles, Pereira, and Brandão as alternates (see Appendix B).

61. Scalapino, *The Communist Revolution in Asia . . .* , pp. 6–9, applies this classification to Asian Communist parties.

62. Jorge Amado, *O cavaleiro de esperança . . . .*

63. See his writings in *Revista Brasiliense*, 1956–64, and *A revolução brasileira*.

64. Michels, *Political Parties*, pp. 298–99, discusses the traditional mistrust between intellectuals and the working class.

65. Ernst Halperin, "Proletarian Class Parties in Europe and Latin America. A Comparison," p. 51.

66. See chapter, Operárias e intelectuais," pp. 325–36, in Peralva's *O retrato.*

67. Quote by Halperin, "Proletarian Class Parties . . . ," p. 55, where he draws evidence from Jorge Amado's trilogy, * *Os subterrâneos da libertade.*

68. The PCB's difficulties with Trotskyist "infiltration" are described by Jorge Amado, * *Homens e coisas do Partido Comunista,* esp. pp. 21–24.

69. Barata's revolutionary experience is recollected in his *Vida de um revolucionário. . . .*

70. See Gregório Bezerra, *Eu, Gregório Bezerra, acuso!*

71. Michels, *Political Parties,* p. 153, recognized that Marxist party leaders in France often distinguished themselves in their party through service in parliament where they demonstrated their competence and capacity. There the power of the parliamentarian is derived from electoral base and not entirely from the party selecting him. Michel's observation implies the possibility of friction between party parliamentarians and party bureaucrats, although in Brazil the period in which Communists held elective public office was brief. These Communists were subject to limits according to the organization and policies of the parties and were unable to establish a power base independent of the party. Elected Communists also tended to be the party decision-makers.

72. Prestes himself at first attacked Prestimo and so too did another party leader, Fernando Lacerda, for "its belief in elites, heroes, or cavaliers of hope." See note 38.

73. Pereira, *Formação do PCB,* pp. 110–13.

74. This maneuvering for party control supports Michels' observation (p. 102) that "new arrivals begin by detaching the masses from the power of old leaders, and by preaching a new evangel which the crowd accepts with delirious enthusiasm . . . . the old leaders, filled with rancor, having first organized for defense, end by openly assuming the offensive."

75. The new Partido Comunista de Cuba was formally established after the 1959 Revolution, and although it includes some leaders of the old Communist Partido Socialista Popular, it is dominated by younger individuals around Fidel Castro and his brother, Raúl.

76. This classification drawn from Duverger, *Political Parties,* pp. 90–116.

77. Attendance at party meetings and subscription payments are two useful indices for measurement of militancy. Duverger (p. 111) cites information suggesting that only one-third to one-half of the members of the French Communist party was militant in the early fifties.

78. Electoral data from Tribunal Superior Eleitoral, *Dados estadísticos,* Vol. I, pp. 74–75. In the Federal District the party polled 105,652 votes in contrast to the PTB (84,548 votes), UDN (82,574), and PSD (54,075). The PCB came out third in voting in five state legislative elections (Rio Grande do Norte, Paraíba, Pernambuco, São Paulo, and Mato Grosso), and fourth in eight states (Pará, Maranhão, Bahia, Espírito Santo, Paraná, Santa Catarina, Rio Grande do Sul, and Minas Gerais).

79. In his study of Communist behavior in France and Italy, Cantril utilizes the concept of faith which "reflects a sense of the worthwhileness of the values that keep our reality system from falling apart and that serve as guides or preconditions to purposive action in the midst of change." Quoted from *The Politics of Despair,* p. 64. The following discussion is based on pp. 62–74.

80. Basbaum, *História sincera . . . ,* Vol. II, p. 315. Octávio Brandão in "Com-

bates da classe operária," pp. 67–71, emphasizes the role of the worker in the party and refers to 20 workers who contributed significantly to early developments.

81. U.S. Department of State, *World Strength of Communist Party Organizations*, Washington, D.C., 1964, p. 81.

Notes to Chapter 6

Titles preceded by asterisk on first appearance have complete entries in Bibliography.

1. Neumann (ed.), *Modern Political Parties: Approaches to Comparative Politics*, pp. 395–421.

2. From "The Tasks of the Proletariat in the Present Revolution," *Pravda*, 26 (April 20 [7], 1917); reprinted in V. I. Lenin, *Lenin, Selected Works*, Moscow: Foreign Language Publishing House, 1947, Vol. II, p. 17–21.

3. A list of major strikes is in Inquérito Policial Militar No. 709, *O comunismo no Brasil*, Vol. III, pp. 339–44, and a description of Communist involvement is in pp. 277 ff. Also useful is *O movimento sindical no Brasil* by Communist labor leader Jover Telles, esp. the Appendix, "O movimento operário e a política sindical dos comunistas," pp. 285–301.

4. See Chapter 3 for details of the November revolts.

5. Prestes, "A Aliança Nacional Libertadora e as lutas de novembro de 1935," *Novos Rumos*, November 22–28, 1963, cited and reprinted in Inquérito Policial Militar No. 709, *O comunismo no Brasil*, Vol. IV, pp. 228–32; a series of PCB documents on the 1935 event are included in pp. 228–43.

6. The first revolt, occurring in El Salvador during January 1932, is described briefly in Poppino, *International Communism in Latin America*, pp. 141–42.

7. Information on these guerrilla activities is provided by Dulles in *Unrest in Brazil*, p. 219 and note 3, citing report of a Fidelista agent whose baggage was found near the crash of the plane in which he had left for Brazil, bound for Lima, on November 27, 1962. The report appeared in *O Estado de São Paulo*, January 29, 1963.

8. Brizola's pronouncement is reprinted in Inquérito Policial Militar No. 709, *O comunismo no Brasil*, Vol. IV, pp. 393–95, and also in Glauco Carneiro, *História das revoluções brasileiras*, Vol. II, pp. 611–16.

9. For secret instructions to regional commands of the Grupos dos Onze, see Comando Supremo de Libertação Nacional, "Instruções secretas aos comandantes regionais para conhecimento, com as devidas cautelas e resalvas dos companheiros dos groupos dos 11," Rio de Janeiro, May 1966, reprinted in Inquérito Policial Militar No. 709, *O comunismo no Brasil*, Vol. IV, pp. 396–415.

10. Interview with Brizola, "Brizola Offers a Self-Criticism," *World Outlook*, II (November 27, 1964), 12–15.

11. Emílio Castor, "Brazilian Communist Party Objectives Discussed," *Joint Publications Research Service*, 50344, Translations on Latin America, No. 323, VIII (1970), 7–30. Trans. of article from *O Globo* (March 24, 1970), 16–17.

12. Capture of the Serra do Caparaó group was sensationally reported in the press. An especially interesting report was Fialho Pacheco, "O diário do chefe guerrilheiro," *O Cruzeiro*, XXXIX (April 22, 1967), 15–18, with excerpts from the diary of ex-sergeant and guerrilla leader Amadeu Felipe da Cruz. The failure of the Caparaó operation was attributed by Marighella to location in an area whose terrain was not the best for guerrilla operations (e.g., vision was obscured by fog); to the proximity of concentrated forces of the First Army; to the guerrillas' failure to identify with or to politicize the peasants of the area; to the immobility of the group,

which remained in one encampment and had no general strategy; and to the poor physical preparedness of the guerrillas. See Marighella's statement in "Los Tupamaros en Uruguay y Marighella en Brasil," *Punto Final*, 87 (September 9, 1968), Supplement, 15–16.

13. *Jornal do Comércio* (Recife), December 3, 1967.

14. For his important statement on revolution in Brazil, see "Marighella apresenta guerrilla rural como tática certa de luta," *Jornal do Brasil* (September 15, 1968), 20. His statement is dated August 1968 in Havana.

15. Marighella, "Minimanual of the Urban Guerrilla," *Tricontinental* 16 (1970), 15–56. See also the collection of his writings under the heading, "Por la revolución brasileña," *Pensamiento Crítico*, 37 (February 1970), 3–106, and Carlos Detrez (ed.), *Carlos Marighella por la libération du Brésil*, Paris: Editions du Seuil, 1970. His analysis of guerrilla warfare is summarized in "Algumas questões sôbre as guerrilhas do Brasil," *Jornal do Brasil*, (September 15, 1968), 20. Other writings are in *Pensamiento Crítico*, 46 (November 1970).

16. Keiros, "The Eve of Revolution in Brazil," *The Communist International*, XII (May 20, 1935), 583–84. The author, who acknowledged that he participated in the 1922 revolt, was particularly optimistic about the revolutionary potential of the army and even the police in Brazil.

17. Skidmore, "Failure in Brazil: From Popular Front to Armed Revolt," *Journal of Contemporary History*, V, No. 3 (1970), 37–57. Author emphasizes PCB's efforts to win allies within the army officer corps. See details of the 1935 revolt in chap. 3 of the present volume.

18. Basbaum, *História sincera . . .*, II, p. 405, who was a member of the committee.

19. *New York Times*, (February 22, 1930), 17; (August 10, 1930), Section II, 1; (March 28, 1935), 1.

20. Of the 238 persons charged, 151 were imprisoned, including the 8 leaders, 29 ANL organizers, 53 supporters, and 61 other participants (all military).

21. David Capistrano da Costa, Benedito de Carvalho, Luiz Carlos Prestes, Marco Dinarco Reis, Agildo Barata, Francisco Antônio Leivas Otero, Agilberto Vieira de Azevedo, Abel Chermont, and Valério Kondor (See Appendix B). All except Chermont and Kondor were affiliated with the military.

22. See scattered reports in the *New York Times*, for example: (March 14, 1952), 5, (March 20, 1952), 1; (May 9, 1952), 3; (August 30, 1952), 10.

23. Dulles, *Unrest in Brazil*, pp. 36–38.

24. *Op. cit.*, pp. 278–85, states that Communist law students enlisted in the navy in 1961 and helped organize the sailor's association that fomented the meeting.

25. Two studies that do not emphasize the role of Communism in labor but are essential background reading are Luiz Pereira, *Trabalho e desenvolvimento no Brasil*, São Paulo: Difusão Européia do Livro, 1965, and Azis Simão, *Sindicato e estado: suas relações na formação do proletariado de São Paulo*, São Paulo: Dominus Editôra, 1966.

26. Alexander, *Communism in Latin America*, p. 96

27. Pereira, *Formação do PCB*, pp. 77–78; Alexander, p. 96.

28. Brandão, "Combates da classe operária," p. 78.

29. Linhares, *Contribução à história das lutas operárias no Brasil*, p. 92.

30. By the end of the Estado Novo in 1945 only a small number of workers' federations had been established and no confederations had been formed. See Alexander, * *Labor Relations in Argentina, Brazil, and Chile*, pp. 59ff., for details on the federations and confederations after 1945.

31. According to Leôncio Rodrigues, *Conflito industrial e sindicalismo no Brasil*, p. 179, the Vargas suicide "was the decisive event in the reorientation of Brazilian Communism." Earlier the party's efforts to penetrate the labor movement had been stifled by labor legislation, repression under the Dutra government, and competition with the PTB. Not to be ignored was the tremendous impact of Vargas on the labor movement. With his death the PCB moved to establish an alliance with nationalist currents and to emphasize the role of the national bourgeoisie in Brazilian nationalism and development. Thereafter the PCB was able to exert greater influence in labor. Rodrigues gives us a useful interpretative analysis of relations between the PCB and the labor movement after 1945.

32. Harding, "Revolution Tomorrow: The Failure of the Left in Brazil," p. 36.

33. Theotônio Júnior, "O movimento operário no Brasil," *Revista Brasiliense*, 39 (January-February 1962), 105.

34. The majority labor movement was led by Roberto Morena, Benedito Cerqueira, Agostinho de Carvalho, Clodsmidt Riani, and others. See Inquérito Policial Militar No. 709, *O Comunismo no Brasil*, Vol. II, p. 174.

35. Theotônio Júnior, *op. cit.*, p. 105–07, and Timothy F. Harding, "An Analysis of Brazil's Third Labor Congress," *Hispanic American Report*, XIII, 8 (October 1960), 567–72. A Communist interpretation is António Pereira, "Trade Unionism in Brazil," *New Times*, 23 (June 7, 1961), 12.

36. For analysis of labor activity during the Quadros and Goulart administrations, see Harding, "Revolution Tomorrow . . . ," esp. pp.37–44. Harding notes that a radical, independent, and leftist faction emerged from the PTB, having received its labor and political education from the PCB before the party split. This group became independent and expressed itself through the CGT because of the Communist schism and Goulart's loss of control over labor. Some of Harding's analysis was published as "The Politics of Labor and Dependency in Brazil," *International Socialist Review*, XXXIII (July-August, 1972), 6–13 ff.

37. Azis Simão, "O voto operário em São Paulo," *Revista Brasileira de Estudos Políticos*, 1 (December 1956), 134. Author states that in the 1933 elections for the national Constituent Assembly the vote for Communists in São Paulo was small and not counted. Socialists received 10 per cent of the 255,706 vote total, however.

38. *Ibid.*, pp. 133–41. In his excellent analysis Simão briefly differentiates between the PCB and PTB voter, examines their socio-economic background and their motives. In an attempt to demonstrate the labor orientation of the PCB Jover Telles identifies 9 of 14 Communist deputies elected to the National Constituent Assembly as workers; 9 of the 18 Communist councilmen as workers; 7 of 11 Communist state deputies in São Paulo, 2 of 3 in Ceará, 1 of 2 in Bahia, and the single Communist deputy in Pará as workers. See Jover Telles, *O movimento sindical no Brasil*, p. 243.

39. Pelacani withdrew from the PCB in 1958 after defying a party decision that he not contest a seat for federal deputy (he was not elected). He became Minister of Labor under Goulart.

40. Cerqueira was probably a socialist, not a member of the PCB, although he served as a director of the Soviet-oriented World Federation of Trade Unions.

41. Morena did not head a confederation or national federation during the sixties although he was very active in labor affairs.

42. A reliable source indicated in an interview during July 1964 that of 55 state federations in the CNTI, 21 were Communist-controlled and 13 infiltrated but not dominated by the PCB.

43. The UST leadership included José Maria Crispim, who had been expelled from the PCB in 1952.

44. Identification of Communist strength in the Brazilian labor confederations is in C. Maday *et al., U.S. Army Area Handbook for Brazil,* Washington, D.C.: Superintendent of Documents, 1964, pp. 526–28. See also *Este e Oeste,* Nos. 37, 38, and 39 (January and February 1964), report reprinted in Inquérito Policial Militar No. 709, *O comunismo no Brasil,* Vol. II, pp. 201–05. Labor and Communist documents linking the PCB to labor strikes and agitation are in pp. 168–200. These sources are frequently inaccurate and tend to exaggerate the PCB's dominance over the labor movement. The party's role in labor is stressed also by Dulles, *Unrest in Brazil,* pp. 161–68, 250–53.

45. Partido Comunista do Brasil, "Resolução aprovada pela reunião nacional, realizada no mês de setembro de 1959," reprinted in Jover Telles, *O movimento sindical . . . ,* pp. 285–301.

46. Alexander notes that because of this training, unions under Communist leadership "are frequently the most honest and most efficient." See his *Labor Relations . . . ,* p. 74.

47. *Ibid.,* pp. 74–75.

48. A classic study of the paternalistic relations between landowners and peasants is Gilberto Freyre, *The Mansions and the Shanties: The Making of Modern Brazil,* trans. by Harriet de Onis from *Sobrados e mucambos,* New York: Alfred A. Knopf, 1963.

49. Examples of messianic movements are in Maria Isaura Pereira de Queiroz, *O messianismo no Brasil e no mundo,* São Paulo: Dominus Editôra, Editôra da Universidade do São Paulo, 1965.

50. An excellent analysis of these changes is in Benno Galjart, "Class and 'Following' in Rural Brazil," *América Latina,* VII (July-September 1964), 3–23.

51. That Brazilian agriculture has in fact been oriented toward production for export tends to undermine the traditional theses, abundantly posited in PCB documents, that the Brazilian land system is and has always been feudal. An interesting analysis is developed by Andrew Gunder Frank, "A agricultura brasileira: capitalismo e o mito do feudalismo," *Revista Brasiliense,* 51 (January-February 1964), 45–70; and Prado Júnior, "Contribuição para a análise da questão agrária no Brasil," *Revista Brasiliense,* 28 (March–April 1960), 165–238 and "The Agrarian Question in Brazil," *Studies on the Left,* IV (Fall 1964), 77–84 as well as his *A revolução brasileira.* An excellent synthesis is Andrew Gunder Frank, * *Capitalism and Underdevelopment in Latin America,* esp. pp. 254–77.

52. Brandão, "Combates da classe operária," p. 78, cites the PCB organ *1° de maio,* which in 1926 published a program oriented not only toward industrial and agricultural workers but also toward landless peasants; also, he states, the BOC "launched the idea of a political alliance of workers with peasants."

53. Information on Communist peasant leagues in the Northeast is in *Fôlha do Povo,* 114 (April 6, 1946), 4; 125 (April 21, 1946), 1; 140 (May 11, 1946), 3; 147 (May 19, 1946), 2–3; 160 (June 4, 1946), 2; 167 (June 12, 1946), 3; 178 (June 26, 1946), 1, 2, 3; 184 (July 3, 1946), 4; 185 (July 4, 1946), 14; 229 (August 24, 1946), 1, 3, 4; 341 (January 4, 1947), 3; 388 (February 28, 1947), 4; 431 (April 30, 1947), 3; 697 (March 2, 1948), 4; 698 (March 3, 1948), 1, 2; 703 (March 9, 1948), 4; 715 (March 23, 1948), 2, 4; and in *O Popular,* 23 (September 23, 1948), 1; 26 September 26, 1948), 1; and 27 (September 28, 1948), 1, 2.

54. By 1962 ULTAB claimed to have 9 federations, 319 associations, and 500,000 workers. See a report by its Communist leader, Lyndolpho Silva, "Divi-

sionismo e traição dentro do movimento camponês," in *A Hora* (Recife) (June 2-8, 1962), 7.

55. See details on the Galiléia developments in Francisco Julião, *Que são as Ligas Camponesas?*, p. 24; also see Antônio Callado, *Os industriais da sêca e os 'Galileus' de Pernambuco: aspectos da luta pela reforma agrária no Brasil*, Rio de Janeiro: Editôra Civilização Brasileira, 1960, especially pp. 33–44. The legal name of the first Liga was Sociedade Agrícola e Pecuária dos Plantadores de Pernambuco.

56. According to an army source, by late 1963 there were 218 peasant leagues, including 64 in Pernambuco and 15 each in Paraíba and São Paulo. See Inquérito Policial Militar No. 709, *O comunismo no Brasil*, Vol. IV, pp. 380–81.

57. Julião advocated ten "commandments" for the Ligas Camponesas; these demands are described by Manuel Correia de Andrade in *A terra e o homem no Nordeste*, São Paulo: Editôra Brasiliense, 1963, pp. 247–49. Julião's memoir and analysis of the Ligas and the structure of peasant life appear in his *Cambão: la cara oculta de Brasil*, Mexico City: Siglo Veintiuno Editores 1968.

58. Shepard Forman in "Disunity and Discontent: A Study of Peasant Political Movements in Brazil," paper presented at the Brazil-Portuguese Africa Colloquium, Riverside: University of California, February 21, 1968, p. 14, states that "there can be no doubt that he is a member of the national elite" and refutes Horowitz, *Revolution in Brazil*, p. 21, who describes Julião as "born of a family of small tenant farmers." Julião's elite status is attested by his graduation from the University of Recife, and he early established himself in the Recife intelligentsia with a book of short stories, prefaced by Gilberto Freyre, *Cachaça*, Recife: Editôra Nordeste, 1951.

59. Forman, *op. cit.*, p. 30, notes Julião's observation that in Brazil there were 40,000,000 peasants in contrast to 5,000,000 rural wage earners; see Julião, *Que são as ligas camponesas?*, p. 67.

60. Roughly in 1962 Julião initiated a newspaper, *A Liga*, in Rio; irregularly issued, this paper apparently was oriented toward urban areas rather than the rural Northeast.

61. The program and other MURB documents are reprinted in Inquérito Policial Militar No. 709, *O comunismo no Brasil*, Vol. III, pp. 553–64.

62. His "mysticism" was an asset among peasants but tended to alienate labor and student leftists, according to Harding, "Revolution Tomorrow . . . ," p. 51. Julião's revolutionary thought is infused with admiration for Mao Tse-Tung, Fidel Castro, and Jesus Christ. In an interview with the Rio weekly, *Manchete* of July 29, 1961, Julião stated: "If we could combine the ideas of Christ, the Buddha, St. Francis, Lincoln, Lenin, Mao Tse-Tung, and Fidel Castro, the problems of Brazil would be solved." Quoted in *Atlas*, III (January 1962), p. 52. See F. Novaes Sodré, *Quem é Francisco Julião?*, São Paulo: Redenção Nacional, 1963, p. 28; and Lêda Barreto, *Julião—Nordeste—revolução*, Rio de Janeiro: Editôra Civilização Brasileira, 1963, pp. 64 ff.

63. A review of legislation relating to rural unions is in Mary E. Wilkie, "A Report on Rural Syndicates in Pernambuco," Rio de Janeiro: Centro Latinoamericano de Pesquisas em Ciências Sociais, April 1964, mimeo., pp. 5–6. Under a 1903 law 13 short-lived unions were founded and dominated by landowners. Based on decree #7038 of 1944, individual unions were established in 1946, 1952, 1955, 1956, and 1957. Only since 1962 were rural unions recognized in larger numbers.

64. These differences were reflected in *Ultima Hora*, a Recife daily that began publication on July 18, 1962.

65. See Barreto, *Julião—Nordeste—revolução*, p. 132, for negative reaction by Giocondo Dias in *Novos Rumos* and Paulo Cavalcanti in *A Hora*, to a speech of Julião, reprinted in *O Semánario* on May 31, 1962.

66. Antônio Callado, *Tempo de Arraes, Padres e comunistas na revolução sem violência*, p. 58.

67. *Ibid.*, pp. 13, 15.

68. Communists were concerned about the revolutionary potential of the peasant leagues once they had been politicized and radicalized by Julião's call for reforms. Anthony Leeds places Julião's behavior in perspective with a penetrating analysis: "Julião is distinctly a member of the controlling class even if he represents a somewhat aberrant and individualistic but not, properly speaking, dissident faction of it . . . . Julião has distinguished himself by uniqueness in his method of manipulating them while operating in the political system of the elites." Quoted in Leeds, "Brazil and the Myth of Francisco Julião," in Joseph Maier and Richard W. Weatherhead (eds.), *Politics of Change in Latin America*, New York: Frederick Praeger, 1964, p. 196.

69. Wilkie, "A Report of Rural Syndicates . . . ," p. 7. Forman, "Disunity and Discontent . . . ," p. 31.

70. This is Padre Crespo's interpretation in "Pequeno resumo do movimento sindical rural em Pernambuco," Recife: Serviço de Orientação Rural de Pernambuco, May 31, 1961, MS p. 4. Crespo describes the intense struggle with Communists for control of his rural union.

71. Since federations were sometimes constituted for each of these three groups, as many as three federations were allowed for each state. Most of the rural unions established between 1962 and 1964 were paper organizations.

72. The breakdown on the 27 federations is in Dulles, *Unrest in Brazil*, p. 222, although Neale P. Pearson states that delegates from 29 federations, representing 19 states and 743 rural unions (263 officially recognized), attended the founding meeting of CONTAG. See Pearson's "Leadership Characteristics of the Emergent Small Farmer and Rural Worker Pressure Groups in Brazil," p. 16 of a paper presented to the annual meeting of the Midwest Association of Latin American Studies, Muncie, Ind., October 30–31, 1969.

73. A solid report on the two priests is Fanny Mitchell's "Padre Crespo and Padre Melo. Two Approaches to Reform," Letter FM-17 to the Institute of Current World Affairs in New York, November 9, 1967, 12 p.

74. See e.g., the important statement of Ação Católica Operária, *Nordeste: desenvolvimento sem justiça*, Recife, May 1, 1967.

75. For a Communist analysis of organization and class, with respect to urban and rural workers in São Paulo, see Moisés Vinhas, **Operários e camponeses na revolução brasileira*.

76. Barreto, *Julião—Nordeste—revolução*, pp. 83–84.

77. By the early sixties the association had a membership of 2,000, according to Paulo Singer, "A luta dos camponeses no Brasil," *Política Operária*, 4 (October 1962), 8.

78. At Formoso in Goiás the defense organization became a large cooperative. The evolution of Formoso is described by Rui Facó in *Novos Rumos*, 124 (July 21–27, 1961), 8.

79. Land disputes in Caxias, Itaquaí, and other places near Guanabara are described in *Novos Rumos*, 138 (September 29–October 5, 1961), 5. The linkage between these defensive organizations and the PCB is suggested in Inquérito Policial Militar No. 709, *O comunismo no Brasil*, Vol. IV, pp. 386–93.

80. Barreto, *op. cit.*, pp. 110–11, describes peasant reactions to Communism as "something cruel and terrible" and to the Communist as "a satanic agent, diabolical destructor of all that is Christian."

81. A brief summary of Bezerra's activities is in Callado, *Tempo de Arraes* . . . , pp. 74–78; Callado describes him as "a good Communist . . . genuinely interested in the good fortune of the peasantry" and compares him to a "good" Catholic priest named Padre Edgar Carício.

82. The PCB's conservative position was attacked by Marcos Peri (probably a pseudonym for a dissident former Communist), who called upon the PCB to take up armed struggle in the countryside. See his * *Perspectiva da revolução brasileira,* pp. 159–61.

83. The document was published in a Communist journal; see "Declaração do 1 Congresso Nacional dos Lavradores e Trabalhadores Agrícolas sôbre o caráter da reforma agrária," *Estudos Sociais,* III (April 1962), 433–37. The results of an interesting opinion survey of delegates at the congress are in José Chasin, "Contribuição para a análise da vanguarda política do campo," *Revista Brasiliense,* 44 (November-December 1962), 102–29.

84. A useful survey of the student movement is Arthur José Poerner, *O poder jovem. História da participação política dos estudantes brasileiros,* Rio de Janeiro: Editôra Civilização Brasileira, 1968; includes a section of 12 documents in general related to events after 1964.

85. Pereira, *Formação do PCB,* pp. 70, 131–32.

86. See Apolônio de Carvalho, "O aniversário da União Juventude Comunista," *Problemas,* 10 (May 1948), 15–21.

87. For historical developments of the UJC during the fifties, see Jarbas dos Santos, "A UJC, o Manifesto de Agôsto e a situação atual," *Novos Rumos,* Supplement to 75 (August 5–11, 1960), 3.

88. "Problems of Subversion in Brazil Reviewed," *Joint Publications Research Service,* 47, 950, Translations on Latin America, No. 170, VII (1969), 59–60.

89. The AP views were projected in the biweekly *Ação Popular* in 1962 and *Brasil, Urgente* during 1963. The publication *Política Operária* was issued 1962–64, and sporadically thereafter, finally coming under the aegis of the POC in about 1968.

90. The military's investigation after 1964 implicated UNE activities as Communist-inspired. See Inquérito Policial Militar No. 709, *O comunismo no Brasil,* Vol. II, pp. 206–25.

91. *Intercontinental Press,* VII (January 13, 1969), pp. 14–15.

92. "Problems of Subversion in Brazil Reviewed," *op. cit.,* pp. 66–67. At this time it was difficult to assess PCB strength in the student movement, although the party was able to disseminate its views through occasional mimeographed handouts, e.g., *Insurreição,* a biweekly first issued in August 1966.

93. Fernando Secalva, "Estudiantes de Brasil por la lucha armada," *Punto Final,* 73 (January 1969), 19–20.

94. See the UFB program in *Fôlha do Povo,* 1 (July 9, 1935), 3.

95. A brief history of the FMB is in Olga Maranhão, "Ganhar milhões de mulheres para o programa do partido," in *Problemas,* 64 (December 1954–February 1955), 271–76.

96. Julia Arévalo, "El trabajo del P. Comunista del Brasil entre las mujeres," *Estudios,* I, 3–4 (August-November 1956), 92–94. The title of the periodical was *Movimento Feminina.*

97. Inquérito Policial Militar No. 709, *O comunismo no Brasil*, Vol. II, pp. 314–30.

98. *Op. cit.*, Vol. III, pp. 357–65; this source cites several references to *Novos Rumos.*

99. *Ibid.*, pp. 365–68.

100. *Ibid.*, pp. 370–74, for the program of the Popular or Progressive Front. The PCB response to this program is in pp. 382–88.

101. *Op. cit.*, Vol. II, pp. 233–34.

102. *Ibid.*, pp. 235–44. This source lists leaders and members of the Brazil-Soviet exchange institute and the Comando dos Trabalhadores Intelectuais, linking all names with the PCB. Although many were indeed members of the party, the PCB's role and influence were greatly exaggerated in the military police report.

103. See, e.g., Giocondo Dias, "Teses errôneas e nocivas," *Novos Rumos*, 176 (July 1, 1962).

104. See Partido Socialista Brasileiro, Comissão Executiva Nacional, **Estatutos;* and for the moderate PSB program, see *Programa do Partido Socialista Brasileiro, n.d., 2 pp.

105. Differences between the PSR and the Vanguarda Socialista are apparent in João Matheus, "Um trotskista sem aspas," *Vanguarda Socialista*, 5 (September 28, 1945), 3, 5 and in Murilo, "O Partido Socialista Revolucionário está com o boi na linha," *Vanguarda Socialista*, 11 (November 9, 1945), 6, 8.

106. The Latin American Bureau headed by J. Posadas and representing certain Trotskyist parties in Brazil, Argentina, Bolivia, Chile, Cuba, and Uruguay (with headquarters in Montevideo), was a dissident element claiming affiliation to the Fourth International.

107. Information on the 35 military men, Clemachuk, and the meeting with Brizola is in Dulles, "Brazilian Communism and the Military Movement of 1964," p. 40.

108. Information in Inquérito Policial Militar No. 709, *O comunismo no Brasil*, Vol. III, p. 442. José Maria Crispim, formerly a Communist but now a Trotskyist, published an article under the name of the Frente: see Le peuple brésilien et les événements de Saint-Dominique," in *Sous le Drapeau du Socialisme*, 18 (June 1965), 21–22.

109. Although written before the formation of the alliance, an interesting article critical of the PCB and PC do B appeared in the PORT publication, *Frente Operária.* See J. Posadas, "A crise dos Partidos Comunistas no Brasil," *Frente Operária*, 98 (first half of July 1963), 3, 5.

110. Partido Comunista do Brasil, Sixth Conference, *"Resolução da Sexta Conferência do Partido Comunista do Brasil (Junho de 1966): União dos Brasileiros para livrar o país da crise, da dictadura e da ameaça neocolonialista." Cited in Dulles, "Brazilian Communism and the Military Movement of 1964," pp. 38–39 and note 57.

111. Emílio Castor, "Brazilian Communist Party Objectives Discussed," pp. 8–9.

112. Partido Comunista Brasileiro, Comitê Estadual de Guanabara, Maioria Revolucionária, "A reunião histórica," *Jornal do Brasil,* (August 25, 1968), 19. Trans. as "Brazilian CPs Analyze Split, Side with Mao," *Joint Publications Research Service,* 46539, Translations on Latin America No. 98, VII (1968), 49–55.

113. Partido Comunista do Brasil, "Nacionalismo e demogogia," *A Classe Operária* (January 1970), 5–7. Trans. as "Military Solution to National Crisis Rejected," *Joint Publications Research Service* 50394, Translations on Latin America, No. 327, VIII (1970), 17–21.

114. Antônio Palmares, * "La izquierda brasileira, história y perspectivas," p. 66.

115. POLOP views are in its journal *Política Operária*. See issue No. 1 of January 1962 for its program. Some documentation is in Inquérito Policial Militar No. 709, *O comunismo no Brasil*, Vol. III, pp. 467–502.

116. Política Operária, Fourth National Congress, * "Declaração política do 4° Congresso da OBMPO," and "Organização revolucionária marxista—Política Operária: programa socialista para o Brasil (approvado no IV Congresso Nacional, Setembro de 1967)," N.p., September 1967, 24 p., mimeo. Both documents cited in Dulles, "Brazilian Communism and the Military Movement of 1964, note 61.

117. Luís Alberto Moniz Bandeira, "Escola de delatores," 3 ed., N.p., July 1967, 13 p., mimeo., cited in Dulles, *ibid.*, note 60.

118. POLOP's journal, *Política Operária*, apparently had become the central organ of the Partido Operária Comunista by 1968.

119. Background on these Church-sponsored organizations is in Emanuel de Kadt, "Religion, the Church, and Social Change in Brazil," pp. 192–220 in Claudio Veliz, *The Politics of Conformity in Latin America*, New York: Oxford University Press, 1967. First issue of the biweekly newspaper *Ação Popular* is dated January 6, 1962.

120. Dulles, notes 70 and 71 in "Brazilian Communism and the Military Movement of 1964," cites a series of documents issued by AP during 1966 and 1967 in which may be found its Marxist orientation. The Marxist radicalization of priests in São Paulo was evident in the publication, *Missão Operária*, ed. by Father Antônio Almeida Soares as early as 1968; see *O Globo* (March 21, 1969), 17. In December 1969, 11 Catholic churchmen in São Paulo were sentenced to indefinite prison terms for supporting Marighella's ALN; see Leonard Greenwood, "21 Sentenced for Aiding Red Leader," *Los Angeles Times* (December 14, 1969).

121. Ação Popular, "A alternativia revolucionária," Guanabara, June 1968, a document explaining the adherence of one AP faction to the PCBR. The document appeared in *Jornal do Brasil* (July 28, 1968), 33, and in "Communist Dissident Group Attracts AP Membership," *Joint Publications Research Service*, 46,251, Translations on Latin America, No. 88, VII (1968), 42–50. Apparently the AP still existed in 1969; see Ação Popular, "Popular Action Urges Struggle by Masses," *Joint Publications Research Service*, 48,076, Translations on Latin America No. 181, VII (1969), 1–2, trans. from *Resistência* (clandestine; March 11, 1969), p. 3.

122. The FLN statement was released by the Brazilian First Army and published in *Correio Brasiliense* (May 30, 1970), 3, and trans. in *Joint Publications Research Service*, 50,747, Translations on Latin America No. 347, VIII (1970), 1–3.

123. Câmara Ferreira himself was captured in October 1970 and died, according to police reports, of a heart attack.

124. See the interview with Lamarca, "Un trabajo político-militar junto a las masas," *Punto Final*, 88 (September 30, 1969), 8–10.

125. Reportedly the congress was a failure, with "theoretical debate without positive results." See Castor, *op. cit.*, p. 19. Closely affiliated with the VPR at this time was the Movimento Revolucionário 8 de Outubre (MR-8), led by Jorge Medeiros Vale. MR-8 was named for the October 8 (1967) death of Ernesto "Ché" Guevara, and it was apparently an outgrowth of the Fração Universitária do PCB, another dissident youth group that broke with the PCB.

126. Document quoted in "Problems of Subversion Reviewed," *Joint Publications Research Service*, 47,950, Translations on Latin America No. 170, VII (1969), 42–43.

127. The PCBR reply to Jover Telles statement of late August 1968 was in-

cluded in "PCs do Brasil continuam se dividindo," *Jornal do Brasil* (September 1, 1968), 35.

128. Formation of the POC is described in *Política Operária* 17 (May 1968).

129. "O que é o Partido Operário Comunista (POC)," *Jornal do Brasil* (August 11, 1968), 26. Like the PCBR, the POC advocated the party as the vanguard force of the proletariat.

130. See Elias Chaves Neto, "Emancipação nacional e defesa da constituição," *Revista Brasiliense*, 5 (May-June 1956), 1–11; "O quadragésimo aniversário do Partido Comunista do Brasil," in 40 (March–April 1962), 1–10; "A liberdade de Luiz Carlos Prestes," in 15 (January–February 1958), 1–7; and "Legalidade do Partido Comunista, marcha para a revolução socialista," 38 (November–December 1961), 39–46.

131. The ISEB director edited a series of pamphlets, called "Cadernos do Povo" which focused on themes of nationalism, revolution, and imperialism. By 1963 many of the ISEB founders had resigned, and a reorganization had been underway.

132. Ronald H. Chilcote, Introduction to *Revolution and Structural Change in Latin America. A Bibliography on Ideology, Development, and the Radical Left (1930–1965)*, Stanford: Hoover Institution Press, 1970, Vol. I, pp. 9–21.

133. See Horowitz, *Revolution in Brazil* . . . , pp. 84–99, for a useful discussion of charisma and personalist power.

134. This regroupment of radical forces is analyzed in *Intercontinental Press*, VII (January 13, 1969), pp. 14–15.

Notes to Chapter 7

Titles preceded by asterisk on first appearance have complete entries in Bibliography.

1. Partido Comunista Brasileiro, Comitê Estadual de Pernambuco, "Os comunistas e as eleições em Pernambuco," *Novos Rumos*, 238 (September 13–19, 1963), 6.

2. *Fôlha do Povo* published weekly except for the periods August 16, 1959, to August 14, 1960, and after October 19, 1960. *A Hora* appeared from August 4, 1961, until March 29, 1964. During the periods in which *Fôlha* did not appear, 26 of the 46 Prestes pronouncements appeared in *Novos Rumos*. Many of the documents in *Fôlha* were reprints of earlier statements. The image of Prestes was obviously visible on the state and local levels.

3. "State CP's Denounce CC Stand on Insurrection," *Foreign Radio Broadcast Service* (November 7, 1967), 1–4. The following discussion of Communist splintering at the state level is not exhaustive nor intended to be definitive. A useful indepth and more detailed analysis is João Quartim, * *Dictatorship and Armed Struggle in Brazil*.

4. Analysis of the three São Paulo factions is in Luis Carrera, "Marighella, el profeta armado del Brasil," *Punto Final*, 73 (January 1969), 16–18.

5. São Paulo State, Secretaria de Segurança Pública . . . , * *Relatório: inquérito instaurado contra Luiz Carlos Prestes* . . . , p. 75.

6. *Ibid.,* p. 99.

7. *Ibid.,* p. 103.

8. *Ibid.,* p. 160.

9. *Ibid.,* p. 219.

10. Emílio Castor, "Brazilian Communist Party Objectives Discussed," *Joint Publications Research Service*, 50344, Translations on Latin America, No. 323, VIII (1970), 11.

11. Brazilian Communist Party, São Paulo State Committee, "CP State Committee Airs Differences with CC," *Foreign Radio Broadcast Information Service* (November 21, 1967), 1–7.

12. São Paulo State, Secretaria de Segurança Pública . . . , * *Relatório inquérito* . . . , p. 217.

13. *Ibid.*, p. 231. Further comments on the split between the state and municipal party leadership were made by state party leader Amaro Valentim do Nascimento.

14. David Capistrano da Costa, *et al.*, "Tese para discussão," Recife? May 1964, 5 p.

15. Details of the formation of the Guanabara dissident groups are in chap. 6 of the present work; see esp. notes 112, 124, 125, 127, 128, 129.

6. Partido Comunista Brasileiro, Convenção Municipal de Curitiba do PCB, "Resolução."

17. Ferdinando de Carvalho (ed.), *IPM sôbre atividades comunistas, Paraná e Santa Catarina.*

18. Jover Telles, remarks quoted in Prestes' notebooks and reprinted in São Paulo State, Secretaria de Segurança Pública . . . , *Relatório: inquérito* . . . , p. 197.

19. See comments by João Adelino Susella in above-cited *Relatório* . . . , p. 245. In 1962 or 1963 the regional party expelled Adamastor Antônio Bonilha, Otto Alcides, and Paulo Dias.

20. Inquérito Policial Militar No. 709, *O comunismo no Brasil,* Vol. IV, pp. 374–75.

21. For details on the FER, see "O que é o Partido Operário Comunista (POC)," *Jornal do Brasil* (August 11, 1965), 26.

22. Interview with Carlos Lamarca, "Un trabajo político-militar junto a las masas," *Punto Final,* 88 (September 30, 1969), 27.

23. See sources for Table 7.2.

24. Age levels are based on the age recorded for each leader according to our sources for three periods—1946, 1956, and 1961–64.

25. The autobiographical writings are Agilberto Vieira de Azevedo, *Minha vida de revolucionário,* 1967, 64 p., with preface and conclusion by Spartacus Ribeiro; and Gregório Bezerra, *Eu, Gregório Bezerra, acuso!* The following quotations and facts are drawn from these works.

26. Josué de Castro, *Death in the Northeast,* New York: Random House, 1966, p. 22.

27. Quoted in Castro, *op. cit.*, p. 25. See also the important section on the history of federal policy toward the drought problem in Albert O. Hirschman's *Journeys Toward Progress: Studies of Economic Policy-Making in Latin America,* New York: Twentieth Century Fund, 1963.

28. *Fôlha do Povo* was published in Recife from No. 1 (July 9, 1935) through No. 110 (November 21, 1935) under Osório Lima and José Cavalcanti.

29. *Fôlha do Povo,* 1 (July 9, 1935), 1, in editorial "Este jornal."

30. *Fôlha do Povo,* 94 (October 29, 1935), 3 and subsequent issues.

31. On banditry, see *Fôlha do Povo,* 2 (July 10, 1935), 4; "Cangaço, luta de classe," 5 (July 13, 1935), 3; and 65 (September 25, 1935), 1.

32. *Fôlha do Povo,* 87 (October 21, 1935), 4, and 91 (October 25, 1935), 4.

33. According to a police report that may well be unreliable, the Pernambuco PCB supported only one strike during the period 1936 to 1945. See Alvaro Gonçalves Costa Lima *et al.,* * *Aspectos da atividade do comunismo em Pernambuco,* p. 12.

34. Tribunal Superior Eleitoral, *Dados estatísticos. Eleições federal, estadual e municipal realizadas no Barsil a partir de 1945*, Vol. I, Rio de Janeiro: Departamento de Imprensa Nacional, 1950, p. 75.

35. See Paulo Cavalcanti, "As urnas! Pela vitória de Juscelino, João Goulart, Pelópidas e Vieira de Menezes," *Fôlha do Povo*, 550 (October 3, 1955), 1, 2; and his "Eleição de Pelópidas, vitória do povo no Recife," *Fôlha do Povo*, 570 (October 23, 1955), 7.

36. Costa Lima *et al., op. cit.*, p. 18.

37. The PCB also backed Cid Sampaio, who was elected Governor of Pernambuco in 1958. The role of PCB in the campaigns is described in a somewhat exaggerated manner by Adirson de Barros, * *Ascensão e queda de Miguel Arraes*, esp. pp. 43–90.

38. Even Prestes visited Recife during 1958–60; see *Fôlha do Povo*, 39 (July 26 to August 1, 1959), 1, and 36 (September 25, 1960), 1, 5.

39. Adirson de Barros, *op. cit.*, p. 63.

40. *Ibid.*, pp. 94–95.

41. See, e.g., David Capistrano, "A propósito da entrevista de Julião e da carta a Paulo Cavalcanti," *A Hora*, 66 (October 20–27, 1962), 7, 8.

42. Precise details and a complex organizational chart of the Pernambuco party are in Costa Lima *et al., Aspectos da atividade do comunismo em Pernambuco*, pp. 21–24. Although this source is dated, the party structure today remains approximately the same as that during the mid-fifties.

43. Biographical information in Costa Lima *et al., op cit.*, esp. pp. 91–144. The evaluation is based on biographies of Ramiro Justino da Silva, Adalgilsa Cavalcanti, Hugo Ferreira (Fragmon Carlos Borges), Clodomir Morais, Hiram de Lima Pereira, Rildo Souto Maior, Paulo de Figueiredo Cavalcanti ,and Amaro Luiz de Carvalho. Autobiographical information on Bezerra is in his *Eu, Gregório Bezerra, acuso!*, esp. pp. 5–11. From other sources we have drawn biographical details also for Agostinho Dias de Oliveira, Miguel Batista da Silva, Antônio Guedes da Silva, and Amaro Valentim do Nascimento.

44. Costa Lima, *et al., op. cit.*, pp. 98–100.

45. *Ibid.*, pp. 138–44.

Notes to Chapter 8

Titles preceded by asterisk on first appearance have complete entries in Bibliography.

1. Rollie Poppino, *International Communism In Latin America*, p. 151.

2. Antônio Palmares (pseud.), * "La izquierda brasileña, historia y perspectivas," p. 4.

3. Moniz Bandeira, Clóvis Melo, and A. T. Andrade, *O ano vermelho: a revolução russa e seus reflexos no Brasil*, pp. 291–92.

4. *Ibid.*, pp. 290–91. The authors document this early contact with references to writings and interviews with Afonso Schmidt and Edgard Leuenroth.

5. *Ibid.*, pp. 296–97. The authors document the proceedings of the founding party congress with an extensive quotation from issue No. 7 of *Movimento Comunista* (June 1922).

6. Canellas' rebuttal was partially reproduced in Bandeira, *et al., O ano vermelho*, pp. 408–18. Having withdrawn or been expelled from the party, Canellas founded a clandestine journal, *5 de Julho*, in 1924, focused on activities of the Prestes Column.

7. Pereira, *Formação do PCB*, p. 132.

8. *International Press Correspondence*, August 1, 1928, and November 21, 1928, cited in notes 22 and 23, pp. 97 and 412, of Alexander, *Communism in Latin America.*

9. See a summary of Prestes' statement in *Information Bulletin* (supplement to *World Marxist Review*), 117–119 (March 14, 1968), 28–29.

10. The 21 conditions are reprinted in Robert V. Daniels (ed.), *A Documentary History of Communism*, New York: Vintage Books, 1962, Vol. II, pp. 95–99.

11. Reported in Afonso Schmidt, *Apud bom tempo*, São Paulo: Editôra Brasiliense, 1958, cited in Bandeira *et al., O ano vermelho*, pp. 290–91.

12. See Pereira, *Formação do PCB*, "Encontro com Luiz Carlos Prestes," pp. 105–09.

13. Rollie Poppino, in a letter to the author, November 21, 1969.

14. A position accepted by Peralva, who claimed that when the PCB and the Soviet party restored close relations in 1949, Soviet leaders attempted to work through the PCB in order to ensure close ties with Communist parties elsewhere in Latin America. See Peralva, *O retrato*, pp. 274–75.

15. Poppino, *International Communism* . . . , pp. 141–42, 144–45. Only in Chile was a popular front able to come to power through election. The uprising in Brazil was aided by substantial amounts of Soviet funds, according to Poppino.

16. Poppino, p. 161.

17. Instituto Brasileiro de Geografia e Estatística, *Anuário Estatístico do Brasil,* Rio de Janeiro, 1963, p. 163, and 1965, pp. 185–86. See N. S. Patolichev, "Soviet-Brazilian Relations," *New Times*, 21 (May 23, 1962), 16–17, which gives trade figures three times larger than the official Brazilian figures.

18. These differences were summarized in the *New York Times*, Western Edition, July 16, 1963, 4. See also Horowitz, "Latin America and the Sino-Soviet Split," *Liberation*, III, 3 (May 1963), 11–15.

19. Peralva, *O retrato*, pp. 39–42.

20. *Ibid.,* pp. 168–84.

21. Background for the split was reported by the PC do B in "Reply to Khrushchev, Resolution of the Central Committee of the Communist Party of Brazil," *Peking Review*, VI (September 13, 1963), 39–43. The PC do B attributed the split to the removal of 12 of 25 members of the PCB Central Committee at the Fifth Congress and to the change in name adopted in August 1961.

22. See, e.g., the policy position in Partido Comunista Brasileiro, "Proposta acêrca da linha geral do Movimento Comunista Internacional," *Novos Rumos,* Special Supplement, July 26–August 1, 1963, pp. 3–9.

23. According to Halperin there was apparently no regular subsidy to the PC do B, whereas the PCB received support from the Soviet Union in the form of peace prizes, payments for the Brazilian edition of the Cominform journal, payments for the organization of congresses, and money and gifts to delegates visiting the Soviet Union. See Halperin, * "Peking and the Latin American Communists," p. 19. Halperin cites Peralva, *O retrato*, for information on Soviet financing of the PCB.

24. Halperin, *op. cit.,* pp. 49–50, states that the first officially recognized pro-Chinese splinter party in Latin America was that in Peru, founded in January 1964. The PC do B's "Reply to Khrushchev . . . " in *Peking Review*, however, would appear to be clear evidence of recognition of the Brazilian party.

25. *Ibid.,* pp. 48–49. For a general and not always reliable survey of Chinese influence in Latin America, see U.S. Senate, Internal Security Subcommittee, *Red Chinese Infiltration into Latin America*, Hearing . . . 89th Congress, First Session,

August 4, 1965, Washington: U.S. Government Printing Office, 1965. See pp. 42–43 for Brazil.

26. A report on the agreement is "Comunicado de la Conferencia de los Partidos Comunistas de América Latina, "Estudios, 33 (January-February 1965), 61–63.

27. One might compare the tactics and strategy in Ernesto "Ché" Guevara, Guerrilla Warfare, New York: Monthly Review Press, 1961, and in Mao Tse-tung, Guerrilla Warfare, New York: Frederick A. Praeger, 1961.

28. From a speech in Cuba Socialista, cited by D. Bruce Jackson, Castro, the Kremlin, and Communism in Latin America, p. 83. Jackson's book provides a useful synthesis of Cuban-Soviet relations and their impact on Latin America for the period 1964–67.

29. Carlos María Gutiérrez, who attended the conference, reported his impressions in "The Internal Struggle at the OLAS Conference," World Outlook, V (September 22, 1967), 778–81.

30. Quoted in a press release of Agence France Presse, printed in Jornal do Commercio (Recife), August 2, 1967.

31. Reported in Jornal do Commercio (Recife), July 30, 1967. Cuban-Brazilian differences were analyzed also by Clóvis Melo in "Fidel e o PCB," Tribuna da Imprensa, July 31, 1967.

32. Prestes, "Outstanding Event in the World Communist Movement," World Marxist Review, XII (August 1969), 19–21.

33. Peralva, O retrato, pp. 275–76.

34. Communist Party of Brazil and the Communist Party of Argentina, "Joint Statement by the Communist Parties of Brazil and Argentina," Information Bulletin (supplement to World Marxist Review), VII, 137 (January 24, 1969), 59–61. Although Fidel Castro also supported the Soviet invasion of Czechoslovakia, he criticized other Soviet policies in a Havana speech on August 23, 1968. He also condemned the Venezuelan, Guatemalan, and Bolivian parties as well as the PCB. Curiously, Blas Roca, an old Cuban Communist and member of the new party's Central Committee, had visited Prestes in prison in July 1942. See Alexander, Communism in Latin America, p. 114.

35. Antônio Palmares (pseud.), "La izquierda brasileña, historia y perspectivas," p. 20. Prado Júnior in A revolução brasileira, pp. 47–48, refers to the Hispanic orientation of the South American Bureau of the Comintern, "which completely ignored Brazil."

36. Palmares, "La izquierda brasileña . . . ," p. 25.

37. Ibid., p. 24, cited from Abguar Bastos, Prestes e a revolução social.

38. Ibid., p. 25.

39. Ibid., pp. 25, 27.

40. Ibid., p. 45.

41. Ibid., p. 49.

42. Prado Júnior, Revolução brasileira, pp. 77–79, critically assesses the program and its impact on subsequent party activities. See also Ribeiro de Lira (?), "Tres etapas do comunismo brasileiro," Cadernos de Nosso Tempo, 2 (January-June 1954), 123–38.

43. A critical portrayal of the party's image appears in Jaguaribe, "Porque venceu Jânio Quadros?" Cadernos de Nosso Tempo, 1 (October-December 1953), 100–101.

Chronology

Chronology of Events: 1917–1972

1917 Russian Revolution.

1917–20 Strikes organized in Brazil by anarchists and anarcho-syndicalists.

1918 Liga Comunista de Livramento formed in Rio Grande do Sul.

1919 Centro or União Maximalista established (in 1921 became Grupo Comunista de Pôrto Alegre).

1919 (April 13). Epitácio Pessoa of Paraíba elected in special presidential elections—departure from federal machine politics.

1920 Third COB Congress.

1921 (November 7). Grupo Comunista do Rio de Janeiro formed.

1922 (March 1). Artur Bernardes, governor of Minas Gerais, elected President.

1922 (March 25–27). First Congress of Partido Comunista do Brasil; Executive Central Committee elected, and the 21 principles of the Comintern and party statutes approved.

1922 (July). Abortive revolt of Fort Copacabana.

1923 (June). PCB printing press and files confiscated by Rio police.

1924 (January). Juventude Comunista organized by PCB.

1924 (July 5). São Paulo uprising; state of siege until December 31, 1926.

1924 (October 24). Rio Grande do Sul revolt. Prestes commanded revolutionary movement and the "long march."

1925 (May 1). *A Classe Operária* began publication.

1925 (May 16 to 18). Second Congress of PCB.

1926 (November). Washington Luiz Pereira de Souza elected President.

1927 (January 3–August 11). *A Nação* carried bulk of PCB propaganda.

1927 (February 24). João Batista de Azevedo Lima elected federal deputy under the Bloco Operário (BO) and with PCB support.

1928 *A Classe Operária* reappeared, published to mid-1929, when finally closed.

1928 PCB, after changing name of Bloco Operário to Bloco Operário e Camponês (BOC), elected two members (Octávio Brandão and Minervino de Oliveira) to Rio Municipal Council.

1928 Joaquim Barbosa, PCB trade union secretary and Executive Central Commission member, initiated internal debate in party magazine, *Auto-Crítica*. Formation of Oposição Sindical, a factionalist group opposed to ultra-left Comintern line.

1928 (December 29) to (January 4) 1929. Third PCB Congress held in Niterói.

1929 Trotskyists in PCB withdrew to form Grupo Comunista Lenino, reorganized two years later as Legião dos Comunistas.

1929 World financial crisis; Brazil hurt as coffee prices collapsed.

1929 (July). Leôncio Basbaum, PCB representative, met with Prestes, Siqueira Campos, and Juarez Távora in unsuccessful attempt to unite PCB and petty bourgeoisie. Prestes offered candidacy of President. PCB continued negotiations with *tenentes* through South American Bureau of Comintern and a Comitê Militar Revolucionário.

1930 (January). Candidacy of Getúlio Vargas for Presidency.

1930 (March 1). Election won by Vargas' rival, Júlio Prestes de Albuquerque of São Paulo.

1930 (March). BOC defeated, and a few months later dissolved.

1930 (July 25). Assassination of João Pessôa, Vargas' Aliança Liberal running mate.

1930 (October 3). Outbreak of revolution against administration of Washington Luiz Pereira de Souza.

1930 (October 24). Overthrow of Washington Luiz.

1930 (November 3). Vargas accedes to power as head of provisional government.

1931 (March 12). In "open letter," Prestes declares himself a Communist.

1932 (July 9 to October 2). Unsuccessful *constitucionalista* revolution in São Paulo directed against Vargas. Seventy-three PCB leaders imprisoned.

1932 (November). PCB Central Committee reconstituted.

1933 (May 3). PCB elections to Constituent Assembly.

1933 (November 15) to (July 16). Constitution drawn up.

1934 PCB's First National Conference. Antônio Maciel Bomfim named secretary general.

1934 (July 13). Vargas elected President by Constituent Assembly.

1934 (October 14). Congressional elections. Near-disaster for the *tenentes*, who lost in the Northeast.

1935 (March). ANL founded as a coalition of diverse groups and individuals, including Communists and *tenentes*.

1935 (March 12). Five-point program approved at first meeting of ANL Executive Committee.

1935 (July 5). Prestes "open letter" published, calling upon the masses to assault the government, and calling for defeat of "fascism" and the "odious Vargas regime" (prompting the government to ban ANL).

1935 (October). Great Western Railway walkout, suported by ANL.

1935 (November 23). Barracks revolt in Natal; revolt collapsed on November 27.

1935 (November 24). Recife uprising of soldiers; collapsed on November 25.

1935 (November 27). Rio outbreak by group of officers, ended when government troops recaptured School of Military Aviation.

1936 (March). Prestes sentenced to prison (until 1945) and his wife deported to Germany.

1936 (July). Vargas pressures Congress to create a National Security Tribunal to punish subversives.

1937 Presidential campaign, in which PCB faction supported candidacy of José Américo de Almeida and eventually formed a Trotskyist movement, the Partido Socialista Revolucionário (PSR).

1937 (April). State of siege declared in Rio Grande do Sul. Vargas aided opponents of Gov. Flores da Cunha.

1937 (June). Plínio Salgado nominated by integralistas for Presidency in elections of 1938, opposing Vargas.

1937 (September). Document outlining plan for Communist revolt "discovered" by Army general staff. Known as "Cohen Plan," fabricated by the integralistas as pretext for a coup.

1937 (November 10). Coup materialized. Congress closed on the same day. A new constitution granted Vargas authoritarian powers and provided for plebiscite in six years to choose a President; new regime called the *Estado Novo*.

1937 (December 2). All political parties banned, including integralistas.

1938 Fourth International organized; joined by Partido Operário Leninista and PSR, the official representative.

1941 (June). Russia invaded by Germany. Brazilian support of allies accompanied by relaxation of police suppression of Communist activities.

1943 (May). Realignment of world powers, with anti-revolutionary dissolution of Comintern as supreme goal of Communism became victory over fascism.

1943 (August 27). PCB Second National Conference known as the Conference of Mantiqueira convoked by a São Paulo group. Prestes elected secretary general.

1944 (November). A Constituent Assembly urged by Constitution's author Francisco Campos—thus revealing opposition to Vargas.

1945 (January 22). First Congress of Brazilian Writers, including many Communist intellectuals, met in São Paulo.

1945 (March–April). União Democrática Nacional (UDN) organized as a political party by leftist intellectuals in São Paulo, including Communists and socialists. Socialists formed Esquerda Democrática, known as *ala moça* (youth wing) of UDN.

1945 (April). Political amnesty and release of hundreds of prisoners, including Prestes, announced by government.

1945 (April 25). Esquerda Democrática established.

1945 (May 9). Partido Social Democrático (PSD) organized by politicians and military leaders closely associated with Vargas regime.

1945 (May 23). Prestes statement that Vargas' departure from office would bring "civil war" and chaos; calls for postponement of Presidential election.

1945 (July 1). Dutra endorsed for President by PSD.

1945 (October 29). Vargas deposed by army after attempting to appoint his brother federal police chief.

1945 (November 10). PCB officially registered as political party.

1945 (December 2). Elections. Prestes elected senator in the Federal District; Dutra elected President.

1946 (January 4). Plenary session of PCB National Committee. Prestes called for a powerful Confederação Geral dos Trabalhadores Brasileiros (CGT).

1946 (April 25). At First National Conference, Esquerda Democrática officially becomes a party.

1946 (April). União da Juventude Comunista suspended by government.

1946 (May). Known Communists in bureaucracy purged by government.

1946 (May). PCB policy "to struggle for peaceful solutions to national problems" restated by Prestes: but government is warned that the masses would oppose "police and fascist provocations against the legality of our party."

1946 (July). PCB Third National Conference.

1946 (August 30–31, November 27). *Tribuna Popular,* party daily, closed down briefly.

1947 (January 19). State and supplementary Congressional elections. PCB retained fourth rank among parties adding two deputies (under another party) to 14 already in Congress; 46 members to 15 state legislatures and gaining a plurality of 18 in Municipal Council of Federal District.

1947 (April). Second National Conference of Esquerda Democrática; name changed to Partido Socialista Brasileiro (PSB).

1947 (May 7). Supreme Electoral Court ruling to outlaw the PCB won by government.

1947 Theses published for PCB's (aborted) Fourth Congress. They reflected changes corresponding to policy shifts that most Communist movements had taken in late 1946.

1948 (January 7). Measure passed purging Communist membership in Congress.

1949 Minimal program published by PCB.

1950 (August 1). Prestes manifesto set new "line" by announcing break with "progressive bourgeoisie."

1950 Movimento Nacional pela Proibição de Armas Atômicas supported by Communists.

1951 Third Congresso do Movimento Brasileiro dos Partidários da Paz.

1952 José Maria Crispim expelled from PCB.

1954 (August 4). Suicide of Vargas.

1954 (November 7–11). PCB Fourth Congress; new program and statutes approved.

1955 (October). Kubitschek and Goulart elected President and Vice President, respectively.

1955 (November 11). Intervention by Gen. Henrique Lott, Chief of Staff under interim President Café Filho, to ensure President-elect's assumption of power.

1956 Federally-financed Instituto Superior de Estudos Brasileiros (ISEB) initiated.

1956 (February). Anti-Stalin denunciation at Twentieth Congress of Soviet Communist Party.

1956 (June). President Kubitschek moves against PCB and suppresses Liga de Emancipação Nacional.

1956 (October). Debate opened by PCB on issues of Soviet Twentieth Congress.

1957 (April). PCB debate closed.

1957 (May–October). Barata withdrew from PCB; Peralva resigned (on May 22), other party members, in October.

1958 Prestes emerges after decade of clandestinity.

1958 (March). PCB Central Committee declares new party line, marking official beginning of de-Stalinization in Brazil.

1959 (February). PCB weekly, *Novos Rumos,* launched.

1960 (August). PCB Fifth Congress affirms support of Soviet party's "peaceful coexistence" policy, and approves eight theses, appealing for party's legality and supporting nationalist movement.

1960 (October). Communist-supported Lott lost Presidential bid to Jânio Quadros, although Communist-backed Goulart won Vice Presidency.

1961 (August–September). Quadros resigned, and Goulart assumed Presidency under parliamentary system.

1961 (September). PCB National Conference approves new program and party name change to Partido Comunista Brasileiro (PCB).

1962 Comando Geral dos Trabalhadores (CGT) formed.

1962 (January). Expulsion of Stalinist PCB faction led by Amazonas, Grabois, and Pomar, who then formed the Partido Comunista do Brasil. *A Classe Operária* reappears.

1963 (January). Goulart given full Presidential powers in national plebiscite.

1963 (March 28–30). Congresso Continental de Solidariedade à Cuba held in Niterói.

1963 (September 12). Revolt by non-commissioned officers in Brasília.

1964 (February). PCB Central Committee approves theses for Sixth Congress, scheduled for November.

1964 (March 31 to April 4). Revolt by military; Goulart flees to Uruguay. Gen. Humberto Castelo Branco "elected" President ten days later, assuming special powers to suppress leftist activities and PCB.

1964–67 Dissension in PCB State Committees in Pernambuco, Guanabara, Rio Grande do Sul, São Paulo, and Paraná.

1965 (October). Opposition wins gubernatorial elections in Minas and Guanabara, and the government issues Second Ato Institucional on October 27, by which the old party system was dissolved and future elections for the Presidency would be held within the Congress.

1966 (February 5). Third Ato Institucional replaces direct election of governors with selection by state legislatures. Two parties organized: the official Aliança Renovadora Nacional (ARENA) and the opposition Movimento Democrático Brasileiro (MDB).

1966 (June). PCB Central Committee approves theses of Sixth Congress.

1966 (December). Carlos Marighella resigns from PCB Executive Commission; later attends conference of Organization of Latin American Solidarity (OLAS) in Havana.

1967 (December). PCB Sixth Congress condemns OLAS for its advocacy of armed struggle. Carlos Marighella, Mário Alves de Souza Vieira, Jover Telles, Jacob Gorender, Joaquim Câmara Ferreira, Apolônio de Carvalho, and Miguel Batista expelled.

1968 (August). 30th UNE Congress held clandestinely in São Paulo state; 1,000 arrested; "new" UNE emerges thereafter.

1968 (December 13). Brazilian Congress ended as military consolidates dictatorship. Later, Congress and universities purged, censorship imposed, and political prisoners tortured.

1969 (June–September). Visit of Gov. Nelson Rockefeller followed by increased activity by resistance groups and kidnapping of U.S. Ambassador Elbrick.

1970 (March and June). Japanese Consul General and West German Ambassador kidnapped; released later.

1971 (September). Guerrilla leader Carlos Lamarca killed by police. His death together with that of Carlos Marighella in 1969 and that of Joaquim Câmara Ferreira in 1970 signified at least a temporary setback for advocates of armed struggle.

1972 PCB policy attacks the government's "economic miracle" and reaffirms position of the Sixth Congress that a broad anti-dictatorial front consisting mainly of workers, peasants, and petty bourgeoisie should be formed.

Index

Persons

General Topics